D0487568

Jonathan Swift

Jonathan Swift
The Irish Identity

Robert Mahony

Yale University Press
New Haven & London · 1995

For
Christina Hunt Mahony
So little gets for what she gives

Set in Goudy by Best-set Typesetter Ltd, Hong Kong
Printed and bound in Great Britain by St Edmundsbury Press

Library of Congress Cataloging-in-Publication Data
Mahony, Robert.
Jonathan Swift: The Irish identity/Robert Mahony.
Includes bibliographical references and index.
ISBN 0-300-06374-1 (hardback)
1. Swift, Jonathan, 1667–1745—Homes and haunts—Ireland.
2. Swift, Jonathan, 1667–1745—Political and social views.
3. National characteristics. Irish, in literature.   4. Ireland—
Politics and government—18th century.   5. Nationalism—Ireland—
History—18th century.   6. Authors, Irish—18th century—Biography.
7. Nationalists—Ireland—Biography.   8. Statesmen—Ireland—
Biography.   9. Irish question.   I. Title.
PR3728.I67M34   1995
828'.509—dc20
[B]   95-18352
CIP

A catalogue record for this book is available from the British Library.

Contents

Acknowledgements

As is appropriate for a work on Swift and Ireland, my main obligations are to Irish scholars and institutions, most prominent among them the academic and library staffs of the University of Dublin. Begun during a sabbatical in Dublin in 1986–7 and concluded during another in 1994, this study has been greatly assisted by the access to resources afforded me by the School of English and the Library of Trinity College. The many courtesies of Geraldine Mangan and Louise Kidney in the English School and of Charles Benson, Rosarii Dunne, Aine Keegan, Vincent Kinane and Lydia Ferguson in the Library's Department of Early Printed Books deserve particular acknowledgement. I am, moreoever, heartily grateful for the friendship, encouragement and hospitality of Nicholas and Eleanor Grene and their family.

I am happy to record my gratitude as well to the staffs and resources of the National Library of Ireland, the Library of the Royal Irish Academy, Archbishop Marsh's Library, the Dean and Chapter of St Patrick's Cathedral, all in Dublin; the libraries of St Patrick's College, Maynooth, and University College, Cork; the British Library, and the Victoria and Albert Museum, London; the Library of Congress and the Folger Shakespeare Library in Washington, D.C.; the New York Public Library, the Free Library Company of Philadelphia, and the Houghton Library, Harvard University. To the library staff of The Catholic University of America and to my clerical assistants at CUA over the years, Matthew Hurley, Daniel McGrath, Michelle Prunty and Melissa O'Leary, I owe heartfelt thanks.

For financial assistance I am grateful to the Rose Saul Zalles Memorial Fund of the Center for Irish Studies, the Richard N. Foley Memorial Fund of the Department of English, and the University Research Fund, all at CUA.

At various stages this work has been read, criticized and encouraged by Denis Donoghue, Roy Foster, Christopher Fox and Elizabeth Malcolm. To each I am deeply obliged, though of course I alone am responsible for any errors of fact or emphasis. For accommodating my research in various other respects, I thank Terence Brown, Andrew Carpenter, Anthony Clare, the late Irvin Ehrenpreis, Tom Garvin, the late Barbara Hayley, David Hayton, Cheryl Herr, Robert Hogan, Colbert Kearney, Elizabeth Kirwan, Eugene McCabe, Tom McIntyre, Michael and Judy McGinn, Joseph McMinn, Patrick Maume, Ulick O'Connor, Betty Rizzo, Christine St Peter, Beverly Schneller, Susan Schreibman, Ruth Sherry and Mary Thale.

The love and encouragement of my whole family prompt the warmest gratitude I can express, while to my wife is due that well beyond expression.

Illustrations

Introduction

This study traces the shaping of Jonathan Swift's Irish identity over the two and a half centuries since his death. That identity is at once an Irish one, and generated mainly within Ireland; it is a versatile construction which accounts for quite a different perception of Swift in Ireland from that in most other countries. Outside Ireland, Swift is recognized as a literary figure, and indeed, owing to the enormous and enduring popularity of *Gulliver's Travels*, he is one of the best-known classic writers in English. Whilst few other than students and scholars of English literature are more widely acquainted with his works, within that academic circle his writings have proved so amenable to a host of critical and theoretical approaches as to ensure his canonical stature. Yet, even as his scores of biographers and hundreds of literary commentators have acknowledged Swift's Irish concerns, most have attended more vigorously to other features of the writer: his attentions to the human mind or body, to women in general or particular, to language and to religion. Studies of his politics, too, have usually kept well within their English dimensions. The consequence of this tendency in international literary scholarship has been the construction of quite a few Swiftian identities which slight his Irish origins and concerns. Throughout the years of this century, studies such as Donald Berwick's *The Reputation of Jonathan Swift, 1781–1882* and Milton Voight's *Swift and the Twentieth Century* have been similarly concerned with his literary reception outside the land of his birth and long residence, the country which prompted both his strenuous defence and deep despair.

Within Ireland, conversely, Swift still cuts a figure as much popular as literary, and one which for well over a century was also politically evocative. Thus his Irish identity transcends and diverges from his literary reputation in development and function. The underlying reasons for this are simply stated. In the first place, Swift was born in Ireland and for most of his life lived there, though, it must be said, never as happily as he had in England when he was

the friend and advisor to Robert Harley (later Earl of Oxford) and to Henry
St John (later Viscount Bolingbroke), who headed the Tory government of
Queen Anne's last years, 1710–14. Secondly, the oddities of Swift's personal
behaviour, during his years in Irish public life after 1713 as Dean of St
Patrick's Cathedral in Dublin, gave rise to a general impression of eccentricity which lingers still, not least through a substantial body of anecdotes
long preserved in folk memory. Last, and most important to his Irish identity,
Swift was cherished during the final decades of his life as an Irish champion
against British oppression. Precisely whom he championed, and why, and
indeed the nature of the oppression, have exercised numerous Irish commentators in the centuries since his death, largely according to their own social
and political affiliations. Yet general agreement among them emerged long
ago that at least he articulated energetically the defensive resentment constant in Ireland's long relationship with Britain; this proved an enduring
consensus for his early and honourable place in the litany of Irish patriots.

Swift's exertions for the good of Ireland were not confined to its relationship with Britain. He promoted Irish economic self-sufficiency, for instance,
and criticized an unjust system of land ownership and management. But in
these matters his arguments were largely unavailing, while he had his greatest
success in a conflict with the ministry in London. In 1722 that ministry, now
controlled by the Whigs who had replaced Swift's friends, awarded a royal
patent for minting a large consignment of farthings and halfpence for Ireland
to an English ironmonger, William Wood. Because Ireland was a subordinate
kingdom, its own administration and parliament had not been consulted or
even officially informed about the award and, stung by this affront, they
criticized the patent over the next two years as excessively profitable to Wood
and potentially ruinous to Ireland's currency regime. But Wood had secured
the patent through a bribe to a former mistress of George I, the Duchess of
Kendall, and the government were determined to proceed with it despite the
Irish objections. The whole matter typified British high-handedness in dealing with Ireland, and Swift responded in 1724 with a series of open letters,
signed 'M.B. Drapier', which so sharpened public resentment against 'Wood's
halfpence' that the patent was eventually withdrawn. It was thus that Swift
became a popular hero, to be remembered ever since as a victorious patriot,
one of the earliest of a rare breed in Irish history.

In considering that reputation and the Irish identity it has so driven, this
study assumes of its readers a basic awareness of Ireland's history in general
from Swift's time to the present, and of its literary history in the twentieth
century. As an introduction to either, or to the life or writings of Swift
himself, this work makes no pretence to adequacy. Rather it describes the
process by which Ireland has 'adopted' Swift, a process that still continues –
though not always with unremitting enthusiasm on either side. Conor Cruise
O'Brien once suggested that 'Swift was perhaps "adopted", much against his
will, by Ireland', and yet that

Irishness is not primarily a question of birth or blood or language; it is the condition of being involved in the Irish situation, and usually of being mauled by it. On that definition Swift is more Irish than Goldsmith or Sheridan, although by the usual tests they are Irish and he is pure English.[1]

Of course, Swift was 'mauled' by life in general as much or more than by the Irish situation, his involvement with which during the 1720s, indeed, made him exceedingly popular in Ireland for the remaining decades of his life. But while his patriotism was the force driving his 'adoption' by Ireland in these years, and the more gradual construction of an Irish identity for him over the centuries to come, the authenticity of that patriotism began to be disputed in England during his own lifetime, and later in Ireland as well. His birth of English parents, his personal cultural orientation to England, his considering life in Ireland a long exile – especially after his high-flying years in London – and his disparagement of Irish customs and conditions (whether directly, ironically or compared to those in England), were all laid against his validity as 'The Patriot Dean'. They seemed to render his patriotic efforts hypocritical or opportunistic, a means of attacking the Whigs who had replaced his Tory friends, or even occasions for glossing his putative misanthropy in a positive character. Although scholars outside Ireland can still argue along lines like these,[2] the Irish have in the main been willing, for much of the twentieth century, to consider Swift's Irishness a fact. It is one of many paradoxes befitting a master of literary irony; and if it be added that he was 'mauled' by the barrage of disappointments his life offered, his suffering lends his Irishness the greater appeal and fitness, since Ireland, particularly if compared with its nearest neighbour, old conqueror and longstanding governor, has certainly been mauled by history.

This provides the essential background to the argument of the present study, that Swift's Irishness has been accreted very largely through the course of his reputation since his death. And the thesis takes its sanction from Swift's own claim upon Irish memory. The conclusion of his 'Verses on the Death of Dr. Swift' maintains 'That Kingdom he hath left his Debtor', while the famous epitaph at his grave site implies that the debt should be discharged by defending human liberty as he had done. Though both quotations have a moral, humanitarian import – the context of the former is Swift's bequest to found Ireland's first mental hospital, while the epitaph applies beyond Ireland – the circumstances behind each were indisputably local. It was perhaps inevitable, then, that the Irish should have interpreted his claim upon them in the first instance by claiming him as one of their own; it was more certainly inevitable, given the developing context of Ireland's history, that at length they were drawn to apply his injunction to defend human liberty in political terms. Students of Swift's own political thought have quite justifiably tended to consider his principles apart from his putative Irishness, even to regard his long residence in Ireland as an opportunity for him to exercise beliefs and attitudes acquired without, necessarily, specific reference to it. Such recent biographers of Swift as Irvin Ehrenpreis, David Nokes and Joseph McMinn have understandably been more willing to take his concern with Irish affairs into sympathetic account; but they, too, could hardly be expected to attend at any length to an Irish identity so posthumously shaped. But within Ireland, Swift's principles have tended to become compounded with his Irishness.

This study highlights those perceptions of Swift which have connected his political principles with his Irishness, and are consequently least familiar outside Ireland. Yet even there, invoking those perceptions has been much more common than following their development, mingled as they are with the shifting politics of Ireland's long-evolving relationship with Britain and of shifting diversities among the Irish themselves. Interpreting the dynamic of these politics is difficult and controversial (Swift himself reckoned the political case of Ireland to be terminal), but we can definitely say that the country he served is vastly different from modern, or even nineteenth-century, Ireland. Though its demographic majority was Catholic, for instance, his Ireland was a Protestant kingdom,[3] composed mainly of second- or third-generation descendants of British 'planters' whose settlements there had been encouraged by successive governments in London to ensure a Protestant presence. More exclusively still, this Ireland was an Anglican polity, effectively unchallenged through most of the eighteenth century either by the native Catholics or the large, mostly northern, Presbyterian community, both of which were legally obliged to support the established Church of Ireland. Whilst the government had advantaged the Protestant population as a whole at the expense of the Catholics, and defended them in military conflicts with the Catholics in the seventeenth century, it had also imposed serious disabilities upon Irish commerce, to the real detriment of the settlers' prosperity. Ireland was further disadvantaged by the subordination or neglect of its interests by the British administration even when these would not have conflicted significantly with British interests – as in the case of Wood's halfpence. Thomas Carte, a contemporary of Swift, saw the issue starkly, reflecting on medieval history when in 1736 he considered a measure imposed by the London parliament in 1663 to restrain the importation of Irish cattle and sheep:

The *English* seem never to have understood the art of governing their provinces, and have always treated them in a manner, as either to put them under a necessity, or subject them to the temptation of casting off their government, whenever an opportunity offered. It was a series of this impolitic conduct, which lost them *Normandy, Poictou, Anjou, Guyenne,* and all the Dominions which they had formerly had in France. . . . It is not a little surprising that a thinking people, as the *English* are, should not grow wiser by any experience, and after losing such considerable territories abroad by their oppressive treatment of them, should go on to hazard the loss of *Ireland* and endeavour the ruin of a colony of their own countrymen, planted in that Kingdom.[4]

Or, as Swift's friend Sir Richard Cox put it more succinctly, if the government 'are afraid we should rebel . . . they should use us so as to make us run some Risque in doing it, they should allow us something that we might *fear* to lose.'[5]

From a late twentieth-century perspective it seems anomalous that such rhetoric concerning British unfairness toward Ireland in the 1730s (the decade following Swift's own greatest prominence as a patriotic rhetorician) should have come from exponents of the Anglican governing elite rather than from among the comparatively oppressed Irish populations, Catholic or Presbyterian. Against the standard of British–Irish and inter-Irish antagonisms that the twentieth century has inherited from nineteenth-century Irish nationalism, eighteenth-century Ireland diverges in a number of respects, among them that the relatively disadvantaged were, prudently, less likely to articulate in print grievances against the London government than the relatively advantaged, who could even flirt with disaffection. Yet the latter too felt hobbled, because they compared themselves with their counterparts in Britain; observers such as Carte and Cox, and indeed Swift, often appear to argue that their fellow Protestants deserved better of the British because they were *not* Irish, or at least not so much as, say, the Catholics. But as Swift's patriotic rhetoric was preserved beyond his own time – largely owing to his literary eminence and a rather earlier recognition in Britain than in Ireland of the canonicity of such rhetoric – it was available to remind later ages that Ireland had long had grievances against Britain. Ultimately, if paradoxically, he could be invoked as an ancestor expressing grievances that by then Catholics felt more deeply than Protestants. Swift grew the more useful as the passage of time eroded historical anomalies to fit the simpler standard of British–Irish antagonisms characteristic of nineteenth-century nationalism, and seemed thereby to resolve his own inconsistencies. For instance, at the time his defence of Ireland seemed mainly *defensiveness* on behalf of the political sensitivities of an elite, while his attacks on the Irish system of land management directly confronted that elite. Yet in the nineteenth century this contradiction could be occluded by its concurrent validation of Swift as a patriot for Ireland and a prophetic voice for a peasantry still oppressed. Or, though he never disputed the Penal Laws against Catholics and indeed favoured their effects, he was less overtly anti-Catholic than many of his fellow Anglican clergymen, which allowed him to become adopted in the nineteenth century as an ancestor for an Irish nationalist movement mainly composed of Catholics.

Through the phases of Ireland's history, then, the political applicability of his patriotic rhetoric could endure, ensuring that the construction of his Irish identity would continue, adapted constantly to new circumstances. Swift himself, as his epitaph implies, regarded his defence of liberty as the key to his survival in memory, evidently mistrusting the permanence of the literary standing that he had achieved in life. Yet, ironically, in the decades following his death his name survived in Ireland mainly because of that literary eminence, his popularity as an author and the currency of anecdotes about him. Half a century would pass before his patriotic efforts would begin to be widely perceived as relevant to contemporary conditions in Ireland, offering principles in which to anchor a distinctly Irish identity. His literary reputation had no similarly intensive force in nineteenth-century Ireland, though its worldwide recognition continued to evoke Irish pride and served to draw attention to his patriotism from beyond her shores. And once most of Ireland achieved its independence, as the values of nationalism have had to be understood in terms broader than British–Irish antagonisms, and as the necessity of invoking ancestral patriots has diminished, his Irish identity has undergone further construction.

Toward the end of the twentieth century, Swift remains a presence in Irish culture more vivid than that of any other from eighteenth-century Ireland – more vivid, indeed, than most from any historical period. To examine the many aspects of that sturdy presence in Ireland since Independence could fill a book in itself. However, since Swift's literary eminence figured early and markedly in promoting him as an Irish patriot, the final chapter does take account of his Irish identity mainly within the context of modern Irish literature. For this, as for Irish nationalism, he has been accorded an ancestral status; indeed, given the wide critical notice of his significant influence on the major figures in twentieth-century Irish poetry and fiction, further treatment of it here could appear summary or even superfluous. That significance, moreover, arises from a series of essentially private experiences. Hence it seems fitting to conclude a study of Swift's Irish identity, whose posthumous development within Irish nationalism was carried on very much in public, by taking stock of the Dean rather as a subject in drama, the most public of literary forms (though not one of his own). This approach has drawn comparatively little attention before now, even though, like the generations inspired by his patriotism, Irish playwrights in almost every decade of this century have been drawn to the dramatic possibilities of Swift the man. His potency for Irish literature extends well beyond the drama, of course, and the treatment chosen here has unavoidably meant slighting his importance in modern poetry and fiction; James Joyce's fascination with Swift, for instance, deserves incomparably better than the barely cursory attention given it in these pages.

Swift the patriot remains important to Ireland's history, both for his success in the 'Wood's halfpence' affair and for the reverberations of that victory among later generations. But the image of Swift fostered by that patriotic reputation could not absorb fully the popular memory of Swift the man – the eccentric Dean, the frustrating lover – nor, indeed, many of the contours of that man shaped by his numerous biographers. On the other hand, the record of Swift's treatment in the twentieth-century Irish drama offers a series of attempts to grasp that fuller character, a man of palpable conflicts in faith, hope, love and even in patriotic purpose. The presentation of Swift on the stage, more than in other literary media, has reflected both the early development of Swift's Irish identity and its extensive currency two and a half centuries after his death.

1

Swift and George Faulkner: Cultivating Irish Memory

I

Jonathan Swift is buried in St Patrick's Cathedral, Dublin, of which he was Dean from 1713 to 1745; a brass plaque set in the floor marks his grave, close to another for his friend Stella. Nearby is a bust of him set in a niche on the wall, and above, to the right, a black marble funerary tablet bearing the Latin epitaph Swift composed for himself. Among the translations of the epitaph, that of W.B. Yeats is best known: its closing description of Swift, *Strenuum pro virili Libertatis Vindicatorem* ('Earnest champion of liberty for men'), he rendered 'He served human liberty.' Obviously it was as a public benefactor that Swift wished to be remembered at his grave site. The history of the bust, however, betokens the guardianship that his Dublin publisher, George Faulkner, exercised over his reputation and implicates also the particularly Irish patriotism for which Faulkner wanted Swift to be memorialized. Even in his own day the Dean had achieved international standing as an author, but he had also recognized that his patriotic service to Ireland was the likeliest basis for an enduring reputation. And in Ireland Swift is still remembered as a patriot: as the author of the *Drapier's Letters* in 1724, who rallied Irish national feeling against English oppression, who promoted Irish economic self-sufficiency and attacked rackrenting and absentee landlords, who founded St Patrick's Hospital, the first Irish asylum for the mentally ill, and whose portrait stared gruffly from the Irish ten-pound note between 1978 and 1993. Swift definitely served *Irish* liberty.

The proximity of the white marble bust to the epitaph on the black marble tablet tends to combine their memorial effect. But they are not a single monument, of course, and in Swift's own day his admirers anticipated something grander than either, and more public. Such a monument was, indeed, envisioned as early as 1724, at the height of the popular acclaim for Swift's thwarting the 'Wood's halfpence' scheme. At that time, one of many anonymous songs hailing the Drapier's patriotic services looked forward to the endurance of his popular memory:

> WE ne'er shall forget,
> His Judgment, or Wit,
> But Life, you must know, is a Vapour;
> In Ages to come,
> We well may Presume
> They'll Monuments raise to the DRAPIER.[1]

The balladeer had taken as his epigraph Horace's '*Exegi monumentum aere perennius*' (*Odes* 3: 30): 'I have erected a monument more lasting than brass.' Apart from fitting the import of the song and almost jokingly tricking out its doggerel with classical dignity, the allusion neatly encapsulated both the 'brazen' arrogance of Wood's project as an English imposition upon Ireland and the remembrance of the Jacobite 'brass money' of 1689 invoked during the halfpence controversy by persistent allegations that Wood's coins were sub-standard.[2] The imagery of brass thus touches neatly upon the poles of ambivalence in Irish Protestants' sense of identity: pride in their still newly secure political and social position in Ireland (which had been gained for them by the Williamite victories in 1689–91), and resentfulness at their ultimate dependence upon the British connection to maintain it.

A more ambitious plan for a monument to Swift in 1732 provoked an anonymous pamphleteer to express this ambivalence quite differently:

> An ingenious weekly Writer amongst ourselves was pleased not long since to propose erecting a Statue of our celebrated *Drapier*, on account of his Assistance in putting an end to a famous project for overstocking the Kingdom with Copper Farthings. No man can have a juster sense of the *Drapier's* Merits than I have, yet . . . [he proposes instead a second statue of William III]. For though Popery and Slavery were the most harmless and innocent Things, yet King *James's* Brass Money, from which we were delivered by the Revolution, was an Evil of a hundred Times greater Consequence than that which provoked the *Splendida Bilis* of the honest *Drapier*.[3]

Projects for a Swift monument were to resurface repeatedly after his death. In the meantime, the Irish Protestant assertiveness he represented, which the anonymous writer of 1732 valued less than reminders of dependence upon Britain, continued to be celebrated otherwise. Swift as the Drapier was lionized in the 1720s, his portrait struck on medals, painted on shop signs, printed on souvenir handkerchiefs. In the years afterwards, his birthday was marked by processions and bonfires,[4] his approval was sought by economic projectors,[5] and though dismayed often that his own economic advice was ignored by the Irish governing class, he enjoyed the affection of ordinary people. When he walked the streets, he told Alexander Pope in 1733, he was never 'without a thousand blessings from my friends the Vulgar'.[6]

Their champion he might be, but Swift had his own deeply rooted ambivalence about Ireland, which such adulation, however welcome, could not displace. As it had from the commencement of his deanship in 1713, Ireland remained to his mind a place of exile, and from that standpoint its internal flaws were as sharply apparent as England's unfairness. Indeed, the arrogance and economic short-sightedness of the gentry, and the slovenly, deceitful character of the peasantry were more often rehearsed in his Irish writings than the disadvantages of Ireland's relationship with England. With an objectivity nourished by his ambivalence, he could wonder whether the contemporary popular acclaim for his patriotic efforts would provide an enduring basis for his posthumous reputation. 'Drapier's Hill,' a poem of 1729, half-mockingly celebrates his purchase of land in the countryside, on which he planned to build a house:

> And call the Mansion *Drapier*'s Hill;
> That when a Nation long enslav'd,
> Forgets by whom it once was sav'd;
> When none the DRAPIER's Praise shall sing;
> His Signs aloft no longer swing;
> His Medals and his Prints forgotten,
> And all his Handkerchiefs are rotten;
> His famous LETTERS made waste Paper;
> This Hill may keep the Name of DRAPIER,
> In Spight of Envy flourish still,
> And DRAPIER's vye with COOPER's Hill.[7]

Though the house was never built, the interplay here between the imaged ephemeral mementoes of his patriotic eminence and the anticipated stability of the mansion veils the literal sense in a haze of irony. This is somewhat dispelled at the close by the allusion to Denham's poem, which mentions no house surmounting Cooper's Hill; for by that token it is only necessary for Swift's hill to last, as it would, for the Dean's memory to be preserved. The fact that in our time Swift is better remembered than Denham threatens to dispel the irony altogether, undercutting Swift's suspicion that ultimately memory cannot be controlled by the one remembered.

Though handled ironically, 'Drapier's Hill' evidences Swift's 'long pre-occupation with his own death'[8] and a concern for his posthumous reputation that grew markedly in the 1730s. These are instanced playfully in a poem of 1733, jostling with a more obvious consciousness that his literary powers were failing. When the Rev. Patrick Delany and Lord Orrery gave him a paper book and a silver standish for his birthday, each accompanied by a tribute in verse, he responded:

> Let both around my Tomb be plac'd,
> As Trophies of a Muse deceas'd:

> And let the friendly Lines they writ
> In praise of long departed Wit,
> Be grav'd on either Side in Columns,
> More to my Praise than all my Volumes.[9]

The genuine complaint about the decline of his wit underpins the light mockery of a lasting monument, itself a neat reversal of Horace's '*exegi monumentum*'; as in 'Drapier's Hill', the irony is at his own expense. But the fear of being forgotten was serious. According to Laetitia Pilkington, who knew him well in these years, 'the *Dean* could not abide the thought of being like other Mortals, forgot as soon as his venerable Dust was convey'd to the Earth; and therefore he always endeavour'd to render himself worthy of a grateful Remembrance in the Hearts of the People.'[10]

And what sounder foundation might there be for such fame than his patriotism? However ephemeral the devotion of the public, Swift was certain that he had performed enduring service for Ireland; and it would have been difficult to measure the impact of such literary work as was not directly concerned with his native (albeit reluctantly embraced) country. Horace could take account of the whole contribution he had made to literature and judge that he had written himself a monument more lasting than brass, but Swift seems to have decided in the 1730s that patriotism offered his surest claim to memory. 'Verses on the Death of Dr. Swift', written in 1731 but not published until the end of the decade, begins with the transitoriness of literary fame and even friendship, but moves to a climax by dwelling on his patriotism. That emphasis determines the poem; its overstatements, as James Woolley has shown, are typical of eulogy, matters of convention rather than indicating Swift's usual irony.[11] Only at the end of the poem is irony manifest, as he describes his bequest to found St Patrick's Hospital:

> He gave what little Wealth he had
> To build a House for Fools and Mad
> And shew'd by one satyric Touch
> No Nation wanted it so much.

Even here, forecasting his most material benefit to Ireland while implying criticism by noticing the country's inferiority in needing it, his irony reveals the ambivalent nature of his patriotism without subverting his actual contribution.

Beside Swift's inclination towards his patriotism as the rock of an enduring reputation, his popularity as a hero among the Irish 'vulgar' was often paralleled in the 1730s by a recognition among the more literary in both England and Ireland that he was a living classic. In each country this most commonly took the form of linking him to Greek or Roman authors, an allusive shorthand for the rhetoric of literary immortality suggesting that English letters could claim parity with those of the classic lands.[12] Or a writer might draw out the implications of such Augustan parity in particular modern circumstances.

A poet in the London *Universal Spectator* in 1731, for instance, depicts the god of poetry disgusted at the contemporary proliferation of hacks and preparing to flee 'these isles', but leaving 'his commission with Swift and with Pope'; their joint deputyship demonstrates that British literature could still boast exponents of ageless classical standards.[13] Since the objective of such rhetoric was as much to assert a British–classical parity as to exalt a particular modern writer, Pope and even Gay were as frequently as Swift the beneficiaries of classical linkages. But it was true that Swift's eminence in England was unprecedented for a writer Ireland could plausibly claim, and to Irish eulogists the classical link was more than an assertion of parity with the ancients; for they particularly admired Swift's combination of the patriot with the writer, a fusion that lent an august veneer to Protestant Ireland. Proud of the Drapier's successfully defiant articulation of their grievance in the Wood's halfpence affair in the 1720s, and more pleased still at the literary stature he had achieved in English eyes, they saw in Swift a model of citizenship. An anonymous Dublin poet could conclude his *Essay on Preferment* in 1736 with a 'just Character of the Reverend Dean Swift', noting that as he neared seventy he remained 'warm with Patriot, and with Poetick Heat!' The vigour of his age was owing to the fidelity of the Muses, but as much again to

> A Treasure gather'd all your Life before,
> And long preserv'd, to combat with Three score . . .
> . . . .
> A *kind Concern*! if not to break her Chains,
> To help your Country, and to ease her Pains.[14]

The strongest evidence of such Irish admiration of Swift in the 1730s, however, is the collected edition of the Dean's works undertaken by the Dublin printer and newspaper proprietor, George Faulkner; for only by preserving his writings could his standing as at once a patriot and a literary man be secured. Swift would have preferred that a selection of his works be compiled by a consortium of booksellers for publication in London 'long after my death'.[15] While that preference seems counter to his reliance on Irish patriotism as a basis for his reputation, it had in fact been Swift's general practice during his Dublin career to have his works published first, and anonymously, in London. There were exceptions – outstandingly the *Drapier's Letters*, for which speed in publishing to achieve a local effect was a major consideration – but in the main Swift kept to his preference. This might suggest some lack of confidence in Dublin printers, but he felt rather differently about Faulkner, who came to his attention by publishing the collected *Drapier's Letters* in 1725 as *Fraud Detected: or The Hibernian Patriot.* Faulkner accommodated Swift further by placing pieces presumably by him, or favourable ones about him, in the newspaper he had begun at about the same time, the *Dublin Journal.* For some of these he got into trouble with the Irish parliament, enhancing his own stock incidentally as a patriot and ensuring Swift's favour. He was well placed, then, to project in 1733 a

Faulkner began publishing *The Works of J.S., D.D., D.S.P.D.* (Jonathan Swift. Doctor of Divinity, Dean of St Patrick's Dublin) with four volumes in 1735; the fourth of these was devoted to Irish writings. Its frontispiece, engraved by George Vertue, depicts the Dean, about to be laurelled for his patriotism, handing a paper to a gratefully kneeling Hibernia while stepping on a struggling purveyor of coinage, representing William Wood.

collected edition of the Dean's works, and the next year sought Swift's approval, making it clear, however, that he would proceed even without this sanction.[16] Swift was left with little choice but to ensure the correctness of the edition, through his friends' and his own supervision, even though he was averse to having his literary reputation so strongly linked to Dublin. That connection, on the other hand, was very important indeed to Faulkner, both for patriotic reasons and because he was 'intent upon making his own reputation through that of the Drapier'.[17]

The *Dublin Journal* was the mainstay of Faulkner's own long career in publishing, but the edition really made his fortune, as an anonymous poem in his paper foresaw:

> *To the Author of the Dublin Journal*
> Poor, honest George, SWIFT's Works to Print!
> Thy Fortune's made, or Nothing's in't.
> Subscribers, a vast Number shew

> There is no want of Money now.
> The DEAN's so great a Man of Taste,
> All covet to read him in haste;
> More from thy Press than any other . . .[18]

If Faulkner's attitude toward Swift mixed respect with opportunism, he was by no means alone, especially as the Dean in 1745 neared death. In that year Henry Jones of Drogheda, County Louth, a bricklayer who had acquired some local fame as a poet, welcomed the arrival of a new Lord Lieutenant, the Earl of Chesterfield, whose literary prestige Jones hoped would spark a revival of the arts in Ireland. Jones represented the country's current 'drooping' state with a picture of the aged, senile Dean:

> Tho SWIFT be Dumb, for SWIFT IERNE weeps
> The Pride, the Pillar of his Country sleeps,
> His clouded Soul emits no dazling ray,
> But faintly warms the animated Clay.
> Not ROME's sad Ruins such Impressions leave,
> As Reason bury'd in the Body's Grave.
> His living Lines shall mix their sacred Fire
> In Nature's Blaze, and with thy Works expire.[19]

Jones's confused syntax in the final line cannot disguise his negation of Swift's permanence: the Dean's seeming imbecility informs at once the poet's melancholy and his dismissal from enduring memory. It becomes equally fitting to mourn Swift's fate and to anticipate his being forgotten, especially to enforce the contrast with the promise of Chesterfield. The new Lord Lieutenant may himself have been responsible for a pair of pamphlets, also in 1745, which showed that Swift's reputation as a patriot could be put to use while he yet, if barely, lived. Taking advantage of his high standing, the two *Drapier's Letters to the Good People of Ireland* warn Irish Catholics against siding with the Pretender in the 1745 rising. According to the *Second Letter*, the first, arguing that even a Stuart victory would hardly improve their lot, was 'bought, with great Eagerness', though whether actually thought to be Swift's it is impossible to say.[20] Of the many pieces spuriously attributed to Swift, these were the last in his lifetime, though others followed after his death.

II

Neither Jones's poem nor the final Drapier's imposture was intended, of course, to have any effect on Swift's reputation, but merely to use it. Faulkner's interest was more proprietary, and it was to his advantage to promote Swift while he lived, as much for his wit as for his patriotism. New

THE

D R A P I E R's

L E T T E R

TO THE

GOOD PEOPLE

OF

I R E L A N D.

D U B L I N:
Printed in the Year MDCCXLV.

The final spurious ascription to Swift as the Drapier in his lifetime, this *Letter* (possibly written by the Earl of Chesterfield, then Lord Lieutenant of Ireland) was apparently intended to dissuade Irish Catholics from joining the Stuart rebellion in 1745.

editions of the *Works*, and additional volumes, appeared in the first half of the 1740s; and after Swift's certification as incompetent in 1742, Faulkner never published anything in the *Dublin Journal* that reflected upon his decline. Then, when Swift died on 19 October 1745, the *Dublin Journal* eulogized him as 'a great and eminent Patriot' whose 'Genius, Works, Learning and Charity are universally admired'. Obviously Faulkner's own composition, the obituary continued in a more personal vein:

> That for a News Writer to attempt his Character would be the highest presumption, Yet, as the Printer hereof is proud to acknowledge his infinite Obligations to that Prodigy of Wit, he can only lament that he is by no means equal to so bold an Undertaking.[21]

However genuine his affection, Faulkner was hardly likely to neglect an opportunity to capitalize on the Dean's death. Accordingly, on the page of

October.   GEORGE FAULKNER.   Numb. 1943

The Dublin Journal.

From SATURDAY October the 19th, to TUESDAY October the 22d, 1745.

A Circular Letter from the Right Rev. the Lord Bishop of Leighlin and Ferns to the Clergy of his Diocese.

My Reverend Brethren,

LET it not seem to speak the least Distrust of your doing, at this important Juncture, every Thing which your Duty to God, your King, and your Country demand from you, but rather my earnest Desire to concur with, and assist you in the Discharge of those Duties, that I take this Method of suggesting to you, by what Expressions of our Zeal and Loyalty, I imagine, we may most effectually contribute to blast the Hopes and wicked Designs of our Enemies, to preserve the Peace and Stability of his Majesty's Government, and in consequence of that, our own Happiness and Prosperity.

However easy and obvious it may be to account for the Dangers that threaten us upon the Principles of human Policy, and to discern in particular, for what Ends a Rebellion in North Britain, in favour of a Popish Pretender to his Majesty's Crown, is at this Time raised, and by what Powers supported, yet it becomes us to lift up our Thoughts to an higher Cause; to that Providence which ruleth in the Kingdoms of the Earth, and is generally seen to punish national Sins with national Calamities.

Let us awaken in the Hearts of our People an awful Sense of this great Truth, and in consequence of it, urge upon them the Necessity of a speedy and effectual forsaking of their Sins, that they may become fit Objects for the Almighty Protection. And let us lead them on to this important Service of our Country by beginning in our own Persons and Characters the blessed Work of a national Improvement.

You will at the same Time think it your Duty, both from the Pulpit, and in private, to admonish them of the Evil of Rebellion, and the horrible Guilt of that Perjury and Ingratitude, which, in the present Case, must attend it,—to shew them how egregiously those Men trifle with the solemn Oaths by which they have bound their Allegiance to his most sacred Majesty King George, who think it sufficient, that they are not themselves the Promoters of Commotions and Treasons, whilst through Indolence or Fear, they suffer them to gather Strength and be-

There having been a great Demand for the following Letter, it is again reprinted at the earnest Request of several Protestants, as well as Roman Catholicks.

The Bishop of CLOYNE's Letter to the Roman Catholicks of his Diocese.

My Countrymen and Fellow Subjects,

NOtwithstanding the Difference of our religious Opinions, I should be sorry to be wanting in any Instance of Humanity or good Neighbourhood to any of you. For which Reason it would be highly imprudent as well as ungrateful to forfeit these Advantages, by making yourselves Tools to the Ambition of foreign Princes, who fancy it expedient to raise Disturbances among us at present; but as soon as their own Ends are served, will not fail to abandon you, as they have always done.

Is it not evident that your true Interest consists in lying still, and waiting the Event, since Ireland must necessarily follow the Fate of England; and that therefore Prudence and Policy prescribe Quiet to the Roman Catholicks of this Kingdom, who, in Case a Change of Hands should not succeed, after your attempt to bring it about, must then expect to be on a worse Foot than ever?

But we will suppose it succeeds to your Wish. What then? Would not this undermine even your own Interests and Fortunes, which are often interwoven with those of your Neighbours? Would not all those, who have Debts or Money or other Effects in the Hands of Protestants, be Fellow Sufferers with them? Would not all those who hold under the Acts of Settlement, be as liable as Protestants themselves to be dispossessed by the old Proprietors? Or, can even those who are styled Proprietors, flatter themselves with Hopes of possessing the Estates which they claim, which, in all likelihood, would be given to Favourites, (perhaps to Foreigners) who are near the Person, or who fought the Battles, of their Master.

and they will lose the last drop of Blood in their Veins to preserve the former, and to destroy the latter. This you may assure the Publick of, and if I prove to be a false Prophet, I will submit to be burnt at a Stake; which by the bye is the least I expect, should it please God in his Wrath, for the just Punishment of our Sins, to curse us with a Popish King. I have four hundred brave Fellows ready to follow me at an Hour's Warning, and I shall not scruple to set myself at their Head. Would to God I were able to furnish them with Arms. Give us Arms, and if we don't use them to good Purpose against our Enemies may we lose our Heads. I am, dear Sir, your faithful humble Servant.

D U B L I N

Last Saturday at three o'Clock in the Afternoon dyed that great and eminent Patriot the Rev. Dr. Jonathan Swift, Dean of St. Patrick's Dublin, in the 78th Year of his Age, who was born in the Parish of St. Warburg's, Dublin, the 30th of November 1667, at his Uncle Counsellor Godwin Swift's House in Hoey's Alley, which in those Times, was the general Residence of the chief Lawyers. His Genius, Works, Learning and Charity are so universally admired, That for a News Writer to attempt his Character would be the highest Presumption. Yet, as the Printer hereof is proud to acknowledge his infinite Obligations to that Prodigy of Wit, he can only lament, that he is by no Means equal to so bold an Undertaking.

The Dean hath bequeathed the Bulk of his Fortune which is about 11,000 l. to build and endow an Hospital for Lunaticks, Idiots and Incurables, which said Hospital is to be called St. Patrick's, and to be erected near Stevens's. Dr. Sterne, late Bishop of Clogher left 600 l. towards carrying on the said Hospital, and Williams Coningham, Esq; 300 l.

Yesterday both Houses of Parliament met according to Adjournment.

The following is recommended by several Roman Catholick Gentlemen and published at their Request to shew their peaceable Disposition and Loyalty at this Time, to the present Government.

The Roman Catholick Clergy have for three Weeks past earnestly recommended to their People to behave themselves peace-

The brief eulogy on the front page of The Dublin Journal, 19–22 October 1745, noting Swift's death as the lead item under the heading 'Dublin'.

Some Masters of Ships who lately arrived here from Scotland, report, that the City of Edinburgh is laid in Ashes; and that the young Chevalier has thought proper to remove his Quarters further from the Castle.

Letters from Philadelphia advise, that the two French East India Ships, that put into Martinico are taken by the English; as also, the Spanish South Sea Ships that made her Escape from Captain Talbot.

At a Quarter Assembly held last Friday at the Tholsel, the Sheriffs and Commons came to the following Resolution, Nem. Con. That the Thanks of this House be given to Alderman John Walker, late Lord Mayor of this City, for his faithful Services to the Public, in carefully and diligently discharging all the Duties incumbent on that great Office during his Administration.

The Grand Biche Privateer of 36 Guns is taken by Admiral Martin, and sent into Falmouth.

Mr. Henry Bridges of London, Author of the Microcosm, is arriv'd in this Kingdom, and purposes immediately to exhibit his Grand Machine or Microcosm to the View of the Curious. It hath carefully been inspected into by the Virtuoso's of London, and to their great Content and inmost Satisfaction.

The Merchants and Traders of Dublin are desired to meet at Guildhall on Thursday next at 12 o'Clock at Noon.

Now in the Press and will speedily be published by the Printer hereof, The Posthumous Works of the Rev. Dr. JONATHAN SWIFT, D. S. P. D. which will be printed in single Pieces, as well as in Volumes. To which will be added, a few Tracts published in his Life Time, with some Corrections by himself, for the Satisfaction of the Publick, to make his Works compleat.

N. B. These Works, with the seven Volumes in Octavo and Duodecimo, will compleat his Writings. And, for the Satisfaction of the Publick, (as some Volumes may be lent, or lost, or mislaid) any single Volume of either Edition may be had alone to compleat Setts.

This Day is published by the Printer hereof, Price 6d. Halfpenny. VERSES on the Death of Dr. SWIFT, D. S. P. D. occasioned by reading a Maxim in Rochefoucault. Dans l'adversité de nos meilleurs amis nous trouvons, quelque chose, qui ne nous deplaist pas. In the Adversity of our best Friends, we find something that doth not displease us. Written by Himself.

Also, just published and sold by the Printer hereof, Price 13 d. each, a very fine engraved Print of the Rev. Dr. Swift, D. S. P. D. taken from the original Picture painted by Mr. Gervais; and the other a Metzotinto taken from the fine original Portrait in the Deanry House in Kevin-Street, which Picture was painted by Mr. Bindon at the Expence of the Chapter, and is universally allowed by all the Friends and Acquaintance of the Dean to be the most exact Likeness that ever was taken.

The Business carried on by Mess. David Latouche, Nathaniel Kane, and David Latouche the Younger, in Castle-Street, is, and will be continued in the same House and Manner, by Na-

Faulkner's advertisements in The Dublin Journal, 19–22 October 1745, overleaf from his notice of Swift's death.

A mezzotint portrait of Swift by Andrew Miller in 1743, taken from the painting by Francis Bindon commissioned in 1739 by the Chapter of St Patrick's Cathedral, which is very similar if not identical to that which Faulkner advertised for sale in *The Dublin Journal*.

the newspaper following the obituary, he advertised a volume of Swift's *Posthumous Works* as forthcoming, to 'complete' his edition, and announced as well a $6\frac{1}{2}d.$ pamphlet of 'Verses on the Death of Dr. Swift' as available at once, along with a 13 d engraved portrait and a mezzotint. And in the next issue of the newspaper, which reported Swift's private funeral at midnight, 22 October 1745, the advertisements for the volume and the pamphlet were repeated. The portraits were no longer mentioned; they may have sold out, for Swift remained a popular figure, attracting a crowd of Dubliners to pass by his bier when he was laid out in the Deanery.[22] The same issue of the *Dublin Journal* also reported that the sophister students of Trinity College had decided unanimously to apply the funds already collected for a 'grand Entertainment' instead to the purchase of a bust of Swift for the college library.[23]

This may have prompted Faulkner to devise his own plan for a memorial, a means of continuing his association with Swift that would at once serve to mark his gratitude, preserve the Dean's memory, and, incidentally, foster sales of the *Works*. Within three weeks Faulkner launched an appeal for funds to erect 'a handsome Monument over his Grave in St. Patrick's Cathedral', since 'many Strangers as well as Natives of this Kingdom who are well-wishers to the Glory of their Country, are earnestly desirous that the Ashes of the Great Dr. SWIFT do not lie undistinguished among the common Dead'.[24] Couched literally as an appeal for a tombstone, Faulkner's new project would testify to Swift's distinctly patriotic claims, which Ireland at large (rather than Trinity's students and scholars alone) would gain glory by remembering. But Faulkner's advertisement for subscribers, though repeated a few times before the end of the year, met with few if any takers, and the project languished. One reason may have been that it would so transparently have promoted his own edition; even before 1745 ended, the plan for a volume of *Posthumous Works* attracted scathing notice in a pamphlet which had Swift's ghost appear to Faulkner and complain

> . . . thou, O avaritious Slave!
> Not content my better Works to have,
> Must tinker-like recoin my Dross,
> And half-form'd Embryo Works engross;
> Works that can never stand the Test,
> But rust and canker all the rest.[25]

Faulkner's thrusting himself forward as a guardian and promoter of Swift's patriotic memory may also have been compromised by his growing closeness to the Irish administration. Even before Swift actually died, Faulkner joined a deputation of Dublin merchants to greet Chesterfield as the new Lord Lieutenant. The printer and the Viceroy became quite friendly in the ensuing months, and in Chesterfield Faulkner gained an entree into Irish government circles that effectively replaced the patronage of the dying, and soon dead,

Swift. Indeed, Faulkner saw no reason not to make use of both of them at once. He saw Chesterfield as a patriot and man of letters cast from the same mould as Swift: both were eminent for literature and both had 'preserved' Ireland, the one from Wood's scheme and the other from involvement in the ongoing Jacobite rising. On account of these traits, Faulkner dedicated to the Lord Lieutenant in January 1746 the eighth volume of Swift's *Works* (the volume advertised as *Posthumous Works* on the Dean's death), since 'no person living bears a greater Resemblance [to Swift] than the Earl of Chesterfield'.[26] The Lord Lieutenant was drawn to the printer as well, whom he thought deserved a knighthood and to whom he apparently offered one, which Faulkner declined.[27] An anonymous lampoon later in 1746 presented Faulkner, after Chesterfield's lieutenancy was over, regretting this refusal and recalling that the earl, who plied him for anecdotes of Swift, was attracted to him by the same qualities that endeared him to the Dean.[28] Such a public impression hardly fostered Faulkner's credentials as the moving spirit behind the monument project he had billed as a patriotic campaign.

For whatever reason the monument campaign was unsuccessful, and at the end of 1747 the Governors of St Patrick's Hospital, founded by the major bequest in Swift's will, themselves decided to remedy the lack of a monument over his grave in the cathedral. Meeting on 11 December, they ordered that a memorial be made and called for designs; one of two submitted was chosen at their meeting of 27 February 1748,[29] and on 8 August 1749 the *Dublin Journal* reported that it had been erected. It bore Swift's arms and the epitaph he had composed, which the newspaper printed in capitals. Meanwhile the bust of Swift ordered by the Trinity students, sculpted by Roubiliac in London, had arrived, as the same paper reported 21–25 March 1749, printing 'VERSES propos'd as an INSCRIPTION':

> We, Youth of ALMA, Thee, her Pride and Grace,
> Illustrious Swift, amid these Heroes place;
> Thee, of such high Associates worthiest found,
> In Genius, Fancy, Sense, alike renown'd
> Rich in unborrow'd wit, thy various Page
> By Turns displays the Patriot, Poet, Sage;
> Born to delight thy Country, and defend;
> In life, in Death to human race a Friend,
> For Mad and Ideots, whom alone to teach
> Thy Writings fail, thy Will's last Bounty Reach.

Whether or not Faulkner's own lines, these would have fulfilled much of the intention behind his monument project, namely to affirm Swift as at once a great writer and an Irish patriot, his image – however sequestered in Trinity's Library – fitly joining those of the classical 'heroes' of learning there.

The bust of Swift by the prominent London sculptor Louis-François Roubiliac for Trinity College Library. It was mounted in the Long Room in 1749.

III

The final lines of this poem propose Bishop Berkeley as the next Irish patriot-sage suitable for inclusion among these heroes. But by 1749 Dublin was embroiled in a political controversy which thrust into prominence a very different successor to Swift, Dr Charles Lucas. Swift was invoked by both sides in this dispute, but only tangentially, indicating a degree of reserve in popular reverence for his memory which may also have contributed to the failure of Faulkner's plan for a monument. Lucas, a Dublin apothecary and dissenter, had been elected to the common council of Dublin corporation in 1741 and began soon afterwards to agitate for municipal reform. He was supported by James Digges Latouche, of a successful Huguenot banking family, but opposed by the Dublin corporation's controlling body, the aldermen (who comprised the upper house of municipal government) and lord mayor, and both Lucas and Latouche lost their places in 1744. The deaths in

1748 and 1749 of two aldermen who also represented Dublin in the Irish parliament prompted Latouche, followed by Lucas, to declare for the vacant parliamentary seats, the by-elections for which would take place in November 1749.[30] Lucas's campaign, marked by a sustained barrage of speeches and pamphlets, moved from the promotion of municipal reform to much weightier considerations of Ireland's status as a dependent kingdom. His assertions at once of the country's constitutional attachment to the king and of her properly autonomous relationship with England recall Swift's arguments in the fourth *Drapier's Letter* of a quarter century earlier, moving later commentators to judge that Lucas, as Stephen Gwynn put it, 'inherited Swift's principles'.[31] But to Lucas himself, strongly anti-Catholic and a rhetorically violent Whig, Swift was entirely a Tory, even a Jacobite in his politics, and the government he had served in 1710–14 'the *wicked Ministry* of the *much misguided Queen Anne*'.[32] Lucas preferred to compare himself to the English Whig patriots Hampden, Sidney and Russell, and their Irish counterparts Molesworth and William Molyneux, as a champion of constitutional liberty,[33] and in 1758 anonymously asserted that greatly though he admired the literary Swift, whom he 'long knew', he

> was no stranger to his politics, connexions, tendencies, passions, and the whole oeconomy of his life. He [Lucas] has long been hardily singular in condemning this great man's conduct, amidst the admiring multitude; nor ever could have thought of making an interest in a man, whose principles and manners he could, by no rule of reason or honour, approve, however he might have admired his parts and wit.[34]

There is only one allusion to Swift in support of Lucas, appearing on 29 July 1749 in the ninth number of *The Censor*, a paper Lucas edited to further his cause; though probably by Lucas, it could have been supplied by another hand:

> . . . though my poor, inconsiderable Labors, [sic] must have contributed little, if anything, to the Service of Mankind, yet conscious that my Intentions and Wishes for the Public, are not inferior to those of PYM, HAMPDEN, or SHEPPIN, MOLYNEUX, KING, or SWIFT, though my Abilities be infinitely inferior to theirs, I soar and steer, in mine own Imagination, towards the lofty sphere of these, and other great and immortal PATRIOTS, and look down, with as much contempt or pity, as any of them could shew, on those poor Wretches, who from *selfish* or *slavish Motives*, oppose every Tendency to Reformation.[35]

If Swift is numbered here, by Lucas or one of his supporters, for his literary talents and public spirit rather than his principles, it would still be strange to include him in a list of otherwise professed Whigs. Whoever the author, then, Swift's inclusion seems most likely a rhetorical flourish. That is the more probable because Lucas's ally Latouche, in a campaign address of 20

October 1749, recalled the Wood's halfpence affair without the barest mention of Swift:

> What defeated Wood's vile *scheme* to ruin us? Was it not the *Representation* of our several Corporations, the inflexible *Integrity* of our Grand Juries, not withstanding the *Insinuations*, *Flattery* and even Menaces of an eminent Lord Chief Justice . . .[36]

The election campaign did, however, prompt a reprint of Swift's *Story of the Injured Lady*, with a preface 'By A. Freeman, Barber and Citizen of Dublin', which does not place Swift decidedly on either side of the issue, but describes him merely as the Lady's (i.e. Ireland's) 'faithful Confessor and Counsellor . . . one of her most true and sincere friends and most intimate acquaintance'.[37] Even more ambiguous, considering that Lucas had adopted Molyneux as a political ancestor, was the announcement of a reprint of Molyneux's *Case of Ireland* at the end of an anti-Lucas tract, which noted that the original publication, 'instead of meeting with the approbation dean Swift and others of our patriots thought it deserved, was condemned to the flames. . . . The DEAN, when living, had this book in so great esteem, that he was often heard to say, "It ought to be printed in letters of gold".'[38] And another pamphlet suggests that Swift's memory should not be invoked in definite support of Lucas. This presents a rural discussion of the campaign between a curate and an apothecary (Lucas's own profession), who notes that Lucas had been honoured by a Dublin guild, adding, ' "What more could they have done for SWIFT, or any other Patriot?" "Softly", says the *Curate*. . . . Let us not compare him to Swift, till we know him better." '[39]

Nor were Lucas's opponents, the anti-reform Dublin establishment, forward in claiming Swift for their side. They preferred more direct methods to undermine Lucas himself, and easily convinced the Irish House of Commons to examine his constitutional assertions, determine that they were seditious, and resolve unanimously that he was an enemy to his country who should be prosecuted and imprisoned. Lucas consequently fled Ireland, and for some years resided in London, eventually to return and gain election to the Irish parliament in 1761. His adherents in the autumn of 1749 continued their campaign, however, by supporting Latouche. He was a strong candidate, and in the open polling that ran from 24 October to 11 November 1749, he was attracting such support among the franchised merchants that his establishment opponents decided to resurrect Swift's ghost to hammer the constitutional positions that Lucas, and by extension Latouche, held – though not by confuting any that Swift himself had asserted. Instead, the ghost admonished the weavers in particular, whom the Dean had championed when alive, to remember where their best interests lay:

> It is said that you are *disaffected*, that you have been the *Aiders* and *Abettors* of Lucas's *Doctrine*. Depend upon it, such a Report can be of no *service* to you.

REMEMBER that it is in your *interest, more particularly than any other set of People*, to be well with those in *Power*, who can *serve* or *disserve* you! you may have Favours to ask of them! Then be wise – be prudent – do not *offend* them – do not kick against the Pricks![40]

Weavers, like others trading in wool and cloth, were historically vulnerable to trade legislation, and this threat may have had some effect. Latouche was elected nonetheless, but was unseated by the House of Commons on the grounds that he had been allied with Lucas. If for the latter 'the term "nationalism" is a perfectly valid description of his ideology . . . a forerunner of the constitutional nationalism of Grattan and O'Connell',[41] it was too soon after Swift's death for an Irish Whig nationalist to forget the Dean's Tory associations and claim his patriotic mantle, even as his establishment opponents took remarkable, even absurd, care not to vilify Swift along with Lucas. All the same, the references to Swift during the controversy are so peripheral as to suggest a general uncertainty about his relevance.

IV

All this should have augured poorly for a revival of Faulkner's plan to erect a monument to Swift by public subscription. By the end of 1751, however, Faulkner was printing the Irish edition of Lord Orrery's *Remarks on the Life and Writings of Dr. Jonathan Swift* and had published a further volume of Swift's *Works*; still another would appear in 1752. For his commentary, the first full-length book devoted to Swift's works, Orrery had used Faulkner's edition, and it is likely that each spurred sales of the other; in this context it could hardly be coincidental that Faulkner's monument project emerged again in 1752. But the moving spirit this time was Thomas Sheridan, the manager of the Smock-Alley Theatre and son of a friend of Swift, the Rev. Thomas Sheridan. In the *Dublin Journal* of 21–5 January 1752, Sheridan proposed a benefit performance at the theatre, the profits of which would 'go towards erecting a Monument by public Gratitude to that glorious Patriot and great Genius, Dr. Jonathan Swift, D.S.P.D., which worthy example, it is hoped, will encourage all the lovers of Ireland, to get on foot a Subscription for this purpose'.

Faulkner himself was to receive contributions, the first of which, for fifty pounds, was announced at the same time, and the sculptor Van Nost was to draw up a plan for the monument. The *Dublin Journal* heartily promoted the subscription campaign, which Faulkner himself probably orchestrated, with poetry, letters and reports of subscriptions coming in. A month after the proposal was published, Steele's *Conscious Lovers* was chosen as the play to be performed, and the date set for 23 March. The play was, apparently, well attended, with a prologue written for the occasion by John Marshall and spoken by Sheridan himself.[42] Faulkner's paper duly reported the 'very full audience' (21–4 March) and then, curiously, was silent for a month about the monument project it had promoted so vigorously. Then, a long letter from 'HIBERNICUS' in the 24–8 April issue recalled the large attendance at the play as well as reflecting Swift's reputation for selfless patriotism, but wondered about the progress of the monument campaign it was intended to benefit:

> as this undertaking is the first of its kind which has been attempted in this Kingdom . . . I am in much Pain about the Success of it; which must in a great Measure depend upon the Conduct of the Undertakers. I fear lest the Management of a few bring a Reflection upon the Nation. If something be not done worthy of the Memory of that great Man, and worthy of the Publick, it were better no such Attempt had been made; lest whilst we think we are erecting a Trophy to SWIFT'S Honour, we in fact give to Posterity a lasting Monument of our own Poverty of Spirit.

'HIBERNICUS' concluded by calling for a meeting of all subscribers to the project, to select trustees who would direct it thereafter. Without naming them, the letter suggested little confidence in either Faulkner or Sheridan, and Faulkner's printing it nonetheless is some mark of his devotion to the project. The paper's ensuing near-silence about the campaign, however, points to its failure.

Indeed, nine months passed before the *Dublin Journal* of 9–13 January 1753 announced that a meeting of actual or intending subscribers was to take place on 10 February following. The announcement was repeated in all succeeding issues until that date, but then the paper fell silent again on the matter. The next year an anonymous pamphleteer took Faulkner implicitly, and Sheridan directly, to task for the delays and, indeed, mismanagement bedevilling the project:

> . . . no man ever exerted a greater portion of public Spirit, nor had the *Vox Populi* more on his side than *Swift*; and I really think it has been an Occasion of just Reproach to this Kingdom, that one, who was not only an Honour, but of material Service to the Nation, should, many Years after his Death, be sent about begging in News Papers, for a Monument to mark his Ashes from the common Clay: But I think it still more extraordinary, that the Publick has not yet call'd upon the Manager [i.e. Sheridan] for some account of above an hundred Pounds, which was raised upon that Occasion [i.e. the 1752 benefit performance]. . . .[43]

Notwithstanding the harsh tone here, four more years elapsed before the two projectors mounted any defence of their behaviour. At that point, after Sheridan had been criticized in print for raising money for a monument to Shakespeare that was never erected,[44] an anonymous letter in response appeared in the *Journal* of 4–7 February 1758. The letter notes that it was a monument to Swift, not Shakespeare, that was intended, and that Sheridan had in mind one costing between £800 and £1,000, but that only £101 had been raised by the benefit play in 1752. Sheridan had duly called a subscribers' meeting for February 1753, but only three attended: the Rev. John Lyon, Swift's assistant and Secretary to the Governors of St Patrick's Hospital; John Marshall, author of the prologue to the benefit play; and Faulkner. Sheridan decided that another benefit performance was the only means of renewing interest, but had to leave Ireland before this plan could be put into effect. The letter concludes by calling for 'a set of Gentlemen public spirited enough to undertake' the monument project, to whom Sheridan would gladly give the funds already collected; and it is endorsed by a note from Faulkner. Thenceforth, however, the paper resumed its silence about the project, from which no one, clearly, had emerged very well.

One reason for its failure seems to have been Faulkner's involving himself in the campaign once again. The 1752 letter from HIBERNICUS reflects obliquely on 'the Management of a few', and there was also the lingering taint of Faulkner's eagerness to publish whatever he could find of Swift's, however unworthy; this may not have damaged sales of his edition, but did little credit to his proprietorship of Swift's reputation. Nor was this impression much altered by Faulkner's publishing Orrery's *Remarks* in Ireland. A nobleman well known as Swift's friend, Orrery was actually quite critical of his character, and his book met with little praise in Ireland. While this provided further evidence of Faulkner's poor guardianship of Swift's memory, it seemed equally base of him to have supported the administration in an ongoing dispute with the Irish House of Commons through the 1751 and 1753 sessions about Money Bills which had been so phrased by the government as to offend Irish patriotic sensibilities. The insult in the first instance seemed gratuitous, but after a majority in the House voted down the 1751 Money Bill to make its point, the government's use of the same phrasing in the next session appeared deliberately arrogant, and unlike the Lucas controversy it generated a discernible 'patriot' grouping within the Irish parliament.[45] The 'Money Bill' dispute wound down slowly, with no remarkable enthusiasm among the patriots to invoke Swift. One anonymous pamphleteer in 1753, for instance, called attention to the demise of Wood's halfpence scheme thirty years earlier, and, like Latouche in 1749, avoided alluding at all to Swift's part in it.[46] Yet when a pro-government pamphlet signed 'Patricius' quoted at length from Swift's early *Discourse of the Contests and Dissentions* to bolster the argument that the patriot side was self-interestedly inflaming the issues,[47] it was quickly answered. The anonymous patriot rejoinder, however, mistakenly took Swift's *Discourse* defending Whig lords in 1701 to be serving instead the ministry he was more actively assisting a decade later, 'supporting the highest Tory Administration ever *England* saw, to break the Power of the Whigs, and set aside the *Hanover* Succession'. Hence Swift's piece 'leaves too much Room to suspect the Honesty of one, to whom this Kingdom has been so much obliged. But let the latter Part of his Life attone for the former, *and Peace to his honoured Shade*.'[48] If the 'Money Bill' patriots were uneasy, in other words, at Swift's apparent political inconsistencies, they were hardly about to let the government party claim the Dean for itself. This extended to vilifying Faulkner, a government supporter, for publishing Orrery's criticism of Swift. Thereby Faulkner showed 'Ingratitude to his deceased Patriot-Creator, and Petulance to those in Being'; he 'Ungratefully endeavour'd to be-spatter the Noble Patriot, who rescu'd him from Poverty and Slavery, a Patriot whos [sic] laurels will ever Bloom, while the Word Liberty is understood in Ireland'.[49]

Just as calling Swift to mind seemed generally inappropriate or irrelevant to the actual political controversies surrounding Lucas and the Money Bills, so Faulkner seemed ill-placed to conduct a patriotic campaign to commemorate him. By contrast, an independent effort to honour the Dean in the County Mayo countryside far from Dublin was quite successful in these years. John Browne, a gentleman with whom Swift had actually quarrelled but was later reconciled, had grown impatient that Ireland was 'so long and so shamefully negligent in erecting some monument of gratitude to his memory'. At his estate in Neale, near Ballinrobe, he sought to remedy the situation in 1750, raising a column surmounted by Pegasus, with a Latin inscription on its pedestal hailing the Dean as '*divine poeta*' but maintaining that the hearts of the Irish people ('*gentis Iernae pectora*') cherished a greater memorial still. Browne also instituted an agricultural fair to celebrate Swift, taking place annually in the first three days of May and starting with contests in dancing and 'singing the praises of this ingenious patriot'.[50] Faulkner, perhaps hoping to spark emulation in the capital, published a report of the events held in May 1753.[51] In Dublin, indeed, even references to his monument campaign were rare outside the pages of his own newspaper, silent itself as the project faltered. A poet in 1754 may have been alluding to the notion of a statue for Swift:

> The *Bard* who triumphs o'er a single vice
> Or saves his Country by his sage Advice;
> Deserves as much a *Statue* to his Name
> As he who conquers in a martial Fame;
> And *Drapier, Dublin, Wood* in Times to come,
> Shall sound like *Tully, Cataline and Rome*.[52]

But the image of a statue juxtaposed with the encomium on the Dean may simply have been a coincidence. And other newspapers all but uniformly ignored the project, though an obituary notice for John Marshall in the *Universal Advertiser*, 11 March 1755, gave most of its attention to his prologue for Sheridan's benefit performance of three years before. If, however, Faulkner's proprietary attitude toward Swift's continuing literary eminence and patriotic inspiration was a major factor in his involvement in the abortive monument project, it remained unshaken. When the Dublin booksellers

George and Alexander Ewing announced an edition of Swift's *History of the Four Last Years of the Queen* in 1758, Faulkner was incensed; the ensuing minor paper war was marked by his charges of piracy, theirs of his arrogance, and his promoting his own competing edition as more authentic and 'complete'.[53]

As the monument project surfaced one last time, moreover, Faulkner may again have been involved, though only on the margin. In mid-1762 the construction of a new roadway, Parliament Street, forced him to move his shop from Essex Street, where he had long conducted business, to temporary quarters in the Blind Quay.[54] He was to move a few years later into a new house, to be built at the corner of Parliament Street, opposite Essex Bridge, and in the interval took the opportunity of commissioning a marble bust of Swift from Patrick Cunningham, formerly an apprentice of Van Nost, the sculptor who was to have produced the monument to Swift projected a decade earlier. Faulkner announced in the *Dublin Journal* of 19–22 November 1763 that Cunningham had completed the bust, 'which is allowed by all people, who have seen it, to be the most compleat Piece of Sculpture ever seen in this Kingdom, and equal to any of the Antiques of Egypt, Greece or Italy'. The bust was intended for display in a niche on the outside of the new premises Faulkner planned to occupy; and shortly after finishing it Cunningham advertised plaster of Paris models available by subscription, at a guinea each.[55] The subscription apparently went well, for in 1820 Monck Mason noted without enthusiasm that plaster of Paris busts of Swift 'are pretty numerous, almost all of them are however taken from the same model, and are very indifferent representations'.[56]

Perhaps buoyed by this success, Cunningham designed 'A model of a monument to the memory of the Late Dr. Swift' and displayed it at the first exhibition of the Society of Artists in Ireland, which opened on 12 February 1765;[57] Faulkner had assisted the Society in launching this show[58] and may have had a hand in Cunningham's plan to interest subscribers and the public at large in this last project for a major memorial to Swift. Cunningham intended the monument to be erected on College Green, where an equestrian statue of William III had long stood.[59] As noted earlier, a pamphlet of 1732 had countered a previous proposal for a monument to the Drapier with the suggestion that Dublin needed a second statue of King William instead;[60] now, over thirty years later, Cunningham's proposal to memorialize Swift near William was a forthright assertion of the Dean's parity with the King as a hero of Protestant Ireland. The model prompted a protégé of Swift, Dr William Dunkin, to compose an inscription:

> Say, to the Drapier's vast unbounded fame,
> What added honours can the Sculptor give?
> None. – 'Tis a sanction from the Drapier's name
> Must bid the Sculptor and his Marble live.

Patrick Cunningham's bust of Swift (*right*), completed in 1763, which Faulkner displayed in his shop, using an engraving of it (*left*) as the frontispiece for volume fourteen of a duodecimo edition of Swift's *Works* in 1767.

If these verses show little enthusiasm for Cunningham's design, they moved William Bowyer, the London printer, to adopt a more positive conventional vein in some of his own:

> Which gave the Drapier birth two realms contend;
> And each asserts her Poet, Patriot, Friend;
> Her mitre jealous Britain may deny;
> That loss Iernia's laurel shall supply:
> Through life's low vale, she, grateful, gave him bread;
> Her vocal stones shall vindicate him dead.[61]

Others, however, seem to have shared Dunkin's lack of admiration for Cunningham's memorial, for like the previous campaigns in which Faulkner's part was clearer, this one came to nothing and the project for a Swift monument on any heroic scale was not revived again. Even Cunningham's design seems not to have survived. But Faulkner's new house was soon ready for business, and presumably the Cunningham bust was mounted.[62] The

This engraving for the *Hibernian Magazine*, April 1802, is the first depiction of the Cunningham bust in place in St Patrick's Cathedral where it was mounted on a column above the tablet featuring Swift's famous epitaph.

sculptor borrowed it for display at the second exhibition of the Society of Artists in Ireland in 1766,[63] and thereafter it was returned to Faulkner, whose pride in the bust is evident from his inclusion of an engraving of it as the frontispiece to the fourteenth volume of Swift's *Works* in 1767, with the legend, 'SWIFT. From the Original in the Possession of G. Faulkner.' And he was happy to show it off: writing in 1826, the actor John O'Keeffe recalled that in his youth he passed one day by Faulkner's shop to 'stare in at a bust, on the counter'. Faulkner noticed the boy and 'invited me in to look at the bust, saying it was the head of his friend and patron Dean Swift. To display it in all its different views, he turned it around and about for me and then brought me upstairs to see the picture of Swift,' which hung in Faulkner's dining room.[64]

A poem by Richard Lewis published about 1775, 'An Elegy written in a Cathedral', imitates Gray's 'Elegy' with St Patrick's Cathedral as its setting; meditating at Swift's grave, Lewis seems to recall the abortive projects for a monument: 'And Though defrauded of the promis'd tomb/His image lives

THE
IRISH PENNY MAGAZINE.
T. & J. COLDWELL,] PUBLISHED WEEKLY. [50, CAPEL-STREET.

No. 29. DUBLIN, SATURDAY, JULY 20, 1833. VOL. I.

DEAN SWIFT'S MONUMENT, ST. PATRICK'S CATHEDRAL, DUBLIN.

Drawn by Samuel Lover, Esq. R. H. A. for the Irish Penny Magazine.

ILLUSTRATIONS OF IRISH TOPOGRAPHY.—NO. XXIX.
[From Original MS. Collections.]

ST. PATRICK'S CATHEDRAL, DUBLIN.
[RESUMED AND CONTINUED FROM NO. XXVIII.]

1434, The Mayor and citizens of Dublin were obliged to perform penance publicly, by proceeding bare-footed to this cathedral, for assaults which they had committed on the Abbot of St. Mary's Abbey, the Earl of Ormond, &c., with intent to murder.

1443, The Pope confirmed the establishment of minor canons and choristers here.

1450, About this time Archbishop Mey, at the petition of the dean and chapter of St. Patrick's, granted forty days' indulgence to all people who should be contributors to the providing a great bell in that cathedral, and to the making some new windows and other repairs therein.

1468, It was enacted in parliament, that if any canon of this cathedral should absent himself, half the benefit of his prebend should be divided among the residentiaries in the close.

1476, The dean, chapter, &c. having represented to parliament that their benefices and possessions lay for the most part in places subject to the power of Irish enemies and English rebels, and that they could not obtain Englishmen to favor the same, it was enacted that they should have liberty to lease their lands and tithes to rebels or enemies, or any other persons without impeachment.

Thirty years later, when St Patrick's was in poor repair, the artist and writer Samuel Lover made this engraving of Swift's bust and tablet for the *Irish Penny Magazine*, 20 July 1833.

within each grateful breast.'[65] Faulkner, meanwhile, who had been elected an alderman in 1770, died on 30 August 1775. His nephew and successor, Thomas Todd Faulkner, evidently did not have the same measure of proprietary interest in Swift's reputation. Considering that the bust of which George Faulkner had been so proud 'would be an appropriate ornament to the Dean's monument', the memorial tablet in St Patrick's Cathedral, he presented it to the Cathedral Chapter within months of his uncle's death.[66] At the Chapter meeting of 20 March 1776 thanks were returned for his gift, and two months later, on 24 May, they commissioned the sculptor Simon Vierpyl to construct a niche for it.[67] With its classical margin recording the bust as the gift of T.T. Faulkner, the niche was installed with the bust presumably while the cathedral was closed for improvements in mid-1776; early in October it was reopened for worship.[68]

More than half a century had passed since a popular ballad, with light-hearted assurance, first forecast a monument to the Drapier. Now, thirty years after Swift's death, a series of campaigns for a fittingly grand memorial had come to no more than the mounting, in Swift's cathedral, of the bust formerly adorning George Faulkner's shop. In time, the simplicity of the bust would come to seem elegantly appropriate to the sad and challenging epitaph chiselled nearby. But when it was installed in 1776, as a kind of Faulkner family tribute to Swift, the bust was so modest a substitute for what Faulkner had envisioned as to reflect the failure of his projects. Richard Lewis might deny in these years the significance of that failure, implying that no public monument was necessary for one whose 'image lives within each grateful breast', but there is little other evidence in later eighteenth-century Ireland of such widespread gratitude for Swift's efforts on behalf of the country's liberty. On the other hand, the public in large numbers continued to buy his books. They respected and admired the author, and found the character of the man fascinating, even if esteem for the patriot was not so broadly expressed as Faulkner had hoped a monument would signify.

2

The Early Biographers:
Preserving Mixed Impressions

I

The most impressive monument to Swift that George Faulkner left is, clearly, not the bust in St Patrick's Cathedral but the editions of Swift's *Works* he assembled and published. He evidently expected to turn a profit from his extensive publishing project, and the sheer number and variety of the editions published suggest that he did.[1] Without such a prospect, he was ready enough to cut his losses; his abandonment of a *de luxe* edition proposed in 1758, and intended to be printed by subscription at the press in Trinity College, was apparently owing to its failure to attract enough subscribers.[2] And his vigorous reaction to the Ewings' publication of a rival *History of the Four Last Years of the Queen* the same year suggests that this infringement upon the monopoly of copyright he had assumed to himself threatened him commercially as much as it affronted his sense of personal proprietorship over Swift's memory. The same monopolistic attitude may well have been partly responsible for the failure of the campaigns for a monument, but the feeble response to them cannot be laid wholly to Faulkner's account. It indicates also, like the paucity of references to Swift during the Lucas and 'Money Bill' controversies, a considerable public diffidence about Swift's patriotism for many years after his death, even as Faulkner continued successfully to publish and sell editions of the *Works*.

The discrepancy between the reception of the patriot and that of the author is revealing. While Swift may have expected that he would live in memory most securely as a patriotic benefactor, his posthumous reputation in fact long preserved a complex of other, sometimes conflicting, impressions that he had given his readers while still alive. In part these derived directly from his habitual resort to various authorial masks for publication, a feature to which Pope had drawn attention when dedicating *The Dunciad* to Swift:

O thou! Whatever title please thine ear,
Dean, Drapier, Bickerstaff, or Gulliver . . .[3]

More darkly, but not unrelated, a number of negative images were current as
well in Swift's lifetime – the irreligious divine, political turncoat, ribald
parson, and, ultimately, misogynist and misanthrope. These too all generally
coloured Swift's prominence as a 'character', authorial, personal and anecdotal. The extent of this prominence was largely determined by his reception
in England, where inevitably he had his greatest audience, and mostly before
he became known as an Irish patriot, about which his English audience would
care little. Such impressions, positive and negative, were moreover animated
after his death by his earliest biographers, Laetitia Pilkington, Lord Orrery,
Rev. Patrick Delany and Deane Swift. These four shared Irish origins (or in
Orrery's case, associations), but all except Pilkington wrote for initial publication in London, and therefore mainly for English readers, to whom their
personal acquaintance with the Dean would matter most. Hence all emphasized his personality traits and displayed the writer in his works, building
moral portraits, each somewhat differently complementing or complicating
Swift's classical literary stature. But none concentrated upon his Irish patriotism, which was all but subsumed in their attention to the Dean's other
features. Among both the English and the Irish reading public, the character
studies fostered interest in Swift and spurred sales of his *Works* but they also
perpetuated a host of negative or ambiguous impressions Swift had left upon
readers and observers during his lifetime. Orrery in particular effectively
constructed an identity for Swift which would continue, over more than a
century, to clash with or compromise that of the disinterested Irish patriot
Swift had asserted for himself and Faulkner had assumed in his monument
propaganda.

II

Thus Swift was throughout his writing career a more controversial figure than
the eminence he gained as a living classic in the 1730s would suggest. His
satire upon the abuses of religious faith in *A Tale of a Tub* (1704) was
commonly interpreted as itself irreligious, the work of an articulately jocular
filth-monger. This was an impression that determined Queen Anne against
Swift's preferment to a bishopric during the Tory ministry at the end of her
reign. The reaction in 1704 of Dr William King, an eminent lawyer (not to
be confused with the Archbishop of Dublin or the Oxford Jacobite of the
same name), was significant. Posing as one not usually averse to literary
cloacality, he was offended nonetheless by the author's 'great affection for
everything that is nasty' in a work of which 'almost every part has a tincture
of such filthiness, as renders it unfit for the worst of uses'.[4] A decade later

Swift's reputation had become sourer, especially among the Whigs, because of the scathing wit of his political writings. This was the more provoking since he had shifted from courting the Whig junto before 1710 to serving the Tory ministry thereafter, both as a propagandist with *The Examiner* and *The Conduct of the Allies* and as an intimate of Oxford and Bolingbroke, who were suspected in Whig circles of being covert Jacobites. The perception grew that Swift was a high-flying Tory, as zealous as Dr Henry Sacheverell, or even a Jacobite himself, as Bishop Atterbury proved to be, but subtler than either.[5] His cultivation of subtlety was itself ironized by a Whig writer in 1714, who posed as Swift and dedicated this work, like the *Tale*, 'To Prince Posterity':

> I know very well how, after the Perusal of some of my works, I have been represented for an *Atheist*, or a *Lewd Town-Rake*, or both, and People are from thence induc'd to believe, that I am such, rather than a *Clergyman*, and *Dignitary* of the Church. This is *Strange*, but *True*! Nay, some will hardly allow me to be a Christian, tho' they know me to be the Author of that Divine Treatise, the *Tale of a Tub*. The Generality of Mankind, I mean the *Vulgar*, are unacquainted with the Polite Modern Way of Writing, and will not allow a Man to make a Jest of Religion, tho' he does it never so Wittily.[6]

Others could be more pointed, describing Swift as 'Smut' in a lampoon on Oxford as court physician: 'SMUT (says the Doctor) is the Darling, he is the Wittiest Knave of my whole Family', though regrettably 'an Infidel'; or likening Swift to a Jesuit.[7] In the blizzard of Whig pamphlets and broadsides following the Hanoverian succession in 1714, Swift could be warned to abandon his partisanship:

> Would S[wif]t and H[iggin]s leave their tricks
> And never more their Sermons mix
> With Raillary [*sic*] and Politicks,
> > *This is the time*.[8]

For Tory politics among the clergy was tantamount to irreligion:

> And are these mercenary Men, the *Welton's*, *Higgins*, *Bretts*, *Smith's*, *Swift's*, &c, mended by the late Ministry? Are they grown obedient to the Laws, more dutiful to the Government? Are their Consciences less sear'd, and do their oaths stick more upon them?[9]

Other Whig Writers accused him outright of Jacobitism, or worse; one included the 'Tide of cursed *Examiners*' among the products of 'all the letter scribbling Hirelings of the *French and Popish Faction*', while a second had a Jacobite Oxford fellow boast that his loyalty to the Devil exceeded that of the 'True blue' Swift.[10]

There was a greater display of wit, however, by Jonathan Smedley, a young Whig clergyman in London, who devoted a whole pamphlet to blackening Swift's character. Purported to be the Dean's diary for the week of Queen

Anne's death in 1714, *A Hue and Cry after Dr S—t* displays a clergyman–politician utterly lacking in principle. A convinced Tory when his men are in power, who even connives at bringing in the Pretender, he quickly shifts to support the Hanoverian succession once it occurs, and actually canvasses for Whig votes in the election to follow.[11] Smedley's view of Swift as hypocritical opportunist was quickly challenged by the publication of what claimed to be Swift's genuine diary for the same week, which reverts to the image of the Tory partisan, consistent in his politics but by habit slovenly and irreligious, who recalls from the printer his ode welcoming the Pretender only to save his neck.[12] But Smedley's caricature achieved the greater currency, both because the *Hue and Cry* had at least six editions and on account of the poem appended to it, which gained celebrity in its own right:

Copy of Verses fastn'd to the Gate of St P[atrick]'s C[hurc]h D[ubli]n, on the Day of the I[nstallmen]t of a certain D[ea]n.

I

To *Day* this *Temple* gets a *D—n*
Of *Parts*, and *Fame* uncommon;
Us'd both to *Pray*, and to *Prophane*:
To serve, or God, or Mammon.

II

When *W—n* reigned, a *Whig* he was   [Wharton]
When *Pem—e*; that's *dispute* Sir: [Pembroke]
In *Ox—*'s Time, what *O—d* please,   [Oxford; Ormond]
Non-con, or *Jack*, or *Neuter*.   [non-conformist;
                  Presbyterian (from John Calvin); atheist]

III

This *Place* he got by *Wit* and *Rhime*,
And many Ways most *odd*;
And might a *Bishop* be in a Time
Did he *believe* in God.

IV

For *High-Church-Men*, and Policy,
He *swears* he prays, most hearty;
But wou'd pray *back* again, wou'd be
A *Dean* of *any* Party.

V

Four Lessons, *Dean*, all in *one Day*,
Faith it is hard, that's certain;
'Twere better hear *Nown Peter* say,   [contr:thine *own*]
God *D—n* thee *Jack* and Martyn   [Luther]

VI

Look down St *Patrick*, look we pray
  On thine own *Church* and Steeple;
Covert thy *D—n* on *this great* Day;
  Or else *God help* the People.

VII

And now, whene'er his D-n-sh-p dies
  Upon his *Stone* be graven,
A Man *of God* here buried lies
  Who never thought of *Heaven*.[13]

Although these verses are unlikely actually to have greeted Swift at his installation in St Patrick's, they would have been a rather mild rebuke, considering that strongly Whig sentiment was much more extensive among Irish Protestants than in England, and that they were governed by a Lord Lieutenant, the Duke of Ormonde, who was to turn Jacobite. As an instance of Irish Whigs' political antipathy to Swift the poem is little enough, certainly, compared to the story the Dean himself related of being threatened with physical injury or even death by Lord Blaney while riding at Howth one day.[14]

The image of the irreligious Tory parson was renewed in Ireland after the publication of the *Universal Use of Irish Manufactures* in 1720. 'I am a stranger to the Author of this Project,' opened one retort,

> but I am sure he is not a Christian, and by this Mark I have nobody to suspect amongst all my Acquaintance, but a *Tory* Doctor of Divinity. It may seem improbable, that one who has done all that in him lay, to ruin his own Trade, should have so much Charity as to set up for an Improver of other Peoples.[15]

Apparently current also was a suggestion that his advocacy of Irish interests was simply an excuse to strike at the English Whigs he despised, a notion that a Dublin balladeer of 1726 tried to parry by showing that the Drapier had united Irishmen of all persuasions against Wood's scheme:

God prosper the DRAPIER! When we were in Fears,
  He cur'd all the Sickness, that lay at our Hearts;
Yet some, with most impudent Faces, declare,
  R[obi]n he aim'd at, by using those Arts.   [Sir Robert Walpole]

But let these consider, how firmly united,
  Were *Whigs, Tories, Trimmers* and the *H[anoverian]s*;
And with what Delight he all others invited,
  Even *Quakers, Conformists*, and the *Presbyterians*.
              To their shame be it spoke.[16]

Nonetheless, Swift was as yet commonly charged with hypocritical opportunism less on account of his Irish activities than because of his shift in
attachment from Whig to Tory years earlier in England. After the appearance
of *Gulliver's Travels* in 1726, Smedley refreshed this charge in *Gulliveriana*
(1728), a collection of satirical squibs including 'Verses fastn'd to the Gate'.[17]
The accusation continued to be repeated, as for instance in 1735 by the Whig
publicist and historian John Oldmixon, who recalled succinctly that in 1710
Swift was

> an ingenious but ambitious clergyman, who had some time before devoted
> himself to the *Whigs*, and written against the *Tories*; . . . [but] being disap-
> pointed in his Hopes of Preferment, upon the Revolution in the Ministry he
> immediately tuck'd about, listed himself in the Service of High Church,
> and . . . was employ'd in writing a Weekly Paper, call'd *The Examiner*; the
> Design of which was to inveigh against the late Ministers with all possible
> Bitterness.[18]

Whether taken as embodying opportunistic Toryism or a lack of principle
altogether, Swift's political activities before and during the Oxford–
Bolingbroke ministry fed Whig perceptions of his irreligious character first
evident to many readers of *A Tale of a Tub*, whatever their politics.

Related to his godlessness was the inclination to scatology perceived in the
Tale – and not only by Whigs, especially since descriptions recurred in
Gulliver's Travels of what a contemporary reader called 'Things, which are
much more necessary to be done than said'.[19] Carole Fabricant has shown
convincingly how the sanitary conditions of London and Dublin gave ample
warrant for Swift's scatological play, and Hermann Real and Heinz Vienken
have demonstrated that Swift's 'excremental vision' cuts a very small figure
indeed in the poetry and *Gulliver's Travels*, taken as a whole.[20] Such critics
offer valuable correctives to a misapprehension still quite current in the
twentieth century. But in Swift's own era his scatology, whatever its extent,
was particularly notable for its origins in the work of a clergyman. Its intensity
and its provenance together characterized Swift within the convention of the
ribald parson. The image of Swift as a revived Rabelais persisted because a
stereotype tends to draw affirmation beyond any accurate instances that
might justify it. Hence, even as his authorship was claimed during his lifetime
for works not his,[21] within a decade of his death works were attributed to him
which had not been so at their first appearance years before.

The London *Daily Advertiser* of 3 November 1748, for instance, advertised
Human Ordure botanically considered. The first Essay of the Kind ever published
as 'wrote by the late Dean Swift'. This brief dissertation on the variety of
stools originally appeared in 1733, in Dublin, and there may have been an oral
tradition for Swift's authorship that would explain the 1748 attribution.[22] The
same newspaper a year later, on 26 December 1749, advertised *D—n S—t's
Medley, containing His Scheme for making Religion and the Clergy useful; with
his observations on the cause and Cure of the Piles; and some useful Directions*

about wiping the Posteriors [with] *Reason against Coition, a discourse deliver'd to a private Congregation.*[23] The assignment to the Dean is curiously, even comprehensively, apt, since the work embraces the interests in the Church, the toilet and the bed that generations of critics since have explored in Swift, while also indicating an English taste (which has persisted) for jokes on such themes. But at least two of the pieces here included, the *Scheme for making Religion and the Clergy Useful* and *Reason against Coition*, had been published in the 1730s accompanied by no suggestion that they were Swift's.[24] An edition of *The Nut-Cracker*, furthermore, a standard joke-book of the mid-eighteenth century, was advertised in the *Salisbury Journal* for 11 February 1754 as containing an appendix, 'The Benefit of F—NG explain'd. By Dean Swift.' This jocular argument for the ladies to resort more openly to that kind of relief first appeared in 1722, and was described by Swift at that time as by 'one Dobbs a Surgeon'.[25] He may have feared that it would be claimed for him (it is included in the 'List of Spurious Productions' compiled for Faulkner),[26] but the actual edition of *The Nut-Cracker* in 1754 which published it made no such claim. The provincial advertisement-writer may have attributed it to him because it was often bound with the fourth edition of Swift's *Miscellanies*, also published in 1722,[27] or because of its putative Irish provenance, or simply to trade on Swift's already considerable reputation as a cloacal jester.

That reputation had expanded considerably beyond its basis in the *Tale* and its affirmation in *Gulliver's Travels* with the chronologically concentrated publication of *The Lady's Dressing Room* (1732), *A Beautiful Young Nymph Going to Bed* (1734), *Strephon and Chloe* (1734) and *Cassinus and Peter* (1734). These poems all use scatology overtly, to satirize either romantic love or female pride in physical attractiveness, and have long been criticized for both their dirtiness and apparent misogyny.[28] The latter, indeed, is a factor in his attitude toward sexuality, evident in *Cadenus and Vanessa*, published some years earlier, where Swift had tried to explain his bachelorhood to Vanessa while she still lived. It is noteworthy that he had himself laid the issue open, for earlier published references to his single state or his sexual character are sparse. In *Dr S—t's Real Diary* (1715), for instance, the response to Smedley's more popular *Hue and Cry*, the mock Swift's mock dedication to Oxford recalls the heady days 'when I was to your Lordship *a Mensa & Secretis* (the world was, never so wicked as to say, *a Thoro*)', and that Oxford had 'so often favour'd me with a CLAPP on the shoulder'.[29] While this might have been intended to imply of Swift a degree of homoerotic heartiness, it more strongly suggests sexual looseness, at the least, in the general picture of Swift as a dissolute Tory partisan-parson. The latter impression occasionally recurs in the course of Swift's reputation, though the whispery hint of homosexual association did not get picked up.

Nor did a more pointed suggestion from the opposite political pole, a very early published reference to Swift's relationship with Vanessa. While Swift was visiting England in 1726 to arrange publication of *Gulliver's Travels*, Faulkner published an anonymous Irish poem portraying a link between the

A young Lady's Complaint for the Stay of Dean SWIFT in *England*.

BLOW ye Zephyrs gentle Gales,
Gently fill the swelling Sails,
Neptune with thy Trident long
Trident three-fork'd, Trident strong,
And ye Nereids fair and gay,
Fairer than the Rose in May,
Nereids living in deep Caves
Gently wash'd with gentle Waves,
Nereids, *Neptune* lull asleep
Ruffling Storms and ruffled Deep,
All around in pompous State
On this richer *Argo* wait,
Argo bring my *Golden Fleece*,
Argo bring him to his *Greece*,
Will *Cadenus* longer stay?
Come *Cadenus*, come away;
Come with all the haste of Love,
Come unto thy Turtle Dove;
The rip'ned Cherry on the Tree
Hangs and only hangs for thee,
Luscious Peaches mellow Pears,
Ceres with her yellow Ears,
And the Grape both red and white
Grape inspiring just Delight,
All are ripe and courting sue
To be pluck'd and press'd by you;
Pinks have lost their blooming Red,
Mourning hang their drooping Head,
Every Flower languid seems,
Wants the Colour of thy Beams,
Beams of wondrous Force and Pow'r
Beams reviving every Flow'r.
Come *Cadenus*, bless once more,
Bless again thy native Shore,
Bless again this drooping Isle,
Make it's weeping Beauties smile,
Beauties that thine absence mourn,
Beauties wishing thy Return:
Come *Cadenus* come with haste,
Come before the Winters Blast,
Swifter than the Lightning fly,
Or I like *Vanessa* die.

Dublin: Printed by George Faulkner in Pembroke-Court Castle-street. 1726:

Dean's bachelorhood and a lady representing Ireland, grateful for his patriotic exertions, fruitfully feminine and eager for his harvest alone (see opposite).

That Ireland should be cast as a faithful female lover awaiting the return of her deliverer and consort is at least very rare, if not unique, for contemporary poetry in English; the imagery, with its sexual overtones, recalls instead Gaelic Jacobite verse. The speaker's conclusion is a climax of sorts, as she identifies Ireland with herself and adverts to Swift's personal history:

> Come *Cadenus* come with haste,
> Come before the Winter's Blast
> Swifter than the Lightning fly,
> Or I like *Vanessa* die.[30]

If this notice of Vanessa hints at Swift's non-sexual or anti-sexual past, it also fits with the interplay of his elusiveness – here seen geographically – and the yearning of Ireland, or the speaker, that informs the whole poem. Certainly there is no implication of misogyny, whatever the poet's familiarity with the Vanessa story, for that would subvert the celebration of Swift's patriotism.

In personal terms, *A Young Lady's Complaint* seems to take Vanessa's as a story of a singularly thwarted romantic attachment. But with the publication of Swift's birthday verses to Stella after her own death (1728) and especially the four pungently scatological satires on female beauty and romance in 1732–4, quite different responses were inevitable, mingling imputations on Swift's sexuality (or lack of it) with the longer-standing complaint of his scatology. Thus the *Lady's Dressing Room* was quickly answered in 1732 with *The Gentleman's Study*, by 'Miss W—', which emphasized the even more disgusting arrangements of a socially superior rake.[31] Responding to both, Samuel Shepard whimsically suggested that the two authors marry, since Swift was a bachelor and they had a mutual interest in the cloacal.[32] Thus contemporary readers first noticed not Swift's misogyny so much as his non-sexual or anti-sexual character, apparently borne out by his bachelorhood; the complex uncertainty of his relationships with women as presented in *Cadenus and Vanessa* and the Stella birthday poems; and the scatology of the poems of 1732–4. Such a character, associated with an ecclesiastic given generally to irreligious wit, scatology and, to English eyes, increasingly old-fashioned political views, made Swift seem an extraordinarily eccentric figure. However these impressions might be made to fit the classical literary stature granted to Swift in politer circles, they presented real difficulty for his image as a selfless Irish patriot.

III

The impression of Swift's eccentricity was reinforced by Laetitia Pilkington's *Memoirs*, which appeared in three volumes in 1748, 1749 and 1754; the last volume assembled by her son and published five years after her death in 1749. She and her clergyman husband Matthew were introduced to Swift by his friend, the Rev. Patrick Delany, in 1730. Matthew Pilkington, respectful of Swift to the point of obsequiousness, was little more than tolerated by the Dean, but his wife gained his favour immediately. Both were very short – Swift once measured her height at three foot two – hence 'Mr. Pilkington was stiled Thomas Thumb, and I his Lady fair.'[33] Mrs Pilkington quickly became a 'bosom friend of Dr Swift',[34] perhaps not only for her attentiveness and apparent devotion but also because she cut such a comic figure, seeming to play his fool as she put up ungrudgingly with insults and beatings from him. At the same time he opened himself unusually to her, and she took careful notice, memorizing the 'Verses on the Death of Dr Swift' which he showed her in manuscript and retaining a great variety of impressions and anecdotes that eventually found their way into print. They were not close for long, as in 1732 she left Dublin for London, accompanying her husband who was to take up a chaplaincy for which Swift had recommended him, and the picture of Swift she presents in her *Memoirs* is thus intensely observed rather than judiciously considered. The *Memoirs* were, furthermore, written hastily and with an eye to public appeal after Colley Cibber, the poet laureate, had secured her release from debtors' prison. In the interval, after leaving Dublin, she had been discovered in adultery – which led Swift to term her 'the most profligate whore in either Kingdom'[35] – was divorced, and for a decade lived meagrely on her literary talent and her charm, ingratiating herself with writers and nobles alike.

The *Memoirs* range over her miscellaneous acquaintance, with the first volume particularly concerned with Swift. Interspersed with the narrative of his biography and hers is a hotchpotch of vignettes, both personal and more generally anecdotal, which amount to a character sketch of a gruff, bitterly incisive old man, often sourly jocular but at the same time unusually generous to the poor. Neither his bitterness nor his charity had been much noticed in previous published references to Swift, but the disjointed structure of the *Memoirs* diminished whatever effect her presentation of these characteristics might have had in altering the persistent image of the Dean, especially in England, as an irreligious wit and scatological jester. Indeed, she fleshed out that image with details that emphasize his eccentricity, whether humorous or in such intimate respects as Swift's virginity, which she noted he maintained though wedded to Stella, not even acknowledging the marriage.[36] She also mixed admiration of the Dean with what could easily be taken as disparagement. He undertook his ecclesiatical duties with 'becoming Piety' for instance, but also 'bowed to the Holy Table like a Papist'. While he was regarded as a saviour in Ireland, she quoted Swift as holding that 'I never preached but twice in my life, and they were not serious, but pamphlets' against Wood's halfpence; implicitly subordinating his religion to his politics,

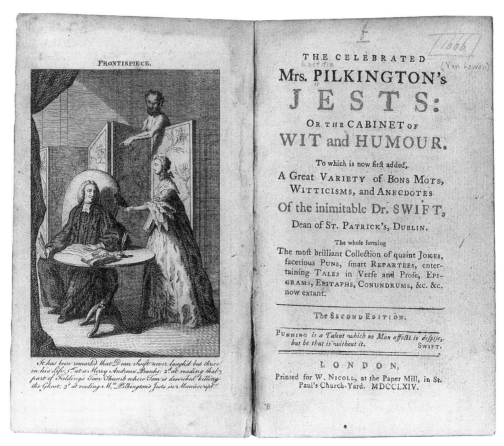

It has been remark'd that Dean Swift never laugh'd but thrice in his life. 1st at a Merry Andrews Pranks: 2d at reading that part of Fielding's Tom Thumb where Tom is described killing the Ghost: 3d at reading Mrs. Pilkington's Jests in Manuscript

THE CELEBRATED

Mrs. PILKINGTON's

JESTS:

OR THE CABINET OF

WIT and HUMOUR.

To which is now first added,

A Great VARIETY of BONS MOTS, WITTICISMS, and ANECDOTES

Of the inimitable Dr. SWIFT,

Dean of ST. PATRICK's, DUBLIN.

The whole forming

The most brilliant Collection of quaint JOKES, facetious PUNS, smart REPARTEES, entertaining TALES in Verse and Prose, EPIGRAMS, EPITAPHS, CONUNDRUMS, &c. &c. now extant.

The SECOND EDITION.

PUNNING *is a Talent which no Man affects to despise, but he that is without it.* SWIFT.

LONDON,

Printed for W. NICOLL, at the Paper Mill, in St. Paul's Church-Yard. MDCCLXIV.

The frontispiece of the second edition of *The Celebrated Mrs. Pilkington's Jests* which depicts a smiling Dean and reflects on the legend that he rarely laughed. It is part of the joke that the book included a number of anecdotes of Swift himself.

this incidentally rendered his politics irreligious.[37] Pilkington's collection of Swiftian anecdotes, whether her own observations or stories she had heard, thus amplified the current popular image of Swift, rather than revising it. Hence selections from the first volume of her *Memoirs*, illustrating his verbal wit and taste for practical jokes, were quickly reprinted in the *Gentleman's Magazine*.[38] Even years later, well after all three volumes of the *Memoirs* had appeared, a sizeable collection of the anecdotes was included in *The Celebrated Mrs. Pilkington's Jests*, the full title of which advertised the Swiftiana.[39] She was 'celebrated', of course, not only for her stories of Swift and other notables, but also for her notorious life; the latter contributed to Horace Walpole's reference to hers among other 'bawdy books'.[40] And in its pages, however accurate in detail, Swift is confirmed as an oddity indeed.

IV

Though the first of Swift's biographers, Pilkington had obviously not attempted to satisfy the hope, expressed shortly after his death, that 'some among his friends will oblige the Publick with a full and particular Account of his Life and Writings';[41] her work was essentially, instead, an entertainment. Against the background of her book and the popular images of Swift disseminated during his lifetime, the Earl of Orrery's *Remarks on the Life and Writings of Dr Jonathan Swift* sought to provide the desired balance and comprehensiveness.[42] Pilkington had never denied Swift's genius, but she was an observer rather than an analyst; Orrery, who knew Swift longer if less intimately, combined the fact of his personal acquaintance with the stance of a literary critic. To modern readers that stance is pretentious, since he recognized the obvious without any accompanying intellectual or aesthetic penetration, but at least he understood that Swift's standing as a modern classic called for literary analysis. It was equally as a moral critic, however, that he concerned himself with Swift; it is not simply coincidental that the *Remarks* were cast as a series of tutelary letters to his son (whose bastardy, however, ironizes somewhat the father's moral stance). Hence Orrery's frequently negative judgements arose in the main from the discrepancy he noticed between the writer's undoubted literary powers and the vulgarity with which they are exercised.

This amounts to a paradox Orrery was ill-equipped to resolve, for while he accepted that satire must attend to foolishness, hypocrisy and vice, his own view of human nature was too benign or sanguine to account for Swift's manner of proceeding. He lay the faults of the great writer, consequently, to the failings of the man, which he also held responsible for a popular reputation that was ambiguous if not outright negative. Early in the *Remarks*, citing his personal acquaintance with Swift, Orrery justified his procedure: 'He was in the decline of life when I knew him . . . I have beheld him in all humours and dispositions, and I have formed various speculations from the several weaknesses to which I observed him liable.'[43] Opposite the same page, in Orrery's own interleaved copy of the *Remarks*, he noted

> The Light in which Dr Swift's character generally stands, makes him rather appear in the manner of a drol [sic] buffoon wit, than of a distinguished eminent writer. His manner in writing and conversing have put him in this disadvantageous situation. Name him, and some ridiculous jest is expected to follow. His Puns and Rebuses are still hoarded up in Cabinets: I mean the few which have escaped Print.
>
> All dignity of character seems lost, partly owing to the low stuff which he has printed, and partly to the want of distinction in the generality of readers. They mistake and confuse the pictures for the painters, and think it impossible that a man can laugh at folly without being drest up in a fool's hat.

MEM. (4.)

The Light in which Doctor Swift's character generally stands, makes him rather appear in the manner of a Drol buffoon wit, than of a distinguished eminent writer. His trifling manner in writing and conversing have put him into this disadvantageous situation. Name him, and some ridiculous jest is expected to follow. His Puns and Bulasses are still hoarded up in Cabinets: I mean the few which have escaped Print.

All dignity of character seems lost, partly owing to the low Stuff which he has pointed, and partly to the want of distinction in the generality of readers. They mistake the pictures for the painters, and think it impossible

5.) He that a man can laugh at folly, without being drest up in a fools coat.

If a man writes the life of a Pickpocket, or a Highwayman, must he therefore be a Highwayman, or a Pickpocket?

Swift wants dignity more in the choice of his subjects, than in the manner of treating them. Yet I own, Dignity is far from being his characteristic. A more correct writer, I have never seen.

If a man writes the life of a Pickpocket, or a Highwayman, must he therefore be a Highwayman or a Pickpocket?

Swift wants dignity more in the choice of his subjects, than in the manner of writing them. Yet I own, Dignity is far from being his characteristic. A more correct writer, I have never seen.[44]

A 'distinguished eminent writer', in brief, ought to have an appropriate reputation; and because most readers cannot differentiate between the writer and his subject, Swift's own lack of literary dignity largely accounts for his undignified reputation. Orrery could not compensate for Swift's want of dignity, but he could present a view of the Dean's character that would, in some measure, explain that deficiency.

It has frequently been maintained that Orrery's often disparaging *Remarks* dealt the first significant blow to Swift's posthumous reputation.[45] In fact the damage he caused was more complicated. The first effect of his method was to confirm the negative aspects of that reputation already perceptible during his lifetime – perceptible in the variety of reactions to Swift's works and judgements upon his character that were published then, and even in the anecdotes whose general effect Orrery decried. Secondly, he countered the somewhat lighthearted image of the eccentric and the jester by suggesting its darker implications, more in harmony with the negative picture of Swift as irreligious, opportunistic and cruel to women, refining Swift's character as perceptibly misogynistic and clearly misanthropic. The ultimate impression was the more marked for being supported by a great deal of detail and presented in as coherent a context as his epistolary format would easily allow. Unlike Pilkington, for instance, he gave details of Swift's relationships with Stella and Vanessa, providing (for the first time) details of the former's secret marriage to the Dean (whose refusal to live with her Orrery ascribed to her low birth), emphasizing Vanessa's forwardness in her affair with Swift, and arguing that his treatment occasioned Vanessa's death and hastened Stella's. So developed upon widespread earlier impressions, the general picture of Swift's character offered little with which a partisan Whig moralist of thirty years before might have disagreed. Setting out the basis for his view of Swift as misanthrope, Orrery described him as a proud and capable man whose ambitions were thwarted, 'and the anxiety of that disappointment had a visible effect upon all his actions'.[46] This included his efforts on behalf of Ireland, for 'his perpetual views were directed toward power; and his chief aim was to be removed into *England*; but when he found himself entirely disappointed, he turned his thoughts to opposition and became the patron of *Ireland*, in which country he was born'.[47]

Thus Orrery attributed Swift's Irish patriotism directly to his bitter personal frustration, rather than to any selfless motive. In context, moreover, his more specific references to Swift's involvement with Ireland demean both the man and the country. His account of Swift's receiving the deanship of St Patrick's, instead of becoming a bishop in England as he had hoped, begins with the observation 'A man always appears of more consequence to himself than he is in reality to any other person. Such perhaps was the case of Dr. SWIFT,' and shortly afterwards, 'I am much inclined to believe that the temper of my friend SWIFT, might occasion his *English* friends to wish him happily and properly appointed, at a distance.'[48] The Irish people, in turn, regarding him as a Jacobite, 'received him with great reluctance', as did his chapter in St Patrick's; though the latter were quickly induced to respect and even venerate him, 'whether fear or conviction were the motives of so immediate a change, I leave you to consider'.[49] The popular abuse and indignity he had to endure in Ireland 'soured his temper, confined his acquaintance, and added bitterness to his style'.[50] Orrery pictured the state of Ireland as wild, with a populace temperamentally violent in their political emotions, to explain the hostility of Swift's initial reception, and, implicitly, his decision to keep silent about politics in his first years as Dean. But in these years also 'his sayings of wit and humour had been handed about, and repeated from time to time among the people, and had pre-engaged all readers in his favour', and thus Swift's adopting a patriotic position in the *Universal Use of Irish Manufactures* 'turned the popular tide' altogether,[51] a movement that rose to its zenith with the *Drapier's Letters* a few years later.

> Every person, of every rank, party and denomination, was convinced, that the
> admission of Wood's copper must prove fatal to the commonwealth. The
> Papist, the Fanatic, the Tory, the Whig, all listed themselves under the banner
> of M.B. DRAPIER, and all were equally zealous to serve the common cause.
> Much heat, and many fiery speeches against the administration, were the
> consequence of this union.[52]

The ironic tone here, taken together with the earlier pictures of Ireland's
wildness, suggests that Swift simply studied the country well and then clev-
erly transformed the people's antipathy toward him into devotion.

Orrery's method, then, militated against a view of conviction as the basis
of Swift's patriotism; instead, he implied, it arose from his disappointed
ambition, and was expressed with hypocritical demagoguery. Considering the
Proposal for the Universal Use of Irish Manufactures, Orrery supposed that Swift
occupied the time between taking up his deanship and the publication of this
pamphlet by composing *Gulliver's Travels*. Hence

> when that was finished, he found an opening to indulge his love of politics, and
> to commence a patriot for *Ireland*: and he made use of the opportunity, by
> increasing the natural jealousy which the lesser island constantly entertains
> of the greater. His treatise, or proposal, immediately raised a very violent
> flame.

The overt disparagement Orrery qualified quickly, though with a hedge:

> But his greatest enemies must confess, that the pamphlet is written in the style
> of a man, who had the good of his country nearest his heart, who saw her
> errors, and wished to correct them; who felt her oppressions, and wished to
> relieve them, and who had a desire to rouze, and awaken an indolent nation
> from a lethargic disposition, that might prove fatal to her constitution.[53]

The hedge, of course, is the phrase 'written in the style of', which leaves the
passage hinting at hypocrisy. Orrery took the hint further in dismissing
Swift's picture of deplorable Irish conditions in *A Short View of the State of
Ireland* (1727) with 'Of this I need take little notice, since the present state
of *Ireland* is, in general, as flourishing as possible.'[54] Not that Orrery was
absolutely consistent in this view. Having in the course of the *Remarks*
developed a more general case for misanthropy as Swift's primary motive, he
was willing, when considering Swift's letter of 10 January 1721 to Pope, to
displace his former implication of patriotic hypocrisy while reinforcing the
image of Swift's misanthropy:

> In it is displayed his immutable attachment to *Ireland*. Such a kind of patri-
> otism must have proceeded from a true love of liberty; for he hated individuals,
> and despised most of the men of property and power in that kingdom; he owed
> them no obligations, and while by his writings he laboured to make their
> posterity happy, he forced from themselves an involuntary, but universal

applause. His conduct was so uniform, and constant in the cause of *Ireland*, that he not only gained the praise, but the confidence of that whole nation, who are a people seldom, if ever, inclined to study and pursue their own interest, and who are always exceedingly apt to suspect any advice that is contrary, or in defiance to a ministerial direction.[55]

This is Orrery's last extended comment on Swift's patriotism, and reads as though, in the course of examining each work as it appears in Faulkner's edition, he was finally converted to the sincerity, if perhaps not altogether to the accuracy, of Swift's pronouncements upon Ireland. Perhaps the Dean's articulation of his attitudes in what was a private letter, not originally intended for publication, convinced Orrery that Swift meant what he wrote in general about Ireland. Or perhaps this conviction arose from Orrery's seeing such views expressed in Swift's outline of his general political outlook to Pope to an extent that had, for Orrery, a comprehensiveness that other expressions of patriotic sentiment lacked. But this concession on Orrery's part did not lead him to revise his earlier opinion of those other expressions as hypocritical or demagogic. His portrait of the Dean remained unflattering or even condemnatory, as he pressed his argument for misanthropy as its mainstay with greater consistency and at greater length. Swift's politics are in a general sense seen as basely motivated, his scatology as inhuman, his relationships with women unbecoming at best, and often tyrannical. Throughout, what Orrery praised was Swift's style, the form but not the substance of his wit. Countering the image of Swift as simply an eccentric, a coarse jester, by tying these aspects of his character to a comprehensive misanthropy prompted, like his Irish patriotism, by an acute sense of disappointment, Orrery articulated a coherently negative judgement assembled from the implications of the popular views current in his lifetime.

Orrery was credited as well with rectifying inaccuracies in those preceding popular views. A notice in the *Monthly Review* thanked him on behalf of the 'Republic of Letters,' since 'never was there beside the immortal Dean *Swift*, so famous a writer with whose birth and private life, the public have been so much misinformed'.[56] To Samuel Richardson, Orrery's character of Swift, especially with reference to Stella and Vanessa, corroborated the literary evidence: 'it is of a piece with all those of his writings, in which he endeavours to debase the human, and to raise above it the brutal nature.'[57] But Orrery's effect on popular impressions of Swift was also quickly satirized in England. The *Remarks* had appeared during one of London's frequent paper wars, this one involving Dr John Hill, a purveyor of patent medicines and the author of a bombastically philistine periodical, *The Inspector*, which took on writers like Henry Fielding and Christopher Smart. Fielding's *Covent Garden Journal* frequently ridiculed Hill, and in an early number dealing with satire hailed the classic immortality of 'that great Triumvirate, Lucian, Cervantes and Swift'.[58] In a similar but more extended vein, an anti-Hill pamphlet published in mid-July 1752 presented Hill descending into the underworld and meeting Lord Orrery, to whom he behaves obsequiously, while showing scant respect on meeting Swift, Pope and Dryden. Hill is presented as reflecting the sort of opinion Orrery had fostered, dismissing the works of these English classics as antique and worthless, and now supplanted by his own.[59]

In Ireland, Orrery was attacked with equal cleverness and more concern for Swift's patriotism. An anonymous Irish 'gentleman' in 1752 ironically doubted the ascription of the *Remarks* to Orrery, since, if they were indeed written by the Earl, their picture of Swift would be a foul violation of the code of friendship.[60] Later he explicitly exposed Orrery's covert ironies about Swift's devotion to Ireland: 'The Remarker truly would have us believe that it was nothing but a mock-patriotism; and therefore describes its Operations and Effects, with all the Mockery of pompous Burlesque'.[61] More circumspect about Orrery was a contemporary pamphlet which took Faulkner to task for publishing the *Remarks*.[62] Orrery and Faulkner were both satirized for their ingratitude in an epigram, unpublished until 1778, written by the curate of Orrery's parish in Ireland:

> A sore disease this scribbling itch is!
>   His Lordship, in his Pliny vein
> Turns Madame Pilkington in breeches
>   And now attacks our patriot Dean.
>
> What! Libel his friend when laid in ground:
>   Nay, good Sir, you may spare your hints,
> His parallel at last is found,
>   For what he writes, George Faulkner prints.
>
> Had Swift provok'd to this behaviour,
>   Yet after death resentment cools,
> Sure his last act bespoke his favour;
>   He built an Hospital for – Fools.[63]

But Orrery's harsh character of Swift also had a palpable influence in Ireland. In a Dublin newspaper in March 1753, an unsigned review of Lord Bolingbroke's recently published *Works* noted

> I presume it will be granted, *Bolingbroke* in arrogance, *Pope* in Vanity, and *Swift* in Insolence, are the true Originals; the last was probably the greatest wit of his time. . . . Swift's Letters might be, as he said, written without Art or Care, but at the same time, if there was little Labour lost, there is little Profit to be gained.[64]

And an anonymous pamphlet during the 'Money Bill' dispute of 1753, recounting the conversation of the ghosts of the Dean and Thomas Prior, founder of the Dublin Society, had Prior criticize Swift's political skills and motivation:

> I never saw or heard any eminent proofs of your extraordinary skill as a
> Politician; except a vast Crowd of Pamphlets. . . . You was [sic] a pretty good
> Patriot, but you had so much of the Politician, that next to taking care of
> others, you loved to take care of yourself . . . You kept a good Byass on your
> Bowl to get near the Jack at long run and secure a Mitre; and tho' when you
> were disappointed, you furiously attack'd the Ministry and pleaded your
> Country's Cause with due Resentment; yet even then . . . while you watch'd
> for the publick Good, you should not overlook your own.

Such criticism was the more pointed coming from Prior, whose patriotic
exertions were agricultural and commercial rather than rhetorically political
or economic, and were recognized widely for their practical effectiveness.
And the response of the ghost of Swift is in keeping with the character Orrery
had drawn: remarking 'you seem to be in a great Fury with little Reason for
it', he all but termed Prior a fool.[65]

The morally coloured picture of Swift that Orrery drew, as splenetic and
self-interested, abetted the antipathy or ambivalence that already existed in
Ireland toward the Dean as a disinterested patriot – hence the paucity of
favourable comment on him from the patriot side during the 'Money Bill'
controversy of 1751–4. And Orrery's dismissal of Swift's patriotism as hypocritical is reflected in the ascription to the Dean of *Some Account of the Irish*,
published in London in 1753. This portrayed the Irish peasantry in absurdly
negative terms, as lacking in culture, honesty and even the rudiments of
civilized behaviour.[66] Its authorship is uncertain, but though expanded from
genuine comments in Swift's correspondence, *Some Account* is definitely not
in Swift's style. It was attributed to him on its title page, however, and signed
by him at the end, implicitly discrediting any real concern on his part for the
condition of the Irish poor while confirming the idea of Swift as sour and
impatient. The date of its appearance, indeed, and its conformity to the
picture of Swift that Orrery presents, suggest that its publication was
prompted by Orrery's.

V

Nonetheless, in the *Remarks* overall, Ireland features rather scantily.
Addressing the book to his son, 'who is so little interested in the present, and
much less in the past affairs of *Ireland*',[67] Orrery justified giving little attention
to Irish matters, and his English readership could be assumed equally unin-
terested. Thus in replying to Orrery, Swift's friend the Rev. Patrick Delany
adopted in general a similarly English perspective, and until the end of his
book alluded little to Swift's Irish patriotism or eminence. His few references
to it were usually disparaging, as when Delany noted that Swift regarded
Ireland as a place of exile, or once remarked that Ireland offered too small an

area for his political genius.[68] Delany's general dismissiveness toward Ireland and characteristically deferential attitude to Orrery undercut his infrequent approval of Swift's Irish exertions, as in commenting on the *Drapier's Letters*:

> his genius never shone out in greater strength than in that, and the subsequent occasions that called it forth. The performances best praise themselves. (*O si sic omnia!*) and your [Orrery's] account of them and him, is clear, succinct, judicious, and just; and therefore I shall not presume to add one tittle to it.[69]

Therefore the conclusion of his book is singular indeed:

> No man ever deserved better of any country than SWIFT did of his. A steady, persevering, inflexible friend; a wise, a watchful, and a faithful counsellor under many severe trials, and bitter persecutions, to the manifest hazard, both of his liberty and fortune!
>
> He lived a blessing, he died a benefactor, and his name will ever live an honour to *Ireland*.[70]

Respectful as Delany was, however, his intention was to correct Orrery. Hence he took some issue with the Earl's notion that Swift was more interested in politics than religion, maintained that Swift was received as Dean in 1713 more warmly than Orrery had allowed, and objected to the Earl's tone and characterizations in treating the story of Stella and Vanessa.[71] Yet he hardly succeeded in painting a distinctly more favourable picture of Swift's behaviour, and while Orrery's *Remarks* were popular, reaching five editions in 1752–3, Delany's *Observations* struck no such chord. The work probably had so little immediate effect because of his inhibited style and a format so dependent on Orrery that it almost necessitated having the earlier book at hand.

With a harsh allusion to the conduct of the Dean's relatives in his final years, however, Delany seems to have provoked Swift's cousin Deane Swift to write his own biographical account.[72] While Orrery became Deane Swift's main target as the book proceeded, the latter's verbose and digressive style, coupled with a marked personal ambivalence about Swift's character, made it no match for Orrery's pointed criticisms. Deane Swift made use of Swift's own autobiographical fragment, which concentrates on the family's history, but had personally known his older cousin best only late in life, and a degree of bitterness towards Swift is frequently perceptible; in addition, the Dean's nature seemed such a mixture of pride, eccentricity and charity as to defy any accurate rendering.[73] Nonetheless, his relationships with Stella and Vanessa appeared altogether above board – though Deane Swift had his cousin, long pursued by Stella, marry her at length to satisfy her, and the better-born Vanessa, disappointed in her own pursuit, die 'a martyr to love and constancy'.[74] Such a version could not counter Orrery's inferences of misogyny very effectively, nor was Deane Swift able to turn aside the Earl's more general charge of Swift's underlying misanthropy.

But Deane Swift was more knowlegeable about Ireland than Orrery and able to hold his ground, certainly on the subject of Swift's patriotism. Remarking that though the Whigs had poisoned the popular spirit against him in the first years after his return to Dublin as Dean, Swift was still selfless enough to take up Ireland's cause and defend the rights of her people in the *Proposal for the Universal Use of Irish Manufactures* and the *Drapier's Letters*, Deane Swift argued that his cousin was motivated by his attachment to principle, rather than by any disappointment on account of his English ambitions. Moreover, lest such political tracts 'be thought local and temporary' and hence 'neglected by succeeding generations', Deane Swift insisted upon their enduring relevance to the British and Irish generally: 'founded upon the secure basis of the laws of this country, and supported throughout the whole with the warmest zeal for LIBERTY, they will forever command the veneration of those, who are not wanting to enjoy the blessings of our constitution'.[75] He feared nonetheless that the Irish might neglect Swift's example, and in the future, 'for want of a patriot inspired like Dr. SWIFT to apprize them of their danger, they may be doomed to chains and slavery'; so Deane Swift concluded his impassioned defence of Swift's patriotism as principled by reminding them of the Dean's sacrifices on their behalf:

> Consider therefore, ye sons of *Ireland*, what hardships had like to have been inflicted upon your wise, your couragious [sic] patriot; consider what persecutions were set upon him by slaves and wretches, for no other crime but that of defending your liberties; or rather indeed for maintaining the very existence of your country; against one vile insignificant mechanick ... Read, therefore, and inscribe the political principles of Dr. SWIFT; engrave them on the tablet of your hearts; teach them unto your children's children.[76]

And where Orrery had snidely dismissed Swift's 1727 *Short View of the State of Ireland* as flatly contradicted by the current 'flourishing' condition of the country, Deane Swift responded directly by wondering at the Earl's ignorance or incomprehension. For how could Orrery

> possibly reside for the greater part of eighteen years in *Ireland* without remarking to his infinite regret that no people in the *Christian* world are so destitute of raiment, food, and all the conveniences of life, as the inhabitants of that wretched kingdom.[77]

Even so, Deane Swift's focus on Swift's patriotism was brief, and generally unremarked; the inadequacies of his rejoinders to Orrery in other respects were much more obvious. An anonymous long notice in the *Monthly Review* commented on the story of Vanessa, indeed, that 'this uncommon *defender* of reputations, has actually left the Dean's much worse than he found it ... the Dean stands inexcusable'.[78]

After Deane Swift's *Essay* appeared, the popular writer Thomas Amory also criticized the inadequacies of its portrait of Swift's character, and proposed 'from my own near observations of the man' to compose a better one, including reflections 'on the cases of Stella and Vanessa'.[79] But this seems not to have appeared. Of Swift's first four biographers in the decade following his death, then, Orrery remained the most lasting influence. At his hands, through his synthesizing categorically a moral basis in biographical facts for the scattered wealth of unseemly impressions and negative insinuations current in Swift's lifetime, the unappealing 'character' which had emerged in those years became the misanthrope. The effect was reinforced by ensuing shorter biographies which plagiarized the *Remarks* extensively.[80] Yet it was susceptible to question, too. For Orrery's constant affirmation of Swift's eminence as a man of letters, together with his repeatedly proposing misanthropy as the explanation for the apparent paradox of the great author who was also a morally deficient man, allowed readers to perceive, at the root of his antipathy, a personal animus disguised as moral condemnation. Hence what Orrery recounted as facts could be accepted more easily than the ostensibly moral context he gave them, in which case Swift's literary greatness, the feature most apparent to the mass of readers who never knew him personally, could shine the more clearly.

While Orrery's influence was to persist well beyond the eighteenth century, a number of commentaries during the period itself, especially in Britain, were to react subtly against the Earl, emphasizing Swift's works over the man as they examined and confirmed his place in the literary canon. Moreover, to some extent in Britain that confirmation would be extended to his patriotic rhetoric. However, Swift would continue to figure remarkably rarely in Irish political commentary, a reflection on the lack of sustained public enthusiasm for his patriotic example that the repeated failure of Faulkner's monument campaigns evidenced, and that Deane Swift had feared.

3

British Canonization and
Irish Diffidence, 1755–1800

I

The remarkable concentration of biographical accounts of Swift in the decade following his death culminated with the appearance in 1755, the same year as Deane Swift's *Essay*, of a London edition of the *Works*, edited with an introductory biography of Swift by John Hawkesworth.[1] Drawing from Orrery, Delany and Deane Swift, Hawkesworth constructed an account that on balance was favourable to Swift, both in respect of his political views – and genuine Irish patriotism – and of his personal life. Forthrightly competing with Faulkner's edition, both the arrangement and editorial accuracy of which Hawkesworth challenged, he disputed even the contention that Swift had a supervisory hand in Faulkner's early volumes.[2] Hawkesworth therefore assumed an editorial authority which, together with his convenient synthesis of the earlier biographical treatments and their use for his annotations, and the fact that his edition was published in London, gave it a status in Britain that lent his 'Account' of Swift's life considerable currency. Further, while a number of minor biographies followed Orrery shamelessly in the first few years after the *Remarks* were published, Hawkesworth's became the main source for shorter treatments of Swift in the biographical dictionaries that appeared over the next quarter-century.[3]

Hawkesworth himself regarded Orrery as a biased source, a false friend to Swift: 'Where he has not *found* the appearance of a fault, he has laboured hard to *make* one.'[4] Hence, while relying on Orrery for much of his information, he softened the latter's insinuations of misanthropy or insincerity on Swift's part, particularly regarding the character of his Irish patriotism. Where Orrery had emphasized that the disappointment of Swift's English ambitions marked him ever afterwards and accounted for his misanthropy, Hawkesworth grants the fact of that disappointment, but gives a more positive dimension to Swift's ensuing 'removal from *England* to *Ireland*', in that it 'shewed him at once what he might possess, and for what he might hope'.[5] And in contrast to Orrery's hinting at demagogic hypocrisy in the *Drapier's Letters*, Hawkesworth approved of them unreservedly, quoting Delany and adding his own encomium: 'of these the *Observator* himself says, "his genius never shone out in greater strength than on that and subsequent occasions", a truth which is universally acknowledged'.[6] Indeed, Swift's 'genius' is the burden of Hawkesworth's 'Account', and by such small strokes, in a fairly short biography, he effectively countered Orrery's implications or assertions of Swift's misanthropy. Indeed, rather than stemming from misanthropy, not only is the Dean's patriotism accepted as purely motivated, but his coarseness of wit and peculiar relations with women are taken as features of a character compounded of eccentricities which made the great writer the more fascinating.

Lacking the earlier biographers' Irish associations or personal acquaintance with Swift, Hawkesworth relied upon his own reading to lend his portrait its subtly positive shades. But as an experienced professional writer, he was also more adept than Orrery in fitting his image of Swift to that current among a wide audience, especially in Britain. Orrery had despised the longstanding popular impression of the Dean as a jesting 'character', for instance; Hawkesworth's depiction of Swift's eccentricities suited it better, posing no obstacle to its continuance. A collection of humorous pieces in 1756 egregiously ascribed to Swift a number of lighthearted songs (including a love ditty beginning 'Of all the Girls that e'er were seen/There's none so fine as *Nelly*'), while also presenting poems actually by or about him.[7] This British popular regard is epitomized in the title of *Swift's Jests: Or, a Compendium of Wit and Humour* which collected jokes and anecdotes by and about many others as well.[8] A second edition of what purported to be *The Celebrated Mrs. Pilkington's Jests* did the same, though acknowledging Pilkington for its Swiftiana.[9] In a rather more serious vein, John Wilkes, who described Swift as 'our *arch enemy*' in number 10 of the *North Briton* (1762), considered in number 11 that 'The truth is, Swift is the *father* of all political humour.'[10] And on a level ultimately if not contemporaneously quite respectable, Swift was a constant resource in the tradition of learned humour that Laurence Sterne mined relentlessly for *Tristram Shandy* (1759–67). Obviously, Orrery had not succeeded in displacing the image of the jocular Dean; on the other hand, he had impressed readers as an observer whose bias was evident even to a critic of Swift's harsher than he. An anonymous reflection upon Swift's character, published in Dublin at the end of 1763 by one claiming personal acquaintance with him, thus maintained 'that it was never my fortune to hear anything either humorous or witty fall from him', and further, that though 'that *great genius* Doctor Swift, is become almost appropriated to him . . . yet, I think, was never more improperly applied'.[11] Still, this ill-humoured critic had begun by castigating Orrery as 'prejudiced against the Dean'.[12]

By taking issue with Orrery, then, Hawkesworth had forwarded a pattern set circumspectly by Delany and more vigorously pursued by Deane Swift. Hawkesworth's impetus hardly carried all before it; doubts regarding Swift's sincerity as a patriot, for instance, well pre-dated Orrery and remained easy to invoke. Thus Tobias Smollett, writing as a British historian in 1758, noted snidely of the Wood affair that 'Ireland was a little ruffled by an incident which seems to have been misrepresented to the people of that kingdom . . . by clamour, pamphlets, papers, and campaigns, written by dean Swift, and other authors.'[13] On the other hand, while Hawkesworth's rendering of the patriot had not quite employed the same enthusiastic terms as Deane Swift – as did an Irish writer of 1755, hailing Swift as the 'Guardian-Genius' of his countrymen[14] – his favourable view abetted those who would. Quite significantly, W.H. Dilworth's biography of Swift, also published in 1758, a compilation based extensively upon Orrery and Deane Swift, echoed the latter outright in characterizing Swift's position in the *Drapier's Letters*. He was both 'a warm and zealous defender of the rights of his country', and 'a most loyal subject, whatever might have been insinuated to the contrary by some degenerate wretches and sycophants to the pandars [sic] in power'.[15] By so adopting Deane Swift's stance Dilworth moved further than Hawkesworth in discountenancing Orrery's insinuations. The rap at Walpole's government in the 1720s was hardly courageous by 1758, when Walpole's Whigs had long been out of power and had few current apologists. Dilworth's advance upon Hawkesworth is a mark, rather, of the process in England whereby the literary figures most recognized as enduring from the Walpole era were opponents of his government such as Pope, Gay and Swift (Addison having died before Walpole's consolidation of power).

That process was only in part a matter of acknowledging superior literary merit. The speed of its progress is inseparable from the effects on British political culture of the flourishing 'patriot' opposition to Walpole in the 1730s and early 1740s, under the patronage of the Prince of Wales, and of the demise of Jacobitism as a threat after the 1745 Rising was quelled. In this context, opposition to ministries came gradually to be understood as compatible with loyalty to the crown, with British patriotism itself. Orrery's imputations of Swift's patriotism as insincere recall the insinuations of political opportunism made about him by Whig writers in 1714–15, but these had been coloured with charges of his secret Jacobitism. Orrery had himself absolved Swift of Jacobitism, however, not allowing notions of principle to soften his suggestion that Swift's antipathy to the Whig government (and consequent Irish patriotism) was motivated by disappointed ambition. Orrery's having dispelled the cloud of Jacobitism made it possible for later eighteenth-century writers to dismiss his aspersions on Swift's patriotism and perceive the Dean's stance as otherwise principled, by loyalty to crown and nation. Though pro-Irish, Swift was not to be considered anti-British; he becomes an exemplar of love of country in general terms.

This was not recognized extensively in Ireland, where the failure of Patrick

Cunningham's project in 1765 for a Swift monument in College Green reflects the lingering diffidence about the Dean's patriotism. But in Britain, the advance in Swift's patriotic reputation is particularly noticeable that same year in two reviews of volumes Deane Swift had edited as part of a Hawkesworth edition. Ralph Griffiths, in a long notice for his *Monthly Review*, outlined the circumstances of the *Drapier's Letters* and judged effusively, 'as his cause was just, his resolution steady, his perseverance unshaken, he finally triumphed over all his opponents, who deservedly sunk into the infamy they so justly merited'. Swift was deservedly 'the patriot Dean', who was 'in this part of his character, whatever may be thought of him as a divine, or even as a wit, A TRULY GREAT AND GOOD MAN'.[16] At least in relation to Ireland, Walpole's government could be seen, as Swift had seen it, as a kind of tyranny. But voicing the corollary, that the Irish cause as he had espoused it was more than a local call to liberty (a point implicit in Swift's own epitaph), was appropriately left to Edmund Burke. Burke was to become the first Irishman after Swift to exert significant influence in British ruling circles, but not for a few years more; in 1765 he was still making his way in British letters and politics. More restrained and concise than Griffiths, Burke reviewed two of Deane Swift's volumes in the *Annual Register* for that year, showing more forthright appreciation of Swift as a clergyman and wit, and noting that the Irish tracts generally 'do honour to his heart as well as his head', since they proved, for all his criticism of the Irish, that 'he had their interest sincerely at heart'. The sermon 'On Doing Good', moreover, though 'peculiarly adapted to Ireland and Wood's designs upon it', has a universally instructive application, presenting 'perhaps the best motives to patriotism, that were ever delivered within so small a compass'.[17] This last phrase, however concessive, nonetheless offers a telling if unintended contrast with Orrery's comment in the *Remarks*, ostensibly to his son, that the cosmopolitan young man would not be expected to know or care about Irish affairs. It even contrasts with Delany's recollection that Swift thought his talents were thrown away on so small a stage as Ireland.

That the British, as Burke implies, should or could learn about patriotism from a writer concerned with Ireland was the more noteworthy for the persistence in British ruling circles of a view of the Irish as rebellious.[18] Burke was, of course, an unusually interested party; it is understandable that, as an Irishman with, like Swift, British political ambitions, he would incline to find in the Dean's patriotism a more cosmopolitan potential than had been recognized heretofore. But his recognition of that potential is yet another landmark in Swift's rising position among the British literary establishment as a modern classic whose patriotism contributed markedly to his stature. From Hawkesworth and Dilworth in the 1750s to Griffiths and Burke a decade later, affirmation of that position grew in confidence, in contrast to the scattered indications of Swift's regard as a living classic in the 1730s. The Dean had remained a popular writer, Orrery had not disabled his reputation, and by the mid-1760s his place in the literary canon remained secure. For Burke to note the cosmopolitan potential of his patriotism, then, advanced the process of Swift's literary canonization; according to this process, the local circumstances prompting a work become less important, receding into history, than the rhetorical effects with which they are characterized. Thus the specifically Irish, and indeed potentially radical, aspects of his political writings could be subsumed in the general admiration of Swift as a writer. Whatever his personal faults or eccentricities, however disturbing his satire, or even disgusting in its particulars, he was a wit of genius, and inasmuch as his patriotic writings instanced this, they were also safe.

II

Swift's typically conservative political and religious outlook of course abetted the growth of such an observation. The 1760s and 1770s were a period of Tory political ascendancy in England, which gradually prompted a vocal reaction culminating in sympathy for American agitations. By no means all who took part in that reaction were radicals, as Burke's own sympathy with American claims indicates, but this fostered a climate which gave radicalism a surer foothold in English political culture than it ever had previously in the eighteenth century. And for radicals, or even liberals, Swift was harder to admire. This was certainly true in Ireland, as the case of Charles Lucas had evidenced over a decade earlier, and by the mid-1770s Swift seemed to the Irish writer Richard Lewis an ancestor of contemporary conservatism: 'His political writings may be justly stiled, *The Tories' Catechism*; for they lay down those absurd and slavish doctrines they hold, and contain subtle and jesuitical expositions thereon'.[19] Consistency was not Lewis's strong point: elsewhere he claimed that Swift 'lives within each grateful breast',[20] and while he admired Lucas he was also a eulogist of George Faulkner. But he sympathized with the claims of Catholics and dissenters, and was particularly outraged by Swift's hatred of Presbyterians, perceiving the Dean as an influence fostering the continued division among Irish Protestants that ultimately served British interests. Hence, in the atmosphere of continuing Irish diffidence about Swift's patriotism, or the kind of anodyne admiration that saw his bust eventually placed in St Patrick's Cathedral, Lewis vilified Swift forthrightly and unremittingly, renewing with none of Orrery's subtlety the old Whig charges of his opportunism in British circumstances and his hypocrisy in Irish affairs. These faults, now ignored by the Tory establishment, were the real source of Swift's mighty patriotism; a

> patriotism that has been celebrated, till MODESTY grew sick, and even VANITY blushed. – Had the English *ministry* numbered SWIFT with their *other slaves in lawn*, we had never seen the word *patriot* annexed to the name of

SWIFT: or had the *Irish* ministers paid their court to him, and promise-fed him as the *English* had done, his patriotism had been smothered in embryo. — A PATRIOT! I sicken at the word. — When that term is so prostituted, and applied to such a *slave* as SWIFT, whom *accident* alone determined to write on the side he engaged in, in *Ireland*; it is high time for those *real good men* and lovers of their country, who defend her cause against her foreign and domestic foes, to quit it, and chooe some other term, less liable to *perversion*.[21]

Lewis pointedly refrained from disputing Swift's literary canonicity – he even found a poem he claimed as Swift's first[22] – but whereas Burke in 1765 had sought to distance Irish local circumstances from the Dean's literary value as a patriot, Lewis highlighted those circumstances in order to compartmentalize and discount such value.

Lewis's diatribe is singular, and not just for its intensity. It bespeaks an Irish as well as liberal resentment at the Dean's affirmation as patriot, especially among conservatives and in England. Yet it had no perceptible effect on the course of Swift's reputation; whatever the regard for him as a literary classic, he continued to figure remarkably little in Irish political commentary. He had rarely been invoked by political writers in Ireland during the quarter-century before 1775, while a 'patriot' party established itself gradually even inside the Irish House of Commons. But that comparative silence persisted through the next twenty-five years, which saw the greatest victory of Protestant Irish patriotism in the achievement of legislative independence in 1782–3, and its defeat with the Act of Union in 1800, while Irish republicanism was conceived in the interval. There are notable exceptions to this, but for the most part Swift was at best a rather vague patriotic eminence: a compartmentalization of Lewis's kind, between enduring literary value and political significance, is clearly discernible. Another observer, certainly more sympathetic to Swift than Lewis, could nonetheless reflect such a split in attitude. Thomas Campbell, travelling through Ireland in the 1770s, described Swift's epitaph in St Patrick's as 'very expressive of that habit of mind, which his own disappointments, and the oppressions of his country, had produced', yet later noted that 'Swift, shrunk from a court-favourite into the head of a chapter, became easily irritated against the ruling men and manners here, and led the way in abusing the place.'[23] Irish political writers and speakers do occasionally refer to Swift in these years, but rather as a classic, a source of quotation, than as a political model, a prophet or inspiration to action.

Indeed, Irish indifference or hostility to Swift as any kind of precursive figure could take the form of ignoring altogether his part in Irish history. An anonymous commentator on the Free Trade campaign in Ireland during the later 1770s, against British laws curbing Irish commerce, noted that Ireland had long featured 'a protestant interest, a popish interest, and an English interest', but before the height of the agitation in 1778, 'I never heard of an *Irish* interest in Ireland since the reign of Queen Elizabeth.'[24] This is perhaps an extreme example, but generally in Ireland Swift's patriotic writings seemed characterized by such local and immediate circumstances in the distant past as rendered them outdated and inapplicable to contemporary conditions. As Gerard O'Brien has pointed out, the writings of patriots like Molyneux and Swift dated from a different era entirely from that of Henry Grattan in the 1780s, and though 'we still have little idea of the stage of development through which Irish patriotism passed between 1730 and 1780',

> At some point during this period economic patriotism ceased to be passive and took on some decidedly aggressive features. In 1779 the people who sought Free Trade no longer talked, like Swift, of boycotts but instead displayed cannons. In 1780 the men who sought redress of political grievances no longer looked to a Union as a solution, as Molyneux did, but rather rejected it as the ultimate degradation. In the course of the eighteenth century the colonial identity had taken on a new self reliance, and this was to assert itself through a newer, more aggressive, and more opportunistic type of patriot[25]

than Swift and Molyneux had represented.

The occasional Irish political references to Swift can contrast quite markedly in rhetoric with that of English literary commentators. William Eden, for instance, alluded to Swift during the Free Trade controversy of the 1770s to lend historical weight to his argument against restrictive British legislation. Swift 'ascribed the poverty of his country to a multiplicity of causes', particularly including the system of land ownership and management, and noted that 'there was a want of an industrious disposition among the people, but he attributed that want to the restraint laid upon their commerce, and to the discouragement of manufactures, which had made them mere hewers of wood, and drawers of water, to their neighbours'.[26] By comparison, Samuel Badcock's review of John Nichols' *Supplement to Dr. Swift's Works* in the *Monthly Review* the same year was effusive in holding that the

> high rank he holds in the republic of letters was owing, not to the indulgence of the times in which he wrote, but entirely to his own incontestable merit. . . . The opposition of an unrelenting party in church and state, and the personal enmity that was borne him by several of high rank and great influence, could not eclipse the lustre of his name, nor sink in the smallest degree, that authority in literature which he claimed, and the world granted, as his right.[27]

And in 1781, Samuel Johnson's account of Swift in the *Lives of the English Poets*, while displaying a considerable lack of sympathy for the man, acknowledged the patriot:

> It was from the time when he first began to patronize the Irish, that they may date their riches and prosperity. He taught them first to know their own interest, their weight, and their strength, and gave them some spirit to assert

that equality with their fellow-subjects to which they have ever since been making vigorous advances, and to claim those rights which they have at last established.[28]

The contrast not only manifests a difference in rhetorical heat between an Irish political writer like Eden and British literary critics, but implies quite a different assessment of Ireland's condition and Swift's effect upon it. Eden cites Swift to suggest that little had changed between Swift's time and his own, while Johnson's argument recalls Orrery's judgement on *A Short View of the State of Ireland* (1728) that Ireland was actually prospering. The British views of Swift, articulated with insufficient current or historical understanding of Irish affairs, display a development of the Dean's literary canonization beyond Burke's elevating his rhetoric over its local occasions. Here, less than two decades after Burke's 1765 review, the very durability of Swift's literary significance facilitated the assumption that his influence as a patriot nearer to his own time must have been strong enough to have succeeded in its objectives; thus his patriotism could be relegated, with due gratitude, to history. Ireland's consistent unimportance to the generality of British writers made it all the easier to marginalize Swift's Irish interests even while hailing his canonization. The anonymous British editor of a 1782 collection of short pieces, excerpts and Swiftiana, dedicated to Johnson and including an abridged version of his 'Life', noted Swift's popularity among 'the very indolent' as well as 'the judicious and learned', but nearly ignored his Irish patriotism.[29] Swift acquired great 'esteem and influence' from the *Drapier's Letters*, for instance, 'the purport of which few readers are unacquainted with', while a note to the 'Fable of Arachne and Pallas, Applied to England and Ireland', excerpted from *Irish Manufactures*, reflects Johnson's judgement: 'Since this was wrote, the oppression complained of has been in some measure lightened.'[30] The very process of literary canonization could blunt the image of Swift as a political energizer.

Until fairly recently it would have seemed less evident that a similar process had occurred in Ireland as well, since Henry Grattan was considered to have actually invoked Swift as a precursor and inspiration in his famous 'declaration of Irish independence' on 16 April 1782. For nearly a century and a half this speech was thought to include the memorable sentence 'Spirit of Swift – spirit of Molyneux – Your genius has prevailed – Ireland is now a nation!' We now know that Grattan did not deliver this invocation in 1782, but added it for an edition of his speeches that appeared posthumously in 1821.[31] The emendation instances a delayed historiographical effect similar to the result of Swift's literary canonization seen in Johnson's comment above: since Swift *should* have had influence of this sort in his own century, it is retrospectively accorded to him. Hence also, the son of Grattan's contemporary and rival patriot, Henry Flood, in the 1838 biography of his father, included the *Drapier's Letters* among the sources of Flood's patriotic inspiration.[32] The younger Flood may have been accurate in so specifying Swift's influence upon his father. A generation earlier, however, the biographer of the Earl of Charlemont noted of the *Drapier's Letters* that 'their influence embraced every part of Ireland', without mentioning any formative influence upon Charlemont himself, who as commander of the Irish Volunteers in the late 1770s did as much as Grattan or Flood to bring about Ireland's legislative independence in 1782.[33]

That the younger Flood's citation is more specific reflects the gathering strength in the nineteenth century of the notion that Swift, often with Molyneux, is at the head of a line of patriots that includes such figures as Grattan, Flood and Charlemont in its progress. Such an ancestral line became a characteristic of nineteenth-century nationalist rhetoric, bespeaking the current tendency to frame historical development in genealogical terms. Charles Lucas, who was sometimes included in this patriot line, had himself constructed a prototype, placing Swift in passing among a group of Whiggish ideologues of liberty. Like the process of Swift's literary canonization at Burke's and Johnson's hands in England after the mid-eighteenth century, however, the nineteenth-century idea of the patriot line subordinated the local and immediate circumstances of Swift's political discourse to its rhetoric, which could be endowed with surpassing and enduring inspirational values. Grattan's amendment to involve the Dean thus fits a nineteenth- rather than an eighteenth-century context: it offered an impetus to what James Kelly has described as a tendency among constitutional nationalists in the later era to hearken 'to the late eighteenth century Irish parliament for historical legitimisation. . . . to inflate the scale and implication' of the legislative independence gained in 1782, 'and to depict Henry Grattan as a talismanic constitutionalist who had guided Irish M.P.s toward this triumph and in whose footsteps they were following'.[34]

Since Grattan's eloquently succinct formulation of the patriot line was a nineteenth-century revisionary gloss on eighteenth-century history, it is the more noteworthy that Molyneux and Swift were in fact invoked in 1782 as inspiring antecedents for the patriots of that year, though not by Grattan nor in a speech to the Irish parliament. That distinction belongs rather to Leonard MacNally, later infamous as an informer against the United Irishmen, who reviewed the steps leading to the achievement of legislative independence, recognized Molyneux's contribution and held that Swift 'went still further in opening the minds of the Irish, and preparing them to nurture the seeds of freedom, and to vindicate those rights which heaven has bestowed upon the human race'. The Dean becomes the precursor of the Volunteers: 'The wisdom of his theory has been proved by practice', since, when his injunction against wearing foreign manufactures was finally heeded during the Free Trade controversy of the 1770s, 'this was followed by a military association . . . resolving upon establishing liberty'.[35] It was not Swift's wisdom and prophetic character alone that affirmed his ancestry for the patriots of 1782 but the fact that, like Molyneux's, his writings provoked government attempts to silence him, as also happened to Lucas later.[36] Swift's persuasive advocacy, together with government persecution, made him for MacNally an ancestral champion of two ideas – national autonomy and the freedom of the press – that Irish liberals cherished. This latter theme, though not supplemented by the notion of a patriot line, was restated the next year in William Crawford's *History of Ireland*, the first general history to give Swift's contribution more than a passing reference. Like MacNally, Crawford was an Irish liberal who favoured the Volunteer movement, but his historiographical scope was necessarily broader. That breadth allowed him to refrain from echoing Richard Lewis's complaints about Swift's Toryism or bigotry, for thus he could clarify the Dean's role in the Wood affair as both disinterested and enduringly relevant: 'his country still acknowledges this noble effort of his patriotism. He was in danger of suffering deeply in the cause', which Crawford regarded as that of 'the people of this country' and which he proceeded revealingly to discuss in the present tense.[37]

In so celebrating Swift, MacNally and Crawford could rely upon his canonicity in Britain, the patriotic sagacity and effectiveness accorded him, for at least a generation, as an aspect of his literary eminence. This had long lain available for appropriation in Ireland, though over the years it had been largely ignored, or, at hands like Richard Lewis's, disputed. But soon after MacNally and Crawford, it was quite overtly appropriated, and in a publication more prominent than theirs, by Thomas Sheridan for his edition of Swift's *Works* in 1784. Sheridan, whose father had been a friend of the Dean, was the last of Swift's editors and biographers to have known him personally, and had himself staged a performance of *The Conscious Lovers* over thirty years before to benefit the campaign for a monument to him.[38] Swift had remained an important memory in the Sheridan family,[39] and Thomas Sheridan's 'Life' of Swift introducing the edition is altogether friendly. He prefaced the volumes of Swift's texts, furthermore, with a dedication that elegantly drew Swift and Grattan together in a patriot line:

TO
HENRY GRATTAN, ESQ.
FOUNDER
OF THE LIBERTIES OF IRELAND –
THIS NEW EDITION OF THE WORKS
OF HIS GREAT PREDECESSOR
THE IMMORTAL DRAPIER!
IN WHOSE FOOTSTEPS HE HAS TRODDEN,
AND WHOSE IDEAS REALIZED,
IS RESPECTFULLY INSCRIBED
BY HIS GRATEFUL COUNTRYMAN
(NOW MADE PROUD
OF THE NAME OF IRISHMAN)
THE EDITOR[40]

Here Sheridan encapsulated both MacNally's representation of Swift as precursor to the events of 1782 and Crawford's implication of his continuing relevance. By shifting his focus to Grattan, he neatly prefigured Grattan's own belated invocation of Swift for his 1782 speech, and may actually have planted the seed for it. As British critical affirmation of Swift's Irish patriotism had depended upon his texts rather than his life, Sheridan's dedication of the texts constructed them as a monument anticipating Grattan as Swift's successor.

Sheridan thus stepped slightly beyond the British literary canonization of Swift as a patriot whose efforts for his country had succeeded – a notion derived from his rhetorical power rather than strict factual accuracy – and could now appear safely historical. By imputing to him an enduring inspirational power, Sheridan's dedication refused to relegate him to history. Sheridan's ceaselessly enthusiastic 'Life' of the Dean, moreover, the longest of eighteenth-century biographical accounts, described the arrogant oppressiveness of British policy toward Ireland in Swift's time as though it still continued. Swift himself was presented as disinterested in his passion for principle and charitable to the Irish poor, who had in turn remained unswerving in their admiration. Implicitly, he was constructed as a constant model of the wise, patriotic and virtuous writer. It is a portrait that might have forwarded again the process of Swift's literary canonization had Sheridan been content with softening his faults of character, as Hawkesworth had done, rather than all but excusing them. For the critics reviewing his 'Life' in Britain took most heated issue not with Sheridan's advancement of the patriot's enduring relevance, but with his attempt to exonerate Swift's character as a man. The biographer's attempt to excuse the Dean's conduct toward Stella and Vanessa was especially castigated.[41] Sheridan's exculpatory method seemed all the more inappropriate when an old anecdote of Swift's having raped a farmer's daughter in 1694, during his time as curate at Kilroot, was resurrected in 1786. It had appeared in print first in Nichols's *Supplement* to Swift's works published in 1779, but gained greater currency from being included in an edition of *The Tatler* in 1786 with an attestation to its truth by the then prebend of Kilroot, which was quickly reprinted in the *Gentleman's Magazine*.[42] The story was soon investigated and refuted by Thomas Percy, Bishop of Dromore, publicly disputed in George-Monck Berkeley's *Literary Relics* in 1789, and retracted by the *Gentleman's Magazine* in 1790, but the episode lent little support to Sheridan's treatment of Swift's character.[43] While the British literary canonization of Swift had come so to favour his patriotic rhetoric as to exaggerate its effectiveness, this hardly meant that Sheridan's review of the Dean's behaviour to make it comport with his greatness was plausible; for that behaviour had acquired a reputation, in Swift's own day and through the numerous biographies after his death, for too much peculiarity to warrant justifying his character, whatever his eminence. After Sheridan, it became unusual for Swift's British commentators to exalt the author or patriot without also lamenting the nature of the man.

III

After Sheridan, indeed, decades would pass before Swift's relevance as a precursive voice in the achievement of legislative independence was commonly accepted in the sense that Sheridan and MacNally had promoted: Grattan inserted the later-famous apostrophe in his 1782 'declaration of Irish independence' nearly forty years after the fact. In retrospect, the emphasis given Swift's patriotism by MacNally, Crawford and Sheridan in 1782–4 merely interrupted the general silence about the Dean that had long prevailed in Irish political commentary, and which resumed after 1784. Moral qualms about Swift's character were probably a less significant factor in that relapse into neglect than were the shifting currents of Irish affairs in the 1780s and 1790s. The fact that events in Ireland afforded so little contemporary perception of his relevance highlights a number of ironies. First, it is ironic that in the thirty years before 1782, British literary critics came to recognize (and even to exaggerate) values in Swift's Irish patriotism that went generally unremarked by Irish political commentators. Then, one Irish liberal, Richard Lewis, could revile him as a conservative 'Patron Saint' in 1775; yet a few years later, MacNally, Crawford and Sheridan constructed a patriotic identity for him as an ancestor of the progressive thrust of Irish liberalism. These ironies are explained by the unsettled nature of Irish Protestant patriotism perceived by Gerard O'Brien in the period 1730–80, followed by its growing substantiality during the Free Trade controversy and the Volunteer movement, culminating in legislative independence in 1782. For independence seemed to vindicate for Protestants an Irish identity somewhat elusive in its previous articulation.

As a minority in the population of Ireland, Protestants, and especially members of the Church of Ireland, had always balanced their sense of Irishness against concern for the security of their dominance in the country. The penal legislation enacted against Catholics from the reign of William III through that of George I had provided a basis for that security, and hence a foundation for Protestants' Irish identity. Upon that foundation and, to an extent, offsetting its negative character, there grew a defensive attitude toward the British connection, upon which Protestant security ultimately depended. The oppositional terms of Swift's rhetoric in regard to the London government spoke to that defensiveness during the Wood affair; and it was his success in this which gave it value, for a time, as a primary feature of Irish Protestant identity. Defensive rhetoric, in other words, impelled a unity of purpose among the Irish, which enabled their victory and quickened their national pride; but over the next two generations their defensiveness gained no like success in opposing the British ministry which could vindicate that pride. It is of significance that the focus upon the rights of Ireland's separate parliament, sharpened by Swift's rhetoric, was not sustained, but only resurfaced sporadically until the late 1770s. Hence his contribution to parliament's rights, as indeed to Irish Protestant identity, became difficult to articulate clearly. By 1782, however, some could recognize Swift as precursive in both respects, since the Irish cause that year, as in the time of Wood's scheme, was united and victorious.

The ironies attending Swift's reputation expand subtly thereafter, as the values underlying his patriotism, whether liberal or conservative, were left undeveloped. This is because the unity of the Irish cause was itself short-lived, allowing little space for the sustained development of Protestant Irish identity while relations with Britain eased but Catholics became an issue in Irish politics as they had not been since Swift's time.[44] He had taken the Penal Laws for granted, but even before Independence various pressures, especially from the London government, had begun to erode them. After-wards, pressure for further erosion quickened, and Protestant concerns for maintaining dominance mounted accordingly. The forms these took, how-ever, revealed a fundamental ideological difference between two strands of Protestant opinion, to neither of which Swift's oppositional rhetoric could have appealed. For especially as the 1780s wore into the 1790s, the British connection offered Irish liberals and conservatives kinds of leverage quite distinct from that of Irish loyalty to crown and opposition to ministry advo-cated by him in the 1720s (and meaningful to some, fifty to sixty years later). As the government used the British connection to press the Irish parliament to concede somewhat to the claims of Catholics, the more liberal elements represented in that parliament maintained that these concessions would ensure Catholic allegiance to a polity that, because of the British connection, Protestants could continue to dominate. They considered that connection as good in itself, but liable to extend Britain's economic and political control over Ireland unless it were tempered by the growth of amity and co-operation between Protestants and a deferential Catholic majority. Conservatives saw the matter more starkly, acceding to pressure from London but seeking to blunt it, increasingly, between the mid-1780s and the end of the century by identifying Protestant dominance with Britishness, founded as it was upon the British connection.

While such factors reduced Swift's relevance among Protestants, he might appear to have had none at all among Irish Catholics. To be sure, as we have seen Swift's Tory sympathies led to charges of his Jacobitism or even covert Popery in his earlier career.[45] In fact, however, after becoming Dean of St Patrick's he never championed Catholics as such nor argued for any relax-ation of the Penal Laws except in order satirically to counter the claims of Dissenters.[46] And while such works as *A Short View of the State of Ireland* and *A Modest Proposal* manifested real concern for the condition of the rural

Catholic poor, the misattributed *Some Account of the Irish* in 1753, claimed as Swift's on its title page, abused the Catholic peasantry at length for their filthy habits and boundless ignorance, concluding 'if Ignorance be the true Mother of Devotion, the City of *Rome* itself cannot produce such devout Catholics as these *Teagues*; and Pity it is they should not be transplanted to the Territories of the Holy Church, as the most submissive of all her Members'.[47] Such a misattribution would not necessarily have been recognized as departing from Swift's own beliefs, especially since he had also satirized Irish peasants for some of the same characteristics in poems like 'Dermot and Sheelagh'. An English traveller of 1758 in Ireland saw, indeed, a connection between such a peasantry and the Yahoos:

> Of all the people I ever saw in my life, the common Irish are the most indolent and most dirty. They live in the meanest huts, and feed on the coarsest fare I ever beheld. This shocked me more than I can well describe to you . . . in short, the men are all Dermots, and the women are all Shilahs [sic]; and I am now less surprised that Dean Swift gave such a humbling picture of human nature, in his account of the Yahoos, considering the country he lived in.[48]

Irish Catholics in their turn were hardly forward in advancing Swift's reputation during the eighteenth century. There is again some irony in the fact that, once Jacobitism had ceased as a threat and Irish Catholics in the 1760s and 1770s began to press for relaxation of the Penal Laws, Swift could be enlisted to strengthen their cause. As a patriot he had fostered Irish unity; by extension he might be made to promote the acceptance of Catholics in such unity. Thus Dr John Curry in 1771, taking the guise of a liberal Protestant in his *Observations on the Popery Laws*, notes that Swift, 'who knew the interests of his native country well, and studied them long', recognized the loyalty of Irish Catholics to 'the present establishment'; though his assurances were ignored in his day, a later generation ought nonetheless to be persuaded by 'that great genius' to allow Irish Catholics to become '*useful* . . . in the service of their country'.[49] Curry again complimented Swift as a 'real and venerable patriot' in the 1786 edition of his *State of the Catholics in Ireland*.[50] This was a forthright Catholic apologetic introduced by Charles O'Conor of Belanagar, who cited Molyneux and Swift as ancestral figures for the campaign to repeal some of the penal legislation, which had begun to see success. These were only comments in passing, rather than expressions of firm Catholic appreciation of Swift; they resemble the contemporary praises of British literary commentators, and were obviously aimed to appeal to the good nature and patriotism of Irish Protestants. But the difference in assertiveness, even in respect to these mild comments, between Curry's plaintiveness in 1771 and O'Conor's confidence in 1786, marks the fact and the portent of Catholic resurgence.

   What this resurgence portended for Irish Protestants was becoming clear by the later 1780s, with drastic consequences for the Irish identity of many of

them. Their ideological differences came to the fore in 1786–7 over the issue
of reforming the system of tithes, which were laid upon the whole rural
population, including Catholics and Presbyterians, to support the established
Church. The system was most burdensome, inevitably, for Catholics, and
when Protestant liberals sought to reform it, once tithe exactions had provoked agrarian 'Rightboy' disturbances in Munster, conservatives saw a
threat to 'Protestant Ascendancy' (the term first appeared during this clash)
and thus to the British connection.[51] Prominent among the conservative
proponents of Protestant Ascendancy during the Rightboy controversy were
leaders of the Church of Ireland, and their position had both anti-Catholic
and anti-Dissenter features, of the sort Richard Lewis in 1775 had seen in
Swift himself. But altered circumstances, again ironically, would have
reduced Swift's attractiveness to the conservatives: he had addressed
Protestants defensive about their ultimate dependence upon the British
connection, but now conservative defensiveness brought into question instead whether Irish Protestants were willing to accommodate the claims of
Catholics. At length the conservatives persuaded the administration to adopt
coercive measures against the Rightboys. As liberals and conservatives
clashed frequently in the following years, the administration pitched toward
the former in extending the franchise to Catholics (1793) and establishing
Maynooth College (1795), motivated in each case by the hope of securing
Catholic loyalty in the war against revolutionary France. That tendency
seemed most alarming to conservatives when a coalition government in
Britain appointed Lord Fitzwilliam as Lord Lieutenant in 1795, for he supported 'Catholic Emancipation' – the repeal of the oath barring Catholics
from the Irish parliament – and set about removing prominent conservatives from his Irish administration. After their protests and his quick recall,
however, the government veered toward Irish conservatives, becoming
increasingly severe toward radicals in the years before the Rising of 1798.

   In this process, a large body of Protestant opinion shifted from the Irish
identity articulated in 1782 toward a stronger appreciation of their British
allegiance by the end of the same decade and into the 1790s. Thus, while the
term 'Protestant Ascendancy' had arisen in a context of conservative defensiveness, its growing currency in the 1790s became an index of confidence
among Conservatives. It stood for a concept that supplied the place of the
receding Penal Laws, and the British connection steadily aroused less defensiveness than pride. Conservatives saw themselves as an essential safeguard for
British empire and liberty, particularly once Britain went to war; behind any
concessions to Dissenters, or especially to Catholics, they discerned a weak-
ening of the British bulwark against revolution. Hence they understood their
British connection in terms more comprehensive than simply sharing a
monarch – especially since Catholic claims were frequently pressed with
expressions of unswerving loyalty to the crown. The distinction for which
Swift had argued, therefore, between loyalty to the crown and to the

oppressiveness of ministers, would have drawn few conservatives to him by the end of the century. His oppositional rhetoric would instead, as a final irony, have posed radical implications for their concept of Protestant Ascendancy.[52]

That some Catholics sensed this is apparent from their quoting the fourth *Drapier's Letter* as the epigraph to a pamphlet of 1792 promoting the continued repeal of penal legislation.[53] But there is no evidence that Swift's subversive potential in this respect was apparent to Irish liberals, nor, indeed, that it would have gratified them. Rather, the complex interactions of internal politics and relations with Britain that retrospectively ironize Swift's reputation in the 1780s and 1790s had narrowed, in those very years, the relevance of the rhetorical simplicities that MacNally had found appealing in 1782. As though that relevance depended upon the Irish political consensus in which liberals had then been prominent, Swift was left, once it ruptured, as an historical and literary figure whose patriotic heritage could be viewed with ambivalence, or doubted entirely, even by those who were liberal or moderate themselves. Thomas Campbell is a case in point. He had treated Swift in *A Philosophical Survey of the South of Ireland* (1778) commendably as a literary figure and an honourable, if irritable, man, but gave him no contemporary political relevance. Writing as an historian in 1789, however, Campbell granted the Dean's place in history and even adopted the early phase of the patriot line by presenting Molyneux as his precursor, but devalued the effects of Swift's patriotism after the 'Money Bill' crisis in 1753: 'The incomparable Swift lighted a flame of patriotism in every Irish bosom, which glowed at intervals till the year 1753, when, having lost its pole-star, it took a direction not altogether right.'[54] Hence, while Campbell praised the Volunteer movement, he gave Swift no part in its ancestry. Writing a few years later, James Mullala, another political moderate who opposed Britain's former policies restricting Irish trade and who supported legislative independence and even Catholic emancipation, dealt with Swift more severely both as an historical and a literary eminence. His *View of Irish Affairs* (1795), published in the glow of conservative triumph following Fitzwilliam's recall, repeated Smollett's 1758 dismissal of the agitation over Wood's scheme as an imposition 'kept up in Ireland, particularly by the writings of the celebrated Dean Swift, and some other authors'. In literature, moreover, Swift's 'muse seems to have been mere misantrophy [sic]', for he was 'a cynic rather than a poet', redeemed only by his 'adopting the extravagant humour of Lucian or Rabelais'.[55]

As Swift's standing in Irish patriotic history was ignored by conservatives and subjected to doubts by others, there also occasionally emerge in the 1790s references to Swift by some liberal political observers as an example of neglected vision, an image of the unheeded in his time. Praising the lawyer and scientist Richard Kirwan, a founder of the Royal Irish Academy and thus a patriotic benefactor like Swift, Henry Grattan remarked to the Irish House of Commons on 19 January 1792 that 'The curse of Swift is upon him to have been born an Irishman; to have possessed a genius, and to have used his talents for the good of his country.'[56] In a more ironic vein, a satiric poem addressed to young ministers by 'Obadiah Tithepig' recalled Swift's admonitions to the clergy, though

> Of course Swift's rules, it stands to reason
> Are now completely out of season,
> And Parsons of the present day
> Will leave them to the worms a prey . . .[57]

The next year, the clergyman Michael Sandys compared the inefficacy he anticipated of his own pleading on behalf of the rural poor to Swift's complaint that his economic arguments 'had as little effect as if [they] came from the pulpit'.[58]

At best, then, Swift's historical standing as a patriot evoked only wistful comment from those in the Irish political mainstream as the eighteenth century drew to its close. Yet for Protestant radicals, at the furthest extent of the political spectrum, Swift acquired palpable ancestral significance. Even before his connection with the United Irishmen, Theobald Wolfe Tone noted in his journal in 1790 his belief that political sentiment 'in the middling ranks and indeed in the spirit of the people' had in the past been evoked to great effect when they were 'informed of their interests by such men as Swift, Flood, Grattan, etc. etc.'.[59] It was an early sign that he would see himself too as one of the Dean's descendants, the latest personage in the patriot line. This implication occurs more markedly later in the decade as Tone looked back upon his political development:

> I made speedily what was to me a great discovery, though I might have found it in Swift or Molyneux, that the influence of England was the radical vice of our Government, and consequently that Ireland would never be either free, prosperous or happy, until she was independent, and that independence was unattainable, whilst the connection with England existed.[60]

Tone compared himself to Swift in another respect as well, noting in 1791 that his own journal 'is a thousand times wittier than Swift's', while his frequent quotations from the Dean also indicate his awareness of Swift's literary eminence.[61] Tone's revolutionary colleague William Drennan, meanwhile, reflecting in letters upon the government's investigation of subversive activities, considered as a model of appropriate behaviour Swift's refusal to testify when his own patriotic writings were being investigated.[62]

Yet these were private utterances, and it is only in retrospect that he can be seen to have had some influence on the radical cast of mind that housed the 1798 Rising. In public, at the end of the eighteenth century, and whether in Britain or Ireland, Swift continued to be regarded primarily as a literary figure. This was itself not without some minor political relevance, however, both as to the past and the uses that could be made of it. William Coxe, an English historian writing in 1798 of the Walpole era, recognized the fallacy in that aspect of Swift's literary canonization in Britain which had exaggerated the effectuality of his patriotic works in his own time because of their rhetorical power. Thus of the *Drapier's Letters*, for instance, he noted that 'The inimitable humour of Swift, which places the Kingdom on one side and William Wood on the other, has misled our judgment and captivated our imagination' long after the event, just as, at the time, Swift's 'hardy assertions, and false representations were implicitly believed'.[63] On the other hand, Thomas Somerville's account of Queen Anne's reign, published the same year, commended Swift's Tory propaganda for its literary qualities, 'precision in the statement of facts; perspicuity of language; acrimonious animadversion, and force of reasoning', and took issue with earlier commentators, like the 'bigoted Whig' Oldmixon in 1735, for exhibiting the 'malice of party' when discussing Swift's character.[64] Considered as a literary eminence Swift was common property for commentators on each side of contemporary political issues, cited as an ornament of Ireland's heritage by a pamphleteer opposed to the projected Act of Union and as a model of satiric technique by a supporter.[65] A poem of 1799 deriding Grattan compares his constant antagonist, Dr Patrick Duigenan, to Swift – 'a man to whom Mr. Grattan bears not the least resemblance in the power of his mind' – and Grattan himself to William Wood.[66] And during the debate in the Irish House of Commons in 1800 on the proposed Union of Britain and Ireland, Swift was the subject of passing literary allusions on the same day by George Ponsonby, who opposed the Union, and Duigenan himself, who supported it.[67] Swift's canonization in literature was secure indeed; he had become a modern classic, even for his patriotism, to the British literary establishment; but in Irish political discourse he cut no great figure, and his patriotism seemed certainly more ornamental than inspiring in that debate following which Ireland's parliament voted to abolish itself.

IV

In Britain, then, the efforts of Hawkesworth and other commentators in the latter half of the eighteenth century had influenced much critical opinion to accept Swift's patriotism as an aspect of his literary eminence. Without very probing reference to historical or current Irish circumstances, his defence of Irish interests in the Wood affair, for instance, was capable of interpretation in the abstract terms set forth by Swift's own epitaph in St Patrick's as upholding human liberty in the face of tyranny. That impression diluted the effect of Lord Orrery's attribution of Swift's patriotism to his hostility toward Walpole's government, and as an aspect of his characteristic misanthropy. However, the problem of Swift's character lingered, and in the course of the nineteenth century was to overshadow his patriotic value, and even impinge upon his literary eminence. In Ireland, the perception of Swift as patriot was to change more markedly still from the eighteenth to the nineteenth century. Eighteenth-century British commentators on Swift's patriotism had overlooked the extent to which patriotism tended to be perceived in Ireland less as amenable to abstract definition or general application, and more as bounded by distinct circumstances. Cumulatively, but quite unevenly, these circumstances worked to inform Protestant Irish identity, but for a long time, instances of patriotic activity in one period would not be understood as applicable models for patriots in a later time. Apart from a brief period in the 1780s, in the triumph of legislative independence for which the Dean could be taken as a victorious precursor, the abstract terms of Swift's epitaph would seem to have had little relevance.

But the Union altered the context of Irish patriotism, effectively displacing its dependence upon circumstance and enabling a more sustained conceptualization in terms of identity. Inasmuch as that identity was measurable within Ireland's new British dimension, Swift was soon accorded a role in the development of Irish patriotism never recognized comprehensively in his own time or even later in the eighteenth century. Dogging the perception of that role, however, was a factor of Irish identity that the Union failed to address, the place of Irish Catholics. Some Irish Protestants had argued, even in the Dublin Parliament, for Catholic Emancipation in the years before the Rising of 1798, but the fact and intensity of that rebellion had diminished their numbers and effectiveness. Emancipation became a bugbear to most Protestants as a consequence. Thus many Protestants opposed the Union lest it compromise Ascendancy, while others supported it as a means of enhancing their own security, without endorsing Emancipation. Of course, still others in the Irish parliament were venally motivated to support the Union, by promises of money or titles; and a few liberals opposed the loss of independence that would ensue from it. It was carried at length, however, because enough members accepted that loss of independence as a means of gaining greater security for Protestant lives and property, which was fundamentally more important than the sense of Irish identity a separate parliament encouraged. And in the event, the Union strengthened that security the more because the King would not assent to Catholic Emancipation.

Irish Protestants were quick to recognize as much. Although the underhanded means the London government had employed to push the Act of Union through the Irish parliament were long remembered, opposition to the Union itself among the wide body of Protestant opinion did not long survive its defeat. With the exception of its leader, after all, Irish Protestants did not figure significantly in Robert Emmet's insurrection in 1803, nor did they in later years lament its failure. The liberals among them did not agitate significantly for repeal of the Union, but, like Grattan, who took a seat in the London parliament in 1805, confined their efforts to pressing for Catholic

Emancipation. And among those opposing Emancipation were formerly anti-Union Irish conservatives like John Foster, who acknowledged in 1805 that what Protestant Ascendancy assured, the Union secured.[68] Even so, they could retain some sense of Irish identity. Foster himself, who had resisted the Union strenuously though he soon took a seat and later office at Westminster, complained in 1802 that the Union had been carried by corrupt means,[69] and is said to have retorted 'Take back your Union!' to another member's complaint in 1811 that Ireland was becoming a burden to England.[70] Such outbursts bespoke Foster's personal animus, or more objectively nostalgia of a safe sort, rather than any threat to the reduction of Irish identity to fit the contours of the new British dimension. That narrowing of Irish identity among Protestants, whether embraced or merely accepted, actually made room for a perception to grow that Catholicism was the more genuine mark of it. But for a time, even as the denial of Emancipation enabled the Union to preserve Ascendancy, other voices were to imply the potential of an Irish identity within the British dimension that could comprehend Protestants and Catholics together, a potential to which they took Swift as contributing.

4

A Protestant 'Liberator', 1800–1840

I

Writing of Swift in 1805, the English literary historian Nathan Drake quoted with complete approval the comment of Isaac Hawkins Browne that 'The *Drapier's Letters* were the most perfect pieces of oratory ever composed since the days of Demosthenes.' Yet when he turned to considering Swift's character, Drake saw the bad qualities outweighing the good:

> He was, without doubt, a man of commanding and powerful intellect; almost unparalleled in wit and humour; intimately acquainted with the human heart . . . from principle charitable; free from hypocrisy; and a strenuous defender of the rights of an oppressed people.
>
> These great and estimable qualities were sullied and debased by pride, dogmatism and misanthropy; by a temper harsh, gloomy and discontented. Such is the malignancy of a disposition prone to vilify and degrade human nature, that no abilities, however pre-eminent, can atone for such a tendency.[1]

In so holding that Swift's faults of character 'sullied and debased' his abilities, Drake articulated a stance that within a few decades would become a commonplace among nineteenth-century British commentators on Swift, though later critics were often less willing than Drake to admire Swift's patriotic rhetoric. This trend would counter the success of John Hawkesworth, half a century earlier, in displacing Orrery's picture of Swift with a softer character, more eccentric than malevolent. Before long, Orrery's assessment had regained momentum, and Swift's supposed misanthropy, particularly as evidenced in his treatment of women, drew increasingly severe criticism during the nineteenth century as a fundamental moral flaw. Whatever his literary eminence, it was an inexcusable fault, and though often attributed, following Orrery, to Swift's career disappointment, it could be ascribed instead to more arrestingly intimate causes. Dr Thomas Beddoes in 1803, for instance, traced Swift's misanthropy, 'his behaviour towards several women' and even his eventual 'madness' to a pitiable secret vice – which Beddoes was too delicate to label masturbation – begun in his over-studious youth.[2] More-over, as in Swift's lifetime, the low moral tone of *A Tale of a Tub, Gulliver's Travels* and some of the poems was also regularly noted and often attacked by British commentators.[3]

Negative reflections of this sort were compounded, especially in the case of the poetry, by the gradual shift in taste away from satirical and socially oriented verse that took place during the second half of the eighteenth century. Thus two anonymous essays of 1790 in the *European Magazine* (of which the first originally appeared in the *Dublin Magazine* in 1763) acknowl-edged Swift's talents in satire, dwelling on the prose, but slighted his poetic gifts: in the first, 'his whole talent that way consisted in finding out rhymes that surprise by their oddness, and [he] was little more than an excellent crambo player';[4] to the second (probably later) essayist, Swift's poems 'are nothing more than prose in rhyme. Imagination, metaphor and sublimity constitute no part of their merit.'[5] With varying emphases, British critical opinion for most of the nineteenth century regularly devalued Swift's poetry, both for aesthetic reasons and because of moral reservations about his char-acter, so justifying some ambivalence about his literary greatness. The very frequency of comment, however, attests to an enduring popular regard for Swift as a prose writer. *Gulliver's Travels* in particular was frequently re-printed, and just as it had by 1800 long since entered the allusive stock of educated discourse, it became in the nineteenth century a remarkably general touchstone of freakish fantasy, and even – when suitably expurgated – a good-humoured tale.

Against this British background of continuing innocuous popularity tem-pered by the moral strictures of literary critics, Swift's patriotic reputation in Ireland during the nineteenth century developed very notably. Occasionally there are echoes of earlier English Whig complaints, or those of Richard Lewis in Ireland in 1775, about the motives of his efforts on Ireland's behalf. A sketch of Irish history often prefacing American editions of J.P. Curran's speeches, for instance, maintained that 'Dean Swift having been disap-pointed in becoming a Bishop in England resolved to become a Patriot in Ireland.'[6] But more commonly, Irish writers reflect and expand upon a view such as B.T. Duhigg's in 1806, that Swift was 'as great a genius, and as unbending a patriot, as ever graced this country'.[7] Comments in passing such as Duhigg's are not rare in eighteenth-century Ireland, though their senti-ment was voiced more typically in the middle years, when Swift's memory was still fresh, than toward the end of the period. Certainly, Swift had maintained among his countrymen a strong reputation in literature, rein-forced by the high position British critics had given him, but Irish notice of his patriotic achievement was mainly an ornament to the local pride that derived ultimately from Ireland's political distinctness as a kingdom.[8] It was an underpinning to which Swift's memory was only occasionally granted more than incidental or evanescent importance until, paradoxically, the Union eliminated that distinctness. For in the years following its enactment Irish local pride acquired a new foundation in which Swift's part was notice-able and actively asserted. These years saw the appearance of a number of accounts of Irish history signifying that local pride could be based upon an historical rather than formally political distinctness, and in this context it accorded Swift a consistently positive role.

II

Since Catholics had neither influenced nor invoked Swift's reputation very noticeably in eighteenth-century Ireland, it is especially remarkable that Catholic writers should have taken part in this early nineteenth-century chorus of praise. Underlying their participation, however, were the shifts in attitude among Catholics towards the British government in the latter years of the eighteenth century and the first decades of the nineteenth. On the one hand, ever since the Penal Laws began to be relaxed in the 1770s, Catholic leaders had found in the London government the most effective source of relief from civil disabilities. Notwithstanding the disappointment of Fitzwilliam's recall in 1795 and the refusal of further relief after the founding of Maynooth that year, the Irish Catholic hierarchy could be moved to give at least tacit support to the Union, since Emancipation was promised to follow. The King's refusal to countenance Emancipation, once the Union had been enacted, was a deep disappointment to the Catholic bishops. Even so, in the immediate aftermath of the Union, it could seem to offer improved prospects for Catholics, since it abolished the Irish polity to which alone, as a majority only in Ireland, Catholics might be perceived as a threat. This was the substance of the case for Emancipation advanced by William Pitt, the British prime minister and architect of the Union; failing to persuade the King, he had resigned his office, but his remained an apparently substantial argument for expecting that Protestant fears of, and consequent hostility towards, Catholicism might slacken. On the other hand, the delay of almost thirty years in granting Emancipation had a gradually vitalizing effect upon Irish Catholic political opinion. Despite Pitt's principled resignation, that delay – rather than, at first, the Union *per se* – seemed to reaffirm, after a period of welcome pressure from London for Catholic relief, the notion of British injustice towards Ireland, to counter which Catholics were eventually motivated to seek the undoing of the Union itself.

The English Catholic and former Jesuit Francis Plowden instanced the first of these perceptions in his *Historical Review of the State of Ireland* (1803). Writing soon after the Union, Plowden regarded it as an opportunity for the British government to discourage the official antipathy to Catholicism that had persisted for centuries, and by extension to end its characteristically repressive treatment of Ireland. In his warmth on Ireland's behalf, the country becomes essentially Plowden's metaphor for Catholicism. Thus he emphasized British historical repressiveness, and represented Swift in glowing terms for resisting it. 'Swift ever supported the natural interests of Ireland against the Dissenters and the Whig Party . . . and against the power of the British cabinet, whose system it was to keep Ireland in a state of perpetual bondage and subserviency to the mere nod of the conqueror.' Plowden also took up the concept of the patriot line that Leonard MacNally had proposed in 1782, adopting his phrasing in an extended encomium upon Molyneux and Swift as pioneers of civil liberty in the face of governmental hostility.[9] The second perception, taking a less sanguine view of the Union's potential, is apparent at an early stage of formation a few years after Plowden's work in Denis Taafe's *Impartial History of Ireland* (1809–11). A controversialist who had abandoned and then re-adopted Catholicism, and had opposed the Union, Taafe was less metaphorical than Plowden, concerned with English injustice as a continuing and literal fact in Irish, not simply Catholic, affairs. He applauded Swift's patriotism in the Wood's halfpence affair but saw the Dean's value in more comprehensive terms. Concentrating on the picture of rural Irish degradation that Swift drew in the 1727 *State of Ireland*, he cast the Dean as 'a patriotic genius . . . like lightning illuminating the gloom of a clouded night'.[10] Thus Swift becomes not only a guiding spirit for Irish unity in defence of liberty, but also a defender of the Irish poor. From their different perspectives, and writing at the beginning and end of the first decade after the Union, both Plowden and Taafe trace Ireland's ills to a British habit of injustice thwarting the interests of Protestants and Catholics alike, this despite an historical loyalty to the crown which characterized both communities and which, regardless of their conflicting attitudes towards the Union, the two historians still espoused. Their works can be understood as partaking variously in a 'wholehearted effort' among Catholic writers early in the nineteenth century 'to prove their steadfast loyalty' to the British imperium.[11] Certainly they contributed to a sense of Irish identity in which the Catholic majority could be regarded sympathetically, even benignly – an attitude they ascribe to Swift himself. To a considerable extent, Protestant historians in these same years took a similar view.

To be sure, Plowden's assertions of undeserved English mistreatment of Catholics during the penal era drew a quick rebuttal from Sir Richard Musgrove in 1804. In this context, rather than in terms of Swift as an apostle of liberty, he challenged Plowden to produce evidence for his assertion that Swift had recognized Catholics' loyalty to the House of Hanover, for Swift was a 'true patriot [who] had the interests of Ireland more at heart, and understood them better than any of his cotemporaries [*sic*]'.[12] But succeeding Protestant historians considered Swift as having greater sympathy towards the situation of Catholics in his time. The Rev. James Gordon in 1805 thus praised him as a 'zealous patriot for the Irish nation' in the Wood's coinage affair, and anticipated Taafe in finding him also 'deeply affected by the wretched poverty of his countrymen, occasioned by an absurdly cruel system of government'.[13] John Wilson Croker in 1808 was both more overtly pro-Catholic and more lyrical on the subject of Swift, whom he hailed as a prophetic figure with a patriotic 'mission', such that 'when he is emulated, his country is redeemed'.[14] Croker's eloquence caused his work to be reprinted, and often quoted, in the nineteenth century, but in his emphasis upon Swift as prophet he resembles both Taafe and the more measured Francis Hardy, a former member of the Irish House of Commons. Reviewing the history of eighteenth-century Ireland as background to his biography of Charlemont in 1810, Hardy cautioned that Wood's patent was not so grievous an imposition as Swift had represented it, and was furthermore a weightier matter in Dublin than elsewhere. Yet he hailed the *Drapier's Letters* as transcending their occasion, for they demonstrated the 'eternal lesson' to 'princes and statesmen' that a people could not effectively be deprived of their rights while they supported even one individual prepared to speak for them.[15]

A point common to Catholic and Protestant historians alike was, indeed, that Swift's opposition to Wood had united Irishmen of both persuasions. Taafe's fellow-Catholic Matthew O'Conor repeated this observation in 1813 to show that Swift 'infused into his countrymen a portion of the spirit and patriotism with which his own soul was animated'.[16] Hence it is ironic that from about this time Swift ceased to draw Catholic, or pro-Catholic, admiration. Thomas Newenham's *View of . . . Ireland* (1809), for instance, attributed the depressed state of the country to the religious divisions that Britain fostered. Both Swift – who accepted and, in the case of Dissenters, accentuated those divisions – and the economic remedies he proposed, were ignored.[17] Such silence may be understood within the context of the 'historiographical counter-attack' arising from Catholic writers' conviction, late in the first decade of the nineteenth century, that despite its earlier protestations of loyalty, the government would not move further to relieve Catholic disabilities.[18] Particularly after the veto controversy in these years, when Irish Catholics organized themselves successfully against a proposition that Emancipation be accompanied by a governmental power of veto over the Pope's appointment of Irish bishops, their spokesmen adopted a stronger line to press their claims. Where Curry and Charles O'Conor in the eighteenth century had argued for the expedience of granting concessions to Catholics, proponents of Emancipation in the early nineteenth century argued that it was due as a matter of right, owed not just abstractly, but legally by the terms of the Treaty of Limerick. For the Penal Laws, the last vestiges of which the Emancipation campaign sought to remove, could be understood as a violation of that treaty. A champion of Irish freedom who supported or simply accepted that legislation, like Swift, thus became much less attractive, and, after the bouquets of admiration thrown his way by Plowden, Taafe and

Matthew O'Conor, he was again all but ignored by Catholic writers. It was as though they sensed that, in Thomas Bartlett's neat formulation, 'in the veto controversy the Catholic nation of the early nineteenth century found its voice, just as the Wood's halfpence dispute of nearly one hundred years earlier had enabled the Protestants of Ireland to strut their pretensions to be "the whole people of Ireland"'.[19]

Nonetheless, the chorus of historiographical favour for Swift within a decade affirmed for him a place of importance in Irish history comparable to that accorded him during the eighteenth century in the canon of British literature. All issuing in the aftermath of the Union, the works of the historians suggest that once the Irish Protestant nation was dissolved as a political entity, they were free to give the Dean his due. For unlike their treatment of other features of Irish history, which often betray their Catholic or Protestant standpoints, they were agreed on a perception of Swift clearer and more unequivocal than any recognizable in Ireland during the later eighteenth century. At their hands Swift emerges as the ancestor of a spirit of Irish patriotism renewable in their own time, a very early representative of national identity that could embrace Protestants and Catholics alike, as it had during the Wood affair. The potential appeal was short-lived for Catholics, a victim of the denial of Emancipation. But its viability for Protestants derived from a sense of Ireland's historical distinctness that no Act of Union could efface and for which Swift's rhetorical defence of Irish liberties against English oppression provided a Protestant heritage. Well into the nineteenth century, Irish Protestant writers in particular would attempt to evoke this kind of patriotic spirit, using the memory of Swift's popularity to lend historical legitimacy to the contemporary potential of patriotism as a uniting force. Running counter to the trend of British criticism over a long period, while also participating in the general Romantic emphasis upon individual greatness, they often viewed his flaws of character as outweighed by his patriotism. There persists, indeed, due to the efforts of such historians as Croker, Hardy and Taafe, an heroic image of Swift as uniquely great, a giant in his time and a prophet for later ages.

III

The historians' construction of Swift's patriotism in the context of the Union was compatible, moreover, with the more widely recognized service to his reputation provided by a Scottish Romantic, Walter Scott. As Swift's first and most influential nineteenth-century editor, Scott allied himself to the heroic view of the Dean's patriotism: in the biographical 'Memoirs' introducing his edition (1814), he quoted Croker approvingly on the 'patriotic' nature of Swift's prophetic 'mission'.[20] Scott was drawn to Swift in the first place by his general admiration for the authors of the Restoration and the

earlier eighteenth century. He accepted the publisher Constable's commission for an edition of Swift in 1808, immediately following the publication of
his edition of Dryden;[21] and he projected, though never undertook, an edition
of Pope. Laid against that fascination, his personal parallels to Swift, as a Tory
and an Anglican, seem to have been merely coincidence. Though his acceptance of Croker's view of Swift as prophet may relate to the connection of
both men with the Tory *Quarterly Review*, Croker's judgement was more
obviously important to Scott as praise of Swift from one of the Dean's
countrymen, of the sort Irish writers had long owed, 'that tribute of gratitude,
which is so particularly his due'.[22] While Scott did not dispute the value of
Scotland's English connection, he was himself a stout patriot, and he admired
Swift as a counterpart. The Dean's Irish patriotism, noble in itself, had
instilled national awareness and pride in the Irish, a view that owes much to
Dr Johnson. Scott's argument that for this Swift deserved the gratitude of
Irish writers implies the Dean's ancestral place in a national literature, of
which Scott admired Maria Edgeworth as a contemporary Irish exponent
with an acknowledged influence on his own writing.[23] At the same time,
Scott included the national distinctiveness of Croker's panegyric in a more
general picture of Swift; in just the same way, British literature – for which
Scott's edition secured Swift's canonical place for the nineteenth century –
should properly accommodate the national literature of Ireland and Scotland. Such perspectives as Croker's were obviously of great importance to
Scott, marking British literature as pluralist rather than imperially English,
their value represented by those, like Swift and like the heroes of some of
Scott's novels, who had resisted the centripetal or imperial perspective in the
eighteenth century. Indeed, Scott's edition with the prefatory 'Memoirs'
appeared in the same year as *Waverley*, the first of the novels, in which he
was 'attempting to ensure and articulate Scotland's distinctive place in
Britain . . . conscious of the need both to construct and to reconstruct images
of cultural identity that are other than Anglo-centric'.[24]

While it required British allegiance, then, a truly United Kingdom seemed
also to offer a potential for a pluralism in Scott's time that would encourage
and integrate a strongly articulated national patriotism. J.W. Croker himself
represented an Irish version of this idea, for though a convinced Tory with a
career in London as Secretary to the Admiralty, he retained his fervent Irish
sympathies and favoured Catholic Emancipation. Nor was such patriotism
merely sentimental, whether in Scott or Croker or a more prominent Irish
writer, Lady Morgan, also living in England. Ireland is certainly sentimen-
talized in her works, but Morgan tempered this somewhat by an astringent
personal attitude towards the country that anticipates modern complaints of
grudgingness as a national characteristic. Maintaining her Irish identity
while justifying her career in England as motivated by more than considerations of the literary marketplace, she noted in 1829 that 'In Ireland, there is
as little affection for merit, as there is market; nor could it possibly be

otherwise, in a country so governed as Ireland has been. It is not so much the fault, as the misfortune of the people. . . .' Hence, 'to those who have established claims on the public, or have been fortunate enough to captivate its good will, absenteeism from Ireland is almost a duty to self'. A cautionary illustration makes her point: 'Swift himself, the patriot *par excellence* among Irish literary characters, was a resident in his own land from necessity; and the sense of that necessity pressed for ever on his mind, embittering his latter days, and discolouring all his views, if it were not among the immediate causes of his deplorable insanity.'[25] Morgan's view that Irishness is easier to articulate outside Ireland (which has become orthodox as a justification for Irish literary expatriates) sheds light on the sentimentalism of her novels, implying that modern British pluralism allowed her the opportunity to retain both her Irishness and her sanity. Thus Swift is at once an ancestor for patriotic identity and a victim of its restriction to residence in Ireland.

In a general sense, indeed, the decided cultural inclination of the nineteenth century to sentimentalism fitted the pluralism that Scott's edition of Swift as well as his own novels had encouraged. This taste for the sentimental was in its earlier stages not so conducive to an enthusiasm for Irishness: half a century before, when Oliver Goldsmith was fostering that taste, it was not regarded as a positive feature of his celebrity that he was Irish. But the sentimental trend made the potential for pluralism offered by the Union easier to exploit, for whatever political affront the Union had represented to the Irish, its passage gave those so inclined a larger stage on which to perform in national dress. And it was an attractive costume: George Canning, another Tory advocate of Emancipation, who would eventually become prime minister, boasted to Scott in 1825 that 'Though I was accidentally born in London, I consider myself an Irishman.'[26] The cultural enthusiasm for Irishness fostered by the popularity of the Catholic Thomas Moore extended further, to a degree of sympathy for sentimental patriotic separatism. In such a context, the Irishness of Swift's own anti-English rhetoric was no great obstacle to Scott's installation of him in a British pantheon.

By offering scope for genuine national patriotism, however sentimentally expressed, Scott's view of pluralism represented a modern advance upon the less enlightened eighteenth century. Conversely, the Romantic exaltation of the individual was related to the previous century's attraction to the oddities of 'character', which also made Swift appealing to Scott. Indeed, while anecdotes illustrating the jocular and eccentric aspects of Swift, thus stressing him as a 'character', were popular in the eighteenth century, a great many of them were collected for publication in *Swiftiana* (1804), a compilation that abetted their continuing popularity in the nineteenth century.[27] Having drawn upon a great variety of sources for his 'Memoirs' of Swift, Scott has been criticized for not discriminating sufficiently among them; for so mixing facts, anecdotes and impressions as to leave the reader with an inaccurate and inconsistent view of Swift. 'Thus the *Memoirs* must in large part be held responsible for the development of a nineteenth-century picture of the Dean as a living paradox.'[28] But the Swift thus presented is an eccentric 'character' of the sort that had strong popular appeal in the eighteenth century; furthermore, Swift seemed such a paradox to Scott himself, in that 'a vein of morbid humour ran through Swift's whole existence, both mental and physical, from the beginning'.[29] Of course, Scott may also have been drawn to emphasize Swift's qualities as an eighteenth-century character because he was writing *Waverley* while finishing the 'Memoirs'. It is nonetheless true that much of the material that nineteenth-century critics found to use against Swift had been included in the 'Memoirs'. For while sentimentalism was allied to the popular concept of pluralism that Scott espoused for British literature, it also had a profoundly negative impact on Swift's reputation in Britain in the long term, since the proprieties it exalted were greatly offended by Swift's literary scatology, his seeming misanthropy and especially by the behaviour toward Stella and Vanessa that Scott described.

More immediately, Scott's inclusiveness supplied abundant ammunition for the sharpest contemporary critic of Swift, Francis Jeffrey, who reviewed Scott's edition of the *Works* for the *Edinburgh Review* in 1816.[30] Scott's placement of Swift within a sophisticated, pluralist conception of British literature paralleled the eighteenth-century British critical canonization of the Dean as a classic of literature and patriotism both; and on both counts Jeffrey had reservations. First, he dismissed the canonical triumvirate of Pope, Swift and Addison, regarding it as anachronistic. Although they had set the standard for literature in English long since, when he was a student in the 1790s, that situation 'is now pretty well altered. . . . It is no longer to them that the ambitious look up with envy, or the humble with admiration; nor is it in their pages that the pretenders to wit and eloquence now search for allusions that are sure to captivate, and illustrations that cannot be mistaken.'[31] Then proceeding to Swift, Jeffrey allowed that his merits were 'more *unique* and inimitable than those of any of his contemporaries'[32] and praised Scott's editorial labours, but inveighed at length against Swift's political transformation from Whig to Tory. A Whig himself, Jeffrey echoed the complaints of Whigs a century before against Swift as an opportunist whose ambitions, when forever thwarted by the ultimate triumph of the Whigs, turned to insulting and embarrassing their government when occasion offered.

To this old charge against the authenticity of Swift's Irish patriotism, Jeffrey offered a new and devastating proof:

> A single fact is decisive upon this point. While his friends were in power, we hear nothing of the grievances of Ireland; and to the last we hear nothing of its radical grievance, the oppression of its Catholic population. His object was, not to do good to Ireland, but to vex and annoy the English ministry. To do this, however, with effect, it was necessary that he should speak to the interests

and the feelings of some party who possessed a certain degree of power and influence. This unfortunately was not the case in that day with the Catholics; and though this gave them only a stronger title to the services of a truly brave or generous advocate, it was sufficient to silence Swift.[33]

Jeffrey was not voicing here a complaint already made by Catholics themselves, though at length they would take it up. Nor did he expatiate upon it; this flaw is, rather, just one of a number suggesting that Swift's politics and private character were of a piece. The selfishness and inconsistency of his treatment of Vanessa apparent in Scott's account, to take another example, show the same man who could turn against the Whigs, his erstwhile friends. Jeffrey admired the author of the 'Tale of a Tub, Gulliver, the Polite Conversation and almost half a volume of poetry', for 'they are very extraordinary performances: and considered with a view to the purposes for which they were intended, have probably never been equalled in any period of the world'.[34] But by attacking Swift's character and refusing to accept his patriotic and political integrity, Jeffrey certainly impeded Scott's comprehensive establishment of the Dean in a pluralistically modern British canon, and recurrently provided a rationale for Catholic writers in the nineteenth century to dismiss attempts to forge an Irish identity for Swift.

Jeffrey's composed acerbity makes his review the most negative judgement on Swift's character, personal and political, since Richard Lewis's diatribe of 1775. Scott's publisher, Constable, who had asked that Jeffrey review the edition, heartily regretted doing so, fearing for a time that the review had dampened Swift's popularity.[35] A history of Ireland published the year after the review seems, indeed, to show Jeffrey's influence. In general, the Rev. Samuel Burdy's History of Ireland (1817) was strongly, even slavishly, indebted to the Rev. James Gordon's History of Ireland (1805); but whereas Gordon had celebrated Swift's patriotism unhesitatingly in discussing the Wood's halfpence project, Burdy maintained that it 'was represented as an odious job by Swift, the virulent enemy of the present government, who exposed it with all the acrimony of wit'.[36] Burdy followed Jeffrey in treating Wood's coinage as innocuous, and attributed Swift's arousal of public opinion against it not to the strength of his arguments, but to 'supereminent wit and humour'.[37] Burdy implied what Jeffrey had laid out expansively: Swift was no true patriot but a cynical manipulator.

Further afield, however, a commentator in the North American Review considered that Jeffrey did Swift 'great injustice, considering him as a man, a tory, or an author'.[38] And within two more years Edward Berwick's Defence of Dr. Jonathan Swift rebutted Jeffrey categorically. Contrasting the latter's criticisms of Swift the man with the praises of his contemporaries, the Defence was most trenchant in pointing to Jeffrey's ignorance of Ireland's early eighteenth-century history. For 'the character of Swift is more a subject of History than of Criticism . . . if the History of Ireland is omitted, little can be known of Swift'. But Jeffrey, 'professing to give an idea of Swift, passed over the history of Ireland, and confined his remarks to his literary compositions, and his intercourse with two or three young ladies'.[39] Berwick continued by elaborating upon J.W. Croker's vision of Swift as prophet:

> Swift's character rose in Ireland with his defence of it in 1724; for by his conduct at that time he acquired an esteem and influence which can never be forgotten . . . the Patriot rose above the Divine. He taught his country to protest against her grievances, and gave her spirit by which she redressed them. . . . You will say, he had the Irish People. There was no People; he was to create a People, by whom he was defended.[40]

Nor did Berwick overlook Jeffrey's contention that Swift should have defended Ireland's Catholics. Quoting a bigoted MP's reference to 'Papists' as typical of the era which saw the Irish parliament enact the Penal Laws, he asked rhetorically, 'what would they have said to Swift, had he proposed to them the emancipation of those Papists? And Swift's not having alluded to the oppression of its Catholic population, is set down amongst the crimes with which he is charged.'[41] Jeffrey's view of Swift was also challenged by reviewers of Berwick's *Defence* in the *Gentleman's Magazine*[42] and the *Edinburgh Monthly Review*; the latter was especially critical, finding Berwick too 'feeble' in condemning Jeffrey's exaggerations, suppressions of fact and his generally non-biographical manner.[43]

As these ripostes to Jeffrey would indicate, he had not diminished Swift's popularity so seriously as Constable had at first feared, and the publisher brought out a second edition of Scott's *Swift* in 1824. But no rebuttal of Jeffrey's criticism achieved the currency of his original *Edinburgh Review* article. He had certainly succeeded, for a large body of the British public, in painting Swift anew as a bigoted Tory partisan, in line with Whig resentment toward him in the Dean's own day. What was discovered in Swift's partisanship now, however, was anti-Catholicism rather than the covert Jacobitism the earlier Whigs had perceived, for in addition to Swift's historical conservatism, anti-Catholicism would place him neatly among modern Tories. In the years after Waterloo, British politics was increasingly heated by the issue of Catholic Emancipation, which Tories typically opposed, while support for it was most pronounced among the Whigs who had long been out of power. By the same token, to complain specifically of Swift's indifference to Catholic disabilities in his own time pointed to Jeffrey's own Whig partisanship. This in turn struck William Hazlitt, though hardly sympathetic to conservatism himself, as anachronistically excessive: 'I do not carry my political resentments so far back: I can at this time of day forgive Swift for having been a Tory.'[44]

It was not too much for Thomas Moore, however, who in 1824 broke the general Catholic silence towards Swift prevailing in the decades after the celebratory notices of Plowden, Taafe and O'Conor. Reviewing Ireland's history from the standpoint of the 1820s, Moore insisted through his narrator, the agrarian agitator Captain Rock, that a century earlier 'Swift's own patriotism was little more than a graft of English faction upon an Irish stock – fructifying, it is true, into such splendid produce, as makes us proud to think it indigenous to the soil.' The Jeffrey-like echo of eighteenth-century Whig bitterness is tempered only by a wry acceptance that Swift, however hypocritical his motives, had spurred a tradition of genuine patriotism, 'splendid produce'. But Rock quickly returned to the defects Catholics could not ignore in Swift the man: 'for the misery and degradation of his Roman Catholic countrymen (who constituted, even then, four-fifths of the population of Ireland), he seems to have cared very little more than his own Gulliver would for the sufferings of so many disfranchised Yahoos.'[45] Still, whatever Swift's unworthiness, the effectuality of his patriotism had to be acknowledged; the wonder was that such a man could unite the whole people, and even raise 'that once animating, but now extinguished, question of the independence of Ireland' over the 'affair of Wood's half-pence, upon which so much of Swift's wit was lavished – "*aere* ciere viros"'. Yet this

> though magnified at the time into more than its due importance, is interesting, even now, as having been the first national cause, round which the people of Ireland had ever been induced to rally. What neither Christian charity nor the dictates of sound policy could effect, an influx of brass halfpence brought about at once.[46]

What Moore found 'interesting' here Berwick had embraced a few years earlier as Swift's creation of an Irish 'People', and the contrast involves more than a shift in emphasis. Moore's acceptance of Swift as patriot with such reluctance is informed by a sense of political morality as a continuum: the Dean had neglected Catholic concerns, typifying his Protestant contemporaries' disregard of 'Christian charity' or 'sound policy', and Protestants still disregarded them by thwarting Emancipation. Though implying his own approval of Emancipation, Berwick had dismissed Jeffrey's use of the issue of Catholic grievances against Swift as a historical absurdity, for any overt Catholic sympathy would have negated Swift's effectiveness in other respects. In so signalling a moral continuum himself, in other words, Jeffrey had been as anachronistic as he had seemed, for his Whig partisanship, to Hazlitt. That history should be true to the past as past, underlies a view that the United Kingdom offered the potential for national development (which would include Emancipation in due course), and for the expression of national patriotism. Implicit in Berwick's celebration of Swift as patriotic 'creator', this view is discernible as well among the early nineteenth-century historians, some of them Catholics.

But the delay of Emancipation had sharpened the Catholic counter-view of Irish Protestants, including Swift, that Moore's 'Captain Rock' persona articulated: they had been before, and remained now, inadequately patriotic.

Increasingly attuned to the cause of Emancipation as a matter of right and a badge of national identity, Irish Catholics were becoming less amenable to considering Protestants as truly Irish. Many Irish Protestants conceded the argument for Emancipation as a matter of right, even natural right, but a right to be guaranteed in principle via British citizenship. On the one hand, the rhetoric of Daniel O'Connell in the Emancipation campaign of the 1820s seemed to accord with this, in his protestations of non-sectarianism and loyalty to the crown. On the other, particularly when addressing Irish Catholic audiences, O'Connell also spoke explicitly or in code in terms of longstanding Catholic grievances – such as the position of the established Church and the dispossession of the ancient landowners – that Emancipation (and later, Repeal) would redress. Such an appeal 'could not have seemed other than sectarian to friend and foe alike'.[47] Emancipation was not only a natural right but a national one, justified by the fact that Catholics were the majority in Ireland, quite regardless of the British dimension; and from the concession of it would issue other amendments in favour of the majority, even contradicting the nature of the British dimension. The acceptance of Protestants as Irishmen, though given lip-service, actually diminished among Catholic leaders, even as pro-Emancipation Protestants found congenial the British pluralism of the Union concept as it worked itself out in practice.

Given these circumstances, Swift was an inconvenient patriot for Irish Catholics, one Moore could acknowledge only reluctantly. The same would hold for Swift's appeal as one of a line of patriots, formulated haltingly in the 1780s and taken up briefly in the first decade of the nineteenth century by Protestant and Catholic historians alike – a line seen as an element in the perception of an inclusive Irish identity within the Union. The Catholic drift away from that perception lends a special and ironic poignancy to the most famous construction of the patriot line, in Henry Grattan's April 1782 address hailing legislative independence: 'Spirit of Swift – spirit of Molyneux – Your genius has prevailed – Ireland is now a nation!'[48] As noted earlier, it is now clear that this invocation, rather than forming part of Grattan's speech in 1782, was actually introduced in an edition of his speeches published posthumously in 1821. It had not appeared in earlier separate printings or accounts of that address, nor in the version of it included with the preceding collection of his speeches in 1811. Added to the 1782 speech between 1811 and Grattan's death in 1821, the invocation links Swift and Molyneux with Grattan himself. It is as though he wished to emphasize Ireland's brief semi-independent nationhood as his greatest achievement as a parliamentarian, assuaging somewhat his sense of failure at not accomplishing his major goal of later years, Catholic Emancipation.[49] Grattan's inclusion of Swift indicates clearly the Dean's importance to him as a founding and guiding spirit of the Irish nation. The belatedness of the inclusion, however, suggests that he was willing publicly to recognize that value in Swift not in 1782, nor even in

1811, but only after such a recognition, pressed by the early nineteenth-century historians and affirmed by Scott, had been rather generally absorbed. That absorption bespeaks in turn the willingness of the liberal Protestants Grattan represented to accept for themselves an Irish identity of the sort those historians had promoted by elevating Swift. Based upon Ireland's historical distinctness, such Irish identity would inevitably include Protestants and Catholics both, potentially united as Swift had united them. But if Grattan's disappointment in advancing Catholic claims does in fact account for this revision of the 1782 speech at the end of his career, the broader context of the denial of Emancipation renders the insertion ironic indeed. For not only does the patriot line he invokes and links to himself exclude Catholics, but, as we have seen, by the 1820s the more assertive Catholic leaders were shifting away from considering Protestants as equally Irish.

Swift himself was exempted somewhat from this shift. A parliamentary report in 1825, for instance, found that the *Drapier's Letters* formed part of the curriculum in hedge schools.[50] And in the 1830s the Gaelic poet 'Dick Barret' (Risteard Bairead) was remembered, from at least two decades earlier, as admiring Swift's verse, speaking of him 'with rapture'.[51] On the level of folk consciousness, furthermore, Swift as a character was actually being absorbed by Gaelic Ireland. A great many stories about Swift in Irish, preserved in the Department of Irish Folklore at University College, Dublin, were collected for its predecessor, the Irish Folklore Commission, in the 1930s and 1940s. Dating from as early as a century before, they are sometimes elaborations of anecdotes published in English in the seventeenth or eighteenth centuries, not all of them by any means originally connected with Swift; very often, indeed, they employ motifs quite conventional in folklore. One category features Swift's adventures with a servant, and in these 'Jack and the Dane' stories Swift and the servant trick or outwit each other, sometimes by turns.[52] A story long linked specifically with Swift, for instance, has him reprimand the servant for not polishing his boots, 'upon which the man observed, that if they were clean they would be dirtied again'. Swift's response was to deny the man any breakfast, for 'if the man eat his breakfast he would be hungry again'.[53] In another instance, the 'Dane' is even presented as a deathbed convert to Catholicism.[54] The acculturation of Swift in the stories, however, does not extend to other Protestants, who remain strangers or usurpers. Swift is embraced as an exception because of his wit and eccentricities, the qualities that made for the popularity of anecdotes about him in the eighteenth century. Nor is his patriotism at all defined, but reduced to a vague fellow-feeling with the Gael. That vagueness, of course, is integral to the humour of the stories, as Swift's witty triumphs or concessions dispel the superficial awkwardness of his fitting into a Gaelic context, accommodating him in that most traditional and unambiguous kind of Irish identity. Among the least anglicized elements of the Irish population, at least in jocular folk tales, Swift could seem heroic without specific reference to his patriotism.

IV

Still, among the anglicized Irish in the 1820s and 1830s, Swift was admired more overtly by Protestants than Catholics, and for a contribution to Irish identity drawing less upon his wit than his patriotism. Both features could, of course, be counted equally in Swift's claim upon Irish memory. The Rev. Richard Ryan, for instance, introduced the Dean in his Irish biographical dictionary in 1821 as 'A celebrated wit, and distinguished political writer', and commented further that 'His patriotism was as manifest as his wit, so peculiarly captivating to the natives of Ireland'; Ryan concluded that 'few humorous tales are more frequently repeated than those of Dean Swift'.[55] This projection of Swift's heritage as bringing Catholic Gaels and Anglo-Irish Protestants together recalls the more politically based sense of his uniting the Irish people that the historians had promoted over a decade earlier. But Ryan was unusual. More often, the jocular 'Dane' was left to contemporary Gaelic 'natives' to admire, while the Anglo-Irish preferred to remember the author and patriot, even, as though following Berwick's line, ignoring the specifically Catholic element in the people Swift had united. Thus William Monck Mason in 1820 expressed annoyance at the Swiftian anecdotes that Scott had included in his 'Memoirs' as demeaning Swift's greatness,[56] and then over-looked Catholic Ireland altogether in his own vindication of Swift as an apostle of Irish independence. Assuming a decidedly local stance for his history of St Patrick's Cathedral, Mason both drew upon and criticized Scott's biography, considering Scott's attitude towards Wood's project, for instance, as insufficiently harsh. For what was significant, in retrospect, was not the objective nature of that project (which Scott had accepted as meeting Ireland's genuine needs), but the arrogance of the government's persistence in promoting it in the face of both official and popular Irish hostility. Scott's ability to see both sides of this issue Mason took as tempo-rizing, tending to trivialize 'the character of a zealous and true patriot' that Swift had acquired by so articulating the nation's will. For Mason, Scott also thus compromised the significance of the fact that Swift extended his defence of Ireland to argue for her independence only after it became clear that the government was behaving towards Ireland as it never would towards England. Victorious in 'this first grand struggle for the independence of Ireland', Swift was, to Mason, regarded with complete justice as 'the liberator of Ireland'.[57]

Swift's obliviousness to Catholic disabilities continued generally in these years to be ignored in his presentation by others as Ireland's defender,[58] but by the end of the decade complaints such as Jeffrey's and Moore's were having some effect as well. The liberal historian W.C. Taylor, while noting in 1831 that Swift had united 'for a brief space, both Catholics and Protestants in fierce opposition to the government', also strongly qualified the notion of the Dean's role in so serving the inclusive notion of identity that had been implied by Grattan and the historians earlier in the century. Taylor in fact echoed Moore:

> Swift was actuated on this occasion purely by factious motives. He was one of the numerous class whom disappointed ambition has converted into patriots, but unquestionably he effected great good, not by upsetting Wood's patent, which was really beneficial to the country, but by giving the Irish an example of turning from party politics to a national object. This is the only claim his shade had to be invoked with that of Molyneux, when Grattan, in 1782, for the first time addressed his countrymen as a 'free people'.[59]

In England during these years, moreover, reservations such as those of Jeffrey and Swift's earlier detractors were being renewed in allusions to his eccentricity, brutal treatment of women and misanthropy, suggesting even that they foreshadowed his supposed madness. William Goodhugh in 1827, reviewing briefly a number of authors appropriate for a gentleman's library, gives an anecdotal pastiche emphasizing the strange cruelty of Swift's wit.[60] And while the entry for Swift in the popular *Oxford Encyclopedia* in 1828 was generally favourable to his works and character, it excepted his behaviour to Stella, whose life 'he shortened by his caprice'.[61] Lady Morgan, as mentioned above, could in a single passage acknowledge Swift's patriotism and suggest that his enforced residence in Ireland helped to drive him mad. In the same year, Anna Jameson elaborated ruthlessly upon Jeffrey's accusations of Swift's inhumanity toward the women most intimate with him: in rejecting Vanessa, for instance, 'he had in effect murdered the woman who loved him, as absolutely as if he had plunged a poniard into her heart'.[62] The gathering force of pointed considerations such as these would contend effectively in the English public mind during the 1830s with the older and less fashionable, milder judgement of Scott. The Rev. John Mitford's introduction to his 1833 edition of Swift's poems, though recalling Scott's literary scholarship and asserting again the Dean's Olympian status as writer and patriot, also took a less forgiving attitude than Scott toward his relations with Stella and Vanessa.[63] The tide of English hostility toward Swift's character could even encompass the descriptions of Irish social conditions which had led some historians at the outset of the century to see him as prophetic. On the one hand, their view was shared by J.E. Bicheno, an English economist deeply moved by the state of the Irish poor, who noted in 1830 that the bulk of the population were no better off than in Swift's day. For this, Bicheno placed most of the blame on rackrenting, of which 'scarcely a page of Swift can be opened on Irish affairs, but he inveighs against it',[64] a comment echoed by E.H. Orpen in 1835.[65] To the English radical William Cobbett in 1834, however, Swift was 'the worst of all possible authorities' on Ireland. Advancing the notion that in fact Swift hated the place and its people, Cobbett explained that 'all the world knows, that he was an eccentric sort of misanthrope; and that, into the bargain, he was a disappointed politician of great ambition'.[66] Cobbett's hostility in particular illustrates the growing shift against Swift in popular opinion, for what 'all the world knows' was more worthy of note in 1834 than it had been in 1820, when he recalled in public that his discovery of *A Tale of a Tub* in boyhood delighted him and 'produced what I have always considered a sort of birth of intellect'.[67]

V

If Thomas Moore's view was representative, most Irish Catholics would have inclined towards Cobbett's sharp dismissal of Swift as a patriot in 1834. In the years leading up to Catholic Emancipation in 1829, and for over a decade thereafter, the political rhetoric of their leaders displayed no desire to adopt the eighteenth-century Protestant Dean as a patriotic hero, much less embrace his Irish identity. In the first instance, they had a living, Catholic hero in Daniel O'Connell, 'The Liberator'. Secondly, there had been culti-vated among them, not least by O'Connell, a majoritarian sense of Irish history, a record of such comprehensive, unrelenting oppression that it all but effaced Irish Protestant complaints or agitation in the past at English misgov-ernment or arrogance. A sense, rather, that specifically Catholic suffering at English hands was the badge of authentic Irish identity and patriotism was implicit in O'Connell's rhetoric, as noted above. It was also stirred, overtly, by his use of the diocesan and parochial organization of the Catholic Church as the engine of the Emancipation campaign. The patriotic defensiveness generated by grievance had a further, triumphalist edge, for Emancipation had not been conceded as a result of liberal Protestant pressure, whether British or Irish, but won by the Catholic mobilization behind O'Connell. The strongly sectarian colour that circumstance lent this patriotic victory worked to compromise, perhaps even to vitiate, the value of Irish patriotism, or public spirit, as informing an identity transcending confessional lines. For this, Swift's success in uniting opposition to Wood's scheme provided the outstanding precedent and model, but O'Connell's efforts had left that model, promoted by historians of the early nineteenth century, relevant nearly exclusively to Irish Protestants.

It is all the more remarkable, therefore, that the stoutest defence of Swift's patriotism since Berwick's was mounted in 1834 by an Irish Catholic. The Tory *Fraser's Magazine*, edited by the Cork Protestant William Maginn, began in that year to publish contributions by 'Father Prout'. The pseudonym (taken from a deceased parish priest of Watergrasshill, County Cork) was that of Francis Sylvester Mahony, himself a Catholic priest from Cork, who had that year abandoned the priesthood and settled in London as a journalist. Mahony's 'Prout' pieces in *Fraser's* were humorous, verging occasionally on the absurd; his essay on Swift, which was one of the first, concluded with an account of Father Prout as Swift's son by Stella, kidnapped by William Wood and abandoned in Cork.[68] Yet the body of the article was a literal and forceful endorsement of Swift as a patriot for all Ireland, lamenting the political turmoil for which O'Connell, her current patriot-hero, was obliquely held responsible, while alluding not at all to the religious divisions at their root. Mahony in fact brought together Swift's literary canonization, his patriotic endeavours and his reputed madness to present the Dean as a disinterested lover of his country, implicitly contrasted with O'Connell's contemporary behaviour.[69] Presented as an essay of Prout's written in March 1830 (the year after Catholic Emancipation was enacted), the article noted that nearly a century after the death of Swift, 'whom Britain justly reveres as the most upright, intuitive and gifted of her sages', his eminence in Ireland was still obscured. Only 'when the frenzied hour of strife shall have passed away, and the turbulence of parties shall have subsided into a natural calm' would the Dean be properly recognized as 'the first, the best, the mightiest' of Irishmen:

> The long arrears of gratitude to the only true disinterested champion of her people will then be paid – the long-deferred apotheosis of the patriot-divine will then take place – the shamefully-forgotten debt of glory which the lustre of his genius shed around his semi-barbarous countrymen will be deeply and feelingly remembered; the old landmark of genuine worth will be discovered in the ebbing of modern agitation, and due honour will be rendered by a more enlightened age to the keen and scrutinizing philosopher, the scanner of whate'er lies hidden in the folds of the human heart, the prophetic seer of coming things. . . .[70]

Putatively dating from 1830 but published in 1834 when O'Connell was manoeuvring a noisily fractious occasional alliance of his parliamentary followers with the Whig government,[71] this depiction of Irish political rancour suggested that the agitation of the country was continuing even after Emancipation was achieved. Writing as a Catholic priest, Prout could hardly be accused of sectarian bias; he noted, furthermore, that Swift might be compared with 'Doyle of Carlow' – James Doyle, the Catholic, putatively pro-Unionist, bishop of Kildare and Leighlin – for not only did both have the interests of the Irish poor at heart, but 'Swift demolished, in his day, Woods [sic] and his bad halfpence; Doyle denounced Daniel and his box of coppers', a reference to the 'Catholic rent', O'Connell's weekly national collection to support the Emancipation campaign. To the voices of Doyle and Swift, however, 'our island's best and most enlightened patriots', the British government was deaf,[72] implying that O'Connell had duped it into accepting Emancipation. However genuine Mahony's own sentiments, such opposition to O'Connell fitted well with the Tory appeal of *Fraser's*.

As the title of the article indicates, it was concerned primarily with Swift's madness. More explicitly than Cobbett, Mahony compounded this aspect of Swift's reputation with his patriotism, but to opposite effect. No usual cause could be adduced for the Dean's insanity, no extraordinary passion, except 'pure and disinterested love of country; and were he ever liable to be hurried into insane excess by an overpowering enthusiasm, it was the patriot's madness that had the best chance of prostrating his mighty soul'.[73] Hence the view of Swift as Ireland's champion conventionalized by Protestant patriots such as Croker, Berwick and Mason was developed to a logical extreme that implicitly contrasted Swift's patriotism to O'Connell's: where the one, from love of his country, went mad himself, the other, out of ambition, pushed his country to madness. But Mahony also moved beyond the conventional emphasis upon the *Universal Use of Irish Manufactures* and the *Drapier's Letters* as the literary instances of Swift's patriotism to include *The Story of the Injured Lady, Maxims Controlled in Ireland*, the 1727 *Short View of the State of Ireland* and the *Modest Proposal*. Such works were inspired by the 'intensity and fervour of the dean's love of his oppressed country'; echoing Bicheno in 1830, Mahony saw the *Short View* as exhibiting the Irish peasantry in a condition they retained over a century later.[74] Thus Mahony expanded the focus of Swift's patriotism beyond the issue of Anglo-Irish relations in his day (in which the Dean's resentment at English arrogance and short-sightedness could still vibrate in the Irish Protestant consciousness) to sympathy and rhetorical exertion for the Irish poor. So reflecting Mahony's own Catholic sensibility, this was an appeal at once to Tory paternalism and to those Catholics not seduced by O'Connell. The article, indeed, attempted to affirm Swift's Irish identity by elevating his place in the history of Irish patriotism and marginalizing O'Connell's.

This approach, especially given Mahony's whimsically erudite style, could hardly have been expected to galvanize many Irish Catholics in Swift's favour. It would have made more sense to Irish Protestants, but even so had no effect upon the mounting hostility among British commentators towards the Dean. Writing two decades after Jeffrey, the historian Lord Mahon reinvigorated the old complaints of Swift's political tergiversation and cruelty to women, especially Stella, judging the Dean fundamentally immoral: 'he had a thorough knowledge of all the baser parts of human nature – for they were his own.'[75] Though for Mahon 'my contempt for the man is at once lost in my admiration of the author', whose 'works have been deservedly classed by posterity as permanent productions',[76] Swift's Irish patriotism presented an ambiguous case. Wood's halfpence project, essentially innocent and indeed beneficial, was taken erroneously but genuinely in Ireland as a calamity, giving Swift 'the opportunity to exert and display his powers'.[77] Indeed, the 'warm-hearted and generous Irish', though misled in considering Swift their deliverer from a great public danger, gave him deep and loyal gratitude, despite his 'contempt and aversion to those who thus revered him', and his memory was still venerated among them.[78] He was, in short, a sham patriot but one perceived as effective, a verdict similar to Thomas Moore's, if reached from a completely different perspective. Also in 1836, T.P. Courtenay's biography of Sir William Temple alluded to Swift's lack of polish when he first joined Temple's household, his arrogance and 'unbecoming behaviour';[79] reviewing Courtenay's book, T.B. Macaulay thus cast Swift as an 'eccentric, uncouth, disagreeable young Irishman' in his years with Temple, to point the greater contrast with the literary giant he would become.[80] And in 1837 the biographical compiler George Cunningham could think it 'worse than ridiculous' to regard Swift as an Irish patriot, for exactly the reasons Jeffrey had outlined; rather, here as in other matters, 'abuse is his inspiration, and, when the occasion serves, he pours it forth with all the fertility and exuberance of true genius'.[81] Thomas Carlyle was moved to an uncharacteristically muted defensiveness:

> In his conduct, there is much that is sad and tragic, highly blameable; but I cannot credit all that is said of his cruel unfeeling disposition. There are many circumstances to show that by nature he was one of the truest of men, of great pity for his fellow-men. . . .[82]

Mahony's praise of Swift in *Fraser's* appears the more singular, even aggressive, in such a hostile climate, which was felt in Ireland as well. The publication of two letters of Swift's in 1838, apparently by William Sheridan Le Fanu, a descendant of the Dean's clergyman friend Thomas Sheridan, thus unsurprisingly included a reflection on his misanthropy. Indeed, Swift's satirical bitterness was 'the prevailing and always morbid habit of his mind', producing 'those feelings of bitter isolation, those mysterious repinings, which are the allotted punishment of him who has looked too far into the secret things of nature'.[83] Yet Le Fanu's comments lack the underlying distaste for Swift increasingly frequent among British historians and critics, and even at the end of the decade there persisted in Ireland a recognition of Swift's value in patriotic history. This was the case particularly among Protestants, since the long denial of Emancipation and O'Connell's politicization of the Catholic Church to gain it had diminished for most Catholics the appeal of an Irish identity that transcended religious barriers. As a Catholic himself, Mahony had recognized and struggled overtly against this narrowing of the patriotic ideal that Swift represented, but Irish Protestants could be slow to perceive its effect. At the close of the decade, W.C. Taylor implies a regretful awareness of it, in perceptibly softening his attitude toward the Dean. In 1831, soon after Emancipation, he had criticized Swift's impure motives while accepting his ultimate efficacy as a patriot; in 1839, providing a biographical introduction to *Gulliver's Travels*, he gave more emphasis to the inclusiveness of Irish support for Swift in the Wood affair.[84] Revising his introduction for an illustrated edition of *Gulliver's Travels* the next year, he combined these features of his earlier comments and added greater enthusiasm than he could earlier muster for the Dean as an ancestor of the movement for independence that culminated in 1782:

> Swift's memory is still revered in Ireland, and especially in Dublin; men of every party confess that he gave the first impulse to the exertions made for constitutional freedom and the consequent development of a manufacturing

industry. His exertions themselves were not, perhaps, of great moment, but they were all important as examples.[85]

What Taylor had 'men of every party confess' was manifestly less noticeable among Catholics; it was important to him as a Protestant liberal, since a widespread contemporary acceptance of Swift's historical significance would reinforce Taylor's own inclusion in Irish identity.[86] Notably here, such a general acceptance would extend to Swift's inspiring effect on the work of later patriots, implicitly including Grattan. (Yet in 1831, Taylor had responded captiously to Grattan's acknowledgement of this function in Swift.)

Taylor's comment, however, only hints at his awareness of a conflict over the inclusiveness of Irish identity in the 1830s. A more assertive note was struck, also in 1840, in a journal that had noticed and sharpened that conflict in the decade. The *Dublin University Magazine* was staunchly Irish and Protestant both, and therefore fundamentally opposed to the O'Connellite concept of 'Irish nationality as congruent with Irish Catholicism'.[87] Drawing out an element implicit in the thought of early nineteenth-century historians, and affirmed by the notion of developing pluralism that Scott had encouraged as potential in British literature, the *D.U.M.* espoused and invigorated a fervently Irish cultural identity within the British connection. This kind of 'nationality' could be ferociously opposed to politicized Catholicism as ultimately anti-national, owing to its Roman allegiance; and also opposed to the myopic mismanagement of the English government, which among other instances of short-sightedness tended to accept the synonymity of Irish nationality and Catholicism. Swift's advocacy of Protestantism and opposition to the English government were quite different in origin from the stance of the *D.U.M.*, but they could nonetheless be fitted into its programme as emanations of a patriotic spirit that O'Connell's factionalism had distorted. Hence the *D.U.M.* published an anonymous profile of Swift through four issues, from February to June 1840, offering a view of his patriotism that extends Mahony's of 1834, though from a more sectarian perspective:

> There is not a man who says Irish independence – Irish trade – Irish Protestantism – Irish agitation – who does not breathe the breath and speak the spirit of Swift. It is true, these are the phrases of conflicting parties – of conflicting Irish parties – but all these parties have drank at the same fountain – all are unconsciously adorers at the same altar – all are worshippers of the same divinity – followers of the beckoning shadows of Swift. We have seen but the first rude savage act of the mystic drama, but how much is yet to come! – how and when shall the dark and bloody complexities of the plot be unravelled? – when shall the great spirit of nationality, which the patriot called from the grave, assert its dignity, and be no more seen discoloured and distorted, through the murky medium of dark, stormy faction. But strangely as this *national principle* has been perverted into ill – and long as it has been made

the slave of cruelty and faction – it is, nevertheless, the germ from which must grow whatever prosperity, greatness or dignity our country is hereafter to accomplish, it is through fiery convulsions working out its mysterious task; and when, perhaps centuries hence, it has ended its mission, and that its struggles and vicissitudes and early degradation are passed away and finished in victory – its glorious nature having conquered all the vile agencies which have so long borne it down, will be seen by the world to have slowly, but steadily, through changes, tumults and many sorrows, brought the country safe to grandeur and to happiness. This spirit was evoked by Swift; he stood like the patriarch in a desert, and with the power which God had given him, he smote the dry rock, and living, ever-flowing fountains gushed forth; and though others have tainted the waters with bitterness and blood, the strong river will soon clear itself, and a few fathoms lower down it will be as though none had ever troubled it.[88]

Swift is thus the source and measure of Irish patriotism, whatever forms it might take – including the O'Connellite agitation of which the *D.U.M.* strongly and unceasingly disapproved. As the standard against which the patriotic exertions of others might be judged, of course, it supplies numerous instances of unsurpassed disinterestedness. The immediate, if implicit, butt of comparison for the *D.U.M.* is O'Connell, for

> The patriotism of Swift was a passion of his mind – he sought the honour and happiness of his country, in all things striving for its true advantage, with an inspiring zeal and intrepidity which no meaner motive could have sustained. His exertions were regulated by the occasions which the history of his country presented, and not by interest. There were from him no periodical bursts of patriotism to secure the periodical replenishment of coffers, but a steady and unvaried ardour of advocacy. . . .
>
> The 'agitation' by means of which he wrought, was peculiar: it was an appeal to *all* Irishmen; and its result was not the victory of a faction, but the triumph of a nation. It spoke to the reason, and not to the passions of the people; and, consequently, it was unsustained by crime and blood.[89]

Where Mahony, writing for the English *Fraser's*, sought to highlight Swift by marginalizing O'Connell, and in other respects to present him as the true hero of all Irishmen unswayed by sectarian bitterness, the Irish *D.U.M.* a few years later proposed him as the best of their own, a decidedly *Protestant* guide for all such Irishmen.

In general, as R.F. Foster has noted, the emphasis of the *D.U.M.* 'on the validity of Protestant Irishness was in effect divisive, since it amounted to a Protestant claim on traditions also claimed by Catholics. And by 1840 the two were divided into mutually exclusive political camps.'[90] But since the majoritarian concept of Irish identity to which most Catholics now adhered allowed Swift little, if any acceptance as a formative role model, it was legitimate for the *D.U.M.* essay to develop the implications of Croker's, Berwick's and Mason's commentaries on the Dean, and to celebrate him in the context of its own programme for Irish nationality. And even as British critics increasingly denigrated Swift's character and politics and pointed to his ultimate 'madness', the *D.U.M.* gave him an heroic cast transcending his Irish significance. For although his madness gave Swift's story 'a humiliating and a mournful' moral,[91] his literary talents and force of character in earlier years evince a nobility that squarely faces down a critic like Francis Jeffrey:

> There was an energy in his wrath, a blasting scorn in his sarcasm, a searching fiery scrutiny in his satire; and withal, he had a presence noble at all times, but in the excitement of aroused indignation, actually awful; a presence before which, we venture to say, an Edinburgh Reviewer would have turned pale, even behind his mask.[92]

This 'venture' against Jeffrey was a challenge from the *D.U.M.* itself as much as from Swift, a subtle restatement in its own right of the journal's particularly and proudly Irish claim on the Dean. Here, as throughout the long essay, the diffidence or ambivalence about the nature and value of Swift's patriotism characteristic in Ireland during the latter half of the eighteenth century is displaced by an assertion of his Irish identity. For that identity informs the very heroism granted Swift here to transcend his Irishness. It is rooted in the double defiance then (and still) typical of Irish Unionism; for it contends at once with British misunderstanding, which Jeffrey's hostility to Swift represents, and with the exclusiveness of the Irish identity maintained by O'Connellite Catholic nationalism.

5

A Nationalist Ancestor,
1840–1870

I

The *Dublin University Magazine* article on Swift, by virtue of its length and prominence, gave him a rare stature in its construction of his Irish identity as local patriotism within the Union. Within a few years, however, the Irish standing that this leading Protestant organ of 'nationality' had articulated for him was appropriated by the opposite side, and made to serve the O'Connellite object of repealing the Union. The *D.U.M.* article had viewed him as the ancestor of that sort of agitation too, if only indirectly – as the fountainhead of patriotism. And it was an Irish Protestant, inspired to patriotic feeling by the sort of grouping at Trinity College from which the *D.U.M.* itself arose,[1] and particularly moved by the concept of a largely Protestant line of patriots as a force in Irish history, who was to adapt Swift for nationalist appeal. Thomas Davis, in fact, was the first Protestant of any prominence since Grattan to invoke that line, and in his hands it is both broader and more radical. Henry Grattan, in the biography of his father that began to appear in 1839, had already drawn out the implications of the elder Grattan's own invocation of the spirits of Swift and Molyneux inserted when revising his April 1782 speech in the Irish House of Commons (published posthumously). The younger Henry traced a line of succession from Molyneux to Swift, to Lucas, and thence to Grattan himself, to confirm the ideological legitimacy, the pedigree, of the latest patriot.[2] But his purpose was hagiographical and backward-looking; there is little hint that he regarded his father's patriotism as an inspiration for the Repeal movement. Davis, on the other hand, sought to legitimize that movement as the contemporary embodiment of the inspiration the patriot line had given. As early as 1840, addressing the Historical Society of Trinity College at the close of his term as its president, he hailed 'those who have been the mind-chieftains in the civil strifes of Ireland – Swift, Lucas, Grattan' as patriotic models for his audience.

Davis reminded his audience that though they belonged 'to what are called the upper classes in Ireland', they would have competition for national leadership from the rising men of the middle classes, and that to gain it they would have to learn more about Ireland and her culture.[3]

When Davis and two Catholic colleagues, Charles Gavan Duffy and John Blake Dillon, founded *The Nation* in 1842, he was continuing to address those of his own background, as much or more than those of the Catholic majority, in exhorting his readership to recognize, value and strengthen their Irish identity. Invocations of the patriot line, and of Swift in particular, were important for manifesting that identity. One early instance of this approach sought to distinguish the Irish element in imperially centripetal British culture: the 'quality of the intellectual wares which Ireland contributes to the *imperial* literature', who have been appropriated by the 'mind monopoly, and mind robbery, of England', namely 'Irish Ussher, Boyle and Berkeley, Swift, Sterne and Goldsmith, Lucas, Burke and [Arthur] O'Leary, Flood, Grattan and Curran'.[4] Some commentators on Swift, even in his lifetime, had disputed the recurrent notion that he was actually a native of England, but none before had so reflected upon the place accorded Swift in British culture. By regarding the Dean's having such a place as an English 'appropriation', Davis was implicitly appropriating him instead for Ireland, along with the others listed. Davis's conscious reversal of what the English had done unconsciously – but thereby insensitively – exemplifies what became characteristic of *The Nation* and much succeeding nationalist writing: a provocative overreaction to British slights, meant to heighten Irish awareness and sensitivity. This rhetorical tactic was in fact programmatic, a means of resisting the subtle imperialist programme of homogenizing culture perceptible, for instance, in the English appropriation of Swift.[5]

As an element in *The Nation*'s programme, invocations of the patriot line, usually featuring Swift, could also provide historical precedents for the Irish unity against Britain that, it was hoped, the cause of Repeal could engender. At the end of December 1842, the second of the 'Letters of a Protestant on Repeal' in *The Nation* promoted a united front of Protestants and Catholics in the cause. The writer recalled their separate exertions in the eighteenth century, when Protestants 'battled, under the successive leaderships of Molyneux, Swift, Lucas and Flood, against England for the independence of the Irish legislature and the dignity of the nation' while Catholics pressed for repeal of the Penal Laws; and he noted that both groups joined to agitate for free trade.[6] During a debate in Dublin Corporation two months later, an O'Connellite member argued for unrelenting pressure to secure Repeal, even advocating a movement like the Volunteers of the previous century. They had been inspired by the memory of 'A Swift, a Molyneux and a Lucas' and energized by Grattan, but nowadays they had a leader in O'Connell, 'greater than either Swift or Grattan'.[7] In 1843, indeed, O'Connell's 'Repeal Year', *The Nation* frequently drew parallels between the long struggle for legislative independence in the eighteenth century and the contemporary struggle to restore it through Repeal. One of the better–known instances, reprinted among Davis's essays, extended the parallel to include the act of the Jacobite 'Patriot Parliament' of 1689, declaring that the English parliament had no right to legislate for Ireland; this anticipated the exertions of Molyneux, Swift and Lucas, which Flood and Grattan brought to fulfilment.[8]

Indeed, more than simply historical, the resurrected patriot line was genealogical, intended to display the nationalist heritage of Irish Protestants while at the same time supplying a pedigree for O'Connell's overwhelmingly Catholic movement. Even alone, Swift could be put to unifying effect. In the same issue of *The Nation* that celebrated the Jacobite parliament, Davis continued his appeal to Catholics by promoting the Irish language, concluding, 'Had Swift known Irish, he would have sowed its seed by the side of that nationality which he planted. . . . Had Ireland used Irish in 1782, would it not have impeded England's re-conquest of us?'[9] And later the same month *The Nation* denounced the government's issuing a contract to an Englishman named Croal for coaches to be used in Ireland, a case that might be regarded as trifling; but Wood's patent was just such a trifle:

> . . . and against this 'trifle' SWIFT shouted aloud, and called the nation together. How funny these Irishmen are – they are in a passion now about a Coach Contract, as they were long ago about brass halfpence. Aye, but read the whole story, and you will find that a conviction had then grown up in Ireland that England was a selfish and monopolizing tyrant, who amused the Protestants with an anti-Catholic yell, while she plundered them of wealth, fame and freedom. WOODS' [*sic*] patent was the trifling occasion, SWIFT saw it, and . . . rallied the Protestants. As his voice resounded, even the chained Catholic raised his head and blessed the intolerant patriot, and the British government bent before his demand. He set the precedent for an Irish party – he pioneered the road to success. 'England's fear' – it was his spell; 'Ireland's union' – it was his talisman.[10]

Although Swift had not known Irish, and was even the 'intolerant patriot' – the editorial refers to him later as 'the great Protestant patriot' – he is yet enlisted as an ancestor, not only for Protestants 'malcontent at being treated as the spurious and degraded offspring of England',[11] but also for Catholics; the latter by a fanciful leap in respect to the language, and regarding Repeal, by the implicit admonition that only unity between Catholics and Irish Protestants could bring it about.

Swift represented to Davis not simply an ancestor for the nationalism he himself embraced, but a model of purpose and effect as well. The Dean had long been acknowledged for his dynamism in forming public opinion and, related to this, as a pioneer of press freedom; Edward Berwick in 1819 had proposed him as the creator of the Irish people, and the *D.U.M.* in 1840 had considered him the wellspring of Irish patriotism. But Davis was the first Irish

Protestant nationalist who was, like Swift himself, not a politician but a publicist. In the repeated invocations of the patriot line and of Swift himself, there is latent the notion that nationalist Ireland, led for over twenty years by O'Connell, was in need of a new, disinterested, Protestant voice, which Davis was providing. The parallel is personal as much as national, or collectively Protestant. Thus, declaiming in 1844 against a proposal that the lord lieutenancy be abolished and Ireland centrally administered, *The Nation* invoked the patriot line to recall the successful efforts of the previous century and noted that the new proposal would rid the country of 'costly, uneven and partial local authority' only, ironically, so that 'Ireland be turned into what GOD and Nature meant it to be – AN ENGLISH FARM!' The paper then suggests the parallel between this spur to indignation and that which provoked the Dean – 'What a subject for SWIFT!'[12] Furthermore, just as Davis's literary interests were primarily patriotic, the few references in *The Nation* to Swift's literary eminence appear only in a patriotic context. The neglected poet Thomas Furlong's character and works, for instance, 'entitle him to a high place among the native poets of Ireland. After the illustrious names of Swift, Goldsmith and Moore, we know not one entitled to take precedence of Thomas Furlong.'[13] And the next year the paper complains that the typical boy in a national school has no exposure to the literature of Ireland: 'SWIFT lived, and GRIFFIN wrote, and MOORE sung not for him.'[14]

While Davis's enlistment of Swift in the cause of Repeal may have had a personal impetus, others were also tempted to use the Dean's high standing among Protestants to induce their good will toward the most prominent advocate of that cause. In late January 1844, during the state trials of O'Connell and his lieutenants arrested following the cancellation of the 'Monster Meeting' at Clontarf, Richard Lalor Shiel, counsel for O'Connell's son John, compared the defendants as patriots with Swift. The whole jury was Protestant as a result of government efforts to ensure a prosecution victory, and Shiel appealed to their loyalism by citing Scott's 'Memoir' as his source for references to Swift: 'I do not think that any writer has given a more accurate, or more interesting account of the first struggle of Ireland for the assertion of her rights than Sir Walter Scott.' Drawing the parallel, Shiel noted that Swift in 1720 'published a proposal for the use of Irish manufacture, and was charged with having endeavoured to create hostility between different classes of his majesty's subjects – one of the charges preferred in this very indictment', and he recalled that the ensuing prosecution failed. And in the *Drapier's Letters* 'Swift addressed the people of Ireland . . . in language as strong as any that Daniel O'Connell has employed.'[15] A few days later, James Whiteside, defending *The Nation*'s Gavan Duffy, pushed the tactic further, contrasting the unarmed 'moral force' of the Repeal movement with the armed Volunteers of 1782: 'All that the genius of Swift, the learning of Molyneux, and the patriotism of Lucas failed to obtain – all that was denied to justice was yielded to men with arms in their hands.'[16] But such rhetoric was unavailing: the jury returned a verdict of guilty, though this was set aside by the House of Lords on appeal a few months later.

For Protestants would, in the main, not be swayed from Unionism by recollections of their ancestors' patriotism. Such memories might, indeed, fructify the sense of national pride that the *D.U.M.*, for instance, heartily encouraged. But the nationalism of O'Connell, or of Davis, was hardly theirs. Protestant Ireland would continue to supply patriotic leaders, but these would have, as the nineteenth century progressed, few of their own among their following. To *The Nation* early in 1845, it could therefore seem that the people from whom such leaders sprang were unworthy of their patriotic forebears:

> Poor deluded Irish Protestants! brave! fierce! impotent! You have denied the country for which a race of Protestant patriots – DANIEL O'NEILL, MOLYNEUX, SWIFT, LUCAS, FLOOD, GRATTAN, TONE, and SAURIN – fought and spoke.[17]

Perhaps because rhetoric of this sort could hardly have been calculated to persuade Irish Protestants, *The Nation*'s appropriation of historical Protestant patriotism drew no sustained Unionist rebuttal. That appropriation could quite reasonably, indeed, have been dismissed as an empty, even desperate, rhetorical stratagem, especially after the clear failure of the 'Repeal Year' agitation of 1843. Yet Protestant unresponsiveness effectively conceded the very concept of a patriot line or genealogy to the nationalists, whose movement the *D.U.M.* had regarded in 1840 as a distorted manifestation of Swift's patriotic spirit. Nor was there any obvious Unionist counter to the nationalist adoption of Swift specifically. Articles in the *D.U.M.*, for instance, rarely mention Swift at all in the middle and later 1840s. It is tempting to explain this as a matter of Unionists' recoil from a figure nationalists had claimed for themselves, but it was more probably the case that, after a long article running over four issues in 1840 had been devoted to Swift, there appeared in the short term nothing of substance to add.

In addition, Protestants were inevitably more susceptible to the influence of the mounting tide of aspersion against Swift in Britain. Lord Mahon's *History of England* (1836) had depicted the Dean's Irish patriotism not only as factitious but as deluding a simple people, a judgement echoed by Lord Brougham in 1843[18] and by the patronizing tone of Robert Chambers's enormously popular *Cyclopaedia of English Literature* in 1844:

> His wish to serve Ireland was one of his ruling passions; yet it was something like the instinct of the inferior animals toward their offspring; waywardness, contempt and abuse were strangely mixed with affectionate attachment and ardent zeal. . . . Ireland, however, gave Swift her whole heart.[19]

To Thomas De Quincey in 1847, 'of all Swift's villanies for the sake of popularity, and still more for the sake of wielding his popularity, none is so scandalous as' the *Drapier Letters*,[20] in which William Howitt the same year saw 'nothing . . . more recklessly unjust than his conduct, or more hollow than his pretences'.[21] Probably the best reason for Irish Protestant unresponsiveness to the nationalist appropriation of Swift in particular is that, despite the prominence *The Nation* had given him, no historical character had much perceptible significance in the large context of Irish politics during the 1840s. Many Catholic readers would still have considered Swift, for instance, mainly a figure from the past with an enduring local repute for eccentricity. Thus a short biography of 1844 published in Dublin and aimed at a popular audience, though perhaps prompted by the heightened profile given Swift by *The Nation*'s references, did not follow its patriotic-genealogical line on him but simply condensed Johnson's eighteenth-century account and added a few anecdotes.[22] But just as the long period of Irish Catholic silence towards Swift's reputation before the 1840s had enabled it to be shaped to serve the interest of local patriotism within the British dimension, the lack of Unionist resistance to *The Nation*'s patriotically genealogical treatment of him allowed that paper and the movement it influenced to lay the basis for the eventual acceptance of Swift by Catholic nationalists at large, without demurrals from Irish Protestants.

In the mid-1840s, however, the nationalist consensus behind O'Connell's Repeal programme began to fracture. *The Nation* had become the mainstay of a group within the Repeal movement known as 'Young Ireland', and had for some time taken a more militant – not to say somewhat militaristic – stance than O'Connell had found comfortable; and he was irritated that during the sedition trial of 1844, sentiments published in the paper, with which he had disagreed, were quoted against him.[23] Following O'Connell's release, furthermore, Davis and *The Nation* favoured the proposed establishment of the non-denominational Queen's colleges, in line with the paper's integrationist cultural principles, while O'Connell condemned the colleges as 'godless'. The dispute was temporarily resolved, but only after O'Connell had asserted his espousal of an 'Old Ireland' ethos – more overtly Catholic and non-violent – rather than the non-sectarian values and militance of 'Young Ireland'. The pressures of the growing Famine, and O'Connell's attempts to take advantage of a possibly greater governmental enlightenment in dealing with it, exacerbated the rift after Davis's sudden death in September 1845. At length a split in the movement could be discerned clearly between a more moderate, 'political' majority of O'Connellite Repealers, supported by most of the Catholic bishops, and the more righteous, ideological and interdenominational Young Ireland group.

Attitudes towards Swift were, of course, peripheral to these tensions, but slight evidences of them appear even before Davis's death in the discriminations *The Nation* was drawing among the heroes of its patriotic genealogy. On the one hand, the paper's militance is reflected in a review of Grattan's speeches early in 1845, which prefers him to Swift and Flood for his 'more fervid and more Irish nature', and for achieving an Irish constitution, while

Tone is acknowledged as having superior 'organising power'.[24] A subtler note by far is struck in an advertisement in mid-year for a biographical series in the forthcoming 'Library of Ireland', which lists historical military leaders, the Catholics Brian Boru, Sarsfield and Owen Roe O'Neill, among its subjects, although it also includes Swift.[25] Such a juxtaposition hints, albeit only gently, that Swift might be evoked not solely or even primarily for effect on Protestants; he is classed with men of action who would appeal particularly to Catholic historical sensibilities. But if such an inclusion of Swift suggested that the achievements of a patriotic rhetorician were no less notable than those of military personages, the paper could also note his inadequacies of attitude. In August 1845, *The Nation*'s review of a collection of Irish ballad poetry – a subject of special importance to Davis – commented that Grattan and Swift were but 'partial' patriots, who 'mistook Ireland for a colony wronged, and great enough to be a nation'. The concessive phrasing is significant, both reflecting the paper's impatience with nationalist moderation – still characteristic of most Catholics – and appealing to the Catholic sensibility that would look askance at the authenticity of Protestant patriots. Yet it was also noted that, while Anglo-Irish ballads before Swift's time 'were chiefly written by followers of the court',

> Swift snatched these weapons out of the hands of the English faction, and turned them against their own breasts. He rescued our popular poetry . . . and gave it a vigour and concentration which it has never wholly lost. During his lifetime it became a power in the country; the obscure precursor of a free press.[26]

Thus an admission of Swift's historical inadequacy – considered from a modern nationalist perspective – was combined with admiration for an achievement that joined literary gifts and political passion. This was certainly an advance upon such observations as those of W.C. Taylor in 1831 and Thomas Moore's 'Captain Rock', which mingled contempt for the impurity of Swift's motives as a patriot with a forced or reluctant acknowledgement of his historical value. Their considerations had confined Swift to history, whether history was understood as a heritage of grievance (appealing to the Catholic nationalist sensibility O'Connell had cultivated) or as an objective record of the past (for which a liberal Protestant historian such as Taylor would aim). The rhetorical design here, admitting Swift's defects but concentrating upon his accomplishments, unlocked Swift from those confines, putting directly to contemporary combative use the potential of his historical function of uniting Irish public spirit.

II

While Davis lived, the process of promoting Swift in *The Nation* as an ancestral patriot for nationalist Ireland was well begun. But Davis had rarely stressed Swift's literary eminence, partly because it could be taken for granted, though probably more because the patriot-publicist aspect of Swift's reputation (in which, at least incidentally, he became Davis's own precursor) seemed more amenable to nationalist absorption. After Davis's death, *The Nation* continued to regard Swift primarily in terms of political history. It was left to the Young Ireland poet Denis Florence MacCarthy, a Catholic, to enshrine Swift in a literary pantheon built to nationalist specifications. MacCarthy began his notice in *The Poets and Dramatists of Ireland* (1846), 'The name of Jonathan Swift is unquestionably the greatest in our literature,' placing him at the head of a genealogy of Irish nationalist writers. For while Swift's celebrity as man and author was widely acknowledged outside Ireland, 'he was to us, however, something even still higher. He was the first Anglo-Irish writer who felt that he was an Irishman, and that his injured and despised country was worthy even of the affectation of patriotism.' So granting the possibility of affectation without accepting it as fact, MacCarthy implicitly parried the complaints of those like Thomas Moore, for whom Swift's personal motives and circumstances devalued his patriotism. He traced Swift's influence, furthermore, genealogically from Lucas through Grattan, Tone, Davis 'and the great living embodiment [sic] of the principles of Swift – O'Connell', thereby promoting his respectability as a patriotic ancestor even for Catholics. Like *The Nation*, MacCarthy justified Swift for Catholics not by examining his sincerity, but in functional terms: his writings were forceful in his own time and had been an inspiration to many patriots since. But MacCarthy went beyond praising the writer as patriot, for he recast the paradox of Swift as an unseemly or immoral character of undoubted literary gifts, to which British critics were generally attached, to present the whole man as tragically torn, and precisely on that account appropriate for Irish affection:

> We should have most in our hearts this strong, weak, mirthful, melancholy, light-hearted, gloomy, affectionate, selfish, whimsical compound of light and darkness, of heaven and earth, which for seventy-eight years of penury, dependance [sic], faction-fighting, patriotism, discomfort and insanity, bore the name of Jonathan Swift on this earth! Peace! peace! to his ashes. May his name ever live in the memories of his countrymen![27]

Instead of perceiving a discontinuity between the works and the man, MacCarthy found the Dean's paradox simultaneously internalized in Swift's conflict-ridden personality, and eternalized in Irish memory through his patriotism. Swift was to be loved, in other words, for a patriotic value inextricable from his torment. MacCarthy thus constructed Swift as a sufferer – the more appealing to Catholics for that – whose suffering was integral to a particular concept of Irishness, rendering him part of the nation, and one in whom the nation could see itself.

Considered from the perspective of political function, then, Swift's patriotic achievement transcended inadequacies of attitude or motive, while in a literary-cultural evaluation, all could be integrated. Since a major object of literary study in the nineteenth century was the revelation of an author's character, the paradox of Swift as character and author posed considerable trouble to contemporary British critics. They tended to treat it by alternating contempt and wonder, like Mahon in 1836, or by emphasizing Swift's inadequacy in poetry – an art higher, more 'literary' than prose – so as to denigrate the man and the artist together. The latter procedure is apparent in an anonymous British writer's view, published, like MacCarthy's, in 1846:

> Swift's principal inspiration as a poet is derived, not from the Muse, but Misanthropy, and his verses exhibit that ferocious energy and blistering power of satire, which rendered his prose works so terrible. Still, however, he exhibits none of that exclusive love towards the divine art which is so necessary to constitute a genuine poet; and he seems to rhyme, merely because it afforded a change in the venting of his atrabilious humour, after he had exhausted it in prose.[28]

By contrast, MacCarthy's Catholic-nationalist aesthetic gave value to the assumed defects in Swift's character as the stigmata of Ireland's own oppression. The Protestant writer was acculturated for the educated Catholic in terms that complemented his celebration as a 'character' by the vulgar in such stories as those of 'Jack and the Dane' from this period (stories described by W.J. Fitzpatrick, in a letter to the British literary historian John Forster in 1856, as 'humorous and traditional stories of Swift . . . constantly in the mouths of the lower orders in Ireland, but especially those of Dublin').[29] MacCarthy carried the process of accommodating Swift to Catholic sensibilities much further than had Francis Mahony in 1834, whose attempt to link Swift's decline into madness with his patriotism was compromised by whimsy and antipathy to O'Connell. MacCarthy even advanced upon *The Nation*, which had usually invoked the patriot line as a genealogy with an assumed primary appeal to Protestants. He brought it forward to include both Davis and the prime Catholic himself, O'Connell. He thereby fleshed out the full extent of the line, which the *Dublin University Magazine* itself, however reluctantly, had implied in 1840.

T.F. Meagher followed a like procedure a few months later, at the beginning of 1847. The tensions between the Young Ireland militants and the main body of O'Connell's Repeal Association had erupted again upon O'Connell's vociferous attachment to the principle of non-violence. This was a principle which Meagher in 1846 was the first to reject, followed by a group of 'seceders' from the Association, including William Smith O'Brien, who was to lead the abortive Rising of 1848. After a fruitless discussion about reuniting, the Young Ireland seceders formalized themselves as the Irish Confederation in January 1847. Meagher addressed its inaugural meeting, and to signify the spirit of the Confederation he cited a patriotic genealogy broader, in that it included both Catholics and Protestants, than Davis's formulations. It was the same spirit that had 'made the walls of Limerick impregnable . . . dictated the letters of Swift . . . sanctified the scaffold of the Geraldine, and made the lyre of Moore vibrate through the world', as it had also prompted the Volunteers, Grattan and Davis, and O'Connell himself in his bolder days. [30] For the leaders of the Confederation, like the founders of *The Nation*, history was an important tool. By abandoning O'Connell's emphasis on 'moral force', they were also turning away from the effectively and restrictively Catholic sense of history, informed by longstanding griev-ances, characteristic of his movement. And by constructing instead an Irish history from examples of inspiring defiance with a non-sectarian ethos, they demonstrated a pluralism intended to draw Protestant support.

Swift was ideally suited to such a programme. The Confederation quickly began publishing patriotic historical documents as educational pamphlets, and as its membership grew, it was organized into clubs named for great patriots. John Mitchel, an advanced nationalist already recruited to write for *The Nation*, but in early 1847 not yet a revolutionary, edited the first Confed-eration pamphlet, *Irish Political Economy*, which included Swift's *Short View of the State of Ireland* (1727) and *Proposal for the Universal Use of Irish Manufac-tures* (1720), with the prefatory comment that 'the warnings, advice and remonstrances, which were addressed to our ancestors one hundred and twenty years ago, suit our condition exactly to this day'.[31] Appropriately, when one of the first Confederate Clubs in Dublin was established in July 1847, it was named for Swift and described as 'guided by the spirits of Swift and of Davis', and Mitchel became its vice-president.[32] Mitchel's pamphlet was reviewed in *The Nation*, which noted that Swift had first articulated that 'distrust of foreigners and reliance upon ourselves' characteristic of Irish economic patriotism since; in addition, the fact that the state of the Irish countryside, as described by Swift, was unchanged showed 'how little of political advancement has taken place here for the last one hundred years'.[33]

The suggestion of Swift's prophetic and inspirational value in both Mitchel's 'Preface' and *The Nation*'s review recalls similar comments on the persistence of rural degradation made in the 1830s by the economists Bicheno and Orpen and by Francis Mahony; but it accrued significance in 1847 from the ongoing disaster of the Famine. Thus Swift could be perceived as he had been by MacCarthy, with personality conflicts useful as metaphors to a Catholic-nationalist aesthetic of suffering Ireland; as a father-figure for rhetorical boldness; and as a prophet, without contradiction. In all cases he was heroic. And such a formulation was reinforced by Swift's prominence in a nationalist genealogy of patriotism. Presented in such coherent variety, he could be a source of inspiration to Catholics and Protestants alike, and in contrast to Francis Mahony's effusive promotion of Swift a decade earlier, this strategy did eventually succeed. Before *The Nation* began publishing, Catholics rarely echoed the admiration for Swift frequently expressed by Irish Protestants; in the 1840s the terms of that admiration were so adjusted as, at

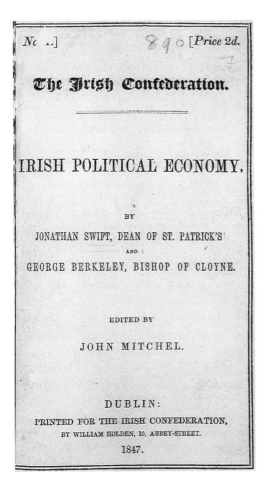

The cover of the Irish Confederation's first pamphlet.

length, to appeal to both. Over the next three decades the articulation of that adjustment remained largely, as during the 1840s, in Protestant hands. Yet Davis's work with *The Nation* and, afterwards, the forward role played by Protestants like Mitchel and Smith O'Brien in the Confederation and the failed 1848 Rising, validated Protestants anew as nationalist leaders in Catholic eyes. Their efforts could only abet the progress of that Catholic favour towards an earlier Protestant hero which MacCarthy had articulated; and the course of that progress ultimately facilitated for Swift a distinctively Irish identity in nationalist terms.

But this consensus on Swift's behalf, its basis laid in the 1840s, was not fully realized for years to come. Many Irish Protestants continued to regard him mainly as a figure from history with no necessarily lingering relevance. And he continued to have British detractors, not without an audience in Ireland, who held that he was driven to a specious patriotism by disappointed ambition, or that he was otherwise opportunistic or misanthropic. A commentator in the *Dublin Review*, for example, a Catholic journal which, despite the title, was published in London, called Swift 'the most intrepid liar whom political controversy, fertile of such progeny, ever brought forth'.[34] And for Irish Catholics, his obliviousness to their ancestors' rights could still be a thorn. Such animosities are acknowledged in a government-sanctioned account of Swift in 1849, designed for use in the Irish national schools:

> A difference of opinion has always existed with regard to the motives by which Swift was actuated in deserting the political party with which he first connected himself; and it is a matter of fact which admits of no dispute, that although he advocated, with unyielding firmness and unrivalled powers of wit and sarcasm popular rights and constitutional freedom in Ireland, yet he was the inveterate opponent of the claims of Roman Catholics and Dissenters to an equality of political power. The important services he rendered to Ireland, at a very critical period of her history, are admitted by Irishmen of every party and every creed.[35]

The passage shows the strains of pursuing that objectivity dear to liberal Protestant historians such as W.C. Taylor, attempting to accommodate strong reservations even while concluding as it does. Earlier, less official school histories of Ireland in the 1840s merely recounted the story of Swift's role in the Wood affair, with no indication that he could be a subject of contemporary dispute.[36] By acknowledging the character of Swift as such a bone of contention, the 1849 schoolbook addressed the question of his modern relevance, ultimately implying that his historical function possessed an enduring potential. Essentially the author followed the line taken by Taylor in 1840, but by the late 1840s, when nationalists had begun seriously to adopt Swift, it was a more accurate line, and thereby forecast the consensus in favour of the continuing relevance of Swift's service to Ireland for which the Young Ireland treatment of the Dean was effectively responsible.

III

That consensus on Swift's behalf was stalled for a time, meanwhile, among some Protestants in particular, by the attention given his putative madness in the late 1840s and 1850s. Like most extended British references to Swift, the 1849 schoolbook, much indebted to Scott's 1814 'Memoir', mentioned the Dean's madness, but concluded its account by commending an Irishman's book on the subject which had just appeared, from which it quotes at length. W.R. (later Sir William) Wilde's *The Closing Years of Dean Swift's Life*, published early in 1849, attempted to show that Swift could not be considered mad in any proper medical sense. Wilde combined observations on his health and attitude from the Dean himself and various contemporaries with the anatomical evidence supplied by his death mask, a bust taken from it and the examination of Swift's skull during an exhumation undertaken while structural work was in progress on St Patrick's Cathedral in 1835. Although material on Stella and other Swiftiana occupies most of Wilde's book, his medical considerations, already published in an Irish medical journal in 1847,[37] led him to conclude that up to the year 1742 Swift showed no symptom whatever

> of medical disease, beyond the ordinary course of nature. That towards the end of that year the cerebral disease under which he had long laboured, by producing effusion, &c., destroyed his memory, and rendered him at times ungovernable in his anger, as well as produced partial paralysis, is quite certain; but all this was the result of physical disease in one whose constitution was of great nervous irritability, a person strange and eccentric in all his thoughts and habits, of strong passions and emotions, who had given his brain no rest, and who had long survived more than 'the years of a man'.[38]

Wilde's objective was scientific precision; though he admits early in the book that any information connected 'with that illustrious patriot, most accomplished scholar, and dazzling wit' ought to be made public,[39] his purpose was not to vindicate Swift's character, but to examine it dispassionately. It had the immediate effect, however, of arousing and confirming the common belief in Swift's insanity. The generally favourable review in the *Dublin University Magazine*, for instance, a journal which had rarely noticed Swift for almost a decade, considered as mere quibbling Wilde's insistence that the Dean was never medically insane, for many would consider as insanity what Wilde had shown was an organic disease. Moreover,

> in Swift's life and conduct – in his violent passions – in his oddities – even in his vindictive patriotism – in his misanthropy, whether it be considered as a pretence or a reality – in the morbid delight in which he dwells on disgusting images, we see very distinct traces of incipient disease.[40]

Such characteristics demonstrate, in other words, what British critics had often implied, that madness was their foreseeable end. In a second edition of his book later in 1849, Wilde clarified that the organic disease he had described during Swift's last years was as much senility as anything more sinister, and compared it with the disease suffered before his death by Sir Walter Scott, whom nobody ever considered insane.[41] The *Dublin University Magazine* reviewer returned to the first edition for an article in the *North British Review*, still in 1849, this time concerned mainly with Wilde's collection of Swiftiana and showing greater sympathy for Swift in general. But he extended the passing reference to Swift's 'vindictive patriotism' in the *Dublin University Magazine* review for a rare comment on Wilde's medical concerns:

> In his Irish politics, we cannot but think the rabid fierceness with which he pursued his antagonists in the battle against Wood and his halfpence in every form of persecution, was symptomatic of mental disease.[42]

Both reviews were written by an Irish Protestant, whose connection of Swift's patriotism to misanthropic madness reflects some departure from the traditional Irish Protestant admiration for Swift as patriot. They appeared at the end of a decade in which the basis for that admiration had been appropriated by nationalists, first attempting to appeal to Protestant, but gradually also to Catholic, sensibilities. As though in reaction, such reviews correspond to the steady British refrain of aspersions upon Swift's character, particularizing it by giving a cast of madness to the patriotic spirit Irish Protestants had long celebrated. Three years later in 1852, when the *D.U.M.* next gave over an article to Swift, such a concordance with the main thrust of British critical hostility towards his character becomes even more pronounced. The writer's repeated comments upon the Dean's boorishness to his friend Thomas Sheridan reinforced the paradox, often perceived in Britain, between Swift's thoroughly admirable writing style and defects of character that 'one laments and revolts from'.[43] Furthermore, 'Swift's claims to genuine patriotism', since these stemmed more from a sense of justice than from love of Ireland or the Irish, 'are sufficiently apocryphal'.[44] If not madness *per se*, at least misanthropy therefore infected Swift's close friendships, as with Sheridan; and perhaps even his patriotic pretensions. Such emphasis upon misanthropy or madness could affect even an Irish commentator who attempted to steer clear of the influence of the British critics for whom it was a commonplace. The Rev. James Wills's biography of Swift, also published in 1852, traced a path between 'some of the most respectable English historians' for whom Swift was 'a ruffianly demogogue', and 'his Irish admirers [who] have exalted his conduct and motives beyond the realities of human character'.[45] Wills maintained that a British critic would hardly attribute Swift's patriotic sentiments 'to any factious motive' had they been expressed 'by an English nobleman . . . risen in his place in the English privy council'.[46] So arguing that Swift's Irishness was instrumental in the British case against him, Wills was able to hail him as a patriot in traditional Irish Protestant terms, though conceding ultimately that Swift's life displayed 'a well marked uniformity in the deeply traced lines of character and conduct, which seemed to converge to the actual result of insanity'.[47]

Even an apologist for Swift, then, could not dismiss the imputation of madness that Wilde's book, by disproving it medically in 1849, had renewed. The fixity of that imputation in Britain, indeed in the very heart of the British establishment, was emphasized in a long and prominent essay in *The Times* in 1850. Ostensibly a review of *Stella and Vanessa*, a French novel by Leon de Wailly newly translated by Lady Duff-Gordon, the article applauded Swift's 'great and unconquerable exertions' which rescued Ireland 'from absolute thraldom', but took greater pains to insist that 'from the beginning to the end of his days Jonathan Swift was more or less MAD'.[48] The ground was therefore better prepared for the reception of a judgement upon Swift more damaging, because more popular, than that of any commentator, Irish or British, since Jeffrey. W.M. Thackeray's *The English Humourists of the Eighteenth Century* was first delivered as a series of lectures in London in 1851, then elsewhere in England and Scotland the same year, in America in 1852, and it was finally published in 1853. That on Swift was the first lecture, and at Thackeray's hands the British paradigm of Swift as paradox received its fullest development. He was not Irish, but an Englishman;[49] a believer, but 'an evil spirit';[50] even the *Drapier's Letters* are not what they seem:

> Against men in office, he having been overthrown, against men in England, he having lost his chance of preferment there, the furious exile never fails to rage and curse. Is it fair to call the famous 'Drapier's Letters' patriotism? They are masterpieces of dreadful humour and invective: they are reasoned logically enough too, but the proposition is as monstrous and fabulous as the Lilliputian island. It is not that the grievance is so great, but there is his enemy – the assault is wonderful for its activity and terrible rage. It is Samson, with a bone in his hand, rushing upon his enemies and felling them: one admires not the cause so much as the strength, the anger, the fury of the champion. As is the case with madmen, certain subjects provoke him, and awaken his fits of wrath.[51]

Thackeray's object was 'to point a moral or advance a tale of ambition',[52] and thus the passage above is just a prelude to the more famous observation on the author of the fourth part of *Gulliver's Travels*, 'a monster gibbering shrieks, and gnashing imprecations against mankind – tearing down all shreds of modesty, past all sense of manliness and shame; filthy in word, filthy in thought, furious, raging obscene'.[53] Like the *Drapier's Letters*, it is the product of one 'always alone – alone and gnashing in the darkness'[54] – except in his relationship with Stella, the one area in which Thackeray softened on Swift. Indeed, the rhetoric of the whole essay seems aimed towards resolving the often-expressed paradox of the great writer and the terrible man by absorbing the writer in the exemplary, ambition-induced, lonely madness of the man.

As Thackeray demolished the patriot only incidentally with the man, most British reviews of *The English Humourists* gave little notice to Swift's patriotism; but reactions to the book were hardly all positive, which betrays some erosion of the long habitual British asperity towards Swift the man, even as this was making inroads among Irish Protestants. While *The Critic* found Thackeray 'a thorough despot in his dealings with Swift', but in the main fittingly so;[55] and the approving review in *Hogg's Instructor* could complain only that Thackeray had slighted 'the dash of insanity that tinged his whole life, and which at length brought it to such a melancholy close',[56] that in *Blackwood's* took heated issue with the whole premise of misanthropy. Castigating both Thackeray and the *Times* article of 1850, it contrasted their exaggerated emphasis upon misanthropy with considerable evidence of Swift's charity and kindliness, and compared his treatment of vice with that of Hogarth, who had never been regarded as misanthropic or insane.[57] The

Following the publication of Thackeray's damning essay on Swift, a sentimental view of the Dean's later years became somewhat more popular. This illustration, for a biographical account by J.F. Waller in an 1864 edition of *Gulliver's Travels*, depicts the benign ghost of Stella visiting the distraught Swift.

Blackwood's reviewer only acknowledged Swift's patriotism, but another, in the *British Quarterly Review* the next year, gave it greater space, comparing Swift to O'Connell in popularity and maintaining that 'his having been an Irish patriot and agitator deserves to be particularly remembered'.[58] Swift's madness, on the other hand, was accepted as a constant factor in his life. Finally, in a critical discussion of satire in 1854, James Hannay defended the Dean as 'a huge figure in our literature' and tried to refute the contentions of Jeffrey and, more categorically, Thackeray.[59] Thackeray's book naturally gained more currency than its reviews, but the latter indicate that the vituperative strain toward Swift's character in British critical opinion, the frequent restatement of the paradox between brilliant wit and depraved man, had reached its limit with his judgement. The celebrations of Swift's patriotism in *The Times* in 1850 and the *British Quarterly Review* in 1854, even if both also maintain the perception of his madness, are not entirely undermined by that perception, and stand in marked contrast to the dismissals of his patriotism that had been common previously, and which the *D.U.M.* after 1849 had come to share.

Yet if Thackeray represents the high-water mark of British critical castigation of Swift, a few who followed him could be quite as thorough. T.B. Macaulay's popular *History of England* trenchantly echoed Jeffrey's complaint of Swift's neglect of injustice toward Catholics, and extended it to others in the line of Protestant patriots, disputing even the notion that they had aroused truly popular opinion, for 'neither Molyneux nor Swift, neither Lucas nor Boyle, ever thought of appealing to the native population'. Swift, furthermore, 'was at heart the haughtiest, the most aspiring, the most vindictive, the most despotic of men'.[60] Walter Bagehot in 1855 considered the *Drapier's Letters* 'essentially absurd; they are a clever appeal to ridiculous prejudices' against Britain's appropriately imperial policy in Ireland; and he nearly matched Thackeray on the Dean himself:

> Swift is a detective in a dean's wig; he watched the mob; his whole wit is a kind of dexterous indication of popular frailties; he hated the crowd; he was a spy on beaming smiles, and a common informer against genial enjoyment . . . his sharpness was the sharpness of disease; his power the sore acumen of morbid wretchedness.[61]

A long-winded versifier in 1856 concluded a sad reflection on Stella and Vanessa by accepting Swift only as 'an alien patriot . . . /Whose combat clanged for Ireland's right/In reason half, if half in spite.'[62] Finally, the historian Alexander Andrews condemned him in 1859, not specifically for his patriotism, but comprehensively, as

> one of those beings whom Providence occasionally inflicts upon the world, blighting all they pass, poisoning all they come in contact with, withering all that clings to them. . . . In death he was a wretched Yahoo of his race, as in life he had been a base forgery of the image of his Creator.[63]

IV

Among Irish Catholics, on the other hand, Swift's acceptance as a patriot made headway in the 1850s. Writing in America for a largely immigrant Catholic audience, the Young Irelander Thomas D'Arcy McGee promoted the patriot line and Swift himself as 'director and champion' of national spirit in his day, for while the Protestant minority mostly disregarded him during the Wood affair, 'it was with the people the appeals of Swift took most. . . . From this dispute about the currency we may date the return of public spirit, beaten down and exiled' in the Williamite war.[64] Contrasted with such blatant sectarianism, the Christian Brothers' *Historical Class-Book* of 1859, one of the earliest Victorian school histories designed specifically for Irish

Catholic pupils, briefly noticed the success of the *Drapier's Letters* in the face of English corruption.[65] The next year, Martin Haverty's Irish history noted that Swift 'practically separated' himself from his own people and 'employed his great powers as a writer to uphold the interests of Ireland against the hostile influence of the British cabinet', thereby achieving unprecedented popularity.[66] Significantly, both books avoided any reference to Catholic reservations about the purity of Swift's patriotic motives. Although their comments were brief, they demonstrated an important achievement for the programme in historical education begun by *The Nation* and carried on by the Irish Confederation in the 1840s: a major Protestant patriot was becoming recognized by the Irish popular classes for the efficacy of his efforts on Ireland's behalf, whatever the purity of his motives, his obliviousness to the plight of Catholics, or indeed his character defects or his assumed madness. These negatives had all been addressed by Young Irelanders, particularly D.F. MacCarthy, but what was most important about Swift as patriot was his success in the Wood affair and his inspiring effect upon the common people of his time. The emphasis in these Catholic treatments lay upon that patriotic function: his historical value was implicitly exemplary for modern Irish patriotism, without the necessity of acknowledging the defects of motive in him that earlier liberal Protestants such as W.C. Taylor, or even Davis, had felt it necessary to concede.

Indeed, for all the popularity in Britain of Thackeray's and other negative impressions of Swift, that functional basis for assessing his patriotism was gaining renewed force among Protestants as well. It was articulated in 1861 by two Irish Protestants writing respectively about literary and political history for a cosmopolitan audience. The first, George Craik, made the point succinctly:

> Swift was universally regarded by his countrymen as the champion of the independence of Ireland – the preserver of whatever they had most to value or to be proud of as a people. And perhaps the birth of political and patriotic spirit in Ireland as a general sentiment, may be traced with some truth to this affair of Wood's halfpence and to these letters of Swift's.[67]

Of greater moment was the appearance that same year of W.E.H. Lecky's *The Leaders of Public Opinion in Ireland*. Published anonymously when Lecky was twenty-three and much more sympathetic to nationalism than he was to become in later years, *The Leaders* dealt successively with Swift, Flood, Grattan and O'Connell, giving Swift's patriotism its most extended analysis to date and fleshing out the major eighteenth-century names in the patriot line often invoked by Young Ireland. Lecky's, indeed, was a detailed development of the functionality characteristic in the Young Ireland view of Swift. It presented a picture of 'the prostration of the spirits of the people' and the absence of public opinion, as such, following the Williamite victory; an acknowledgement that 'for the Roman Catholics as a distinct body he did absolutely nothing . . . and his patriotism was in consequence restricted'; as well as a laudatory account of his campaign against Wood, by which he became 'the creator of public opinion in Ireland'. Swift showed the Irish people how to rely upon themselves, a lesson which inspired 'the development of his policy', especially through Grattan's efforts, in the achievement of legislative independence in 1782.[68] Lecky even, inferentially, turned the tables upon Thackeray, who had argued that Swift's avoidance of the florid excesses typical of Irish rhetoric manifested his intrinsic Englishness.[69] To Lecky, Swift was instead 'admirably calculated to be the leader of public opinion in Ireland' because of that very 'freedom from the characteristic defects of the Irish temperament'.[70] Finally, and more forcibly than Wills in 1852, he pointed to Swift's Irishness and Tory affiliation as fundamental reasons for British dismissal of his patriotism:

> He was the leading representative of Irish principles which writers on the other side of the channel are accustomed to treat with ridicule and contempt, and of an English party which has of late years been rapidly falling into disrepute.[71]

In effect, Lecky was a forceful proponent of Swift's Irish nationalist identity, adopting and elucidating the essentials of the Young Ireland position on the Dean. His debt to Young Ireland was quickly recognized and hailed by an old Repealer, W.J. O'Neill Daunt, who also asserted Swift's historical service specifically to Catholic Ireland as a 'bold, manly tone . . . imperatively needed to rouse whatever energies the penal laws had not utterly prostrated'.[72] Lecky seems to have been impelled, at least in part, by a fascination for the concept of the patriot line as strong as Davis's twenty years before, but vastly better informed and, for him, more particularized in Grattan as the ideal of Irish patriotism. Also like Davis, Lecky seems to have imagined himself as potentially the latest embodiment of Protestant nationalist leadership, the heir of the patriot line.[73] Throughout his life he maintained his admiration of Grattan. It was already clear in the first edition of *The Leaders*, especially by contrast to the treatment given O'Connell, and evident again in the substantially similar second edition in 1871. It became starkly, even plaintively obvious in the third edition in 1903, a major revision reflecting his antipathy to the democratic trend of contemporary Home Rule nationalism. By then Lecky had long since become convinced that the aristocratic spirit he celebrated in Grattan was lost to Irish patriotism, and for the 1903 edition of *Leaders* he also dropped the section on Swift. This had found a place in somewhat revised form as the biographical introduction to the first volume of Temple Scott's edition of Swift's *Prose Works* (1897), but its absence from *Leaders* diminished the effect of the patriot line. Though Lecky, frightened by the excesses of the Land League and Parnellism, had avowed his Unionism by the mid-1880s, he retained the respect of nationalists for the services rendered by his earlier works, for having 'done more than any living man to keep

alive the spirit of nationality among the Irish Catholics'.[74] Swift's Irish
nationalist identity was one beneficiary as that spirit was vitalized.

Though of Irish provenance, Lecky's *The Leaders* was published in England
in 1861 and consequently had a British as well as an Irish audience. In this
context, his glowing appraisal of Swift as patriot had been at least cursorily
anticipated by the positive aspects of the *Times* article in 1850 and of those
reviews of Thackeray's *English Humourists* that departed from the usual dismissals of the Dean's patriotic efforts either in a specific sense or as an
illustration of his general misanthopy. In fact, from the 1860s such dismissals
gradually ceased to be the norm among British commentators. With
Thackeray, Bagehot and Andrews, the high-water mark of wholesale condemnation had been reached, and after Lecky, few British political writers
would echo Goldwin Smith's judgement of 1861 that Swift took part in the
Wood's halfpence affair 'principally to indulge a restless and embittered
spirit, which craved for agitation'.[75] Literary commentators in Britain naturally felt the influence of Thackeray more strongly, but for them Swift's Irish
interests were fairly incidental to the view that, though his nature was
'gigantic . . . his was the grandeur of a fallen angel'.[76]

In Ireland itself, some writers during the 1860s were still prone to reflect
the strains upon traditional Irish Protestant admiration of the Dean's patriotism and the longstanding, largely tacit, antipathy among Catholics which
had prevailed before the Young Ireland adoption of him in the 1840s. In 1862
Thomas Arnold, the brother of Matthew and a convert to Catholicism,
published a critical history of English literature based upon his lectures at the
Catholic University in Dublin, treating Swift from an English standpoint
that also recalled Thomas Moore's complaints of nearly forty years earlier. For
'Swift's ambition was for power; he wished that his literary successes should
serve merely as a basis and vantage-ground whence to scale the high places of
the State', while his satire betrayed a cynical, irreligious materialism and his
Irish patriotism was opportunistic.[77] W.F. Collier, Arnold's counterpart at
Trinity College, revealed at once the influence of Thackeray and the greater
willingness to deprecate Swift's patriotism that the *D.U.M.* had sanctioned
for Irish Protestants from 1849: a monstrously tragic man, Swift was a patriot
'more from hatred of England than love to Ireland', however 'laudable' his
effect, and he died an embittered madman.[78]

On the other hand, in 1863 James Whiteside, Gavan Duffy's counsel in the
sedition trial of twenty years before, gave a lecture eulogizing Swift in strongly
Young Ireland, functional terms: 'Swift created a public opinion; Swift
inspired hope, courage and a spirit of justifiable resistance in the people; Swift
taught Irishmen they had a country to love, to raise and to cherish.'[79]
Whiteside's forthrightness provoked a response by W.H. Flood, a descendant
of Grattan's contemporary and rival Henry Flood, that seems captious by
comparison. Insisting upon Flood's primacy among eighteenth-century
patriots, he viewed Swift as a misanthrope, 'a strong anti-Papist in politics',

lacking in originality ('The 'Drapier's Letters' contain the patent grievances of Ireland long existing'), who degraded his clerical office by 'political polemics'.[80] By contrast, Thomas D'Arcy McGee's decidedly Catholic *Popular History of Ireland*, published in America in 1864, maintained that Swift's patriotism exalted his cloth and that he was a pioneer of a free press and a vigorous proponent of legislative independence. Terming him the 'invincible Dean' in whom 'the patriot was the liberator',[81] indeed, McGee implied that Swift was entitled to the same label popularly accorded O'Connell among Irish Catholics; it was as if appropriating the Dean as ancestor of 'The Liberator' would secure Swift's Irish nationalist identity.

The main differences among these Irish viewpoints are at once literary and political in orientation. The critics Arnold and Collier reflected the lingering British habit of deprecation to which Irish Unionists were also occasionally attracted, while Whiteside and McGee, like Lecky just before them, were concerned primarily with political history, and echoed the Young Ireland treatment of Swift in a decade marked by a steady increase of nationalist agitation that often resembles the militance of the earlier movement. Though Lecky, Whiteside and McGee may not consciously have contributed to such a climate, their attitude towards Swift fitted it well. For they emphasized the functional nature of his patriotic reputation, implying if not pointing directly to its continuing relevance for Ireland, but slighting the personal characteristics of the Dean that had loomed so large to British detractors and Irish Unionist writers. Whatever the details of its enthusiastic embellishment, furthermore, the essentials of McGee's Catholic perspective are at one with the non-sectarian and liberal Protestant stances of Whiteside and Lecky. It seems that a consensus was indeed emerging in nationalist opinion towards adoption of Swift as a patriotic ancestor of all Irishmen, and the construction for him of an Irish identity along Young Ireland lines.

Even an Irish Protestant strongly critical of Swift's personality, J.F. Waller, could hint in mid-decade at the attraction this consensus exerted, noting that in the eighteenth century

> his political sins, his faults of temper, his imperious bearing, and his caprices, were almost forgotten in the general sentiment of gratitude, and to this day men remember, not so much his failings and his errors, as his services, his power, and his genius.[82]

The *D.U.M.*, too, was affected, maintaining in a largely adulatory article of 1866 on the Dean that to him 'was committed the charge of cleansing that Augean stable, the eighteenth century; but he could not do so without stirring up a rank, putrescent mass of corruption'; furthermore, 'he was continually fighting with his powerful pen in the cause of Ireland'.[83] The widespread acknowledgement of Swift's high place in literature complemented such efforts, of course, but more ironically, so did the fascination that his personality and career exerted upon generations of disparaging British critics.

With the objectivity of an Irish observer in Britain, William Allingham, contributing to *Fraser's* as 'Patricius Walker' in 1867, sought to explain that fascination in terms such disparagement had seemed to obscure:

> ... Swift's fame is a more conspicuous edifice than could have been built upon his literary performances alone. . . . His strong and peculiar personal character, his distinction, first in the social and literary world of London, and then (much higher) in Irish politics, the interest that belongs to Stella and Vanessa, his position as a church dignitary, which lends so much zest to his humour and to the odd stories and jests reported of him, the terrible eclipse of his intellect, his gloomy death, and the legacy to found a madhouse – all these strike the imagination and impress the memory of mankind. Many have been his predecessors and successors, but Jonathan Swift remains and will remain *the* Dean of St. Patrick's.[84]

The Young Ireland writers and their successors had thus managed, over a quarter-century, to forge an Irish identity for Swift that could appeal to both Protestants and Catholics, channelling and clarifying the vaguer contours of old-fashioned Protestant admiration of him as a patriot and the enduring folk memory of him as a 'character'. An emphasis upon Swift's function, his enduring relevance, as the basis for that identity seemed particularly apt in the later 1860s, as landlord–tenant relations came to the forefront of Irish politics. Yet now also, after more than two decades of appropriation by nationalists, Swift's patriotism was directly challenged from within their ranks. When Swift's *Short View of the State of Ireland* (1727), for instance, was specifically cited as prophetic by Isaac Butt in 1867 and George Sigerson in 1871, they were following a path signposted in the 1830s by Bicheno, Orpen and Francis Mahony.[85] This feature of Swift's identity had also been promoted in the Irish Confederation in 1847 by John Mitchel, but over the ensuing years Mitchel changed his mind almost completely about the Dean, and in his *History of Ireland* (1869), written in America, attacked him with a fury unmatched before the end of the century. For, rather than maintaining the Young Ireland line that Swift's patriotic function granted him enduring relevance and Irish identity, Mitchel had come to the view that the Dean's neglect of Catholic grievances in his time precluded his having 'a broadly national aim'. Hence his patriotism could seem trivial:

> While the Irish Parliament was . . . earnestly engaged in their measures against popish priests, Dean Swift . . . suddenly plunged impetuously into the tumult of Irish politics. His indignation was inflamed to the highest pitch – not by the ferocity of the legislature against Catholics, but by Wood's copper halfpence. The country, he thought, was on the verge of ruin, not by reason of the tempest of intolerance, rapacity, fraud, and cruelty, which raged over it on every side, but by reason of a certain copper coinage. . . .

Mitchel judged from Swift's choice of such 'an occasion, no matter how silly' that the Dean was more a satirist than a patriot. Instead of complementing his patriotism, his literary gifts actually undermined his claim to it: 'any peg would do, to hang his essays upon'. And since 'he opposed English domination over Ireland, yet equally opposed the union of Irishmen to resist it' by ignoring Catholics and persecuting Dissenters, 'the verdict of history must for ever be, that he was neither an English patriot nor an Irish one'.[86] Mitchel's denial of Swift's Irish patriotism thereby challenged the appreciation of his identity that the efforts of Young Ireland – including his own, in its day – had fostered among contemporary Irish people, especially Catholics. Ultimately, however, Mitchel as well had to concede much of the Dean's functional value, in which that appreciation was rooted:

> Yet the tone of independent thought which rings through his inimitable essays, and the high and manly spirit with which he showed Irishmen how to confront unjust power . . . penetrated the character of the whole English colony, and bore fruit long after that unquiet and haughty heart lay at rest. . . .[87]

Mitchel was at pains, then, to deny Swift's Irish identity even while allowing, with a reluctance recalling Thomas Moore's, his function of inspiring later patriotic generations. Compared with Young Ireland's elevation of that function, his was a narrow line. It reflected the majoritarian impulse of his own ideological development, sympathetic to Catholics not *per se*, but because they were the Irish majority. He strongly objected, in fact, to the overtly sectarian attitude, attributed to Paul, Cardinal Cullen of Dublin, 'that there is no Ireland but the Catholic Ireland – the Protestants are not Irish at all'.[88] But Mitchel's viewpoint was obviously liable to sectarian construction, and Fr Thomas Burke, a famous Dominican preacher and Irish nationalist who had much the same attitude, thus took rhetorical ammunition from Mitchel. Burke was prompted in the first instance by J.A. Froude's 1872 history, *The English in Ireland in the Eighteenth Century*, a wholesale assault upon the nationalist historical programme. Forthrightly imperialist, Froude depicted a scene of nearly constant English misgovernment of Ireland, characterized, however, not by oppression but by concession, whether to Catholic backwardness and criminality or Anglo-Irish Protestant patriotic posturing. In this context Swift, by exhorting the Irish to economic self-reliance (however vainly), appeared almost singularly disinterested: 'in the best and noblest sense, an Irish patriot'.[89] Working to an unprecedented degree from state papers, Froude also disclosed more than had been known previously of the government's behaviour in the Wood's halfpence affair in order to underscore his glowing account of Swift as the Drapier. But while such praise of Swift echoes that becoming established in nationalist history, it counted for little in the balance against Froude's antipathy to Catholicism and Irishness in general. Froude's tone would eventually be countered best by Lecky's *History of England in the Eighteenth Century* (1878–92) and that of Ireland drawn from it; but Fr Burke typified the immediate rage of nationalists, attacking Swift in the process. Swift was in fact treated incidentally, in one or two asides, but Burke revealingly extended Mitchel's criticism. Granting nothing at all to Swift's function, he dismissed the Dean's Irish identity outright as vitiated by his personal discomfort with his Irishness. Swift's interests, moreover, were economic, while Burke's concept of Irish identity was sectarian in its essence:

> ... We call Dean Swift a patriot. How little did he ever think, – as great a man as he was – of that oppression ... that beggared and ruined a whole people; that drove them from their land; that drove them from every pleasure in life; that drove them from their country; that maddened them to desperation; and all because they had Irish names and Irish blood; and because they would not give up the faith which their consciences told them was the true one.[90]

Many of the Catholic majority in the nationalist population would have inclined generally to Burke's sectarian view of Irish history – however sharpened it was, like Mitchel's majoritarianism, by trans-Atlantic distance. But in contemporary Ireland neither his nor Mitchel's view specifically of Swift was so widely shared. For Burke had refused to address, and Mitchel had had to concede, the grounds of Swift's functional value to nationalism. These were set forth neatly by two other nationalist historians in these years. Mary Frances Cusack, a Catholic convert and Poor Clare sister, the 'Nun of Kenmare', concentrated on Swift's patriotic singularity:

> A new phase in Irish history was inaugurated by the versatile talents, and strong will in their exercise, which characterized the famous Dr. Jonathan Swift ... [who] in his famous 'Drapier's Letters' told the Government of the day some truths which were more plain than palatable. ... Swift's letters accomplished what the Irish parliament was powerless to effect.

Swift was, moreover, sadly but effectively prophetic in his depiction of rural Ireland:

> He describes the wretched state of the country; but his eloquence was unheeded. He gave ludicrous illustrations of the ignorance of those who governed in regard to those they governed. Unfortunately the state of things which he described and denounced has continued, with few modifications, to the present day.[91]

A.M. Sullivan, on the other hand, hailed Swift's place in a line of Protestant patriots,

> ... men who commenced to utter the words Country and Patriotism. These 'rash' and 'extreme' *doctrinaires* were long almost singular in their views. Wise men considered them insane when they 'raved' of recovering the freedom of parliament ... Nonetheless the so-called doctrinaires grew in popularity. Their leader was the Very Rev. Jonathan Swift, Protestant dean of St. Patrick's. His precursor was William Molyneux. ... Swift took up the doc-

trines and arguments of Molyneux, and made them all-prevalent amongst the masses of the people. . . . Later on – in the middle of the century – Dr. Charles Lucas, a Dublin apothecary, became the leader of the anti-English party.[92]

Neither Cusack nor Sullivan was a disinterested historian, and in the broadness of their strokes, Swift's service to the nationalist historical programme is obvious. For Cusack, writing from a Catholic perspective, what matters about Swift is that a 'new phase' of Irish history opened with his success against the government, by mobilizing public opinion, whereas the (Protestant) parliament failed; and his picture of rural devastation is accurate, indeed prophetic. His uniqueness makes him the more memorable as Ireland's champion. To Sullivan, writing for a less distinctly Catholic audience, Molyneux, Swift and Lucas form a genealogy of nationally minded Protestants specifically defending Ireland's parliament, again by mobilizing public opinion – implicit forebears of nineteenth-century agitation against the Union.

Swift could thus be made to suit conceptions of Irish patriotic history that were either, in essence, Protestant or Catholic, a broadness of appeal generated by Young Ireland in the 1840s. If criticism along the lines of Mitchel or Burke had been voiced against the Young Ireland approach at that time, it might have had a lasting effect on Swift's reputation, at least impeding the promotion of his Irish identity. But by the end of the 1860s that Irish identity, though hardly granted by all, was definitely emerging. Swift's reputation had survived earlier reservations about his opportunism, and others centring on his madness in the late 1840s and 1850s; such reservations would continue to be raised from time to time, but by the 1870s a consensus had indeed arisen in Ireland that he was more properly defined by his achievements than by his defects. The fact of that consensus manifested the success with which Young Ireland had harnessed history for contemporary political use; it reflected the very unity that Swift's own efforts inspired in his time. The practical effect, if a paradoxical one, was to free the influence of Swift from the simple importance of his place in history; that such influence had endured – which Protestants and Catholics alike maintained – was as much a factor in the notion of his Irish identity as his actual achievements in his time.

6

Nationalism and Historicism:
Confirmation and Resistance, 1870–1930

I

In the half-century from the 1870s, while the advance of nationalism quickened the pace of Irish politics toward Independence, the nationalist identity that Young Ireland had fostered for Swift was sustained in the face of both direct and subtle opposition. As pressure for repeal of the Union developed into the Home Rule movement, it acquired institutional cohesion and a disciplined parliamentary party in Westminster; though a force maintained much longer than O'Connell's earlier Repeal agitation, it was itself gradually strained and ultimately overtaken by even more assertive separatist elements. Cultural and politically republican, these were initially distinct, but had allied by the time of the 1916 Rising and were energized by it, bringing forth in turn an independent Irish state, won through armed struggle and negotiation with Britain, and a brief but intense civil war which that state survived. In the context of these developments, which included a shift from Protestant to Catholic leadership of political nationalism, Swift's Irish identity withstood occasional attacks from Catholic nationalist cultural commentators. In Britain, too, Swift's Irish identity was challenged, if much more reservedly and by scholars in history, biography and literary criticism who esteemed his literary eminence more enthusiastically than most earlier British writers in the nineteenth century. With regard to his Irish politics, however, they inclined to an historicist view that granted Swift's achievement in his own time but either disparaged its inspiring viability in contemporary Ireland or displaced it from Irish particularity toward a more general humanitarianism. In treatments of the former kind, Swift's Irish identity is reconfined to history; in those of the latter, which have continued to prevail among British and North American scholars, it has become incidental.

The British resistance to inscribing that identity in the rhetoric of Irish nationalism began about the same time as the Irish one that Mitchel and Fr Burke had pressed, but was subtler and more gradual. At first its shape was indistinct, though certainly, by the end of the 1870s, a marked warming in the British critical climate toward Swift had taken place. There were still only few in 1869 who might have agreed with F.H. Friswell that Swift was a 'wonderful genius', and that his satire, rather than 'nasty', was 'essentially manly and strong' (it dared 'even to point out to women their offensive ways, their want of personal cleanliness').[1] But ten years later, Anthony Trollope spoke for a remarkably diminished number on the other side in denouncing the Dean as one who 'from first to last, was miserable himself, who made others miserable, and who deserved misery' – terms Trollope had borrowed from Thackeray for his biography of the novelist.[2] What emerged in the interval, as Thackeray's grip on English critical perceptions of Swift loosened, was a picture of the Dean conditioned by a better understanding of historical circumstances and a more sophisticated approach to the literary values of satire. With these arose an acceptance of Swift's validity as an Irish patriot and a concomitant recognition of English misrule over Ireland in his time – though not necessarily as something continuing into the later nineteenth century. Even in 1869, D. Laing Purves could characterize the *Drapier's Letters* as an 'exposure of the tyranny and inequality of England's dealings' with Ireland, which 'concluded by not obscurely calling upon the Irish People to assert their independence of England, if the abuses Swift pointed out were not remedied'.[3] The gathering reaction, particularly against Thackeray and Macaulay, is perceptible the next year in reviews by C.H. Pearson and Abraham Haywood[4] and an essay by William Mackay, who suggested that it was Swift's 'touch of madness', rather than 'depravity in natural badness', that accounts for 'the true secret of some chapters of his life, which are sad and strange'.[5] Even Thackeray's disputation of Swift's Irishness – not least on account of his English parentage – seems not to have struck very deep among ordinary Victorian readers. A commentator of 1874 in a popular magazine considered that 'we are so accustomed to think of Swift as an Irishman' that it is 'often forgotten' that he had English parents, though this detracted nothing from his patriotic effectiveness.[6]

The decline in Thackeray's influence is particularly noticeable in the reception of John Forster's 1875 *Life of Swift*, whose scholarly detail prompted a number of reviewers to criticize the factual flimsiness of Swift's earlier detractors, especially Jeffrey, Thackeray and Macaulay.[7] Forster died before completing more than the first volume of the full-length biography he had projected, which thus carried Swift only to 1711, well before he became prominent in Ireland; yet the Dean's patriotic work received at least positive mention in most reviews. None is so favourable, however, as the *Dublin University Magazine*'s, which contrasts sharply with the derogatory, or at least ambivalent, tone of its contributors on Swift a quarter-century earlier.

[Swift,] by the marvellous multiplicity and prodigious power of his writings, reflected honour on the land of his birth, while, by the fearless and successful mannner in which he asserted its rights and defended its interests, he earned a title to its gratitude, which was willingly allowed during the latter part of his life, and ought not to be obliterated by his death.[8]

If the hortatory final clause here falls short of the more prescriptive emphasis that Young Ireland had laid on Swift's function – as the model and inspiration for patriots since his time – it certainly reflects the influence of that emphasis, and the enthusiastic tone of the whole evinces an Irish Protestant gratitude for Forster's scholarly assistance in the critical rehabilitation of the Dean.

Indeed, Forster's critical reception heralded a sporadic debate in Britain about the continuing value for Ireland of Swift's patriotism. In 1878, for instance, Albert D. Vandam, though conceding that Swift had rescued Ireland from the 'absolute thraldom' of England, could not forbear denigrating the Dean's Irish popularity: 'it remains unparalleled up to this day, in a land where the indiscriminate worship of the agitator is, unfortunately, part of the national religion'.[9] Stanley Lane-Poole, on the other hand, took a line on Swift resembling Lecky's version of the Young Ireland position, complementing its emphasis upon the Dean's function with a short patriot line:

> . . . no one can doubt the worth and disinterested sincerity of his work for Ireland . . . the people worshipped him. He taught them that their opinion was a power, that the passive resistance of men's minds could withstand a bad law and turn aside the purpose of a government. He created a public opinion in Ireland, and he guided it. Finally, when it grew strong, he left it to take care of itself, till Grattan and O'Connell came to lead it, in a different way, but towards the same goal of freedom and equal justice.[10]

Lane-Poole's defence of Swift was the more significant for appearing in the early 1880s, when the emergence of the Home Rule movement and the agitation of the Land League were eroding the appeal of Irish nationalism in Britain. In their context, nonetheless, there arose, in Matthew Arnold's words, an 'interest about Ireland which the present state of the country compels even the most unwilling Englishman to feel'. It had prompted Arnold himself to publish in 1881 a collection of Edmund Burke's Irish writings, noting that a century earlier Burke had exposed 'all the causes which have brought Ireland to its present state': English tyranny and mismanagement, and Protestant Ascendancy. Swift received no such specific praise, yet Arnold had introduced the edition by remarking that, like Burke's Irish writings, Swift's had been neglected in Britain, and 'to lose Swift and Burke out of our mind's circle of acquaintance is a loss indeed'.[11] And, the next year, C.G. Walpole, while utterly dismissing Swift's motives, readily granted his function in a genealogy of patriots who 'initiated a line of policy which, under the guidance of pure and single-minded men, was soon to become an irresistible national impulse' – the struggle for legislative independence culminating in 1782.[12]

Whether that struggle the Dean had so inspired had any continuing significance was subtly questioned in a number of biographies of Swift which followed Forster's in the last quarter of the nineteenth century, and gave his Irish career progressively greater positive stress. In 1882 Henry Craik examined the social and political state of Ireland in Swift's time, and vindicated his patriotic writing as prompted by English misgovernment, absentee and rackrenting landlords, and a wretched peasantry driven to thievery and sexual immorality.[13] The historicism of Craik's biography is immediately apparent, manifesting how the British educated classes might accept Swift as a genuine patriot for his time without acknowledging appropriately either his neglect of Catholics or the patriotic function for which Young Ireland had promoted him. Leslie Stephen's biography of Swift for the 'English Men of Letters' series, also in 1882, did consider Swift's continuing Irish relevance. But Stephen proceeded obliquely, hedging enthusiastic praise of Swift's efforts for Ireland with statements such as 'Ireland – I am speaking of a century and a half ago – was the opprobrium of English statesmanship. There Swift had (or thought he had) always before him a concrete example of the basest form of tyranny,' and 'Whether the rousing of the national spirit was any benefit is a question I must leave to others.'[14] Such sly disclaimers undercut the value of contemporary Irish nationalism, while allowing the possibility that Swift had influenced its development. On the other hand, Stephen argued forthrightly that Swift regarded Catholics 'with a sincere compassion for their misery and a bitter resentment against their oppressors', and was more direct than Craik about the neglectful nature of English government, 'not intentionally cruel but absolutely selfish'.[15] Thus, rather than validating the Dean's enduring significance in Irish politics, Stephen took the historicist stance of simply endorsing the validity of his patriotic motives. Pointing to the overstatements in Swift's patriotic rhetoric, for example, he yet stressed its sincerity, and even attributed Swift's madness to rage at injustice.

Dr J.C. Bucknill had already, at the beginning of 1882, published a more scientific diagnosis of Swift's apparent madness as Ménière's disease, a finding that has remained substantially unchallenged since.[16] This had appeared too late for mention by Craik or Stephen, and indeed, as a scholarly article in a medical journal rather than a monograph like Sir William Wilde's *Closing Years of Dean Swift's Life*, it had no similar provocative effect. John Churton Collins, however, summarized Bucknill's diagnosis in concluding a lengthy, two-part review of Craik's and Stephen's books for the *Quarterly Review*, which was itself expanded to a biography a few years later.[17] Collins's was by far the most notable of the reviews of Craik or Stephen (though Edward Dowden on the latter takes the palm for oddity with an account of his meeting Swift's ghost),[18] and he found neither book very satisfactory. Craik, he thought, lacked 'precision and grasp', while Stephen was seriously inadequate in his understanding of the Irish conditions from which Swift's patriotic writings issued.[19] Hence the review, and ultimately Collins's biography, provides details which place the Dean in a very favourable light. His emphasis upon English misgovernment in Swift's time, though, did not extend to attributing to the Dean the inspiration for contemporary Irish nationalism. His hesitancy about such continuing influence seems derived from his antipathy, not to Swift's motives, but to the Dean's intellectual positions in general. For, as he concluded his own book in 1893, 'there is probably no writer of equal power and eminence in whose judgements and conclusions, in whose precepts and teaching, the instincts and experience of progressive humanity will find so little to corroborate'.[20] Instead, Swift is immortalized by his literary style, and by his efforts for Ireland in his time.

II

The historicism that during the 1880s was enabling a readier British reception for Swift's eighteenth-century Irish patriotism had a counterpart in Ireland itself, meanwhile, as concern about his disregard of Catholics resurfaced. The consensus behind Young Ireland's derivation of his Irish identity from his patriotic function was strained by tension between Protestant Unionist sentiment and largely Catholic support for Home Rule and the Land League; this tension despite the nationalist leadership of Charles Stewart Parnell, a Protestant himself. In this context the link between Swift's Irish identity and his function became, for some Catholic writers, strained as well. The Catholic convert and old Repealer O'Neill Daunt, for instance, who had welcomed Lecky's *The Leaders of Public Opinion in Ireland* in 1862, hailed the patriot Swift in 1883 for having 'boldly vindicated the constitutional independence of his country'. Now, however, he also maintained that the Dean's Anglican sympathies demonstrated 'how connection with an alien establishment can vitiate the mind and impair the consistency of even the greatest patriot'.[21] W.A. O'Conor took a more complicated line, denying Swift any love of Ireland or sense of justice that comprehended 'the persecuted Catholics', and indeed dwelling upon his neglect of them. Nevertheless, in the Wood affair Swift 'threw himself into the ignoble contest that flickered around him, and raised it by his genius to the magnitude of a national struggle'; he wrote for Protestants out of a concern for political effectiveness, 'well knowing that all power and all responsibility was with them'; he was aware that the peasantry were 'rack-rented to rags and starvation, not by England, but by their landlords'; and his victory over Wood was momentous mainly for 'the tendency to union between Catholics and Protestants, and the bolder spirit of independence that had been developed in the course of the contest'.[22] O'Conor's was a valiant attempt to square a sectarian circle, a means of accommodating objections to Swift's Irish identity such as those of Mitchel and Fr Burke a decade earlier, while still remaining on the Dean's side because of his function. For a liberal Protestant such as Emily Lawless, it was simpler to adopt the standard Young Ireland line almost completely, readily admitting Swift's defects of motive but concentrating upon his success, for 'High Churchman as he was, vehement anti-papist as he was, he became . . . beyond all question the most popular man in Ireland, and his name was ever afterwards upon the lips of all who aspired to promote the best interests and prosperity of the country.'[23] As a Unionist, however, Lawless would not have included among Ireland's 'best interests' what O'Conor deemed the 'spirit of independence'.

Such reservations about the continuing value of Swift's patriotic function, whether cultivated as historicist doubts by British commentators antipathetic to contemporary Irish nationalism, or troubling Irish Catholic writers dealing with his neglect of Catholics, were still mainly variations in emphasis. In both countries, acceptance of that function itself as genuine had gained critical momentum, a fact which on its own served a nationalist end. 'It has been asserted over and over again that Swift had no real love for the country of his birth,' noted J.H. McCarthy in a nationalist history of Ireland in 1883, adding, 'whether he loved Ireland or no is little to the purpose, for he did her very sterling service'.[24] It was from Swift's effectiveness in uniting the Irish people, after all, that Young Ireland had drawn inspiration, a point marked fittingly by the reappearance of Charles Gavan Duffy, who with Thomas Davis had argued this in the early years of *The Nation*. Duffy had quit Ireland in the 1850s, and soon became prominent in Australian politics, earning a knighthood in the process and demonstrating in his own career how fervent Irish nationalism could be combined with imperial loyalty. One of the few Young Ireland notables surviving into the 1880s, he published *A Bird's-Eye View of Irish History* in 1882 and dealt with Swift very much as though unchanged by the years. When Swift wrote the *Drapier's Letters*, for instance, 'the nation took fire. . . . For the first time, men of all parties, and both religions, were of one mind', and success resulted even though Swift 'was only fair to the Catholics by fits and starts, never indeed gave them any help to redress their special wrongs, and . . . cordially detested Protestant Dissenters'.[25]

It is implicit in Duffy's consideration that the Dean succeeded in uniting the people in the Wood affair in good part because he addressed the question of Ireland's constitutional relationship with England. For Duffy it was equally important that, even before Swift, Molyneux had raised this question, since in his review of eighteenth-century Ireland the venerable tactic of invoking the patriot line is renewed subtly to suggest the organic development of Irish nationalism towards its contemporary manifestation in the Home Rule movement. Thus Duffy represents a link between the Young Ireland treatment of Swift and his usefulness to its Home Rule successors. And even as other nationalist historians continued to stress Swift's Irish identity as 'the only representative of the Irish nation who kept his lamp of patriotism burning through the hours of its deepest darkness',[26] a Home Rule politician emphasized instead his place in the primarily Protestant genealogy of nationalism. Protestant support seemed the more necessary in 1886, when the prime minister, W.E. Gladstone, depending for his majority upon Irish nationalists, adopted Home Rule as government policy, only to be defeated by the desertion of Unionists in his own party. Parnell himself never claimed Swift as his ideological ancestor, but among his Catholic lieutenants John Redmond made a special attempt to convince Protestants of their nationalist heritage by outlining Swift's part in it. Speaking on 'Irish Protestants and Home Rule' at the Rotunda in Dublin in 1886, Redmond repeated the Young Ireland line on Swift and the overarching concept of a Protestant patriotic genealogy. Though no advocate of the Catholic Irish, in the Wood affair the Dean 'united the people of all creeds at his back and in the end he carried his point', was a forerunner of the patriots of 1782, and taught the people 'their first lessons in self-reliance'.[27]

The guide Redmond chose to acknowledge here was not Duffy, however, but Lecky, from whose The Leaders he quoted. The historian's reservations about modern nationalism had been ripening for years; while he continued to fault English policy in Swift's time, and to admire Ireland's Protestant patriots of the eighteenth century, he had come to see the Union in his own day in a vastly more positive light than the disturbingly democratic tendencies of Parnellism. In a forceful letter to The Times of 13 January 1886 he clarified his opposition to Home Rule, prompting a run on copies of the 1871 edition of The Leaders. Sales of the book had been languishing; now it was eagerly sought by nationalists keen to quote the old, apparently pro-nationalist Lecky against the new, and the stock was quickly exhausted.[28] Without adverting to Lecky's now forthright Unionism, Redmond cited him as an admirer of Swift's function as the creator of public opinion, and implicitly thereby the harbinger of constitutional nationalism, so suggesting at once the genealogy and the justice of Home Rule. The next year Gladstone himself, in an essay explaining his advocacy of Home Rule, after this had ruptured his party and brought down his government, acknowledged Lecky and Duffy's Bird's-Eye View among his influences, and considered that Swift 'for the first time called into existence a public opinion flowing from and representing Ireland as a whole'.[29] Gladstone also reasserted the genealogy of patriotism, with Swift as Molyneux's heir and Lucas the heir of both, but in a form designed to stress the persistence of Irish grievances rather than that of Protestant patriotic spirit, as Redmond had done.

As the Home Rule movement cooled somewhat under a Conservative British government, John Bowles Daly published a collection of Swift's Irish writings from the period 1720–34, with an introduction that accommodated Catholic reservations about Swift's Irish identity by adapting historicism to the Young Ireland emphasis upon Swift's function. The Dean was enduringly relevant: the creator of public opinion in Ireland, he 'gave the Press the wonderful position it holds now'; he was a prophet in that his 'pictures of the state of the country present curious parallels to what we find today'. But with an apparently historicist focus on Swift in his own time rather than on his part in the nationalist tradition, Daly adjusted the standard Young Ireland apologetic for the Dean's neglect of Catholic grievances. Unlike O'Conor a few years earlier, he acknowledged neither obliviousness nor bigotry on Swift's part, arguing instead that 'he was the last man who, from his connection with a discarded Tory party, could have taken action with any effect' on behalf of the Catholics. Quite arrestingly, moreover, Daly recalls the Catholic-nationalist aesthetic of D.F. MacCarthy, his predecessor of forty years earlier, in promoting Swift's Irish identity, by drawing a parallel between Swift's experience and the condition of Ireland, which Daly mediated through Christ:

> endowed with heaven-born genius and the pride of an insulted god . . . Swift, like his great Master, was moved by compassion for the multitude. He knew what poverty and scorn were, even at an age when the mind expands and the path of life is sown with generous hopes.

Further, Daly indirectly downplayed Swift's part in a patriotic genealogy by exalting his uniqueness as an Irish saviour, for no agitation since the Wood controversy 'has been so immediately and completely successful. The whole power of the English government was found ineffectual to cope with the opposition that had been roused, and marshalled by one man.'[30] Yet Swift had been neglected. Daly contended that his collection of Swift's Irish tracts was necessary because they 'are now little studied by the people or their representatives; nonetheless, if carefully examined, they will be found useful in throwing light upon the unsolved problem[s]', both constitutional and social.[31] The putative neglect was, of course, overstated; stressing Swift's Irish identity, Daly had overtly ignored the process, begun over a generation since, of establishing it in the nationalist tradition.

The rhetoric of neglect was also useful to the sixteen-year-old William Rooney, embarking on his brief career as a pioneer of the literary revival with an address to the Irish Fireside Club in 1889, who complained that few Irish people 'have studied the beauties' of Swift and other Irish writers of the eighteenth and nineteenth centuries.[32] Yet concerns such as those of Daly and Rooney may have had some element of justice as well, in that the Young Ireland insistence upon Swift's function in nationalist history could obscure even some of the writings which had informed that function. Hence the historians W.K. Sullivan in 1888 and John Ferguson in the late 1890s cited Swift mainly as a prophetic observer of Irish rural desolation, all but ignoring his role as the Drapier.[33] Nor after decades of nationalist appropriation of Swift (however accommodated to Protestant sensibilities), were Unionists agreed upon his place in history. On the one hand, perhaps attempting to

counter that nationalist appropriation, Standish O'Grady in 1894 hailed
Swift's service to the Irish gentry. They were 'wild and irresponsible' when
Swift delivered his patriotic message, which aroused in them 'an angry spirit
towards England', but their considerable improvement late in the century
owed much to his efforts.[34] On the other hand, the Duke of Argyll in 1893
and T. Dunbar Ingram in 1900 reviewed eighteenth-century Irish history
while hardly mentioning Swift at all.[35]

III

More than offsetting the inadequacies of such treatments, however, most
scholarly and popular commentaries during the 1890s, in both Britain and
Ireland, accepted that Swift's patriotism had an enduring function in Irish
nationalism, though not all to the same degree. Their variety ranged from the
renewed enthusiasm of Swift's veteran advocate, O'Neill Daunt, in 1890, to
shades of hesitancy in biographies by James Hay in 1891, and by J.C. Collins
and Gerald Moriarty in 1893. These were most pronounced in the latter two,
who took a hard line on Swift's character and, in Moriarty's case, on the
inconsistency between his patriotism in general and his defence of the Anglican establishment. But Richard Ashe King's extensive account of *Swift in
Ireland* in 1895 and W. O'Connor Morris's survey of Irish history in 1896
reinforced the by then longstanding Young Ireland line on the Dean's Irish
identity as deriving from his function. William Rooney was more succinct,
admiring Swift as attracted to Gaelic literature and as a patriot 'of whom we
can be proud'.[36] Of course, only O'Neill Daunt and William Rooney, among
those listed, could be said to have addressed an Irish popular audience. The
others, mainly English and Anglo-Irish (by now a term in common use for
Irish Protestants of the middle and upper classes), aimed at a more lettered
readership: the literary and historical establishment was endorsing Swift as a
pioneer Irish nationalist, however reservedly, as well as a literary giant. The
closest parallels are Swift's canonization as model patriot and British classic
in the 1760s, and again, at the hands of Scott and others, in the decades
following the Union. Now, from the perspective of the 1890s, he could
appear a herald of Home Rule.

The demurrals from this consensus are important, nonetheless, for exhibiting the potential of lingering historicist and Catholic doubts about such an
anticipatory identity for Swift. W.E.H. Lecky's study of eighteenth-century
Ireland in 1892 expanded the historicism of Swift's British biographers a
decade before and gave it a Unionist imprint. Developing implications latent
in the early editions of his *Leaders*, Lecky here confined Swift's patriotism to
the context of Irish national advance under Protestant guidance during the
period.[37] Unstinting in pointing out British oppression, yet refraining from
finding it paralleled in modern Irish circumstances, his approach preserved

the appearance of objectivity while subtly shifting the basis of the question whether Swift was an ancestor of modern nationalism away from Swift, where it had long stood, and toward the shakier issue of the actual benefits such nationalism offered to contemporary Ireland. This was a very sophisticated Unionist historiography, beside which the Conservative politician A.J. Balfour's disparagement of Swift's patriotic motivation as merely the desire to irritate the English government seems crudely old-fashioned.[38] At the same time, the popular nationalist historians Joseph Glynn in 1887 and P.W. Joyce in 1893 were also more measured in their notices of Swift's patriotism.[39] Underlying their restraint, and especially their disinclination to see Swift as a model for later patriots, there recurs the longstanding Catholic suspicion that Swift was insufficiently Irish. Even as Lecky's nostalgia for Protestant leadership was hardening into Unionist reaction against its absence in contemporary Irish politics, their reservations about Swift's Irish identity are perceptible in a related and broader light, appearing when such leadership was coming to the fore in Irish culture instead.

Home Rule, stalled for a time by Gladstone's defeat in the House of Commons in 1886, gathered strength anew and passed that House in 1893, when Gladstone was again prime minister, only to be defeated in the Lords. But in the meantime the movement was shattered in 1890–1 by the revelation of Parnell's affair with Mrs O'Shea and his subsequent political collapse and death. Nationalist Ireland's last Protestant leader, he could be perceived as martyred by Irish Catholic bishops and English politicians, and a split between Parnellites and the majority in the Home Rule movement persisted for the rest of the decade. In the meantime, Protestants with more literary credentials, foremost among them W.B. Yeats and Douglas Hyde, promoted cultural movements that would ultimately give Irish nationalism a deeper definition than political separatism or religious majoritarianism had lent it previously. The Young Ireland definition of Swift's Irish identity, in terms of a popular political function that anticipated and inspired their own similar efforts – a definition acknowledged or even embraced (with occasional reservations) by the British and Irish intellectual establishment by the mid-1890s – would figure only peripherally in the early efforts of those Irish cultural movements. Yeats, for instance, having refused to consider *Gulliver's Travels* part of the national literature in 1895,[40] only hinted at a link between Swift and those efforts when reviewing King's *Swift in Ireland* in 1896. He exalted Swift for 'a more intense nature, a more living temperament, than any of his contemporaries. He was as near a supreme man as that fallen age could produce.' Yeats praised King's study as 'a beginning of that scholarly criticism of men and things which is needed in Ireland even more perhaps than creative literature'; and Swift himself exemplified the service literature provides, which in Ireland comprised more than 'to give us a good opinion of ourselves by glorifying our past or our future'.[41] Yet beyond this review, until much later in his own life, Yeats left undeveloped Swift's potential for

Ireland's cultural resurgence. Alluding to Swift a few months afterwards in a story, for instance, he simply characterized the Dean as a great hater – perhaps a portent for a theme central to Yeats's own old age, but without a wider Irish significance here than to pose a contrast with the loving Christ.[42] And Swift's cultural potential is only dimly apparent in the passing praises of William Rooney and the university student Arthur Clery, who were rare among Irish Catholics in recognizing Swift as a specifically Irish cultural figure.[43]

Nonetheless, the acceptance of Swift's Irish identity by the literary-historical establishment and the continuing nationalist alignment in his favour comported with the assertiveness of Protestants in the cultural scene – including Yeats and King – in lending an Anglo-Irish tinge to the Irish 1890s. The Celtic Twilight could seem, indeed, a golden Ascendancy sunset, threatening to diminish the Irish identity of Gaelic and Catholic Ireland – the identity that the language revival movement (paradoxically led by a Protestant, Douglas Hyde) was spurring to articulation. Because Swift had never identified himself with that Ireland in the eighteenth century, his acquisition of a nationalist political identity in the nineteenth century betokened just such a threat to D.P. Moran, a strident proponent of cultural nationalism, at the turn of the twentieth. Writing in 1899, Moran's immediate complaint was that a habit of mind at root foreign to Ireland had long flourished in the country; he termed it an 'Anglo-Irish parade of sentimental Paleism'.[44] In its manifestation as Anglo-Irish patriotism, he focused on Swift and his influence, which had nearly extinguished the Gaelic soul of Ireland:

> The spirit of Molyneux and Swift . . . the spirit which 99 out of every 100 of us still look up to as our polar star, was the death of those elements of the Irish race that could have defied the attacks that were to come. It started the spirit of English civilization and English progress in our midst, and the Irish race, ceasing to think for itself, has persistently mistaken this for the spirit of the Irish nation.

Swift himself was a particular irritant:

> . . . that great Irishman, as we love to call him, who had not a drop of Irish blood in his veins, no Irish characteristics, and an utter contempt for the entire pack of us. . . . This Englishman, whom, with characteristic latter-day Irish cringe we claim for ourselves, became a popular hero of the Irish people.[45]

Moran anticipated, in order to reject, the charge of racism, expressing pride in those Protestants 'who dreamt and worked for an independent country' even while stressing their proper subordination to the Gael, for 'the foundation of Ireland is the Gael, and the Gael must be the element that absorbs'.[46]

Moran's overall thesis is not so much crudely racist as anti-cosmopolitan. Like Hyde's Gaelic League, he was raising a barricade against insidious anglicization. But the Gaelic League in these years fostered a cultural prin-

ciple for uniting the Irish people, with the language and its associated customs as that bulwark. It could attract Protestants, even Unionists, because it
addressed social and political issues covertly at best. Moran's principle, on the
other hand, promoted the Gael as a sociological construct for Irish identity.[47]
Latently more powerful than a simply cultural construct, this could not only
offset a lingering Catholic deference to Ascendancy but parry as well the
more recent, urban-based, cosmopolitan thrust of a cultural movement in
which Protestants were prominent, a contemporary analogue to the long-
accepted notion that Irish patriotism had Protestant ancestry. Instead, he
thought the strength of anglicization could only be countered by thorough
gaelicization: 'the Gael must be the element that absorbs'. Moran's concept
of Irish Ireland as outlined in the article is essentially sectarian, a sociological
gloss upon the rawer sectarianism exemplified by Fr Burke a generation
earlier, tempered by a majoritarianism like John Mitchel's. And Moran was as
unbending as Burke on Swift. By contrast, an anonymous reviewer of a
collection of Swift's letters for a Unionist newspaper in Dublin the same year
would maintain that 'for all his cheap and noisy patriotism, Swift did not love
Ireland nor its people', and then add that 'at the same time, the Dean could
see that much of the wretchedness of the country came from English misgovernment and over-taxation'.[48] Separately, these were propositions Moran
could have embraced, but he would have rejected the reviewer's concessive
link as an equivocation typical of 'enlightened' Unionists – such as Lecky –
and mainstream Home Rulers alike.

IV

By disputing the Protestant genealogy of patriotism and Swift's own Irishness,
Moran knew, he was challenging a cast of mind well set among nationalists.
And while the 'Irish Irelandism' he articulated was indeed influential among
the cultural and political associations that blossomed at the fringes of the old
Home Rule consensus, Swift was as yet only incidental to these: even Yeats
had only in passing assigned any relevance to the Dean. Unlike either Moran
or Yeats, however, Arthur Griffith saw the possibility of harnessing Swift's
Irish identity to the task of enriching nationalism, since Swift had espoused
economic self-sufficiency as much as he had promoted Irish political
assertiveness against British arrogance. Griffith launched *The United Irishman*
in 1899 as an Irish Ireland weekly, with his friend William Rooney, whose
influence upon Griffith endured beyond his early death a few years later.[49]
Rooney had always admired Swift, and the new paper's opening editorial
stressed the Dean's continuing relevance to their brand of nationalism:

> To be perfectly plain, we believe that when Swift wrote to the whole people
> of Ireland, 170 years ago, that by the law of God, of nature and of nations they

have a right to be as free a people as the people of England, he wrote commonsense. . . .[50]

As ardent in promoting the language revival as Rooney or even Hyde, Griffith continued after Rooney's death in 1901 as strong an Irish Irelander as Moran. But he had developed a deeper interest in political economy than they, and his emerging advocacy of dual monarchy on the Hungarian model lent conceptual substance to his admiration of Swift. That model embodied principles which, for Griffith, underlay Swift's patriotism: that Ireland was by right a nation equal with Britain; and that a government derived its legitimacy from the consent of the governed. Though Griffith was far from the first to discover these Lockean principles in Swift, the Dean's importance to nationalists had heretofore lain more insistently in his rhetoric of opposition to British policy and his success in rallying the Irish people to unity with that rhetoric: the practicalities of patriotic action mattered more than the specific doctrines at its base. But Griffith, undeterred by Moran's attack on Swift a few months after *The United Irishman* began, also found occasion often during his journalistic career – in that paper, in *Sinn Fein*, its successor from 1906, and in other writings – to celebrate Swift's anti-British rhetoric and cite him in versions of the patriot line. These groupings could be casual or substantial, restricted to common eighteenth-century citations of him with Molyneux and Lucas,[51] or to pairings with later patriots: of Ireland's many leaders between Shane O'Neill and Parnell, for instance, 'there were only two England thoroughly feared, and who could manoeuvre effectively the small resources of Ireland against the great resources of her enemy – Swift and Davis'.[52] Griffith would even pair Swift with his posthumous antagonist, John Mitchel.[53]

Like Thomas Davis, then, Griffith found Swift valuable as a precursor for his kind of nationalism. Much further to the left, James Connolly preferred to commemorate the Dean for describing the misery of the Irish poor, rather than as a patriotic ancestor, though Home Rulers like Justin McCarthy and Fr E.A. D'Alton attested amply to his continuing significance for mainstream nationalism.[54] In Britain at the turn of the century, moreover, only a very few voices, such as that of A.J. Balfour in 1897, still disputed his patriotism in terms characteristic of half a century earlier. Goldwin Smith's attack on Swift's reputation in 1861, for instance, fell in with the temper then current in British criticism. When resuming the offensive in 1905 to promote the Union as Ireland's best chance for prosperity and social advancement, he took on a new edge, impugning Swift not only as a self-interested 'artificer of discord' but one who profited from the Penal Laws. In the process he seems almost to echo D.P. Moran:

> Swift's Drapier's Letters are monuments of his genius for pamphleteering, his intense malice, and his freedom from the restraints of truth. . . . Their author did not mention among the evils of an English connection that he and the

members of his State Church were enabled by the support of the British power to get their feet upon the necks of four-fifths of the Irish people and to wring from the starving Catholic the income of the dean of St. Patrick. The letters ranged far beyond the immediate occasion, and appealed strongly to the growing desire for independence, which we may be pretty sure that Swift, had he been nominated by Bolingbroke to an English bishopric, would have fiercely opposed.[55]

The historicist approach to Swift that Lecky in 1892 had validated for Unionism, on the other hand, captured the scholarly mainstream with Temple Scott's edition of the *Prose Works* (1897–1908). This was a monument of late nineteenth-century scholarship, finally displacing Walter Scott's as the standard edition of Swift's prose, and for it Lecky himself provided a biographical introduction, expanded from the section on Swift in *The Leaders of Public Opinion in Ireland*.[56] As in previous versions of this essay, Lecky found British rule at fault for Irish shortcomings in the early eighteenth century, and thereby vindicated Swift's patriotism while acknowledging his neglect of Catholic grievances. Like his historical treatment in 1892, however, he combined such explicit ancient blame of England with implicit modern exculpation, thereby reducing the usefulness his essay might have continued to offer to contemporary nationalism.

Temple Scott's own introduction to the sixth volume of the edition, containing the *Drapier's Letters*, complemented Lecky's case for Swift as patriot by disparagingly conceding its usefulness to modern nationalism. For to Scott, English misgovernment of Ireland in Swift's day had fostered a 'dangerous spirit of resentment and rebellion which is the outcome of the sense of injustice' and which had 'served, even to this day, to give vitality to those associations that have from time to time arisen in Ireland for the object of realizing that country's self-government'. Conveying in his tone little enough sympathy with nationalism, Scott subtly discounted the aptness of paralleling modern Irish conditions with those of Swift's day, his own historicism locking Swift into the past in a scholarly attempt to justify the Dean's point of view in his own time. Thus 'the injustice from which Ireland suffered was a fact', and accounted alike for the oppressiveness of her ruling class and the contemptibly slavish morals of those it oppressed; and even if one granted Swift's frighteningly passionate intensity in responding to these perceptions, 'it was not the mad man that made the passion; it was the passion that made the man mad'.[57] But if the historicist view of Swift denied him to modern nationalism, the very subtlety of the procedure diminished its utility to contemporary Unionism. It would colour British critical views of Swift for decades to come, but within Ireland it provoked little attention or debate. Nationalists who admired Swift seem not to have perceived Temple Scott's treatment of the patriot Dean, any more than they had the later Lecky's, as a threat to their own politicization of Swift's identity. The historicist approach, by validating the historical Swift, could actually serve their ends, inasmuch as nationalists sensed history as continuous, or at best evolutionary (as invoking the patriot line would suggest), rather than as compartmentalized.

V

The task of fixing Swift's Irish identity among nationalists in the later nineteenth century, as indeed that of his British scholarly rehabilitation at the hands of John Forster and his often historicist successors, was assisted by growing favour for the Dean among popular writers. Even the story of Stella and Vanessa, long repeated in the nineteenth century as evidence of Swift's churlishness, if not utter inhumanity, with his final years of madness lending it a fitting moral, had begun to attract more positive sentimental attention. Taking the lead in this shift were accounts by women, or at least addressed to a female audience. As early as 1874, the anonymous writer in the *Englishwoman's Domestic Magazine*, hailing Swift's patriotism, could celebrate Stella without demonizing him.[58] In 1891 Lady Wilde – in youth the poet 'Speranza' of *The Nation*, who married Sir William Wilde and now, like her son Oscar, lived in London – gave a highly coloured and somewhat fanciful version of the triangular relationship without accusing Swift of any more than an inability to ascend from the most affectionate friendship with Stella to amorous passion.[59] A few years later, the Irish playwright John Todhunter, by contrast, perceived the same failure not as an incapacity but as Swift's 'tyranny' in restraining his own 'instinct'.[60] Todhunter's observation was a passing comment in a play, and indeed from the beginning of the twentieth century the story of the lovelorn ladies and the proud clergyman became the subject of a drama in its own right. In 1850, *The Times*'s review of Leon de Wailly's 1846 novel in French, *Stella and Vanessa*, newly translated by Lady Duff-Gordon, had commended the creative possibilities of the story for an original novel in English.[61] The hint was long ignored, however, and it was as drama in English that the tale was to draw a lasting audience – de Wailly himself having made a French play of it in 1862.[62] Perhaps this was inevitable, since the comparative paucity of historical data makes it difficult to sustain the plot of a novel without a great sacrifice of accuracy, as de Wailly's novel itself shows. On the other hand, the episodic nature of the story and the potential of Swift's own rhetoric for witty or oratorical effects lent themselves to dramatic treatment. But the antipathetic view of Swift's relationship with both women, traditional from Jeffrey's time until the last quarter of the nineteenth century, would have rendered the story a simple melodrama. With the changing understanding of Swift's part in this story, complementing the more positive reception of Swift generally in British circles, it acquired more of the elements of a romantic tragedy.

It was to this genre that Eveleen Bell's *The Dean of St Patrick's* aspired, though it actually reaches little beyond melodrama. A play in four acts published in 1903, but apparently never performed, it follows Swift from his bitter subordination in Sir William Temple's household, through his rise to fame and favour with Queen Anne's Tory ministry in London, to his deanship in Dublin.[63] For the purposes of the play, however, this is less the path of Swift's career than the course of his amours with Stella and Vanessa. His affection for Stella is depicted in the first act, set in Moor Park; the second, in London, reveals Vanessa's passion for him; the last two bring the ladies into confrontation with each other, ultimately in apparent reconciliation. The future Lady Bell, a prolific popular writer, used the still commonly accepted marriage of Swift and Stella as her dramatic fulcrum, presenting Vanessa as driven to distraction by her suspicion of it, and to death by Swift's finally acknowledging it, with Stella present and rushing to her aid. The relationship of sorts between Stella and Vanessa is Bell's only serious departure from received fact, but her structure is wooden and her dialogue too often silly, perhaps reflecting the influence of Lady Wilde's 1891 essay, which sketched a broadly similar treatment in apparent hope that a novelist might develop it. Given Lady Wilde's Young Ireland background, it is surprising that she gives Swift's patriotism only the merest glance; Bell doesn't mention it at all, treating Ireland mainly as the setting for the final two acts, and concluding before the Wood controversy erupted in 1724. But Bell's handling of the Stella and Vanessa story does present Swift's dilemma in a human light, giving him something of the quality of a tragic hero flawed in character by his procrastination in choosing finally between the two women (despite the marriage) until it is too late to save Vanessa's life.

Bell's play draws upon fact and tradition, incorporating into the dialogue passages from the *Journal to Stella* and relaying material from often-repeated anecdotes, which to an extent balances the fanciful climax featuring the three principals together as Vanessa learns of Swift's marriage. There is no such balance in the next Swift play, also titled *The Dean of St Patrick's*, by G. Sidney Paternoster, which was actually produced in 1913 at the Abbey Theatre in Dublin. Though it similarly focuses on the Stella–Vanessa story and neglects Swift's emergence as an Irish patriot, it mixes characters, dates and events in search of dramatic effect. Paternoster's play was never published and no copy exists in the surviving Abbey archive, but the Lord Chamberlain's collection in the British Library preserves a typescript of the work as performed in 1923 at the Vaudeville Theatre, London. Headed '"Jonathan Swift" Dean of St Patrick's', this typescript accords with reviewers' descriptions of the play produced at the Abbey a decade earlier; the quotation marks around Swift's name, with none around his title, suggest that the 1913 script was simply recycled for the single matinee performance in London in 1923.[64] Paternoster, a London journalist who died in 1925, seems to have left no other plays.

When he had submitted his *Dean of St Patrick's* to the Abbey Theatre in 1912, W.B. Yeats, as a director of the company, had read and admired it; directed by Lennox Robinson, it was the first new drama performed by the Abbey's second company while the main one toured North America. Once Yeats saw the play, however, he thought it merely 'commercial drama' and Paternoster himself 'a typical London hack'.[65] But most Dublin reviewers treated it more gently: the *Irish Times*, for instance, noted that 'the charm of the literary subject is heightened by the free weaving of several authentic utterances of the characters with the dialogue'.[66] Only two reviews were at all negative: Arthur Griffith's *Sinn Fein* condemning it as undistinguished and sentimental, while *The Irish Citizen*, a women's suffrage paper, more mildly noticed that the play 'smells over much of the lamp and strains unduly after effect'.[67] The stage-Irish dialogue Paternoster gives Swift's servants at Laracor in the first act is certainly an example of such straining, as are Swift's relegation, in the second act, to the deanship of St Patrick's to keep him from obstructing Bolingbroke's plan to bring in the Pretender, and in the third, Vanessa's confrontation of Swift and Stella in the church as they prepare for their wedding. Paternoster was readier than Bell to employ melodramatic effects, such as an undertone of madness, from fear of which the Dean is unwilling to enter into a normal marriage. Stella, furthermore, as *The Irish Citizen* remarked, 'is oversentimentalised, while Vanessa emerges from Mr. Paternoster's crucible as a shrewish little minx'.[68] The character of Swift that results, though not so misanthropic as the earlier nineteenth-century picture, is yet that of a man embittered and dreading madness, a flatter and less complex portrait than Bell's of a decade before.

Yet both plays, whatever their artistic failings, made for a more human picture of Swift than had been common in the nineteenth century. And though neither Paternoster's nor Bell's seems to have been written with an Irish audience in mind, and neither even alludes to his patriotism, the positive tenor of most reviews would suggest that Dublin playgoers were receptive to the presentation of the tragic Swift that Paternoster, at least, gave them. Their acceptance was a portent of the literary direction in which Swift's Irish identity would develop in later years, when Yeats realized the potential, and successors saw new values, in what that identity might offer Irish society in an independent state. Their achievement connected Swift as never before to the character of popular anecdote, and enabled his identity to broaden well beyond the patriotic function given value by nationalist politics, as nationalism itself, having gained the better part of its objective, slipped into history. But in the troubled decade before Independence, it was still that function which the final generation of nationalist writers would find most evocative in Swift.

VI

In Britain, the scholarly authority of Temple Scott's edition of the *Prose Works* had elevated Lecky's, and his own, historicist validation of Swift's patriotism, which would take a further development before that decade ended. The distinction between this and the Irish nationalist case for Swift's identity, however, unremarked in Ireland at the time, becomes all the clearer in the emphasis given to his inspirational value in nationalist commentary and propaganda during the crisis in British–Irish relations between 1912 and 1922. Arthur Griffith had been the most urgent in sounding that note since the turn of the century, so identifying Swift with the ideals of Sinn Fein that the Irish literary historian and editor D.J. O'Donoghue was tempted to title an article of 1912 on the Dean, 'Jonathan Swift, Sinn Feiner and Cattle Driver'. O'Donoghue's essay is actually a rejoinder to D.P. Moran's criticism of Swift in 1899 as a patriot unrepresentatively Protestant and impurely motivated. As a propagandist, O'Donoghue is less heated and cleverer than Moran, whose Irish Ireland clothes he steals on Swift's behalf:

> I know that English writers, historians and biographers are always asserting that the great satirist was not an Irishman, that he hated Ireland and her people, and that if he did raise his voice against England at all it was solely in the interests of the English settlers. This is a constant and favourite declaration from those who do not like to admit the claim of Ireland to Swift, and it has often been echoed by Irish writers, to whom Swift's work can only be unfamiliar. I am surprised that even Englishmen can hold such a view, but it is quite remarkable that Irish students of history should so readily accept so absurd and unwarrantable a theory. It is so far from the truth and the facts that one might more reasonably take the other extreme view, and say that Swift was fanatically anti-English and an out-and-out Irish-Irelander.[69]

O'Donoghue was, of course, exaggerating to make his case, describing as still dominant the view of Swift fostered by Thackeray and Macaulay over half a century earlier, while ignoring the weight of commentary more favourable to Swift's patriotism which had long since superseded it in Britain. But O'Donoghue could rely on the greater celebrity of Thackeray and Macaulay than that of their successors, and the exaggeration enabled him to refute Moran the more emphatically. 'To stand by Ireland whenever the question is one between this country and England is not a bad definition of an Irishman' for O'Donoghue, and it was one from which Swift emerged 'triumphantly': he 'was with the people and against their oppressors all the time'.[70] This ignored the impurity of motivation and the unrepresentative Protestantism, to say nothing of other evidences of favour for English culture, that Moran complained of in Swift; but it convinced O'Donoghue that Swift's 'suggested identification of himself with the [Protestant] settlers was an unmistakable pose, and that he spoke for the whole of the Irish people'.[71]

Perhaps because of his own sympathy with the ideals of Irish Ireland, O'Donoghue never named Moran outright as his target. Yet O'Donoghue's was the most elaborately unequivocal declaration of Swift's Irish identity pressed to date, forswearing any of the conditions or accommodations that typically accompanied the case made for it since the Young Ireland era seventy years before. He even did without the emphasis upon Swift's inspiring service to later patriots that so often impelled the arguments on Swift's behalf by the Young Ireland writers and their successors. While his treatment of Swift is more reflective than any in Griffith's journalism, moreover, he laid little stress on the doctrines Griffith had hailed in Swift, the equality of Ireland with Britain and the consent of the governed; these O'Donoghue considered simply 'admirable truths'.[72] The forthrightness of his essay, published while the third Home Rule Bill was moving tortuously through the House of Commons, heralded a revitalized nationalist consensus on Swift. And in this, the various aspects of his Irish identity were rehearsed again. Thus Phillip Lee's account of Swift's life for a more restricted audience, running through the two issues of the *Journal of the Ivernian Society* in 1913, insisted more broadly upon Swift's inspiring function as the basis of his Irishness, and upon the singularity of his role: 'the foundations of whatever prosperity we have are laid in the disinterested and magnanimous patriotism of Swift'.[73] Arthur Griffith himself could take the traditional nationalist approach of emphasizing Swift's place in the line of patriots, as when comparing him in 1914 to John Mitchel.[74] Swift's emphasis upon equality and consent, on the other hand, gained more attention in an account of the Wood affair for a religious and literary magazine late in 1915: they 'flamed through Ireland', constituting the focus of Swift's challenge to government.[75] But this was unusual, for just as the British parliament finally enacted Home Rule, its implementation was frustratingly delayed by the outbreak of a war which, by 1915, seemed nowhere near a resolution. In this context, abstract rights could seem less motivating than, for instance, traditional Irish mistrust of British intentions and the need for national unity to resist them, which were repeatedly invoked in a pamphlet of 1915, *Dean Swift on the Situation*, produced by the militant nationalist women's organization Cumann na mBan. This reprinted excerpts from Swift's patriotic writings with an introduction extending O'Donoghue's observation that British writers were ultimately to blame for denigrating Swift's concern for Ireland. The pamphlet, indeed, discovered here a British government conspiracy, 'a policy on the part of the then and now rulers of Ireland which misrepresents Swift to his countrymen'. For 'No single man did so much in his time to arouse his countrymen to an abhorrence of the condition to which they had been reduced by alien fraud and to sow the seed of national union.'[76] There was no need to prove Swift's national identity, nor even to emphasize the doctrines of equality or consent, so much as 'Swift's insistent doctrine that Ireland should never trust the faith of English statesmen, and least of all when they

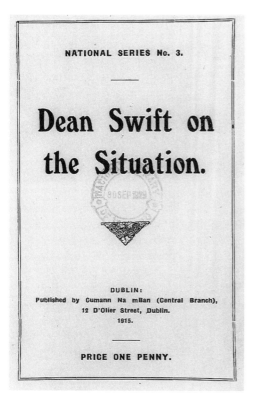

A pamphlet issued by the militant nationalist women's organization Cumann na
mBan in 1915.

professed friendship'.[77] Thus far had Moran's complaints been consigned to irrelevance, or even complicity with British designs.

Nationalists were hardly at one, of course, in so dismissing Moran's conten-
tions. The Christian Brothers' *Irish History Reader* in 1916 gave a very brief overview of the eighteenth century, merely listing Swift, Molyneux and Lucas as 'remarkable men' who 'wrote very able books and pamphlets' against the London parliament's assertion of Ireland's dependence while cautioning that 'it must be remembered that this was altogether a Protestant dispute. These men did not want to give freedom to their Catholic fellow-country-
men.'[78] And among advanced nationalists the same year, Padraig Pearse remarked that though one could construct the case for Irish separation from the writings of Berkeley, Swift and Burke, he preferred as patriotic forbears 'not those who have thought most wisely about Ireland, but those who have thought most authentically for Ireland, the voices that have come out of the Irish struggle itself', such as Tone, Davis, Lalor and Mitchel.[79] A few years later, in a popular history of Ireland, Mary Hayden and George Moonan insisted that Swift was solely a Protestant patriot, whose 'attitude is throughout that of a colonist' in the Wood affair.[80] Compared to Moran's attack, however, such reservations were quibbles, and most nationalist writers in the years between the 1916 Rising and the establishment of the Irish Free State joined in the renewed consensus on Swift's behalf. These ranged across the

spectrum of nationalist opinion, from the old-fashioned Home Ruler J.G. Swift MacNeill, who held that 'to Swift belongs the credit for having sown the seed which afterwards matured and yielded fruit' in the hoary paradigm of the constitutional nationalist, the 1782 settlement; to the Irish-American Patrick Lennox, a devotee of separatism, whose 1917 essay shows considerable indebtedness to O'Donoghue's of five years before; and the spectrum includes the journalist Maurice Dalton, whose brief account of Swift's Irish career laid equal emphasis upon English denunciation of the Dean and Swift's doctrines of equality and consent.[81]

This final outburst of nationalist rhetoric in Swift's favour, then, evoked Swift's Irish identity in terms quite similar to those of its original assertion by Young Ireland in the 1840s. These terms were never entirely adequate to counter the kind of sectarian or majoritarian exception-taking that characterized Hayden and Moonan in 1920, and others before and after. Nor, on the other hand, were they greatly enhanced by Griffith's promotion of Swift's adaptation of Lockean political theory to Ireland, as is clear from the merely occasional references to it – even by Griffith himself. Rather, Swift's identity was secured for nationalist Ireland more on symbolic than theoretical grounds, grounds informed, further, by his actions instead of his motives. For Irish nationalism itself was impelled throughout the nineteenth century and into the twentieth by practical considerations, a record of British misrule constantly refreshed by instances of poor or unresponsive government, foreign and lingeringly insensitive to the character and wishes of the majority of Irish people. That government had propped up oppressive systems of religion and land ownership in previous centuries, and seemed increasingly to heed the northern Unionist minority rather than southern nationalists in the second decade of the twentieth. Whatever his complicity in the system of oppression during his day, Swift could be celebrated as a symbol of Irish defiance of the government that sponsored that system then, and continued to slight the wishes of the majority now. Just as during the Repeal campaign of the 1840s and its aftermath, what contributed most to that symbolic identity in the final years of the Home Rule campaign, the war, the Easter Rising, the struggle for Independence and finally the Anglo-Irish Treaty of 1921, was the tone of his rhetoric and the enduring inspiration of his successful defiance. Certainly these counted more, in popular terms, than the Lockean principle of government by consent that he applied to an Irish situation.

VII

For some influential British commentators in these years, however, it was quite otherwise. Like Temple Scott, they could perceive the strength of the elements that made Swift a nationalist symbol, but showed no interest in the ways current circumstances kept this specifically Irish symbolism fresh. In quite different ways, Charles Whibley and C.H. Firth drew on the historicism fostered by Lecky and Temple Scott to scrutinize and fault English misgovernment and corruption in Swift's time, though not to advance Unionism or degrade nationalism. Whibley's historicist concern for accuracy enabled him, rather, to move in the direction Edmund Burke had laid out in the 1760s, portraying Swift's relevance as transcending Ireland, unlocking him from history; while for Firth a similar concern locked Swift more firmly into the past. Whibley's Leslie Stephen lecture at Cambridge in 1917, argued, for instance, that Swift was an idealist with regard to Ireland, and proposed admiringly the absence of a patriotic motive in him that D.P. Moran had seen as a glaring fault:

> . . . it was in his Irish policy that Swift proved most clearly the pure and lofty idealism that burned within him. In defending the Irish from oppression he was not swayed by the motives of patriotism; he did not yield even to a personal prejudice. He was not an Irishman. No drop of Irish blood flowed in his veins. As he said himself, he was born in Ireland by mere accident. . . . Nor did he love Ireland. . . . But he hated injustice and dishonour, wherever he saw them, and so he became as wise and valiant a champion of Ireland as that unhappy country ever found.[82]

In so disclaiming patriotism as Swift's motive Whibley struck obliquely at the chauvinism widespread in England during the First World War, but also disputed, perhaps inadvertently, the thrust of the mainstream Irish nationalist evocation of Swift. Two years later, in 1919, the historian C.H. Firth addressed the British Academy on *Gulliver's Travels*, revealing the hitherto unexamined extent of Swift's contemporary political allusions. Among them he noticed that

> Gulliver's description of the Yahoos recalls the description given by Swift, in prose pamphlets written about the same time, of the people he terms 'the savage old Irish'. . . . The 'savage old Irish' who make up 'the poorer sort of our natives' were not only in a position similar to that of the Yahoos, but there was also a certain similarity in their natures. If nothing was done to stop the process of degeneration, they would become complete brutes, as the Yahoos were already.[83]

Swift's schemes for the education and acculturation of the poor suggest that unlike the Yahoos, they might be reclaimed, yet if

> . . . Swift's pity for the old Irish seems to be developing into sympathy . . . in reality he reserved his sympathy for the new Irish – that is, the English colony in Ireland. The inhabitants of that country were two distinct races, and he was anxious not for their union but for the maintenance of the distinction between them.[84]

Thus Firth's historicism affirmed Swift's identity as purely a Protestant patriot, a stance that the Christian Brothers' and the Hayden–Moonan histories had maintained against the prevailing trend of Irish nationalist treatments in the decade before the Treaty. But while Whibley, however unknowingly, echoed Moran, Firth appears to have inspired an Irish attack on Swift in 1724, within a year of the end of the Civil War that followed the Treaty, that was even more blatantly sectarian than Moran's. In a series of articles for the *Catholic Bulletin* in 1924, its editor, Fr Timothy Corcoran, under the pseudonym 'Donal MacEgan', was at pains to destroy utterly the notion of Protestant patriotism in eighteenth-century Ireland: Swift, essential to this concept, merited two articles. He began in a tone that recalls Moran: 'Worshippers of an Anglicised Ireland, an Ireland to which some partial measure of local power might be granted as a boon, have, by a convention of long standing, come to regard Jonathan Swift as a notable and typical Irish patriot.'[85] Otherwise, however, Corcoran displayed none of Moran's vitriolic eloquence, continuing on a largely unimpassioned note, rather drily bitter, to demolish the Dean as patriot. He may not have known of O'Donoghue's encomium of a dozen years earlier, but Corcoran's essays amount to a categorical refutation of the weaker points in the earlier argument. Thus he proceeded, armed with such ample quotation from Swift himself as Firth had provided, to dismiss the case for Swift's Irish identity by challenging the idea that the Dean sympathized with the plight of Catholics or had any sense of fellowship with the Gael – two groups which to Corcoran (as to Moran a quarter-century earlier) were essentially the same. Whereas O'Donoghue had suggested that Swift simply posed as a defender of the settlers' interests but really spoke for the whole people, Corcoran demonstrated, like Firth, that Swift was entirely at one with the settlers' interests, complicit with the penal system against Catholics, and had no time for Gaelic Ireland, supporting measures for English education and the conversion of Catholics. Where Firth had seen such support as evidence that the native Irish, unlike the Yahoos, were in Swift's eyes redeemable, Corcoran concentrated on the comparison between Yahoo and Gael as so outrageous to Irish sensibilities that he could not even articulate the comparison clearly; instead, he quoted Firth (without acknowledgement) on the shock that Swift's obvious relation between the Yahoos and humanity produced in generations of admirers.[86]

To Whibley and Firth, then, Swift was essentially an idealist, or 'a charitable and public-spirited misanthropist',[87] more than a distinguishably Irish patriot; to Corcoran, the particulars of his personal attitudes toward Catholics and Ireland belie not only his characterization as a patriot, but by implication even his humanitarianism. Corcoran's historical project ranged well beyond Swift, however. There was actually quite a contemporary purpose in his meticulous dismantling of the edifice of eighteenth-century Protestant public-spirited patriotism in order to reveal instead a systematic attempt to undermine real Irish identity by penalizing Catholicism. The *Catholic Bulletin*, though pietistic from its inception and inclined to identify devotion to Ireland with Catholic fervour, had at least published Maurice Dalton's mainstream nationalist exposition of Swift's patriotism in 1918. After Corcoran became editor in 1922, however, the sectarianism became the more pronounced, and it took a strong, if somewhat discreet, line against the Anglo-Irish Treaty of 1921, which had secured the independence of the Irish Free State as a dominion within the British Commonwealth rather than as a republic, and had confirmed the partition of Northern Ireland from it. Corcoran's opening his first essay on Swift with a rebuke to 'Worshippers of an anglicized Ireland', then, while appearing as a somewhat anachronistic attack on Home Rule nationalism, was actually aimed at the supporters of the first independent Irish government – those who, by accepting the Treaty, seemed to advance little beyond Home Rule. Corcoran's *Bulletin* was in general hard on Irish Protestants, living and dead, and on their institutions, but equally so on those of the flock who consorted, or found any common cause, with them. For, more than simply nationalist, the journal was profoundly anti-British in its mixture of Catholic triumphalism and defensiveness. Nor was it sensitive to irony, whether Swift's or that imposed by circumstance. Directly following Corcoran's second essay attacking Swift, the *Bulletin* printed the continuation of an article promoting economic nationalism and self-reliance that, though with its own characteristic turn of phrase, nonetheless echoes Swift's own thinking:

> We say to England and to England's garrison in Ireland: We don't want your depreciated paper and we don't want your goods. We want to get back for ourselves and to retain our own home market which you have filched from us and which will give ample scope to our industries for many a year to come.[88]

It was thus the more shocking to Corcoran that, in 1926, he should have been taken to task for his articles by W.F.P. Stockley, the Professor of English at University College Cork, in the *Irish Ecclesiastical Record*, a journal published under official Catholic auspices. Asserting that Swift's pejorative comments on Ireland could indeed, taken alone, make him seem a remarkably inappropriate nationalist ancestor, Stockley – himself strongly opposed to the Treaty settlement and a forcefully Catholic scholar – argued that these are outweighed by his efforts on Ireland's behalf and his own distrust of British government. Stockley was not espousing the notion of an eighteenth-century Protestant patriotism; Swift constitutes something of an exception, in fact, to the anti-national character of his fellows. But the professor maintained the need for distinguishing the different registers of Swift's voices, for reading sensitively and for considering the effect of a whole comment of which Corcoran had only quoted part.[89] Stung by this rebuke, in which he was alluded to only as 'the detractor', Corcoran, as 'MacEgan', quickly countered in the *Bulletin*. Naming Stockley and accusing him of pilfering sources from another of his own *Bulletin* articles attacking eighteenth-century Protestant Ascendancy, Corcoran admitted that the *Drapier's Letters* constitute an argument for Swift's patriotism, but dismissed them without even a semblance of the scholarly posture he had assumed in 1924:

> The whole gist of the 'Wood's halfpence' controversy lies in this, that it was a petty squabble between two factions in the Ascendancy, as to who would pocket the profits from minting the token coinage. Swift sided with one party, because of his personal feud with the chiefs of the other.[90]

Stockley's essay may have seemed especially irritating to Corcoran because, in the aftermath of the Civil War, contemporary Protestants such as the Home Ruler Stephen Gwynn and the Gaelic scholar Eleanor Hull were themselves much more reserved about the purity of Swift's patriotism. Gwynn, as a nationalist politician defeated in the Sinn Fein landslide in 1918, was frankly supportive of the Treaty settlement, and as a popular political and literary historian was most interested in Swift as a writer. Hence 'Ireland of the Anglo-Irish', which was generally unconcerned about Gaelic culture, 'began to find expression of its own in Swift's writings', but 'All that he wrote in Ireland and about Ireland, the pamphlets that servant-girls in Dublin read with delight, belonged to English literature.'[91] And to Hull a few years later, more historically minded, Swift was essentially as Whibley and Firth had painted him: no Irish patriot but a humanitarian, though noteworthy as an advocate of legislative independence.[92]

In the Corcoran–Stockley exchange, the Catholic sectarian stance toward Swift's patriotism, foreshadowed by Thomas Moore a century earlier and articulated thereafter by Fr Burke and D.P. Moran, was for the first time challenged directly from within the Catholic community. Irritating as this certainly was to Corcoran, it was unimportant to the substance of their controversy, the terms of which had in fact changed little on either side over the years. But the timing of this intra-Catholic argument lends it some retrospective significance. As before, the case against Swift was founded upon an understanding of Irish identity which excluded him; but even for many in the Gaelic League generation before Independence, and certainly for most other nationalists, this could be subordinated to the question of Swift's function, his patriotic effectiveness and inspiration. Now, with a new state achieved, the question of Irish identity would have exposed the salient vulnerability of Swift's own Irishness, with greater effect than that of earlier complaints against him. Assuring that identity was the overwhelming Catholic temperament of the Free State's population, buttressed by the official elevation of Gaelic culture by successive governments. Had the Irish Free State developed as a Gaelic Catholic nation, it is doubtful that Swift's reputation as a patriot would have survived beyond grudging acknowledgement of his having defended Anglo-Irish 'colonists'. But that was not the direction the country actually took under the moderate nationalist leadership of W.T. Cosgrave in the 1920s, nor during the long administration of Eamon de Valéra and his avowedly republican Fianna Fáil party after 1932. In the first place, the official policy of supplanting Anglophone with Gaelic culture, pressed especially in the area of education, met with widespread and effective, though usually tacit, popular resistance. Secondly, Ireland's lingering constitutional, and even more its economic and social, relationship with Britain, and the impact of partition, maintained from the pre-Independence era a sense of ambiguity about Irish identity. Thus, as a cloudy concept, Irish identity could still be inclusive. It sheltered Swift increasingly, however, on account of his susceptibility to Irish acculturation in other respects than simply his rhetorical patriotism as emphasized by Young Ireland and its nationalist successors. For the ambiguities that Young Ireland had not highlighted in the Dean, those of Swift the man, of the 'character' of legend and anecdote, of the literary genius now generating an international critical industry, were indeed compatible with Ireland's own ambiguities of identity. And abetting the attraction of these features of Swift in the 1920s and 1930s was the rise in popularity of psychology, nourishing literary criticism and new literature alike. In these and following decades, Irish literature so nourished would foster rather than resolve the ambiguous nature of Irish identity, incidentally promoting a new pluralism, in which the figure of Swift would be explored, especially on the stage, as a genuinely Irish type.

7

From Patriot to Personality, 1930–1995

I

The 1920s and 1930s, which saw Ireland coming to terms with its independence, also witnessed an international flowering of Swift studies. Even in his own lifetime Swift had not remained the exclusive property of British and Irish readers: continental translations and commentaries were frequent, and continued to appear in the nineteenth century. In the twentieth, Emile Pons' critical treatment of Swift's early career, *Swift: les années de jeunesse et le 'conte de tonneau'* (1925), was a major advance in scholarship, cited for decades afterwards. And in the United States, Sophie Smith's *Dean Swift* (1910), a favourable biography which sought to rescue the Dean from his major nineteenth-century detractors, marked the beginning of the academic Swift industry in twentieth-century America. Psychological commentaries on Swift, especially those influenced by Freudian psychoanalytic theory, achieved a vogue after the First World War, in both the US and in Germany, and continued in favour for many years.[1] In Britain, more traditional academic commentary remained the norm, occasionally supplemented by editorial and textual scholarship, as in the edition of *A Tale of a Tub* by D. Nichol Smith and A.C. Guthkelch in 1920. The twentieth-century Irish contribution to this surge in academic and biographical interest was seminal in F. Elrington Ball's edition of *The Correspondence of Jonathan Swift* (six volumes, 1910–14) before the war, but slight in the 1920s. With the achievement of Independence Swift's role as an early propagandist for Irish freedom began, among Irish commentators, to recede from contemporary prominence into history; in the growing body of scholarship in Britain and America, it nearly slipped from view altogether. For the Free State's independence, and the autonomy of Northern Ireland, took the country as a whole off the list of pressing British concerns and dispensed with any further need to understand Irish nationalism. The field was clear for the historicism of Temple Scott's approach in Swift's *Prose Works*, at the turn of the century, to harden into orthodoxy, especially along the lines Charles Whibley had laid down in his Leslie Stephen lecture at Cambridge in 1917. When Swift's patriotic work was treated at any length, it could be subsumed into his larger passion for justice.

Little recognized outside Ireland, then, was the Irish particularization of Swift, the establishment of his Irish identity, which over the preceding eighty years had come to dominate consideration of him within the country. Whether in historical scholarship or literary studies, Irish commentary offered little to counter this international trend; Irish arguments, as the Corcoran–Stockley exchange demonstrates, remained parochial. Yet this in itself showed how rooted had become the Irish particularization of Swift within Ireland, and even as its political currency began to fade in the 1920s, its effective service to nationalism completed, that particularization began to acquire significance in Irish literary culture. The potential of this had been largely overlooked at the dawning of the literary revival in the 1890s. Thirty years later, the same homebound attitude that kept Irish treatments of Swift on the margins of international literary critical attention, drew to the surface at last in Irish literature a welcoming response to the persistent popular image of the Dean as 'character'. With varied emphases, this fashion was to continue throughout the twentieth century, endowing Swift in the process with an Irish identity broader and more complex than its function to nationalism.

For James Joyce, himself at once international and homebound, Swift was a recurrent emanation in the pages of *Ulysses*, mostly covert but hailed by critics within a decade of its publication in 1922 and ever since.[2] In *Finnegans Wake* (1939), moreover, he is a pervasive presence, integral to Joyce's Dublin-centric cosmic dream burlesque within the characters of the twins Shem and Shaun, but also in aspects of other characters and as himself, Dean, 'Draper' and Gulliver. His significance is invoked from the very first page of the *Wake*, which yokes him to Dublin and to Stella and Vanessa, both of whom bear the same Old Testament name, spelled variously Esther and Hester, and thus are sisters, wrathful at Swift's treatment of them and given counterparts in a Jonathan split in anticipation of the Shem Shaun divide: 'all's fair in vanessy, were sosie sesthers wroth with twone nathanjoe'. For his final work, Joyce appropriated to Swift a broad identity indeed, a general influence far greater than the sum of its particular, definably Irish referents, at once transcending Irishness and transcendentally Irish.[3] On an equally intimate but more spectral plane, W.B. Yeats was to remark that Swift 'haunted' him in Dublin, exhibiting a sensitivity shared by the usually less phenomenalistic Mary Colum, who recalled that when she returned to Dublin from America in the early 1920s, the city was for her full of ghosts, Swift's pre-eminent among them.[4] In the popular imagination Swift the patriot lingered as well: an old pupil of the Christian Brothers in Dublin recalled in 1928 the Dean's prominence in the roll of (mostly Protestant) locally based patriots in whom he was taught to take pride.[5] And it was this popular Swift who became the subject of the first play featuring his patriotism, Arthur Power's *The Drapier Letters*. Upon its initial submission to the Abbey Theatre in the early 1920s, the play was rejected, but W.B. Yeats was taken by its story of 'Swift saved from English soldiers at the time of the "Drapier letters" by a young harlot he was accustomed to visit', and the author's claim that the Dean's having recourse to such women was a traditional view. 'Country friends' of Yeats confirmed this view, as Yeats remembered in 1926 for a footnote on Swift and Gaelic tradition to his 'Introduction' for Arland Ussher's translation of Brian Merriman's *The Midnight Court*.[6] And indeed, Lady Gregory included in the 1926 edition of her *Kiltartan History-Book* a legend about Swift sending his servant to find him a woman for the night, and dismissing the servant when he woke the next morning to find that the woman was black.[7] Power, who was working in Paris as a journalist, read Ussher's book and was surprised to see Yeats's reference to his rejected play, which he decided to re-submit to the Abbey, this time with success.[8] Yeats may simply have reconsidered the theatre's earlier rejection; he might also have compared Power's play with a very poor one-act 'dialogue' by C.E. Lawrence, 'Swift and Stella', which appeared in the *Cornhill Magazine* about this time: oblivious to Swift as patriot, Lawrence has Swift explain to Stella that they can never marry because they are illegitimate brother and sister.[9] The theme Lawrence could not render dramatically was to be pursued independently and forcefully by Denis Johnston, but it was with Power's play that Swift returned to the Abbey stage, and, for the first time, at the hands of an Irish author. *The Drapier Letters* was first performed on 22 August 1927, as the curtain-raiser for a revival of G.B. Shaw's *Arms and the Man*, and was published later that year.[10] Concentrating the action into a single act, Power made no attempt to represent Swift himself in the drama, though it was, according to a prefatory 'Note', 'an attempt to invent a reason' for the Dean's having moved from despising Ireland to so defending his country in the Wood affair that 'for the first time in Irish history a spirit of national life was breathed into an almost denationalized people'.[11] He was concerned to suggest, in other words, that not only did Swift inspire others, but was himself subjectively motivated to become a patriot, and the vehicle Power invented for this was a young woman of the Dublin slums, Mary-Bridget Cafferty.

The play is set in the Caffertys' slum tenement in 1724; the government has proclaimed a reward of three hundred pounds for discovering the author of the Drapier's letters, Swift is generally suspected, and Mrs Cafferty is fearful because her daughter, an ardent admirer of the Dean, is expecting a visit from him that evening (that Mary-Bridget is a 'harlot', which so intrigued Yeats, is implicit, but may have been more obvious in the first, rejected version of the play). Mary-Bridget's appearance thereafter is followed by that of Sally O'Gorman, a money-lender to whom Mrs Cafferty is indebted for three pounds. When Mary-Bridget learns of her mother's debt she promises to pay

ABBEY THEATRE
— DUBLIN. —

Proprietors   THE NATIONAL THEATRE SOCIETY, Ltd
Directors   W. B. YEATS, LADY GREGORY
WALTER STARKIE, LENNOX ROBINSON
Manager   MICHAEL J. DOLAN
Producer   LENNOX ROBINSON
Assistant Producer and Stage Manager   ARTHUR SHIELDS

All seats in Theatre with exception of Back Pit may be Booked
Seats Reserved but not paid for, will not be kept later than 7.45 p.m.
Telephone 3268

Monday, Aug. 22nd, 1927, and following nights at **8**
Matinee, Saturday at 2.30 p.m.

FIRST PRODUCTION OF
THE DRAPIER LETTERS
A Play in One Act, by ARTHUR POWER

Characters :

MARY-BRIDGET   Shelah Richards
MRS. CAFFERTY (her mother)   Eileen Crowe
MRS. KATE   May Craig
SALLY O'GORMAN   Maureen Delaney
BIDDY   Aoife Taaffe
AN ENGLISH OFFICER   P. J. Carolan
PRIVATES THOMSON AND SMITH   T. Moran, M. Scott
ROBERT BLAKELEY (Dean Swift's servant)   Peter Nolan

SCENE—Interior of a slum in Dublin.

PERIOD—1724.

Play produced by ARTHUR SHIELDS.

NOTE

"One of the chief wants of Ireland in that day (1724) was that of small currency adapted to the daily transactions of life....and a patent for supplying Ireland with a copper coinage was accorded to William Wood on such terms that the profit accruing from the difference between the intrinsic and the nominal value of the coins, about 40%, was mainly divided between him and George I's favourite Duchess of Kendal..... Swift now had his opportunity, and the famous six letters signed M. B. Drapier soon set Ireland in flame. Every effort was used to discover the author, or rather to obtain legal evidence against the author, whom, Walpole was assured, it would have taken ten thousand men to apprehend. None could be procured ; the public passion swept everything before it ; the patent was cancelled, Wood was compensated by a pension, and Swift was raised to a height of popularity which he retained for the rest of his life."

(Encyclo. Brit.)

INTERVAL OF TWELVE MINUTES

ARMS AND THE MAN
An Anti-romantic Comedy in Three Acts,
by GEORGE BERNARD SHAW

Characters in the order of their appearance :

RAINA PETKOFF   Eileen Crowe
CATHERINE PETKOFF   Maureen Delany
LOUKA   May Craig
CAPTAIN BLUNTSCHLI   Barry Fitzgerald
OFFICER   Peter Nolan
NICOLA   Arthur Shields
MAJOR PAUL PETKOFF   P. J. Carolan
MAJOR SERGIUS SARANOFF   F. J. McCormick

ACT   I.—Night. A Lady's Bedchamber in Bulgaria, in a small town near the Drago-man Pass. Late in November, 1885.

ACT II.—In the Garden of Major Petkoff's House. A Spring Morning.

ACT III.—In the Library after Church.

The Orchestra, under the Direction of Dr. J. F. LARCHET, will perform the following selections :

Overture	" Raymond "	Ambroise Thomas (1811-1896)
Fantasia	" Samson and Delilah "	Saint-Saëns (1835-1922)
1st Movement	Symphony in B minor—Allegro moderato	Schubert (1797-1828)
Fantasia	" La Bohème "	Puccini (1858-1924)

ANNOUNCEMENT

Monday, 29th August, 1927, and following nights at **8**
Matinee, Saturday at 2.30

AUTUMN FIRE
A Play in Three Acts, by T. C MURRAY

NOTICE—Ladies sitting in the Stalls are requested to remove their Hats

The programme for Arthur Power's *The Drapier Letters.*

it speedily, and then locks herself in an inner room. Sally leaves, threatening to have not only the three pounds owed but the government's three hundred for the Drapier, since she knows of Mary-Bridget's association with Swift. After a friend arrives with gin and the news that a fourth Drapier's letter is published, a few soldiers appear and demand entry to search for the Drapier, whom they have been told is hiding in the house. They quickly discover the door to Mary-Bridget's inner room and shoot the lock open, but only find the girl herself within, mortally wounded in the chest by the gunshot. As the soldiers depart to continue their search, the dying Mary-Bridget reveals that 'it was I who made him write those letters'.[12] By her account, when they had met some time before the Dean was unhappy and alone; she had told him that his pride was to blame, and that he should dispel it by making common cause with the lowly people of Ireland. Her rambling dying speech also reflects on the hitherto dejected spirit of the Irish people, and alludes to her romantic interest in Swift, whom she leaves to Stella as she dies.

The setting and stage-Irish dialogue of the play suggest the influence of O'Casey, whose Minnie Powell's sacrifice for Davoren in *The Shadow of a Gunman* anticipates Mary-Bridget's dying to defend the apparently hidden Swift. But Mary-Bridget is not deluded in her self-sacrifice; the genuineness of Swift's patriotism is essential to Power's play, in which the major flaw – its undue reliance upon the girl's final speech to clarify her relationship with Swift – owes nothing to O'Casey. As a play, indeed, the work is slight, essentially a patriotic melodrama, with Mary-Bridget implicitly recalling the traditional Gaelic representation of Ireland as a young woman. Power was himself, however, not very nationalistic. Son of a Catholic landed family with a military tradition, he was disaffected with religion because of its rigidities experienced during his upbringing and education, but joined the British army during the First World War. On leave he once visited the Arts Club in Dublin, where he first saw Yeats, who 'seemed to avoid me', evidently because Power was still in uniform. After the war Power based himself in Paris, reporting on the art world for a New York newspaper; once Yeats had accepted the re-submitted play and it was in production Power travelled to Dublin to see it, and there finally met Yeats.[13] Inevitably they fell to discussing Swift, whose nationality they disputed: '. . . I maintained that whereas Irish wit was playful and fantastical as in the case of Shaw and Sheridan, Swift was typically English – the hammer blow to kill. But Yeats maintained that Swift was typically Irish.' Power based his case on Swift's English parentage as well as on the Englishness of his method, 'that logic, the classical build-up, the suppressed violence, the open contempt'; and even on the parallel of the Gaels and the Yahoos, who would

> for want of enemies, engage in what is a civil war among themselves – an indirect allusion, as it was, to the recent events in Ireland instigated by De Valera. . . . However, in the end Yeats smiled a smile of forbearance, and said with a sigh: 'Anyway, we try to claim him for our own for he was Irish by birth, residence and sympathy.' . . . my argument was ill-advised with a man who was anxious to found a distinctive Anglo-Irish school of literature of which Swift was one of the main pillars, and whose sarcastic wit, as Yeats pointed out, was undoubtedly sharpened by his early and long association with Ireland, and whose residence in England had been brief and disappointing.[14]

Both before and after this account of his argument with Yeats, Power noted that the poet was an 'ardent nationalist'; 'it was part and breath of his being', which was not at all his own case.[15] Yet *The Drapier Letters*, for all its faults, is certainly a patriotic play.

Yeats himself in these years was increasingly drawn to Swift, about whom he would write a greater, and less nationalistic play, *The Words upon the Window Pane*, produced at the Abbey on 17 November 1930. Although he had reviewed R.A. King's *Swift in Ireland* in 1896, for years afterwards neither Swift nor other eighteenth-century Anglo-Irish writers had attracted him, as he noted in a reflection on his play published in two parts beginning almost a year after the first performance.[16] It was only in the 1920s that his hope and work 'for some identification of my beliefs with the nation itself' took the form of examining such eighteenth-century predecessors. And now, he noted, 'Swift haunts me; he is always just round the next corner.'[17] With respect to *The Words upon the Window Pane*, this reference is particularly apt. Like Power's a one-act play, and Yeats's only venture towards realist drama, *Words* presents a group of Dubliners assembling for a seance at the hands of a medium, Mrs Henderson, whose recent efforts have been disrupted by the intrusion of a hostile spirit. The venue for the seance is an old house with Swiftian associations; part of a poem by Stella scratched on a window pane gives the play its title. John Corbet, a Cambridge student researching Swift for his doctorate, has joined the group on this occasion, recognizes the scratched quotation, and, as the seance proceeds and is again disrupted, identifies the hostile spirit as Swift. The medium speaks, in fact, as both Swift and Vanessa in conversation, the latter professing her love for the Dean, Swift confessing that he must not marry lest he pass on the madness he suspects in himself. After a pause, Mrs Henderson again speaks as Swift, this time to Stella, explaining the nature of his devotion to her. The seance then breaks off, the medium wakes, Corbet questions her about Swift, of whom she is actually ignorant, and the group leaves. As the play ends, Mrs Henderson, now alone, is once more possessed by Swift, bewailing the sadness of his life.

While the processes of Yeats's thought from which *The Words upon the Window Pane* emerged centred upon Ireland, it is clearly not a nationalist play. To be sure, Swift had 'created the political nationality of Ireland' and at the same time 'found his nationality through the *Drapier's Letters*',[18] but Yeats was considering the Dean's value to the independent new country rather than simply as rhetorician for Irish liberty. And that value he located specifically not in the *Drapier's Letters* or other writings about Ireland, but in the early *Discourse of the Contests and Dissentions*. Here, in what Yeats considered in his 1931 essay Swift's 'one philosophical work', he saw a warning against a tyranny of the democratic mob: 'for the Many obsessed by emotion . . . give themselves at last to some one master of bribes and flatteries and . . . into the ignoble tranquillity of servitude'.[19] The 'discord of parties' that democracy encourages 'has compelled half a dozen nations since the [First World] war to accept the "tyranny" of a "single person" ';[20] to avoid this, Yeats maintains, it is useful to have a governing class which reflects the national temper, without necessarily representing all its particulars. Such a class had existed in Swift's day, which accounts for Yeats's view of the eighteenth as 'the one Irish century that escaped from darkness and confusion'.[21] Though that governing class fell into decline, 'their genius did not die out – they sent everywhere administrators and military leaders, and now that their ruin has come – what resolute nation permits a strong alien class within its borders? – I would . . . gladly sing their song'.[22] Thus, though Yeats, as he admits, refrained from having any character in his play represent his own thinking with precision, he exalts Swift as an intellectual aristocrat, who offers thereby an enduring standard for Ireland, however long neglected, a standard that Yeats vouchsafes himself to disclose. Not only is Swift, in Arthur Power's words, a 'main pillar' of the Anglo-Irish school of literature Yeats hoped to found, but an instructor for the new state. He stands as a symbol of clear-headed thought, of such qualities, ironically, which to Power's mind stamped him as essentially English, but which for Yeats evince a pride that in Ireland's new circumstances may be claimed as a discovered legacy to the nation.

Yeats's play draws upon this view without articulating it directly; it emerges, rather, from the inadequacies of the characters. John Corbet, though the most sympathetic to the notion, is a budding pedant whose interest in Swift's celibacy keeps him from recognizing the Dean's enduring significance. And the other characters, all Anglo-Irish, are similarly preoccupied with their own hobby-horses, all but one of them oblivious to Swift. The decline of their class is palpable in the contrast between Swift's tragic egocentricity and their petty self-concerns. Yet the first part of Yeats's essay on *Words* inclines more to nostalgia for the vanished influence of the Anglo-Irish in society than it challenges their descendants to earn such prominence anew. Implicitly, the essay assigns Swift's modern symbolic value for the Irish nation to the singularity of his intellect; he stands as an ideal rather than a model. And precisely on that account Swift was attractive to Yeats personally, in terms discernible as early as 1896 in Yeats's book review, but becoming clearer and more potent to the older poet of the 1920s and 1930s.[23] In these years, his closer study of the Irish eighteenth century enabled Yeats to find in Swift a personal significance that substantiated, as it were, the image of the Dean's 'haunting' him:

> Thought seems more true, emotion more deep, spoken by someone who touches my pride, who seems to claim me of his kindred, who seems to make me a part of some national mythology, nor is mythology mere ostentation, mere vanity if it draws me onward to the unknown; another turn of the gyre and myth is wisdom, pride, discipline.[24]

Thus, toward the end of Ireland's first decade of independence, Yeats was constructing an identity for Swift that extended to Yeats himself: the modern writer finds his 'pride' quickened by the Dean's 'claim' on him as 'kindred', a claim that fashions Yeats as 'part of some national mythology'.

Yeats thereby acquires a pedigree from Swift, rather as did the nineteenth-century nationalists who traced the ancestry of their movement to the Dean. But Yeats's Swift, a new invention though long gestating, was free from the actual, or previously constructed, effects upon Irish history of the Dean's actions. Yeats had foreseen in his 1896 review that 'The recognition of the expression of a temperament as an end in itself, and not merely as a means toward a change of opinion, is the first condition of any cultivated life, and there is no better text than Swift for preaching this.'[25]

Now, in his 1931 essay, he could clarify that 'In judging any moment of past time we should leave out what has since happened; we should not call the Swift of the *Drapier Letters* nearer truth because of their influence upon history than the Swift who attacked in *Gulliver* the inventors and logicians.'[26]

More even than a spiritual Anglo-Irish ancestor, Swift was a spirit, who for Yeats still lived. Hence he devoted the second part of his article on the play to explaining his concern with spiritualism. Reduced to its essence, his notion is that great spirits (not necessarily the same as the spirits of the great) live beyond death in a sense amenable to the perceptions of the living; as such, this is the most widely apprehensible aspect of Yeats's occult system. That system, of course, is considerably more complex, as shown expansively in *A Vision* (1925, revised 1937); the explanation offered of its simpler features in the essay on *Words*, however, certainly vindicates Yeats's understanding Swift not merely as a literary precursor or political influence, but as a living, even sacral, spirit, one of those 'many strange and beautiful things become credible' once we accept that the world is invested with 'a precise inexplicable teeming life, and the earth becomes . . . not in rhetorical metaphor, but in reality, sacred'.[27]

Yeats's apprehension of Swift as a living spirit, marked both in his play and in the commentary which became its introduction, charted quite a different course for the use of Swift's reputation from that chosen by most earlier nationalist admirers of the Dean. The convention of Swift as a nationalist pioneer, whether on his own or as part of a patriotic genealogy, was losing its potency as propaganda since Ireland had gained independence; in the same way, Yeats himself had found that invoking that genealogy in defence of Protestant traditions – as he did in the Irish senate when opposing the abolition of divorce in 1925 – had little effect. The Drapier's anti-English rhetoric might still seem historically valuable, but for Swift's endurance, indeed his continuing presence, Yeats turned to his singularity of character instead. In national terms, that singularity, Swift's relentless individuality, informs what for Yeats is the Dean's 'Irish' hatred of abstractions, the ideologies engendering social disharmony, disrupting the 'unity of being' to which artists could address themselves in an aristocratic society.[28] Such a unity, still perceptible in the Ireland of the 1920s and 1930s, might be invoked, conceivably invigorated, through renewed attention to Swift, whose memory lived among the vestigial gentry and in folk tradition; though in fact neither the play nor the essay holds out much hope for this. But the value in Swift that was personal to Yeats was inextricable from this; it was a product of the eighteenth-century studies which for him had transformed that whole period in Ireland from an era of dull rationalism into one populated by great 'characters' (using that word in the popular Irish sense of idiosyncratic personality as much as in that of a strong will). In this transformation, Swift became a hero of strenuous intellect resisting the pull of drab mediocrity, and thus an exponent of an Anglo-Irish tradition in which Yeats could see himself appropriately embedded; of which, indeed, he might be perceived as the major contemporary manifestation. The process is not unlike that by which Davis, or Lecky, could project themselves as Swift's heirs – though the integration of that process in Yeats's spiritualist system renders it the more idiosyncratic.

II

In addition to its subjective attractiveness, Yeats's focus on Swift's personality opened a way for succeeding dramatists to emphasize it and so develop the potential latent in the anecdotal Irish popular memory of the Dean. If Yeats could allude to that anecdotal memory, he could not tap much of it in *Words* any more than he could evoke 'Swift's one experience of community, an experience that was to beguile and frustrate Yeats all of his life', as Douglas Archibald terms the Wood affair.[29] But Yeats did manage successfully in *Words*, for instance, to objectify Swift's unacknowledged sense of his own guilt as a major feature of his character. This guilt, as Richard Cave has noted, extends beyond the facts of Swift's relationship with Stella or Vanessa; Yeats's achievement lies in his rendering

> so intricate a mind as Swift's, trapped in a labyrinth of guilt of its own devising that betrays itself to ever subtler forms of irrationality in its efforts to avoid acknowledging the necessary irrationality of so much human behaviour. Ultimately, that mind finds guilt even in the fact of having been born. . . . Swift 'outlives' himself to a most tragic extreme. . . .[30]

The Dean as author of his own horror is the subject as well of Lord Longford's *Yahoo*. Longford's most popular play and among the most popular of those dealing directly with Swift, *Yahoo* came to him in a burst of inspiration during the summer of 1933, and takes much greater liberties with historical fact than any preceding play about Swift. The first full-length play on Swift since Paternoster's effort of twenty years before, it was produced at the Gate Theatre on 19 September 1933.[31] While less theatrically experienced than Yeats, Longford could appeal to an audience with a sure touch, and his Swift exhibits more of the characteristics that inform popular legend, evoked within an interest in psychology typical of the 1930s: patriotism, cruelty to the women who loved him, attendant guilt and madness.

The first act opens in 1724 with Stella listening to Swift in the deanery reading the end of *Gulliver's Travels*; she resents its imputations upon humanity as a race of Yahoos, and tries to convince Swift to attack Wood's scheme. Bishop Berkeley, arriving on a visit, agrees, and no sooner tells him of Vanessa's coming to town than she appears as well. Frantic with lovesickness, she has a letter for Stella, revealing her own relationship to Swift and asking if Stella is Swift's wife; this Swift takes privately. Once Vanessa leaves, he has Berkeley marry Stella and himself, and then shows Stella the letter. The second act opens the next day at Vanessa's house at Celbridge, where she reads Stella's reply acknowledging her marriage, and burns it. Berkeley arrives to tell her that Swift, who spent the previous night in extreme agitation, is on his way to Celbridge, and then departs. Swift appears shortly after Berkeley's exit and throws down Vanessa's original letter to Stella. Though she detains him, pouring out her love, and evokes his pity, he refuses her advances and rages at the Yahoos of the world, and at Wood's scheme in particular, leaving her heartbroken.

The third act begins many months later, with Berkeley again visiting the deanery and learning from a servant of Swift's isolation, distraction and even apparent madness as he devotes himself to Ireland's cause. Vanessa has died, leaving Berkeley half her estate, and as Swift enters he hails Berkeley's patriotism and his good fortune. They discuss Swift's own patriotism in the Wood affair, when Stella arrives, in declining health, and asks on that account for Swift to acknowledge her publicly as his wife, which he refuses. They hear a crowd outside cheering at the news that Wood's patent has been withdrawn, and Swift, responding to their acclamation in a note of triumph, becomes suddenly giddy and the scene fades out. The mode of presentation suddenly changes from realism to expressionism as the lights return, and Swift is confronted in turn by 'The Yahoo', who leers and laughs at him, by Vanessa's ghost, which calls upon him to repent his sin against her, by the figure of Death carrying Stella's body away, and by a series of tableaux representing the course of his reputation. The first is a family at Christmas, presenting a little girl with *The Little Folk's Gulliver*; next, a speaker at a public meeting protests the naming of a road after Swift, 'a man of anti-Irish outlook and degraded morals';[32] there follow an auctioneer selling portraits of Stella and Vanessa, and a lecturer promoting a psychoanalytical approach to Swift. The lights fade again and return, revealing Swift surrounded by the same crowd which had hailed the Drapier and which now contemplate his insanity with growing indifference; seeing how he is and will be perceived, he pleads 'I am what I am,' hears a voice (of God, presumably) asking him to repent, and as the lights dim once more asks divine forgiveness as no more than a Yahoo himself.

What distinguished *Yahoo* in its day was Longford's experiment with expressionism in the third act. Hilton Edwards, who played Swift in the original production but who was also, then and especially in later years, an incisive observer and analyst of the Irish stage, noted in 1934 that

> This is one of the few perfect instances in which expressionism can be utilized in an otherwise realistic play with absolute justification and as the logical expression of the action. When madness descends upon Swift, realism has taken the play as far as it can go; it could only portray madness in an outward expression of eccentricity or gibbering idiocy; instead, the action is held up for a fraction of a second; time stops; the creations of Swift's demented mind take the stage, appearing and disappearing in the blackness surrounding the central figure of Swift faintly lighted at his desk, yet dominating the figures that appear round him.[33]

The expressionistic interruption also enabled Longford to build in the final act a sympathy for Swift that the actions of the character as hitherto presented do not inspire. And at the very end of the play, the lingering

The climax of the third act of Lord Longford's *Yahoo*, 1933, with Hilton Edwards (*centre*) as the Dean.

atmosphere of delirious prophecy that evoked such sympathy, together with the appropriate artifice of the Dean's declaiming his repentance in blank verse, just restrain that declamation from the verge of melodrama. The expressionistic tableaux were especially effective in riveting the audience's attention, and Longford responded to their enthusiastic approval on the first night by explaining 'I wrote this play as a tribute to the man I regard as the father of modern Irish nationalism.' One reviewer, David Sears, noted that 'expressionism is used with striking success . . . some of the reminders of our forgetfulness and ingratitude to Swift came like a slap in the face. The final curtain leaves us ashamed of ourselves, which is probably how the author meant us to feel.'[34]

III

Longford's comment to his audience, of course, restated the old mainstream Irish nationalist view of Swift's patriotic function, which in fact was rarely articulated in the late 1920s and early 1930s. British scholarship in those years hardly acknowledged that Swift's patriotism as such had had any enduring Irish relevance. The elevation of justice over patriotism among Swift's concerns, which Charles Whibley had derived from historicism, had become so orthodox for those considering his Irish interests as occasionally to take a mystical cast. W.D. Taylor asserted in 1933, for instance, that in the fourth Drapier's letter, addressed to 'The Whole People of Ireland', Swift became so sympathetic to the situation of the Catholic poor that he began 'insensibly' to speak for them.[35] Like Longford, other Anglo-Irish commentators in 1933–4 began to take implicit or direct issue with this new critical orthodoxy; but unlike him, not all were content to restate the old nationalist formula. Departing from it in an historicist direction, Joseph Hone addressed the even older notion, which he perceived as still widespread in Britain and even in Ireland, that Swift was motivated by disappointed ambition to take up Ireland's cause. Instead, Hone maintained, Swift's malice toward the English Whig ministry was sparked by his devotion to the established Church (which was threatened more in Ireland than in England by latitudinarian toleration of dissenters) and his belief in old-fashioned economic doctrine (which disputed the modern economics of English imperialism that thwarted Irish trade). So motivated, therefore, Hone's Swift was no spokesman for the masses.[36]

But Stephen Gwynn's biography, also in 1933, put forthrightly the case for Swift's patriotic function, the basis of the old nationalist consensus on the Dean. Paralleling his comments of the decade before, Gwynn would not claim Swift as unambiguously Irish, and indeed alternated between calling him English and Irish, for 'Swift cannot in any ordinary sense be considered an Irish nationalist; but he became a nation-builder' nevertheless. For he 'had led the Irish people to beat the government . . . had shown the possibilities of a combination, even unarmed, to defeat the machinery of land and power. This was the beginning of constitutional agitation in Ireland.'[37] Hone returned to this issue in a biographical study of 1934, in collaboration with the Italian critic Mario Rossi, to present Swift as essentially and consistently egotistical. Contending that, though literally an Irishman, 'he rather exploited than attempted to form and lead the growing sense of an Anglo-Irish nationality', Rossi and Hone yet allow implicitly for his enduring patriotic function, which after all is more a matter of perception than intent. And his intent, regarding Ireland, was certainly sincere, for egotistically he took the Irish people as an extension of himself, badly served by the same governmental practices, like Wood's patent, that antagonized him.[38]

Outside scholarly circles in the same years, a stricter sense of Irish identity was in the ascendant. After the electoral victory in 1932 of Fianna Fáil, a party committed to economic protectionism and to removing the vestiges of British dominion over Ireland, relations with Britain soured and a greater Gaelic or Catholic populism came to the fore than had prevailed among most in the old national consensus. Speaking at the opening of the Radio Eireann broadcasting station in Athlone in February 1933, the head of the new government, Eamon de Valéra, briefly reviewed Anglo-Irish literature – which was 'far less characteristic of the nation than that produced in the Irish language' – noting that 'Ireland has produced in Dean Swift perhaps the greatest satirist in the English language' but alluding not at all to his patriotic efforts.[39] In addition, Fr Timothy Corcoran produced a characteristically

truculent article in the *Catholic Bulletin* in 1933, this time under the pseudonym 'Dermot Curtin'. Since what alone 'counts in our National record is
what the mass of the average people was and worked for', Fr Corcoran argued
that in the eighteenth century Swift was simply an 'acute and determined
thinker in the enemy interest' and the *Drapier's Letters* therefore only
'absurdly thought to be the work of an Irish thinker and leader'.[40] And at the
end of 1933 Fr Corcoran, again taking up the pseudonym of 'Donal
MacEgan' that he had used for attacking Swift in the *Catholic Bulletin* in the
1920s, criticized 'this foul brute and callous bigot, Jonathan Swift' with a
review of Gwynn's biography, repeating the main points of his earlier contributions to the magazine.[41]

While W.F.P. Stockley had met and beaten back Corcoran's earlier
attacks, his successor as Professor of English at Cork, Daniel Corkery, now
joined in the assault on Swift with a review of the Taylor, Gwynn, and Rossi
and Hone biographies in mid-1934. Corkery's impeccable nationalism, however, was vastly more refined than Corcoran's, founded upon a genuine love
and critical appreciation for Gaelic literary culture rather than reflexive
Catholic anti-Britishness. In his 1924 study of the eighteenth-century
Munster Gaelic poets, *The Hidden Ireland*, and in *Synge and Anglo-Irish Literature* (1931), he had argued – in the face of the prominence of Anglo-Irish
writers in the contemporary 'Renaissance' of Irish literature in English – that
to endow Anglo-Ireland with a retrospective, or even current, Irish nationality was simply inauthentic. His 1934 review in *Studies* approached Swift
directly from the same perspective, which he maintained with a sophistica-
tion lacking in the Dean's earlier advanced nationalist antagonists from
Mitchel and Father Burke through D.P. Moran and those of his own day. For
he granted immediately that Swift was Irish, and that Irish national identity
was difficult for a modern Irish commentator to gauge, since 'there is no living
Irishman who is Irish through and through as the first Englishman we may
light upon is English. The best of us, even the people of the Gaeltacht,
practically all of them educated in English, are little better than piebald
nationalists.' But in Swift's own day, this was not the case for him or for most
Irish people, including such Irish poets as Carolan, O'Rahilly and Ó Doirnín,
'poets who were journalists in the sense that Swift himself was a journalist':

> The dominant factor, the scale of values, native to the mind of these poets was
> a 'glow' transmitted from the Gaelic past. The 'glow' in Swift's mind came to
> him from the past of the English nation; the dominant factor in his mind was
> English.[42]

Thus Swift was hardly an Irish nationalist in the eighteenth century; Corkery
had assimilated in his Gaelic perspective Charles Whibley's judgement that
in Swift's 'defending the Irish from oppression he was not swayed by motives
of patriotism'.[43] And the effect of that view carries into Corkery's allowing, in
implicit contradiction of Swift's Irish critics from Mitchel to Corcoran, that

Swift may well have sympathized with the downtrodden native Irish, but that this is an argument for his having been a humanitarian rather than a patriot. His exertions for Irish liberty, furthermore, were also not patriotic, for such liberty meant to him simply the 'freedom of the Ascendancy from British interference'.[44]

For the most part avoiding aspersions upon Swift's character, Corkery's was the most studied, temperate, even commanding statement in Swift's post-humous career against his acceptance as an Irish patriot. However different in nuance from those of Swift's other Irish antagonists, though, it rested upon the same premise: that the Dean was himself insufficiently Irish in attitude to be perceived as a patriot. This slighted, as if their validity were no longer an issue, two notions about Swift deriving from his own century and retaining their force in the twentieth: the paradox of his character – the misanthropic humanitarian, the despiser of Ireland who defended its interests, and so on – and the function of his patriotic efforts in defying the British successfully in his own time and inspiring later generations of nationalists. With the authenticities of Gaelic culture informing his perspective, Corkery could ignore both notions as the ingredients of myth, the one popular and the other political. But not addressing them could not dismiss them, and as Swift's patriotic function underpinned his gradual assimilation into the mainstream of Catholic Irish historiography in the nineteenth century, and his blossoming in nationalist propaganda in the twentieth, so the popularly maintained paradox of his character was vital to the plays of Power, Longford and even Yeats.

To Corkery's fellow cultural nationalist, Aodh de Blacam, whose school history of Irish literature appeared in 1934, that paradox seemed inextricable from the accomplishment of Ireland's first great English writer. Unlike D.F. MacCarthy nearly a century before, however, de Blacam refrained from emblemizing it within a Catholicized nationalist aesthetic. Swift is no symbol of Ireland's wrongs, but simply

> incomprehensible – a sceptic who was a clergyman; a despiser of the old Irish . . . who yet gave Ireland a policy of economic independence and a belief in its own resources . . . a hater of injustice, yet a cynic, often obscene – a genius who died mad.[45]

This paradox may bear some relation to another one de Blacam discovered in his research. Later in 1934, convinced that the works of some Irish Protestant writers from the sixteenth through the eighteenth centuries manifested a real, if variable, sense of Gaelic culture, he was moved to contest the exclusively Catholic outlook of Corkery's *Hidden Ireland*. In an article in *Studies* he argued instead for the existence of a Protestant nationalism that was authentically Irish, and which Swift implicitly served.[46] Earlier in the same issue of *Studies*, Joseph Hone analysed Swift's economic nationalism, with a postscript on Corkery's earlier *Studies* article, retorting that Swift never wrote as sympathetically of the Anglo-Irish as he had on occasion of the natives.[47] In the final issue of *Studies* for 1934, Corkery responded to de Blacam's article, while ignoring Hone's and its postscript, by holding that there was simply no such concept as Protestant nationalism. A Protestant might be 'an Irish nationalist *sans phrase* if his purpose was to conserve the national mind', but the Protestant settlement of Ireland was 'thoroughly imbued with the spirit of English imperialism, to which spirit Bedell the Gaeliciser, as well as Ussher the Angliciser, had both surrendered themselves',[48] and which in Swift is only somewhat diluted. His Irish identity could only be granted notionally; politically, Swift's motives were humanitarian rather than patriotic, while culturally he was foreign to the genuine spirit of Ireland.

This was far from sectarian, but was immediately given such a construction by the *Catholic Bulletin*, which would not be eclipsed as a Catholic champion in the controversy. An editorial applauded Corkery for taking the *Drapier's Letters* as 'the product of the Ascendancy spirit, bluntly and brutally expressed', and criticized both Hone's and de Blacam's articles, confuting the latter in particular with an example of Catholic cultural populism that the more scholarly Corkery had avoided:

> Right down from the time of Elizabeth, our people rightly deemed that one term in Irish, *Sacsanach*, does excellently well as a label for English and for Protestants. They sensed the two elements of alien and apostate influence as being one in their whole essence and purpose: and they have the same true sense of the facts to-day.[49]

While the *Bulletin* was allying itself with Corkery, his former student, Sean O'Faolain, took up the same point to make a case against him. Corkery had argued in *The Hidden Ireland* that Gaelic culture had survived in the eighteenth century as an inspiring reinforcement to popular Irish identity. Instead, O'Faolain held in his biography of O'Connell, *King of the Beggars* (1938), that what survived of Gaelic literary culture was irrelevant to the contemporary oppression of most Irish-speaking country people; what informed their culture was precisely their religious identity, upon which O'Connell was able to construct modern Irish identity.[50] In this sense, of course, that identity would exclude Swift, but even as O'Faolain was more forthcoming than Corkery about the primacy of religious over literary culture among the eighteenth-century rural masses, he was also critical of Corkery's cultural nationalism for excluding the contributions of the Anglo-Irish. In this latter area particularly, Swift's role was central, and in an essay of 1936 O'Faolain had charged Corkery with viewing Anglo-Irish literature from the narrow perspective of political chauvinism.[51] And in O'Faolain's 'character study' of *The Irish* in 1947, he explicitly embraced the Anglo-Irish contribution not merely to literature but to social and political life, while acknowledging the historical responsibility of Protestant Ireland for the oppression of the

Catholic majority.[52] Implicitly, he located this paradox as central to the Irish identity of those Protestants, recalling de Blacam's emphasis upon the paradox of Swift's own identity.

Unlike the *Catholic Bulletin* writers, Corkery was no demagogue but a genuine scholar, respected and influential. Yet on Swift, O'Faolain reflected the temper of his time more accurately than his former teacher. Corkery's effect on the shape of Swift's reputation was not only limited by his ignoring such aspects of the Dean as the paradox of his character and the function of his patriotism. To maintain that 'Irish' was synonymous with 'Gaelic' – and then only to the extent that the latter was free of English influence – manifests in Corkery an historiography so systematic that Emmet Larkin has questioned 'the extent to which he will be overthrown', though conceding the inevitability of some modification.[53] But this consistency in his understanding of Irish cultural and political history, which effectively excluded Swift, and certainly Yeats among his successors, was also too rigid to accommodate two factors gathering force in Corkery's day. First, while the long-secure place Swift had occupied in mainstream nationalist ideology had indeed diminished in propaganda value after Independence, it had begun to gain respect anew among those who wished to validate the Irish state not as progressing toward Gaelic purity, but as it actually was. Thus the genealogical imperative formulated in the nineteenth century, lending nationalism historically distant ancestors and more recent successors, distinguished not by their religion (or even their motives) so much as by their anti-English rhetoric or actions, had combined (perhaps paradoxically) with the steady growth of English as Ireland's popular language, and was complemented by the achievement of independence. Ireland's emergence as a free, modern and (in fact, if not in official preference) Anglophone nation demonstrated an organic development, and to debunk patriots who were Protestant, and indeed so attractive as rhetoricians as Swift, would vitiate the patriotic genealogy central to that organicism. It would also, of course, fly in the face of contemporary official non-sectarianism, however unsteady this may have been in practice. The developmental, genealogical concept both was patriotic and gave a positive cast to contemporary Irish (rather than exclusively Gaelic) identity, as evidenced by writers such as de Blacam and O'Faolain; it would, especially with the passage of time, become too useful a myth for Corkery's logic, however intellectually compelling, to dislodge.

The second proposition Corkery would not accommodate because he had already disputed it: the Irish authenticity of the 'Literary Revival' that Yeats in particular had promoted. This authenticity, however, was already widely accepted, not least for a political value both within and without Ireland. As early as 1922, Ernest Boyd had at once taken the literature of the Revival as 'a creditable manifestation of the awakening of the national spirit', and considered that it 'has done more than anything else to draw the attention of the outside world to the separate national existence of Ireland'.[54] The same

international recognition of that literature gave Irish writers of the generation following Yeats – O'Faolain and Frank O'Connor among them – what
Lawrence McCaffrey has termed 'a vested interest' in that assertion of Irish
identity:

> They were proud of the worldwide opinion that the Anglo-Irish school
> reflected Irish genius. Yeats and his friends developed Dublin into a literary
> capital, making things Irish a subject of international interest and concern,
> enhancing the reputation of every writer calling him or herself Irish.[55]

As Arthur Power recalled, Yeats had himself had a genealogical imperative,
seeing Swift as an ancestral pillar of that Anglo-Irish school. While the Dean
served a useful purpose in an historical myth, then, he was an indispensable
representative of the greatness of Irish literature, a father-figure for an inter-
nationally appealing literary movement.

IV

The Anglo-Irish literary tradition, so perceived genealogically, with Swift as
its progenitor and Yeats as its foremost modern representative, could thus be
understood as a tradition of personality. The most striking of its figures, with
pride of place in this Romantically oriented line and with a patriotic reputation as well, Swift was the more amenable to dramatic treatment, not only as
example but as theme for literary inspiration. For Yeats, Swift's singularity of
character weighed more heavily than his overtly patriotic contribution, since
the modern poet regarded nationalism alone as a poor claim to literary
memory. But Swift's personality could also attest to his Irishness: Corkery
himself, reflecting briefly upon the Dean's character in the first of his 1934
articles in *Studies*, had noted that 'there are men built on the same plan in our
own streets'.[56] And the character which variously fascinated Yeats and
Longford was sufficiently compelling to the dramatist Paul Vincent Carroll
that he found it could work independently of the Dean. In the mid-1930s,
dissatisfied with a play about Swift titled *Farewell to Greatness*, Carroll abandoned it and used the character of Swift for another work, *Shadow and
Substance* (1937), which became his best-known play.[57] As he wrote in
the *New York Times* early in 1938, just as *Shadow* was being produced on
Broadway:

> I decided one day to resurrect Dean Swift, make him not only a Catholic but
> a learned interpreter of Catholicism, and throw him into the modern mental
> turmoil in Ireland, which could be complicated by contact. From him came
> the character of the canon. . . . The rebel schoolmaster and the canon repre-
> sent the conflicting forces that crush Brigid (the spirit of the nation) between
> them.[58]

The play, of course, is not concerned with Dean Swift, but rather with the plight of Brigid, Canon Skerritt's servant, whose claim that St Brigid has appeared to her in their little Mourne village is treated sceptically both by the austere, cultivated Canon and the anti-clerical O'Flingsley, the village schoolmaster, though of course for different reasons. Canon Skerritt's selfishness, his learned, aristocratic manner and disdainful sense of exile in rural Ireland are drawn from Swift's character, and Carroll's fascination with the Dean enabled him to flesh out the character of the Canon more successfully, in fact, than he was able to manage with that of Swift himself when *Farewell to Greatness* was revised as a television play for the BBC some twenty years later.

By 'resurrecting' Swift in the person of Canon Skerritt, Carroll emphasized the tyrant in Swift's personality; it is only the Canon's cultivated manner that keeps him from becoming the stock Irish character of the autocratic parish priest. Denis Johnston, a dramatist of the generation following Yeats who has endured better than Carroll, found the tormented nature of Swift's character more absorbing than the tyrannical. An experienced and accomplished writer, whose first play, *The Old Lady Says 'No!'* (1929), had already gained renown as an expressionist experiment, Johnston 'first became fascinated by the problem of Swift after seeing Lord Longford's play at the Gate Theatre'.[59] His own Swift play was also an experiment, and was initially scripted for broadcast on BBC Radio, 18 June 1938, with the title 'Weep for Polyphemus'.[60] Developing the play for the stage, Johnston retitled it *The Dreaming Dust* and enriched its experimentalism; as produced by Hilton Edwards and Micheál MacLíammóir at the Gaiety Theatre, Dublin, on 25 March 1940, it involved the conventions of acting and of morality as much as the story of Swift. Set in 1835 in St Patrick's Cathedral, where the graves of Swift and Stella have been opened in the course of repairing the cathedral floor, the play presents a group of actors who have just finished portraying the seven deadly sins in a masque. Fascinated by Swift's story, in which each of the actors is attracted to a different individual, they are encouraged by the current Dean of the cathedral to act out different episodes in Swift's career, for all of which he would play Swift's own part. As the episodes take place, it is clear that each features a different failing in the characters variously of Swift, Stella and Vanessa, a failing corresponding to the sin each actor has earlier portrayed. As Richard Cave has noted, 'the theatrical idea of type-casting takes on symbolic resonance, illustrating how perception, and beyond that, judgement are subjectively conditioned reflexes, that acts of creative sympathy are rare movements in the human psyche'.[61] On the one hand, the play allows Johnston to draw out his theory that Swift and Stella never married because he was the illegitimate half-brother of Sir William Temple and she Temple's bastard daughter. On the other, it uses Swift's life and loves as the basis for a morality play about human sympathies – Swift's, the actors', and by inference ours – rather than simply as a story sufficiently dramatic in its own right.

In that story, Johnston's concern is with Swift the man, the subject of popular anecdotes – some of which are enacted in the play – and this allows him to take occasional licence with factual accuracy. To Hilton Edwards, however, who had played Swift in both Johnston's and Longford's plays, Johnston's Swift was 'less playable and less satisfactory than the Swift of Lord Longford's *Yahoo*, which, with all its crudeness, comes off well and really enables the actor to hit on something like theatrical verity', while *The Dreaming Dust* 'sacrifices drama to a thesis'.[62] Yet Johnston's theory of Swift's consanguinity with Stella provides a dramatic fulcrum for the play and gives it dramatic coherence. Johnston was greatly attached to his theory,[63] and he revised the play repeatedly on its account. Indeed, though in the earliest version of the work 'he schemed it too mechanically',[64] the hostile reception of the theory among Swift scholars made him insist upon it the more.[65] The dilemma of integrating it properly meant that 'the composition of this play has cost me more time and trouble than any other play that I have ever written'.[66] In the process of revision, the Dean's patriotic career, never very prominent, became less so. Johnston may not have regretted this, given the sort of ambivalence toward reputation-mongering for historical patriots that remained constant in the successive revisions of *The Old Lady Says 'No!'*. In addition, Swift's patriotism as an aspect of his Irish identity was no longer a subject of very serious dispute; Johnston's focus instead on Swift the man, like that of Yeats, manifested the lure of personality that complemented his patriotism, and to a degree would ultimately even displace it, as the dominant feature of that identity.

Patriotic reputation-mongering, however, became the order of the day when in October 1945 Dublin marked the bicentenary of Swift's death, and though Johnston joined in the tributes, he had quite a different emphasis. In *The Bell* for September the old Sinn Feiner P.S. O'Hegarty had already struck the appropriate note for the occasion, recalling Young Ireland by elaborating a Swift-inspired patriot line and vindicating the Dean's as 'an Irish Patriotism, not a sectarian one'.[67] On the anniversary itself, only the distinctly Anglo-Irish tone of the proceedings would have hinted that his patriotism or Irish identity had ever been disputed; *The Irish Times* devoted a leading article to the Dean, and lectures were delivered at Swift's grave in St Patrick's Cathedral and at Trinity College. But that tone was equally nationalist, at least implicitly anti-English, celebrating Swift as a progenitor of a self-reliant, independent nation. Even the *Irish Press*, the pro-Fianna Fáil newspaper owned by Eamon de Valéra, featured an article hailing Swift, by the Rev. R. Wyse Jackson, a Church of Ireland clergyman, amateur Swift scholar and later Bishop of Limerick. Jackson struck a left-of-centre note, in keeping with Fianna Fáil populism: 'Few men ever saw so clearly and felt more bitterly the plight of the Irish workers and peasants. . . . He fought the corner of the workpeople. . . . As the Drapier he was the first to give them a sense of their strength. . . .'[68] The *Irish Times* editorial saw him as at once 'the first of the great line of Protestant champions of his native country' and a proto-revolutionary:

> He coaxed, bullied, lashed his fellow-citizens into a momentary forgetfulness of their degraded condition: for a few years he made them hold up their heads again: he taught them that, in the event of England's failure to redress their wrongs, they had always the last resort of revolution. It took a man of high courage to preach the doctrine of Theobald Wolfe Tone in the days of the first Hanoverians, and royally the poor of Dublin repaid the man who preached it.[69]

The current Dean of St Patrick's noted in his lecture at Swift's grave that not only was Swift the first modern journalist, 'the originator of the leading article' and of 'the power that the Press wields today', but that he also 'gave Ireland a soul, self-respect, something that she had not had for a long time'. M.J. MacManus of the *Irish Press*, the only non-Anglo-Irishman to join in the tributes, insisted in his lecture at Trinity that 'Swift must be placed in relation to his Irish world if we are to understand him, either as a man or a writer. . . . Whatever his blood or ancestry, . . . Ireland took him and made him largely as he was.' And Sir Shane Leslie, Anglo-Irish but a Catholic convert and old Home Rule nationalist, held in a Radio Eireann broadcast that 'Modern Irish nationalism . . . was born at the tip of Swift's pen. He was the first Sinn Feiner who called on Irishmen to burn everything English but their coal.'[70]

Nearly all the bicentenary observances, in fact, stressed Swift's nationalist identity rather than his contribution to literature or even his personality. That emphasis reflects the renewed strength of the old nationalist formula, which Corkery had denigrated, for Ireland's organic development toward independence. The pronounced patriotism of the Anglo-Irish observers betrays, further, a note of historical self-congratulation; the occasion lent an opportunity to invoke their ancestors' role in founding modern Irish nationhood and demonstrated thereby their own sense of belonging to that nation. But in his own 'Bicentenary Tribute', Denis Johnston cast a jaundiced eye at perfervid nationalist encomia: 'his works are being ransacked to-day as never before for handy epithets and quotations that can be applied to the political problems that confront us still. And never in vain. . . . Here in Ireland we have the Drapiers Letters and the "Modest Proposal" to bolster up the hearts of our tradesmen and justify us in our insularity. . . .' Johnston regretted, furthermore, that even though 'We, who possess his birthplace and his bones, his tradition and his secret, can claim to have a special position on his bicentenary,' comparatively few of the works about him are by Irishmen. Since 'the native contributions to his biography are much the best', however, he instanced a few, and noted that 'above all, Swift was a dominating influence in Yeats's later years, and whistles through the pages of his diaries

like a cold draught in the last bus for Innisfree'.[71] Here Johnston was touching
on the two factors driving Swift's modern Irish reputation that Corkery, a
decade earlier, had not managed to derail: the revived political usefulness he
offered well after Independence (related to the patriotic function for which
nationalists long before Independence, and Johnston's fellow Anglo-
Irishmen the preceding day, had hailed the Dean); and the newer genealogical imperative for an Anglo-Irish literary tradition that elevated Yeats as
well. Snidely ambivalent about both factors, Johnston was yet gentler on the
latter, for a tradition emphasizing personality better suited his own fascination with Swift the man; a year later Hilton Edwards noted that Johnston had
been revising *The Dreaming Dust*.[72]

Johnston's comments hardly deterred a fresh academic interpreter, J.J.
Hogan of University College, Dublin, whose bicentenary tribute at the end of
1945 so unconditionally promoted the old nationalist line on Swift as to
recall the enthusiasm of D.J. O'Donoghue in 1912. Ignoring Corkery's (and
Whibley's earlier) distinction between patriotism and humanitarian
impulses, Hogan insisted that Swift was a true nationalist because in all his
Irish writings he had the good of the nation at heart. Swift even discounte-
nanced 'a system of ascendancy, of privilege and exclusion' for Ireland, since
he 'was no colonial patriot, if by that is meant the patriot of a class; he had
no notion of erecting an Anglo-Irish freedom upon native helotry'.[73] Yet
while the enthusiastic bicentenary observances, culminating with Hogan's
essay, indicated the durability of the approach to Swift laid out by Thomas
Davis and *The Nation* a century before, they comprised the last concentrated
celebration of Swift's nationalist identity along those lines. The bicentenary
coincided with the end of the Second World War, during which the Irish
state had maintained its neutrality, in good part in order to assert the national
independence toward which Young Ireland had looked. The patriotic drum-
beat of the Swift observances reflected the officially sanctioned mood in the
wartime period termed in Ireland 'The Emergency', as well as Anglo-Irish
attempts to validate Swift's Irishness in the context of that mood. Thereafter,
as no major successor emerged in the line from Thomas Moore to Daniel
Corkery to argue against his Irish identity, it stood in no more need of
extended validation than did Ireland's place in modern literature.

As to Ireland's place in the world, on the other hand, wartime neutrality
(especially when contrasted with the Allied participation of Northern Ireland) had imparted a degree of isolation – the 'insularity' of which Johnston
had complained – that the post-war era offered the nation few opportunities
to breach. Politically, Ireland's exclusion from the United Nations by Soviet
veto until 1955, and the declaration of the Republic in 1949, taking the Irish
state out of the Commonwealth, hardened that isolation. Economically,
continued dependence on the British market for agricultural goods forestalled
development. But tourism did present an opportunity, which enthusiastic
interpreters of Swift were eager to exploit. The marketing of Ireland as a

tourist destination meant that travel magazines and brochures included radically condensed versions of Irish nationalist history along with touring suggestions and photographs – those of Dublin often featuring Swift's bust in St Patrick's. Contemporary literary figures were often induced to write such magazine features, as Frank O'Connor did for *Holiday* in 1949. While he noted for its American audience that Swift was 'the first important figure to face up to the fact that England was attempting to make the Norman Conquest a continuous process', he could remark that after Vanessa's death 'Swift hurled himself into Irish politics, perhaps goaded by Stella, who had turned into a red-hot little rebel,'[74] an idea owing more to Longford's *Yahoo* than to history. O'Connor's comments here were less important than their coming from him; genuinely interested in the Dean, of whom he noted in a travel book 'He is the most vivid figure which ever walked in Dublin streets,'[75] he was also following the custom, introduced by Yeats, of modern Irish writers' discussing Swift as though embracing a tradition of personality in Irish literature.

As a writer popular outside Ireland, O'Connor was exposing that custom to a broader audience than experimental playwrights such as Yeats, Longford or Johnston could reach. By emphasizing the authenticity of the patriot as much as the character in Swift's Irish identity, furthermore, he also bespoke the renewed acceptance within Ireland of the old-fashioned nationalist treatment of the Dean. By contrast, it was a foreigner who recounted a reservation almost as old. Accepting that Swift was the first to protest Irish subjugation to British interests in the eighteenth century, the French historian Roger Chauviré nonetheless struck a note resonant of Mitchel and Moran:

> But in spite of everything . . . he seems to be unaware of where the injustice really lay, and to have bypassed the real problem. Swift seems to have no idea that the rule of the Protestants might be questioned; the original inhabitants . . . seemed to him a barbarous people.[76]

When that note was sounded in Ireland itself during the 1950s, however, it was more muted. A history book prescribed for use in the national schools in these years shows the influence of the British orthodoxy derived direct from Whibley, and perhaps also that of Corkery. Stressing Swift's 'showing up the misdeeds of the Ascendancy in Ireland', it was ambivalent, at worst, about his identity, recalling the old nationalist weighting of his effect (here put in Whibley's terms) as greater than that of his motives:

> Dean Swift was not a nationalist and had no love for Ireland's ancient tradition or culture, but he had even less love for the narrow Ascendancy in power. He hated injustice and misery, and these evils he did everything in his power to remedy.[77]

But outright praise was still more common. P.S. O'Hegarty borrowed part of Corkery's thesis in *The Hidden Ireland* in maintaining that Catholic Ireland at the time of the Union comprised an 'Underground Nation', but one that cherished the memory of a 'Patriot Party among the Garrison Nation', the heritage of Molyneux, Lucas, Flood, Grattan and Swift.[78] And there was no ambivalence about his identity in another school history, which claimed Swift as 'one of the greatest Irishmen of modern times', largely on the basis of his economic writings.[79] In the balance positive about Swift's Irish identity, these popular histories seem generally to rehearse the old nationalist consensus on the Dean that O'Connor had invoked. It is remarkable, however, that none of them even mentions the *Drapier's Letters*, whose defensive anti-Englishness had prefigured the attitude of much pre-Independence nationalism. Indeed, Carty's *Class-Book* in particular, by implicitly defining Swift's Irishness in terms drawn from his social observations and economic exhortations, manifests a nascent trend in Irish historiography, anticipating the socio-economic orientation with regard to Swift in *The Course of Irish History*.[80] This popular work of 1967 was based upon an Irish television series, and represented the ascendance of a 'revisionist' school of Irish history which took issue with many features of old-fashioned nationalist historiography, not least its political emphases.

V

Developing from the 1950s much more rapidly than the impact of revisionist historiography on Swift's identity was its part in the Yeats-inspired matrix of a tradition of personality for Anglo-Irish literature. Paul Vincent Carroll revised his early, never-performed play of the 1930s on Swift for a BBC television production in 1956 as *Farewell to Greatness*.[81] Though Carroll was the first non-Anglo-Irish playwright since Arthur Power to compose a Swift play, patriotism is less evident than the Dean's internal conflicts. Having already constructed, in *Shadow and Substance*, a vehicle for one Irish feature of Swift's identity, his focus now, like Denis Johnston's but without any of Johnston's theory or moral aim, was Swift the man. Indeed, Carroll laboured to produce a Swift well-rounded, in terms both of his career and of his emotional life: the play emphasizes the contrast between his influence upon the Tory ministers in Queen Anne's time and the narrow life he had to lead in Dublin, between the sensual Vanessa and a usually stoic Stella, between Swift's increasing misanthropy and the affection his friends had for him. These contrasts were the more easily accommodated by the numerous scene changes that television allowed, while a liberal post-war popular morality is apparent in Vanessa's actual seduction of the Dean, despite all his efforts to resist the temptation she offers. Swift's patriotism is not ignored, but is certainly secondary to the play's focus on more intimate emotions: at the height of the Wood affair, for instance, when Stella is overcome by the continual frustration of her love for Swift and plans to leave him, she is moved to return by the devoted admiration of the Dublin mob for the Drapier. The subordination of the patriot Dean, however, leaves the somewhat contrived early scenes of Swift among the powerful as the major counter balance to his eventually consuming misanthropy. His misanthropy therefore seems mostly the product of arrogance and an internalized sexual tension of which Swift is unaware, obvious though it becomes for the audience. The problem, then, is not that Carroll was unsympathetic to Swift, but that the portrayal of Swift's character does not render credible the magnetism to which the devotion of the crowd and the affection of his friends clearly respond.

While Carroll implied a psycho-sexual interpretation of biographical facts, he was followed within a few years by Sybil Le Brocquy, an amateur Swift scholar, who conjectured a striking addition to those facts. In the course of research on Swift, she discovered some long-lost documents about Vanessa's family, the Vanhomrighs, which led her to interpret well-known correspondence between Swift and Vanessa and other documents and claim that they had had a liaison at the end of Swift's years in London as a result of which Vanessa produced a child. The evidence and her argument Le Brocquy published in 1962 as *Cadenus*, a book-length study; both were pressed again in her play *A View on Vanessa*, produced at the Lantern Theatre, Dublin, in April 1967, during the tercentenary celebrations of Swift's birth.[82] The play presents a small group in modern Dublin who discuss and read selections from the Swift–Vanessa correspondence, alternating with interludes in which the Dean and Vanessa appear themselves, enacting the reconstruction of events arising from Le Brocquy's conjectures. The work is more interesting for its reconstruction than for its dramatic value, yet the emphasis upon Swift the man was in keeping with the general tone of the tercentenary.

Indeed, as Roger McHugh, Professor of Anglo-Irish Literature and Drama at University College, Dublin, noted in his contribution to an issue of *University Review* devoted to Swift: 'By now the enigmatic figure of Jonathan Swift has been woven into the Irish tapestry and, subjected to different lights, has taken on colours and connotations of which he never could have dreamed.'[83] Though McHugh went on to summarize Swift's patriotic exertions, his tone was dispassionate, suggesting that these were common knowledge, almost to be taken for granted. And otherwise in the tercentenary celebration, they generally were. Contrasting remarkably with the observances on the bicentenary of his death, those of the tercentenary of his birth were both more expansive and tended to emphasize the man and author rather than specifically the patriot. The Irish government printed stamps portraying Swift's bust in Trinity College and Gulliver among the Lilliputians; *The Irish Times*, which had published a patriotic leader on the bicentenary of Swift's death in 1945, printed a commemorative supplement for the tercentenary of his birth;[84] and while both Trinity and Radio Eireann had been content with single lectures in 1945, in 1967 Trinity sponsored a

Commemorative stamps issued for the
tricentenary of Swift's birth.

scholarly symposium and Radio Telefís Eireann broadcast a series of Thomas
Davis Lectures.[85] Eliciting both academic and official pride in Swift as an Irish
writer and a forerunner of the Literary Revival, the occasion showed Ireland
well able to take advantage of the scholarly industry that Swift's works had
long since prompted in Britain and North America. An untypical note of
ambivalence was struck, characteristically, by Denis Johnston, who with R.
Wyse Jackson, now Church of Ireland Bishop of Limerick, were the only
celebrants from 1945 to contribute to the 1967 tercentenary. Johnston's essay
in the *Irish Times* supplement was wry where before he had been regretful and
acerbic, noting now that the ambivalences of this occasion, as of much that
had shaped the course of Swift's reputation, were simply matched by the
Dean's own inconsistencies.[86] For his part, Bishop Jackson dwelt on Swift
associations in Dublin, in contrast to the populist political tone of his 1945
essay.[87] The construction of Swift's identity as a pillar of Anglo-Irish literature that Arthur Power remembered Yeats projecting in the 1920s, was by
now soundly established.

But this Anglo-Irish literature was one to which far more than the Anglo-
Irish were attached, whether by affection or participation; and the literary
values accorded to Swift as its pillar could be broadly humane as well as
nationalist. Frank O'Connor's earlier emphasis on Swift as both character
and patriot was qualified shortly before his death, in an appreciation of Swift's
significance to Ireland's literature for an academic audience, by his discerning
that the 'political note' struck in *A Modest Proposal* and other works 'is
characteristic of Anglo-Irish literature. I know of no other literature so
closely linked to the immediate reality of politics.'[88] On the other hand,
the most moving tribute arising from the tercentenary was Austin Clarke's
'A Sermon on Swift', recalling his own lecture of 1967 in St Patrick's on
the Dean's poetry and exploring his affinities with Swift, satirical and
scatological:

> In prose, plain as pike, pillory
> In octosyllabic verse turning the two-way
> Corner of rhyme, Swift wrote on privy matters
> That have to be my text.

Clarke's 'text' is at once the subject of his 'sermon' and of such works as his later scatological poems. But the association extends beyond literary concerns:

> Last gift of an unwilling patriot, Swift willed
> To us a mansion of forgetfulness. I lodged
> There for a year. . . .[89]

Already over seventy, Clarke, a poet whose work and career were always overshadowed by Yeats, found an ancestor, precursor and protective spirit in Swift as surely as Yeats himself had done.

If with a lesser degree of self-involvement, in the years since the tercentenary a further generation of Irish playwrights has embraced Swift as personality, all but eclipsing the patriot. Eugene McCabe's *Swift*, produced at the Abbey on 18 August 1969, is set in 1741, toward the end of the Dean's life; and interwoven with his reminiscences – presented as flashbacks – are scenes of the old man's helplessness as his chaplain plots to have the sub-Dean of the cathedral removed and himself named to the vacancy. The picture of Swift on the verge of senility, softened by his feeble attempts at kindness toward an old servant, contrasts with the chaplain's machinations and even cruelty toward him, and offsets effectively the flashback scenes in which a younger Swift is more resolute and himself harder upon those around him. The scenes of reminiscence often allude to Swift's years of political influence in England and Ireland, but never present any such episodes directly, concentrating instead on his relationships with Stella and Vanessa and, to a lesser extent, with Bolingbroke out of power and with Archbishop King. The pathos of Swift's old age throws into relief the emphasis in the flashback scenes upon his missed opportunities to love better when he was in his prime, so that a generally sympathetic picture emerges, rather than that of a misanthrope. Heightening this pathos, McCabe used Le Brocquy's theory of Vanessa's having borne Swift's illegitimate child, to whom the Dean is unfailingly tender and who dies in his boyhood. Swift's tragedy is perceptible as intensely personal; indeed, his patriotic eminence is largely taken for granted, and the allusions to it tend to be dismissive: 'Posing in pamphlets as M.B. Drapier, I used a tinder that always sparks off patriotism . . . cash!! It worked very well indeed.'[90]

Almost exactly six years later, Ulick O'Connor focused particularly upon the Swift–Stella liaison in his play *The Dark Lovers*, first performed at the Project Theatre, Dublin on 16 August 1975.[91] The two-act drama opens with Swift lamenting Stella's death, then featuring as narrator or participant in a

Eugene McCabe's *Swift*, directed by Sir Tyrone Guthrie (*front right*), in rehearsal. Micheál
MacLíammóir plays Swift and the author is pictured on the extreme right.

series of roughly chronological episodes illustrating the course of their relationship, from the early years in Sir William Temple's household to the point
of Stella's death. The circular time-line emphasizes Stella's centrality in
Swift's life, while encompassing Swift's rise from a humble position with
Temple to social and political eminence in London and then to patriotic
popularity in Dublin. These vignettes are coloured by evidences and anecdotes of Swift's pride, generosity, wit and resentment at English injustice to
Ireland, as well as his attempt to juggle amours at once with Vanessa and
Stella, and his fears of madness. Maintaining the patriotic aspect of the
tradition of personality, O'Connor presents Swift as not only politically but
culturally sympathetic to Ireland, especially in a factually fanciful vignette of
Turlough O'Carolan visiting the deanery and entertaining a group of friends
with a rendition of 'O'Rourke's Feast' on the harp as Swift recites his translation of the poem. But O'Connor focuses upon Swift the lover, attempting
to portray him in as positive, indeed romantic, a light as history would allow.
If this and the occasional departures from attestable fact disadvantage history
somewhat, *The Dark Lovers* is still certainly a historical drama.

Theatrical performances featuring Swift in both Britain and Ireland over
the next few years again rather acknowledged than deferred to history. The
Dean as wit and lover was the focus of *Yahoo*, an 'entertainment' that Sir
Alec Guinness (who took the role of Swift) and Alan Strachan 'devised' for

production in Cambridge and Bath before its London opening in October 1976.[92] A more straightforwardly comedic one-man show, *Patrick Gulliver*, its Dublin-based humour incorporating elements of stage Irishry, was presented by Eamonn Morrissey at the Peacock Theatre, Dublin in 1978 and revived in slightly altered form as *Mr Gulliver's Bags* at the Peacock in 1984. By contrast, *No Country for Old Men* was an ambitious attempt to portray Swift's final years; a film by Tristram Powell with a script by David Nokes (who was soon to produce an influential biography of the Dean), it was broadcast on BBC 2 Television on 28 June 1981. In conveying the impression of Swift as 'trying to maintain the dictates of reason in a world seething with vice and folly . . . the strain [of which] finally almost broke his mind', *No Country* struck one sympathetic reviewer as particularly sensitive to eighteenth-century squalour – not least that of Ireland – becoming in the process 'a gripping and sometimes persuasive fantasia in the grotesque'.[93]

A final Swift drama from the contemporary Irish generation of playwrights, indeed, emphasizes psychology at the utter expense of history. Tom MacIntyre's *The Bearded Lady*, first produced at the Peacock Theatre on 10 September 1984,[94] is a phantasmagoria 'dominated', as MacIntyre put it in a later article, 'by the "woman problem" '.[95] Despite its surrealistic experimentalism, the play was heralded with a quite straightforward historical article by MacIntyre in the Aer Lingus tourist magazine, illustrated with photographs of the players acting Swift, Stella and Vanessa in non-stage settings at Dublin and Celbridge.[96] The two-act play presents Swift as three characters, sometimes simultaneously on stage: the young 'Master Jonathan', the mad 'Old Dean' and Swift himself, essentially as Gulliver, and is loosely constructed around Gulliver's reception among and ultimate rejection by the Houyhnhnms. Female sexuality provides the focus of the play, the set of which features a giant pair of breasts between which the major characters often enter and exit; it fascinates and disturbs the main Swift character (and to a lesser extent the attendant young and old Swift), who is also intensely attracted to the Nazi-like orderliness of the Houyhnhnms. Thus Stella, Vanessa and the Female Yahoo enact a recurrent interplay in Swift's mind with the Master Houyhnhnm and his stormtrooper lieutenants, whether these characters appear separately or together. Concerned to portray Swift's mind rather than abide by any historical timeline, *The Bearded Lady* barely even alludes to the patriot Dean; Swift the man becomes a Swift beset, inescapably but not wholly against his will, by sex, permanently symbolized by the mammary set on stage and vivified by the antics of the women, who highlight the pubic allusiveness of the title. In his 1986 article, MacIntyre recounted his satisfaction at having captured his conception of Swift, yet confessed that about midway through the second act, 'somewhere in the last quarter of the two hour traffic – Swift banished by the Houyhnhnms, resumption imminent of the dark voyage with all its palpitating baggage, somewhere in there he got away from me'. However convinced that sexuality offered the

A scene in Tom MacIntyre's *The Bearded Lady*, from a production at the Peacock Theatre, Dublin, in 1984, directed by Patrick Mason, with Vincent O'Neill as the Master Houyhnhnm and Tom Hickey as Swift.

right approach to Swift, he attributed the Dean's ultimate elusiveness to 'that shadow he has, the genius he has, the amplitude of him'.[97]

If Swift's 'amplitude' escaped MacIntyre, it had also every other dramatist since Eveleen Bell at the turn of the century. Of course, no historical drama can encompass the whole of a character once living. Very few come near to the essence of one; and in Swift, the important aspects of personality and career, of the man, the satirist, the propagandist, the friend, the lover and (more) the beloved of women, are sufficiently discrete that no single essence satisfies. Between Yeats's comment that 'Swift haunts me; he is always around the next corner' and MacIntyre's half a century later, that 'The man Swift pursues me, eludes me; many, no doubt, would say the same,'[98] there is little difference. Probably Longford comes closest to the Dean, tempering temporal linearity with expressionism, taking Swift *and* his posthumous reputation, the friend, lover and patriot (in varying degrees) into account, and eschewing the theory-directedness that flaws Johnston's, Le Brocquy's and McCabe's, and

MacIntyre's plays. Longford's background was different from that of Swift's other modern dramatic interpreters in Ireland, more aristocratic and, somewhat like Swift himself, as much English as Irish. And more than any of them except possibly Yeats, he resembled Swift in his commitment to a mission of improvement, in his case enlarging Ireland's theatrical exposure by means of the Gate Theatre and a touring company. It may have been these aspects of the man, combined with his political nationalism, that ensured his more comprehensive sympathy with Swift. Yet even that sympathy, or comparative success, may be simply more appreciable in the context of examining Swift's identity, to which Longford was better attuned than the others. For Swift's amplitude, naturally and ultimately, resists definition. Irish plays about the Dean attest as much, and in fact are most properly appreciated in the aggregate, less for their particular attempts to capture the man or fix his Irish identity than for demonstrating, in their range of responses to his amply enduring presence in Irish culture, the fluid dynamism of his Irishness in the decades since national Independence.

Epilogue

Independence enabled the development of Ireland's culture beyond the political, inevitably collectivist orientation characteristic of nationalism in the nineteenth century, so that gradually, in the literature of the twentieth, it has accommodated a heightened artistry and individuality. In the course of this transition, Swift's refusal to accommodate himself to the shift in his own time beyond the conventions he had found comfortable in Queen Anne's day, his insistence upon being awkward politically, socially and romantically, could be reconsidered. That refusal had been amenable to nationalist interpretation as analogous to the Irish refusal to accommodate British political control; now it made Swift an emblem of the unconventional. His suffering, rather than implicitly representing Ireland's, appropriated him to the temper of Ireland's writers and intellectuals in the twentieth century. This modern implication, lurking in *Finnegans Wake*, recurs in the Swift plays of three generations of dramatists: Yeats, Johnston and certainly McCabe and MacIntyre. From the nineteenth through the twentieth century, then, Swift has remained an Irish cultural touchstone, 'the most potent and recurrent symbolic presence in modern Irish writing'.[1]

And in contemporary Ireland at large he offers an icon of elastic significance. For school and university literature courses in Ireland – unlike those in Britain or North America – the *Drapier's Letters* are as much standard texts as *Gulliver's Travels*. Yet, while Swift for fifteen years appeared on the Irish ten-pound note, his portrait was superimposed upon an extract not from the *Drapier's Letters*, nor any other patriotic or literary text, but from a letter outlining his intention to found a mental hospital by bequest (only the fact that the note is currency suggests the economic aspect of Swift's patriotism). The reproduction of even this extract on the note stands as official and literal acceptance of a notion that the Dean himself, anticipating the legacy in 'Verses on the Death of Dr. Swift', could treat ironically:

The ten-pound note featuring Swift was issued by the Central Bank of Ireland in 1978; it was discontinued in 1993.

> He gave the little wealth he had
> To build a house for fools and mad
> And showed by one satiric touch
> No nation wanted it so much.

Another creative interpretation, or misunderstanding, of Swift the patriot is the weekly 'Drapier' column in *The Irish Times* devoted to legislative politics and backbench gossip, hardly ever verging into substantive, much less nationalist, commentary. On a more genial level, for over two centuries public houses in Dublin have been named for Swift, and especially since the 1960s a number of restaurants, usually calling themselves 'Jonathan's' – all successors themselves to the 'Drapier's Head' taverns of Swift's lifetime. And a highlight of the 1988 Dublin Millennium celebrations was a huge figure of Gulliver, paraded through the city centre and launched into Dublin Bay, washing up on Dollymount Strand, a popular bathing place, like Gulliver arriving in Lilliput.

These are merely gestures at Swift's amplitude, but their direction has some meaning. Swift has been absorbed so completely into Irish cultural life, at various levels, essentially because he remains a 'character' in the Irish sense of the word. He is remembered still for a fundamentally human impressiveness, as 'the Dane' of the old nineteenth-century 'Jack and the Dane' stories and as a man whose loves and lovers made a fascinating story, even as his patriotic and literary achievements, and the perceptions of him that have flowed from them, have validated preserving that character. In recent times, moreover, his character lingers because Ireland's contemporary circumstances have made a passionate ambivalence about the country – such as his own – familiar.

This plaster bust of Swift, now in the Civic Museum, Dublin, long adorned a public house near his birthplace in Hoey's Court.

This is an ambivalence of many aspects, political, economic, perhaps most perceptibly socio-cultural, as its shapes appear in the 'various forms of doubling [that] are frequently put forward as somehow intrinsic to Irishness'.[2] In Irish literary culture, that doubleness has been recognized as 'an underlying irony of approach' to literary conception among writers,[3] or as a literary feature of 'the relentless reciprocity that binds the colonizer to the colonized', perhaps remediable by an analysis of 'Anglo-Irish literature as a continuation of the colonial enterprise'.[4] An early image of that doubleness, in either aspect, indeed appears in Swift's own ambivalence about Ireland. But the most commonly recognized source of Irish doubleness, the shift from Irish to English as the preferred language in Ireland, transcends Swift; though he advocated this shift[5] he can bear little responsibility for its advance. Nor can he, indeed, for the resonance of his ambivalence in modern Irish society and culture, for his was rooted, for the most part, in inextricably personal circumstances. These latter contribute, however, to the unfading fascination with Swift as a 'character' in Ireland; they make part of his amplitude, as does his

A seventy-foot model of Gulliver, constructed for the Dublin Millennium, was eventually beached on Dollymount Strand where it was photographed for the front page of *The Irish Times*, 13 July 1988.

literary greatness, his patriotism and even his official position in the 'colonial enterprise'. The echo of his ambivalence in modern Ireland has its own euphony, if one far different from that of the ideological seemliness nineteenth-century nationalists found in Swift. That coherence appeared counterpointed by his eccentricities rather than belied by the contradictions that slavish historical accuracy could reveal. Now Swift's contradictions seem to befit Ireland's discontinuities; the unease many have felt at the unrealized ideals of independence presents parallels with his own discomfitures. Such parallels are themselves often untrue to Swift, yet – appropriately to so paradoxical a man and writer – they too contribute to his Irish amplitude, more warrant still for perpetuating his memory in a country he defended but could not love.

Notes

Introduction

1 Conor Cruise O'Brien, 'Irishness,' in *New Statesman* (January 1959), reprinted in *Writers and Politics* (London: Chatto & Windus, 1965), pp. 98–9.

2 See Wolfgang Zach, 'Jonathan Swift and Colonialism', in *Reading Swift: Papers from the Second Muenster Symposium on Jonathan Swift*, ed. Richard Rodino and Hermann Real (Munich: W. Fink, 1993), pp. 91–9; also Warren Montag, *The Unthinkable Swift* (London: Verso, 1994), pp. 157–8, n. 6.

3 For the applicability of this term, rather than the currently more familiar 'nation', I am obliged to the recent work of C.D.A. Leighton, *Catholicism in a Protestant Kingdom: A Study of the Irish Ancien Regime* (Dublin: Gill and Macmillan, 1994).

4 Thomas Carte, *An History of the Life of James Duke of Ormond* (London: J. Bettenham for J.J. and P. Knapton et al., 1736), 2: 317.

5 Richard Cox, *Some Observations on the Present State of Ireland* . . . (Dublin, 1731), p. 23.

Chapter 1

1 'A New Song Sung at the Club at Mr. Taplin's The Sign of the Drapier's Head in Truck-Street' (broadside) (Dublin, 1724); this has been ascribed to Richard Witherall by Bryan Coleborne, 'Anglo-Irish Verse 1675–1825', in *Field Day Anthology of Irish Writing*, ed. Seamus Deane (Derry: Field Day, 1991), 1: 482, 499.

2 Swift had implied as much in a number of his poems at this time, for example 'A Serious Poem upon William Wood'. 'An Epigram on Wood's Brass Money' and 'Prometheus', in *The Poems of Jonathan Swift*, ed. Harold Williams, 2nd edn (Oxford: Clarendon Press, 1958), 1: 333–8, 343–7.

3 *A Letter to the Right Honourable Sir Ralph Gore* . . . (Dublin, 1732), pp. 11–12. The author signs himself 'Philostelus', p. 15.

4 Irvin Ehrenpreis, *Swift: The Man, His Works, and the Age* (Cambridge, Mass.: Harvard University Press, 1962–83), 3: 495.

5 For example, 'nothing on that Subject [trade] can obtain a Currency amongst us, till your Approbation has first stampt a Value upon it, and made it Sterling . . .', from the dedication 'To the Revd. Dean Swift', in *A Reply to the Observer on Seasonable Remarks* (Dublin: S. Powell, 1728), p. ii. The author was probably Sir John Browne.

6 JS to Pope, 8 July 1733, in *Correspondence of Jonathan Swift*, ed. Harold Williams (Oxford: Clarendon Press, 1965), 4: 171.

7 *Poems*, 3: 874–5.

8 Ehrenpreis, 3: 898.

9 'Verses written by Dr. Swift', in *Poems*, 2: 611. Another contemporary text of the poem in *London Magazine*, 6 (August 1737), p. 421, has 'Fame' for 'Praise' in the final line quoted here.

10 *Memoirs of Mrs. Laetitia Pilkington*, vol. 3 (London: R. Griffiths, 1754), p. 54.

11 James Woolley, *Swift's Later Poems* (New York: Garland, 1988), pp. 14–15.

12 See, for instance, Matthew Pilkington, 'The Candle', in *Poems on Several Occasions* (London: T. Woodward, 1731), p. 58: 'Or *Swift's*, or *Pope's*, or *Maro's* Lays, / All blest with universal Praise'; or Richard Barton, 'The Author to his Book', in *Farrago: Or Miscellanies in Verse and Prose* (London, 1739), sig. b: 'Old Horace, Swift and Pope he passes.'

13 'A New Session of the Poets for the Year 1730', *Universal Spectator*, 6 February 1731, repr. in *Gentleman's Magazine*, 1 (February 1731), p. 71.

14 Anon., *An Essay on Preferment* (Dublin, 1736), p. 16.

15 JS to William Pulteney, 8 March 1734–5, in *Correspondence*, 4: 304.

16 JS to Pope, 1 May and 8 July 1733; to Oxford, 30 August 1734, in *Correspondence*, 4: 154,169, 248. Cf. also Margaret Weedon, 'An Uncancelled Copy of the First Collected Edition of Swift's Poems', in *The Library*, 5th ser., 22 (1967), pp. 44–56. Faulkner maintained in 1744 that he had not instigated the edition himself, but that 'many Friends of Dr. Swift's applied to the Printer hereof, who had published many Pamphlets of his, at different Times, to make a compleat Collection of his Works': *Dublin Journal*, 29 September–2 October 1744, p. 2.

17 Joseph McMinn, 'Printing Swift', in *Eire-Ireland* 20 (1985), p. 143.

18 *Dublin Journal*, 1–4 February 1734.

The possibility that Faulkner wrote these verses himself is noted by Robert E. Ward, *Prince of Dublin Printers: The Letters of George Faulkner* (Lexington, KY: University Press of Kentucky, 1972), p. 12.

19 [Henry Jones], 'The Bricklayer's Poem. Presented to his Excellency the Lord Lieutenant. On his Arrival in this Kingdom' (Dublin, 1745), p. 6.

20 *The Drapier's Second Letter to the Good People of Ireland* (Dublin, 1745), p. 2. Years later Matthew Maty, similarly noting that the (first) 1745 *Letter* was 'greedily received', considered it 'much in the Dean's stile' and suspected Chesterfield's hand in it: 'Memoirs of Lord Chesterfield', in *Miscellaneous Works . . . of Chesterfield* (Dublin: Watson et al., 1777), 1: 157. Faulkner, however, thought the style unlike Swift's: *Supplement to Dr. Swift's Works* (London: C. Bathurst et al., 1779), p. 423.

21 *Dublin Journal*, 19–22 October 1745, p. 1.

22 Ehrenpreis, 3: 918; Monck Mason, *The History and Antiquities of the Collegiate and Cathedral Church of St. Patrick . . .* (Dublin: W. Folds for the Author, 1820), pp. 412–13.

23 An anonymous chronicler in 1840 speculated that the College authorities were displeased by the students' plan: see 'Gallery of Illustrious Irishmen: Swift', *Dublin University Magazine*, 15 (June 1840), pp. 659–60.

24 *Dublin Journal*, 9–12 November 1745.

25 *The Draper's* [sic] *APPARITION to G——e F——r, A New Poem* (Dublin, 1745), p. 6.

26 *The Works of J.S., D.D., D.S.P.D.*, vol. 8 (Dublin: G. Faulkner, 1746), sig. a2^v.

27 Maty, 4: 81.

28 *Chivalrie, No Trifle——Or, The Knight and his Lady: A Tale* (Dublin, 1746), p. 2. Attributed to a Rev. Stevens, cf. Foxon, *English Verse 1701–1705: A Catalogue of Separately Printed Poems* (Cambridge: Cambridge University Press, 1975), 1: 119.

29 MS, [First] *Minute Book of the*

Governors of St. Patrick's Hospital (1746–96). I am indebted to Dr Elizabeth Malcolm for this information.

30 The most succinct account of the contest is Seán Murphy, 'Charles Lucas and the Dublin Election of 1748–1749', in *Parliamentary History*, 2 (1983), pp. 93–111.

31 Stephen Gwynn, *Henry Grattan and His Times* (London: Harrap, 1939), p. 9.

32 Charles Lucas, *A Third Address to the Free Citizens and Free Holders of the City of Dublin*, 5 September 1748 (Dublin: J. Kelburn, 1748), p. 6, repr. in *Political Constitutions of Great Britain and Ireland Asserted and Vindicated* (London, 1751), 1: 14.

33 Charles Lucas, 'Dedication', in *Political Constitutions*, 1: xxviii.

34 [Charles Lucas], 'Advertisement', in *The History of the Four Last Years of the Queen. By the late Jonathan Swift . . .* (London: A. Millar, 1758), pp. v–vi; (Dublin: G. and A. Ewing, 1758), p. v. Lucas was first identified as the 'editor' of this work in Samuel Johnson's account of Swift (1781) in *Lives of the English Poets*, ed. G.B. Hill (Oxford: Clarendon Press, 1905), 3: 27–8.

35 *The Censor*, no. 9, repr. in *Political Constitutions*, 1: 494. The possibility that others besides Lucas contributed *Censor* articles was suggested by the attribution of those signed 'B' (including nos 8 and 10) to Edmund Burke, in A.P.I. Samuels and A.W. Samuels, *The Early Life Correspondence and Writings of the Rt Hon Edmund Burke* (Cambridge: Cambridge University Press, 1923), pp. 390–1; G.L. Vincitorio, 'Edmund Burke and Charles Lucas,' in *PMLA*, 68 (1953), p. 1048 n., disputed the attribution to Burke but did not hold that Lucas was the sole author of *The Censor*, while Seán Murphy, 'Charles Lucas and the Dublin Election of 1748–1749', pp. 100–1, supports the possibility of multiple authorship and even that of Burke for the articles signed 'B'. The authorship of the unsigned ninth *Censor* thus remains an open question,

though the style resembles Lucas's.

36 James Latouche, *A Second Address to the Citizens of Dublin* (Dublin: P. Wilson, 1749), p. 11.

37 JS, *The Story of the Injured Lady* (Dublin: J. Byrn, 1749), p. 3.

38 [Advertisement in] 'T. Taylor', *Lucas Refuted: Or Liberty Supported . . .* (Dublin: H. Garland, 1749), p. 15ᵛ. The actual Dublin reprint of Molyneux's work by Augustus Long and Henry Hawker in 1749 has no reference to Swift.

39 *A Letter from Patrick Taylor, of Bally-James-Duff, to his cousin Jemmy in Dublin, upon a late Paper War in the Metropolis* (Dublin: J. Esdall, 1749), p. 4.

40 Anon., *Dean Swift's Ghost, To the Citizens of Dublin. Concluding with a Word particularly to the Weavers*, dated 'Nov. 6th 1749' (Dubin: 1749), p. 7.

41 Murphy, p. 108.

42 See Esther K. Sheldon, *Thomas Sheridan of Smock Alley* (Princeton, New Jersey: Princeton University Press, 1967), pp. 180–1, who suggests Sheridan as the author of the prologue; it is attributed to John Marshall in the notice of his death, *Universal Advertiser* (Dublin), 11 March 1755. A manuscript of the prologue is in the British Library, MS Egerton Add. 26036, ff. 15–16; it was printed in the *General Advertiser* (London), 7 April 1752.

43 Anon., *Remarks on two Letters . . . Published in the Dublin Journal . . .* (Dublin, 1754), p. 4.

44 *The Case of the Stage in Ireland . . .* (Dublin: H. Saunders, n.d.), p. 28.

45 See Declan O'Donovan, 'The Money Bill Dispute of 1753', in *Penal Era and Golden Age: Essays in Irish History, 1690–1800*, ed. Thomas Bartlett and David Hayton (Belfast: Ulster Historical Foundation, 1979), pp. 55–87.

46 Anon., *A Letter to a Member of the H[ouse] of C[ommons] of I[relan]D, on the Present Crisis of Affairs in that Kingdom* (London: R. Scot, 1753), pp. 8–9.

47 'Patricius', *Tyranny Display'd. In a Letter from a Looker-On* (Dublin,

1754), p. 7.

48   Anon., *The Review: Being a Short Account . . . of the Writings offered to the Publick, by the C[our]t Advocates . . .* (Dublin, 1754), p. 25.

49   Anon., *Sir Teague O'Ragan's Address to the Fellows of T——y Col. . . . With some Remarks on Sir Tady Faulkner, Printer in Petto to the C[our]t P[art]y* (London, n.d. [*c.* 1753]), p. 14. See also anon., *The History of the Ministerial Conduct of the Chief Governors of Ireland* (London: W. Browne, 1754), pp. 68, 75.

50   John Browne to George Faulkner, 14 February 1750, *[Swift's] Works*, vol. 14 (London: W. Bowyer *et al.*, 1765), pp. 1–4, repr. in *Correspondence of Jonathan Swift*, ed. F. Elrington Ball (London: G. Bell, 1913), 4: 463–4.

51   *Dublin Journal*, 12–15 May 1753, p. 1.

52   Anon. [probably Paul Hiffernan], *A Dish of Chocolate for the Times* (Dublin, 1754), p. 14.

53   For an account of this dispute, see Harold Williams's introduction to his edition of the work, *Prose Writings*, vol. 7 (1951), pp. ix–xxviii. Faulkner's vigorous disputation of the Ewings' challenge to his virtual monopoly of Irish publication of Swift's work derived not from any legal copyright but from a sense of moral proprietorship, about which he remained defensive. Introducing his next edition of the *Works*, an issue in eleven volumes, in 1763, he reviewed the circumstances of his publishing the first edition (with Swift's supervision of those volumes appearing in his lifetime), justified his inclusion of all the works, however unmeritorious, and noted that he had always declined the Dean's offers of help in raising subscriptions or paying the expenses of legal proceedings associated with his publishing Swift. Thus now, 'the Editor most humbly thinks, that, according to the Laws of Justice and Reason, he is most truly entitled to the Property of these works; the Author having bestowed them to him, and corrected seven Volumes in his own Life-Time,

as well as many small Tracts published of different Periods'. ('To the Reader', dated 'October 1762', *Works . . . in Eleven Volumes* (Dublin: G. Faulkner, 1763), 1: ix–x.)

54   *Dublin Journal*, 1–5 June 1762.

55   *Dublin Journal*, 13–17 December 1763.

56   Mason, *The History and Antiquities of the Collegiate and Cathedral Church of St. Patrick . . . .*

57   J.T. Gilbert, *History of the City of Dublin*, vol. 3 (Dublin: McGlashen and Gill, 1859), p. 353.

58   See unsigned letter to 'Mr. Faulkner', *Dublin Journal*, 12–16 February 1765.

59   W.G. Strickland, *A Dictionary of Irish Artists* (Dublin, 1913; repr. Shannon: Irish University Press, 1968), p. 248.

60   See note 3, above.

61   William Dunkin, 'INSCRIPTION intended for a MONUMENT to Dr. Swift. 1765', and 'EPIGRAM (by Mr. Bowyer) occasioned by the above INSCRIPTION. 1766', reprinted from the end of the collection of Swift's poems, vol. 40 of Samuel Johnson, *English Poets*, 1779, in *Gentleman's Magazine*, 49 (November 1779), p. 552. Dunkin hadn't long to live after composing his inscription; his death was memorialized later in the year in verses noting 'with SWIFT and POPE in Virtue's Paths he trod / . . . with them our DUNKIN shall for ever live' (*Dublin Journal*, 23–26 November 1765).

62   *Dublin Journal*, 28 May–1 June 1765. The bust may not have been placed in a niche outside the house, but rather 'on a bracket in a bow window looking towards Essex Bridge' (Strickland, *Dictionary of Irish Artists*, p. 248).

63   *A Catalogue of the Pictures, Sculptures, Models . . . Exhibited by the Society of Artists in Ireland . . . March the 10th, 1766* (Dublin: H. Saunders, n.d.), p. 9.

64   John O'Keeffe, *Recollections of the Life of John O'Keeffe. Written by Himself* (London: Colburn, 1826), 1: 17.

65   *The Pleasing Moralist: Or, Polite Philosopher* (Dublin, n.d. [vol. 1 dated 1775, p. 189]), 2: 242; Lewis reprinted the poem (with the reading 'public'

for 'promised' in the line quoted) in his *The Dublin Guide; Or, A Description of the City of Dublin* (Dublin, n.d. [National Library of Ireland catalogue dates *c.* 1787]), p. 94.

66 Rev. Alexander Leeper, *Historical Handbook to the Monuments, Inscriptions &c of the Collegiate, National and Cathedral Church of St. Patrick, Dublin* (Dublin: Hodges, Foster & Figgis, 1878), p. 63.

67 MS. 'Minutes of Meetings of Chapter, Cathedral Church of St. Patrick', vol. for 1764–92, n.p.

68 *The Hibernian Journal*, 23–26 March 1776, records that 'Both our Cathedrals have been closed for several months.' *Dublin Journal*, 1–3 October 1776, notes that the improvements to St Patrick's (on account of which, apparently, the cathedral had been closed) were almost complete and that services would soon be held there.

Chapter 2

1 To arrive at a specific number of editions is not simple, as the original four octavo volumes issued in 1735 were supplemented by others, often in conjunction with reissues (sometimes with textual revisions) of the earlier volumes; editions were also published in different formats.

2 The project was announced in Faulkner's *Dublin Journal*, 15–18 July 1758, and conditions for subscribers appeared in the same paper, 1–5 August 1758, with further description given, 16–19 September and 28–31 October 1758. See also Vincent Kinane, 'The Dublin University Press in the Eighteenth Century' (unpublished fellowship thesis, Library Association of Ireland, 1981), p. 71.

3 Alexander Pope, *The Dunciad*, ed. James Sutherland, 1: 19–20 in *The Poems of Alexander Pope*, gen. ed. John Butt (London: Methuen; New Haven: Yale University Press), vol. 5 (1943), p. 62.

4 William King, 'Remarks on A Tale of a Tub,' in *Original Works* (London: N. Conant, 1776), 1: 216.

5 For a contemporary summary of the continuing controversy over Swift's political opinions see Ian Higgins, *Swift's Politics: A Study in Disaffection* (Cambridge: University Press, 1994), pp. 1–37.

6 Anon., *Essays Divine, Moral and Political . . . By the Author of the Tale of a Tub . . .* (London:1714), p. iii.

7 Anon., *The Enigmatical Court . . .* part 1 (London, repr. Dublin: 'G. Risk', 1714), p. 15 ('Smut' is identified as 'The Reverend Dr. Swift,' p. 3); anon., *A Letter to the Examiner . . .* (London: J. Moore, 1714), p. 2.

8 Anon., 'All's out at LAST; Or See who has been in the wrong', Dublin, 1714.

9 Anon., *The Justice and Necessity of Restraining the Clergy in their Preaching* (Dublin: J. Roberts, 1715), p. 36.

10 Anonymous, *Neck or Nothing: Or the History of Queen Robin . . .* part 1 (London: M. Budenell, repr. Dublin, 1714), p. 11; anon., *Magdalen-Grove; Or, a Dialogue between the Doctor and the Devil* (London: J. Carrett, [*c.* 1714]), p. 9.

11 *A Hue and Cry after Dr. S—t . . .* (London: J. Roberts, 1714).

12 Anon., *Dr. S—t's Real Diary . . .* (London: R. Burleigh, 1715).

13 *Hue and Cry*, pp. 21–3.

14 JS, 'Dean of St Patrick's Petition to the H. of Lords, Against the Lord Blaney', *Prose Writings*, 5: 199–200.

15 Anon., *An Answer to the Proposal for the Universal Use of Irish Manufactures . . .* (Dublin, 1720), p. 2.

16 'A.R. Hosier', 'A Poem to the Whole People of IRELAND, Relating to M.B. Drapier' (broadside) (Dublin: Elizabeth Sadlier, 1726).

17 Jonathan Smedley, *Gulliveriana . . .* (London: J. Roberts, 1728).

18 John Oldmixon, *The History of England During the Reigns of King William and Queen Mary, Queen Anne, King George I . . .* (London: Thomas Cox, . . . Richard Ford, and Richard Hett, 1735), p. 471.

19 Anon., 'To the Author of the *Flying Post*', *Gulliveriana*, p. 280.

20 Fabricant, *Swift's Landscape* (Baltimore: Johns Hopkins University Press, 1982), pp. 24–42; Real and Vienken, 'Psychoanalytic Criticism and Swift: The History of a Failure', *Eighteenth-Century Ireland* 1 (1986), pp. 127–41.

21 A typical example is *The Grand Mystery, or Art of Meditating over an House of Office, Restor'd and Unveil'd . . . Published by the Ingenious Dr. S—ft . . . The Third Edition, Corrected* (London, 1727), which argues that the character and even fate of persons can be determined by examining their stools.

22 *HUMAN ORDURE, Botanically Considered. The First Essay, of the Kind, Ever Published in the World* (Dublin: S. Powell for John Watson, 1733). A 'List of Spurious Productions' in the *Supplement to Dr. Swift's Works*, vol. 14 of *Works* (London: C. Bathurst, 1779, pp. 771–2), includes the 1748 ascription but not the original 1733 edition.

23 The book was advertised slightly differently in the 'Monthly Catalogue', *London Magazine* 18 (November 1749), p. 532.

24 See H. Teerink, *A Bibliography of the Writings in Prose and Verse of Jonathan Swift, D.D.* (The Hague: Nijhoft, 1937), p. 334.

25 *The BENEFIT of F[ART]ING EXPLAIN'D . . .* (Long-fart [Longford in *Ireland*]: Simon Bumbubbard, 1722). JS to Knightly Chetwode, 13 March 1722, *Correspondence*, 2: 421.

26 See note 22.

27 See Teerink, p. 326.

28 The issues they raise are discussed at length, and Swift absolved of misogyny, by Margaret Anne Doody, 'Swift among the Women', in *Yearbook of English Studies*, 18 (1988), pp. 68–92.

29 *Dr. S—t's Real Diary*, sig. A2^v, A3^v.

30 *A Young Lady's Complaint for the Stay of Dean Swift in England* (broadside) (Dublin: Faulkner, 1726).

31 ['Miss W—'], *The Gentleman's Study, in Answer to The Lady's Dressing Room* (London, printed; and Dublin, reprinted, 1732). The attribution to 'Miss W—' is made by Samuel Shepard (note following).

32 Shepard, 'Thoughts upon Reading the *Lady's Dressing Room* and the *Gentleman's Study*', in *Chloe Surpriz'd: Or, The Second Part of the Lady's Dressing Room* (London printed, and Dublin, reprinted, 1732), pp. 7–8. Foxon, 1: 726, identifies the author as Shepard and maintains there 'was probably no London edition'.

33 *Memoirs of Mrs. Laetitia Pilkington* (London: R. Griffiths, 1754), 3: 65.

34 Mary Delany, *The Autobiography and Correspondence of Mary Granville, Mrs. Delany*, ed. Lady Llanover (London: R. Bentley, 1861), 1: 301.

35 JS to John Barber, 9 March 1737–8, *Correspondence*, 5: 95.

36 *Memoirs of Mrs. Laetitia Pilkington* (Dublin printed, London reprinted, and sold by R. Griffiths and G. Woodfall, 1748; Griffiths, 1754), 1: 107; 3: 56–7.

37 *Memoirs of Mrs. Laetitia Pilkington*, 1748, 1: 52–3, 56.

38 *Gentleman's Magazine* 18 (March, May and July 1748), pp. 153–8, 243–5, 309–12.

39 *The Celebrated Mrs. Pilkington's Jests: Or the Cabinet of Wit and Humour. To which is now first added, A Great Variety of Bons Mots, Witticisms, and Anecdotes of the inimitable Dr. Swift, Dean of St. Patrick's Dublin . . . The Second Edition* (London: W. Nicoll, 1764). A first edition, apparently published in 1751, may also have contained Swiftiana, but has not been found.

40 Horace Walpole, letter to Horace Mann, 2 April 1750, in *Correspondence*, 20: 134. On the other hand, the Irish writer Paul Hiffernan regretted that 'the late unhappy Mrs. PILKINGTON' had not confined herself to 'the Account of Dr. SWIFT', which would have made 'a small, yet valuable work': *The*

Hiberniad (Dublin, 1754), p. 30.

41 Walter Harris, translating Sir James Ware's *Writers of Ireland* in *The Whole Works of Sir James Ware concerning Ireland. Revised and Improved* (Dublin: S. Powell, 1745), 2: 301.

42 [John Boyle], Earl of Orrery, *Remarks on the Life and Writings of Dr. Jonathan Swift* (London: A. Millar, 1752).

43 Orrery, p. 4.

44 MS Eng. 218, Houghton Library, Harvard University.

45 For example, Donald Berwick, *The Reputation of Jonathan Swift, 1781– 1882* (Philadelphia, 1941), p. 7.

46 Orrery, p. 4.

47 Ibid., pp. 5–6.

48 Ibid., pp. 46, 47.

49 Ibid., pp. 50, 51.

50 Ibid., p. 62.

51 Ibid., p. 70.

52 Ibid., p. 73.

53 Ibid., pp. 196–7.

54 Ibid., p. 199.

55 Ibid., pp. 247–8.

56 *Monthly Review*, 5 (November 1751), p. 407. The reviewer was probably Ralph Griffiths, editor of the magazine.

57 Samuel Richardson to Lady Bradshaigh, 23 February 1752, *Correspondence of Samuel Richardson* (London: R. Phillipps, 1804), 6: 153.

58 Henry Fielding, *Covent Garden Journal* no. 10, 4 February 1752. *The Covent Garden Journal*, ed. G.E. Jensen (New Haven: Yale University Press, 1915), 1: 194. Fielding admired Swift heartily, considering him 'one of the greatest Enemies that Dulness ever had' in the *Journal*, no. 18, 3 March 1752 (1: 244).

59 Anon., *The Inspector in the Shades. A New Dialogue in the Manner of Lucian* (London: T. Swan and E. Cooke, 1752; advertised London *Daily Advertiser*, 16 July 1752), quoted by Jensen, 1:76–7.

60 *A Letter from a Gentleman in the Country to his Son in the College of Dublin. Relating to the Memoirs of the Life and Writings of Doctor Swift, Dean of St. Patrick's, Dublin. Ascribed to the Right*

Honourable the Earl of Orrery (Dublin: O. Nelson, 1752), pp. 4–9.

61 *Letter III. From a Gentleman in the Country* [etc. as n. 60] (Dublin: Booksellers, 1753), pp. 89, 93–4.

62 Anon., *Sir Teague O'Ragan's Address to the Fellows of T[rinit]y Col. . . . With some Remarks on Sir Tady Faulkner, Printer in Petto to the C[our]t P[art]y* (London, n.d. [c. 1753]), p. 14. See also chapter 1, note 49 of the present study.

63 Quoted in [Thomas Campbell], *A Philosophical Survey of the South of Ireland* (Dublin: W. Whitestone, 1778), p. 427.

64 *Universal Advertiser* (Dublin), 17 March 1753.

65 Anon., *A Dialogue Between Dean Swift and Tho. Prior, Esq; In the Isles* [sic] *of St. Patrick's Church, Dublin* (Dublin: G. and A. Ewing, 1753), p. 124.

66 *Some Account of the Irish. By the late J.S. D.D. D.S.P.D.* (London: M. Cooper, 1753).

67 Orrery, p. 198.

68 Patrick Delany, *Observations upon Lord Orrery's Remarks on the Life and Writings of Dr. Jonathan Swift* (London: W. Reeve and A. Linde, 1754), pp. 89, 218.

69 Ibid., p. 106.

70 Ibid., p. 291.

71 Ibid., pp. 37–42, 87–8; for Stella and Vanessa, 54–8, 64–8, 111–30.

72 Deane Swift, *An Essay upon the Life, Writings, and Character of Dr. Jonathan Swift* (London: C. Bathurst, 1755). Delany's provocation of Deane Swift is outlined in Phillip S.Y. Sun, *Swift's Eighteenth-Century Biographies* (Ph. D dissertation, Yale University, 1963); Ann Arbor: University Microfilms, (1971), p. 74.

73 Deane Swift, especially p. 359.

74 Ibid., pp. 86–95, 253–64.

75 Ibid., pp. 196–7.

76 Ibid., pp. 197–8.

77 Ibid., pp. 199–200.

78 *Monthly Review*, 12 (April 1755), p. 250.

79 Anon., *Memoirs of Several Ladies of Great Britain . . .* (London: J. Noon,

1755), pp. xxvii, xxx; the account is promised in an appendix to the second volume of the *Memoirs*, for which no record of publication has been found.

80 These are summarized in Sun, pp. 52–5.

Chapter 3

1 John Hawkesworth, 'An Account of the Life of . . . Jonathan Swift', in *The Works of Jonathan Swift, D.D., Dean of St. Patrick's, Dublin* (London: C. Bathurst, *et al.*, 1755), 12 vols, 1: (1)–76 (second pagination).

2 Ibid., 'Preface', 1: 7–16 (first pagination); see also George Faulkner, *Dublin Journal*, 29 September–2 October 1744; Orrery, *Remarks*, pp. 79–81.

3 See Phillip S.Y. Sun, *Swift's Eighteenth-Century Biographies* (Ph. D dissertation, Yale University, 1963; Ann Arbor: University Microfilms, 1971), p. 108.

4 Hawkesworth, 'Preface', 1: 6–7.

5 Ibid., 'Account', p. 32.

6 Ibid., p. 41.

7 *The Comic Miscellany* (London: M. Cooper, 1756), 1: 177–8. Swift appears, incorrectly or otherwise, throughout the two volumes of this work.

8 *Swift's Jests: Or, a Compendium of Wit and Humour, Being the Facetious Jokes, and Witty Sayings, of the most eminent English Wits* . . . (London: H. Dell, 1759).

9 *The Celebrated Mrs. Pilkington's Jests . . . The Second Edition* (London: W. Nicoll, 1764).

10 John Wilkes, *The North Briton* (London: G. Kearsley, 1762), pp. 59, 62.

11 Anonymous, 'Some Outlines of the Character of Dr. SWIFT', in *Dublin Magazine* 2 (December 1763), pp. 715, 716.

12 'Some Outlines', p. 712.

13 Tobias Smollett, *A Complete History of England* (London: J. Rivington and J. Fletcher, 1757–8), 4: 502–3. Smollett, of course, would have taken

justifiable offence at Swift's hostility to the Scots.

14 R. Sharp, *A Letter to the People of Ireland; On the Present State of the Kingdom* (Dublin, 1755), p. 5.

15 W.H. Dilworth, *The Life of Dr. Jonathan Swift* (London: G. Wright, 1758), p. 55; cf. Deane Swift, *Essay* (London: C. Bathurst, 1755), p. 187.

16 Ralph Griffiths, 'The Posthumous Works of Dean Swift', in *Monthly Review*, 33 (August 1765), p. 149.

17 Edmund Burke, *Annual Register* [8], 1765 (2nd edn, London: J. Dodsley, 1778), p. 304.

18 A recent Irish disturbance had refreshed the English bias against the Irish as disloyal: see Seán Murphy, 'The Dublin Anti-Union Riot of 3 December 1759', in *Parliament, Politics and People: Essays in Eighteenth-Century Irish History*, ed. Gerard O'Brien (Dublin: Irish Academic Press, 1989), p. 58.

19 Richard Lewis, *The Pleasing Moralist: Or, Polite Philosopher* (Dublin, n.d. [dated in 1: 189 as 1775]), 1: 195–6.

20 Lewis, 'An Elegy Written in a Cathedral', 2: 242.

21 Lewis, 1: 199.

22 Lewis, 'An Original Poem of Dr. SWIFT, being his first poetical attempt, written at Oxford in 1690', 1: 233–7, an attribution Williams dismisses: *Swift's Poems*, 3: 1068. Lewis's 'Elegy Written in a Cathedral', 2: 236–47, especially p. 242, seems to admit Swift's patriotic value or function while disputing his motives.

23 Thomas Campbell, *A Philosophical Survey of the South of Ireland* (Dublin: W. Whitestone, 1778), pp. 22, 428.

24 Anon., *The First Lines of Ireland's Interest in the Year 1780* (Dublin: R. Marchbank, 1780), p. 40.

25 Gerard O'Brien, 'Illusion and Reality in Late Eighteenth-Century Irish Politics', in *Eighteenth-Century Ireland*, 3 (1988), pp. 151–2.

26 William Eden, *A Letter to the Earl of Carlisle* (Dublin: R. Marchbank, 1779), p. 10.

27 *Monthly Review*, 61 (November 1779),

p. 356, attributed to Samuel Badcock in B.C. Nangle, *The Monthly Review. First Series. Index of Contributors and Articles* (Oxford: Clarendon Press, 1934), p. 206.

28 Samuel Johnson, *Lives of the English Poets.* ed. G.B. Hill (Oxford: Clarendon Press, 1905), 3: 50. Johnson's final clauses refer to the repeal in 1779 of laws restricting Irish trade.

29 *The Beauties of Swift: or, the Favourite Offspring of Wit & Genius* (London: G. Kearsley, 1782), sig. A^v.

30 Ibid., pp. xvi, 111–12n.

31 Discussed by Gerard O'Brien, 'The Grattan Mystique', in *Eighteenth-Century Ireland*, 1 (1986), pp. 190–4.

32 Warden Flood, *Memoirs of the Life and Correspondence of the Right Hon. Henry Flood, M.P.* (Dublin: J. Cumming, 1838), p. vi.

33 Francis Hardy, *Memoirs of the Political and Private Life of James Caulfield, Earl of Charlemont* (London: Cadell and Davies, 1810), p. 49.

34 James Kelly, *Prelude to Union: Anglo-Irish Politics in the 1780s* (Cork: University Press, 1992), p. 1; this work argues that the Irish parliament between 1782 and 1800 was more conservative and more controlled by the British administration, while Grattan was less influential upon its workings than nineteenth-century nationalists preferred to acknowledge.

35 Leonard MacNally, *The Claims of Ireland and the Resolutions of the Volunteers Vindicated* (London: J. Johnson, 1782), pp. 14–15.

36 Ibid., pp. 15–16.

37 William Crawford, *A History of Ireland, from the Earliest Period, to the Present Time* (Strabane: J. Bellew, 1783), 2: 289.

38 See pp. 16–17 of the present study.

39 In the same year that Sheridan's edition appeared, his son had published a letter written in the manner of the *Drapier's Letters*, 'To the People of England', in the *Morning Chronicle*, 2 March 1784: see *The Letters of Richard Brinsley Sheridan*, ed. Cecil Price

(Oxford: Clarendon Press, 1966), 1: 158–60.

40 Thomas Sheridan, ed., *Works of the Rev. Dr. Jonathan Swift* (London: W. Strahan *et al.*, 1784), 2: (A2).

41 Anonymous reviews, *Gentleman's Magazine*, 54 (August, September 1784), pp. 603–4, 676–8; *European Magazine*, 6 (October 1784), pp. 282–6.

42 *Supplement to Swift's Works* (London: J. Nichols, 1779), 1: 258–59; *The Tatler* (London: J. Nichols, 1786), 5: 142–5; *Gentleman's Magazine*, 56 (August 1786), p. 694.

43 Correspondence between Thomas Percy and John Nichols in J.B. Nichols, *Illustrations of the Literary History of the Eighteenth Century* (London: J.B. Nichols, 1858), 8: 78–87; George-Monck Berkeley, *Literary Relics. . . . To which is prefixed, An Inquiry into the Life of Dean Swift* (London: C. Eliot and T. Kay, 1789), pp. xlv–lii; *Gentleman's Magazine*, 60 (March 1790), p. 189.

44 This discussion is generally indebted to Thomas Bartlett, *The Fall and Rise of the Irish Nation: The Catholic Question 1690–1830* (Dublin: Gill and Macmillan, 1992), pp. 45–201, and James Kelly, *Prelude to Union, passim.*

45 See for example JS as the 'Examiner' condemned as one of the 'Hirelings of the *French and Popish Faction*', in *Neck or Nothing: Or, The History of Queen Robin . . .*, Part 1 (London: M. Budenell, repr. Dublin, 1714), p. 11.

46 See especially JS, 'Reasons humbly offered to the Parliament of Ireland for Repealing the Sacramental Test, in favour of the Catholicks . . .' (1733), in *Prose Writings*, ed. H. Davis, vol. 12 (1955; 1971), pp. 283–95.

47 *Some Account of the Irish. By the late J.S. D.D. D.S.P.D.* (London: M. Cooper, 1753), p. 42.

48 Letter from James Grainger to Thomas Percy, 18 October 1758, in *Illustrations of the Literary History of the Eighteenth Century*, ed. J.B. Nichols (London: Nichols, 1848), 7: 265.

49 [John Curry], *Observations on the*

Popery Laws (Dublin: T. Ewing, 1771), p. 50.

50 John Curry, *State of the Catholics in Ireland* (Dublin: L. White, 1786), 2: 246, 1: iii–iv.

51 Discussed by James Kelly, 'The Genesis of "Protestant Ascendancy": The Rightboy Disturbances of the 1780s and their Impact upon Protestant Opinion', in Gerard O'Brien, ed., *Parliament, Politics and People*, pp. 93–127, to which much of the following summary is indebted.

52 The currency of this term and the issues it has continued to present are discussed by W.J. McCormack, 'Eighteenth-Century Ascendancy: Yeats and the Historians', in *Eighteenth Century Ireland*, 4 (1989), pp. 159–81.

53 'In reason, all government without the consent of the governed is the very definition of slavery . . . a man upon the rack was never known to be refused the liberty of roaring as loud as he thought fit'. Quoted in *Proceedings of the Catholic Meeting in Dublin duly convened on Wednesday, October 31, 1792 . . .* (Dublin: H. Fitzpatrick, 1792), title page.

54 Thomas Campbell, *Strictures on the Ecclesiastical and Literary History of Ireland. . . . Also, An Historical Sketch of the Constitution and Government of Ireland . . . down to the year 1783* (Dublin: L. White, 1789), p. 362.

55 James Mullala, *A View of Irish Affairs since the Revolution of 1688, to . . . 1795* (Dublin: T. Henshall, 1795), 1: pp. 233, 237–8.

56 Henry Grattan, *The Speeches of the Right Honourable Henry Grattan, In the Irish, and the Imperial Parliament. Edited by his Son* (London: Longman et al., 1822), 2: 355.

57 'Obadiah Tithepig', *Pastor Evangelicus: A Poem* (Dublin: H. Fitzpatrick for G. Folingsby, 1795), p. 2.

58 Michael Sandys, *A Letter to the Right Honourable Henry Grattan, on the State of the Labouring Poor in Ireland* (Dublin: B. Dugdale, 1796), p. 32.

59 MS. 2041, fol. 1^v, Trinity College Library, Dublin; quoted in Marianne

Elliott, *Wolfe Tone: Prophet of Irish Independence* (New Haven: Yale University Press, 1989), p. 87.

60 Theobald Wolfe Tone, *The Life of Theobald Wolfe Tone . . . Edited by his Son* (Washington: Gales & Seaton, 1826), 1: 32.

61 Quoted in Elliott, p. 142; noted, p. 145.

62 Drennan, *The Drennan Letters*, ed. D.A. Chart (Belfast: Stationery Office, 1931), p. 145.

63 Coxe, *Memoirs of the Life and Administration of Sir Robert Walpole* (London: Cadell & Davies, 1798), 1: 216, 226.

64 Somerville, *The History of Great Britain during the Reign of Queen Anne* (London: Strahan et al., 1798), pp. 474, 532, 551n.

65 Anon., *Proofs rise on Proofs, that the Union is totally incompatible with the Rights of the . . . Kingdom of Ireland* (Dublin: Marchbank et al., 1799), p. 9; anonymous, *Cease Your Funning* (Dublin: J. Moore, 1798), pp. 3–4.

66 W.J. Mathias, *The Shade of Alexander Pope on the Banks of the Thames* (London: T. Beckett, 1799), p. 6.

67 *Parliamentary Register*, Session 1800 (5 February 1800), pp. 168, 234.

68 John Foster, speech of 14 May 1805, *Hansard*, 1, 4: 1003–4.

69 Foster, exchange of 7 May 1802, *Parliamentary History*, 36: 652.

70 Quoted in Henry Grattan (jr), *Memoirs of the Life and Times of the Rt. Hon. Henry Grattan* (London: H. Colburn, 1846), 5: 422, but not so recorded in *Hansard*, 1, 20: 311.

Chapter 4

1 Nathan Drake, 'Jonathan Swift', in *Essays, Biographical, Critical, and Historical, Illustrative of the Tatler, Spectator and Guardian* (London: C. Whittingham for J. Sharpe, 1805), 3: 160,171. The contrast between a view of Swift still common in the eighteenth century and that foreshadowing the harsher judgements of nineteenth-century critics is palpable

in the Rev. Mark Noble's *Biographical History of England . . . Being a Continuation of the Rev. J. Granger's Work* (London: Richardson *et al.*, 1806), 2: 163–7, in which Noble's generally negative assessment of Swift precedes the glowing tribute that Granger had given in manuscript preparatory to a continuation of his own *Biographical Dictionary* (1769) before his death in 1776: 'The more we dwell upon the character and writings of this great man, the more they improve upon us. . . . He did the highest honour to his country, by his parts; and was a great blessing to it, by the vigilance and activity of his public spirit' (2: 166).

2   Beddoes, *Hygeia: Or Essays Moral and Medical . . .* (Bristol: J. Miller, . . . for R. Phillips, 1802–3), 3: 186–96.

3   For a more thorough account of Swift's reputation at the hands of British critics during this period see Donald M. Berwick, *The Reputation of Jonathan Swift: 1781–1882* (Philadelphia, 1941; repr. New York: Haskell House, 1965), pp. 18–50.

4   Anon., 'Some Outlines of the Character of Dr. Swift', in *Dublin Magazine*, 2 (December 1763), p. 716; *European Magazine*, 18 (September 1790), p. 185. The commentator's harshness may reflect an Irish desire to keep pace with English developments in taste, for he notes that Swift's verse is more admired in Ireland than in England.

5   Anon., 'Character of Jonathan Swift, D.D., Dean of St. Patrick's, Dublin', in *European Magazine*, 18 (November 1790), p. 332.

6   *Forensic Eloquence . . . Including the Speeches of Mr. Curran . . . accompanied by certain papers Illustrating the History [of Ireland]* (Baltimore: G. Douglas, 1804), p. 16; repr. as *Speeches of John Philpot Curran . . . To which is Prefixed, A Brief Sketch of the History of Ireland* (2 vols) (New York: Isaac Riley, 1809, 1811), 1: 16.

7   B.T. Duhigg, *History of the King's Inns* (Dublin: J. Barlow, 1806), p. 216.

8   J.C. Beckett has argued in *Literature and Society in the Age of Swift and Grattan* (New Orleans: Graduate School, Tulane University, 1977), p. 13, that the Irish Protestant agitation for constitutional rights in the eighteenth century, rather than manifesting a 'colonial nationalism', derived from the 'fundamental assertion that Ireland was, and always had been, a distinct kingdom'; so that the achievement of legislative independence in 1782 'restor[ed] an ancient kingdom to its rightful place in the world'.

9   Francis Plowden, *An Historical Review of the State of Ireland . . . to its Union with Great Britain* (London: C. Rowarth for T. Egerton, 1803), 1: 258n, 389–91.

10   Denis Taafe, *An Impartial History of Ireland . . . to the Present Time* (Dublin: J. Christie, 4 vols, 1809–11), 4: 21.

11   Donald MacCartney [*sic* for Donal McCartney], 'The Writing of History in Ireland, 1800–30', in *Irish Historical Studies*, 10 (1957), p. 355.

12   Richard Musgrove, *Strictures upon an Historical Review of the State of Ireland* (London: F.C. and J. Rivington, 1804), pp. 73–4. It is ironic that Musgrove here should have so closely echoed Dr John Curry's encomium on Swift, used to press the contrary argument, in *Observations on the Popery Laws* (Dublin: T. Ewing, 1771), p. 50.

13   James Gordon, *A History of Ireland . . . to the Accomplishment of the Union with Great Britain in 1801* (Dublin: J.Jones, 1805), 2: 209, 211.

14   John Wilson Croker, *A Sketch of the State of Ireland Past and Present* (Dublin: M.N. Mahon, 1808), pp. 10, 11.

15   Francis Hardy, *Memoirs of the Political and Private Life of James Caulfield, Earl of Charlemont* (London: Cadell and Davies, 1810), p. 49.

16   Matthew O'Conor, *The History of the Irish Catholics from the Settlement in 1691 . . .* (Dublin: J. Stockdale, 1813), p. 194.

17   Thomas Newenham, *A View of the*

Natural, Political and Commercial Circumstances of Ireland (London: Cadell and Davies, 1809), p. 177.

18 MacCartney, p. 355.

19 Thomas Bartlett, *The Fall and Rise of the Irish Nation* (Dublin: Gill and Macmillan, 1992), p. 294.

20 Walter Scott, 'Memoirs of Jonathan Swift, D.D.', in *Works of Jonathan Swift, D.D.* (Edinburgh: Constable, 1814), 1: p. 306.

21 See J.G. Lockhart, *Memoirs of the Life of Sir Walter Scott* (Edinburgh: Cadell, 1837), 2: 170.

22 Scott, 'Memoirs', 1: 305.

23 In the final chapter of *Waverley* (1813), Scott expressed his hope 'to emulate the admirable Irish portraits drawn by Miss Edgeworth', and Lockhart noted that Scott hailed Edgeworth a 'sister spirit' when visiting her in 1825: *Memoirs*, 6: 60.

24 Robert Crawford, *Devolving English Literature* (Oxford: Clarendon Press, 1992), p. 15.

25 Morgan, 'No One a Prophet in his Own Country', in *The Book of the Boudoir* (London: H. Colburn, 1829), 2: 311–13.

26 Letter to Scott, 24 July 1825, quoted in Lockhart, 6: 62.

27 *Swiftiana* (ed. by Charles Henry Wilson) (London: R. Phillips, 1804), 2 vols.

28 Donald Berwick, *The Reputation of Jonathan Swift 1781–1882*, p. 51.

29 Lockhart, 3: 122–3.

30 Francis Jeffrey, 'Jonathan Swift', in *Edinburgh Review* (27 September 1816), pp. 1–58.

31 Jeffrey, pp. 1–2.

32 Ibid., p. 9.

33 Ibid., p. 22.

34 Ibid., p. 25.

35 See Lockhart, 3: 123.

36 Samuel Burdy, *The History of Ireland from the Earliest Ages to the Union* (Edinburgh: D. Stevenson for Doig and Stirling, 1817), p. 383.

37 Ibid., p. 384.

38 Anon., 'No. 53 of the Edinburgh Review', in *North American Review*, 5 (May 1817), p. 146.

39 Edward Berwick, *A Defence of Dr. Jonathan Swift . . . in Answer to . . . the Edinburgh Review* (London: Nichols & Son, 1819), pp. 37–8.

40 Ibid., pp. 38–40.

41 Ibid., p. 35.

42 *Gentleman's Magazine*, 89/1 (February 1819), pp. 156–7.

43 *Edinburgh Monthly Review*, 4 (July 1820), pp. 1–37, especially 3, 5, 7.

44 William Hazlitt, *Lectures on the English Poets* (London: Taylor and Hessey, 1818), p. 222.

45 Thomas Moore, *Memoirs of Captain Rock* (London: Longmans, 1824), pp. 123–4.

46 Ibid., pp. 126–7. By italicizing 'aere' (from Vergil, *Aeneid*, vi, 165), Moore emphasizes the literal value of what is usually a metonymy; 'to rouse men by the trumpet' can be taken as 'to rouse men by brass', thus wryly fitting the Wood controversy.

47 Gearóid Ó Tuathaigh, 'Gaelic Ireland, Popular Politics and Daniel O'Connell', in *Galway Archaeological and Historical Society Journal*, 34 (1974–5), p. 31.

48 *Speeches of the Late Rt Hon. Henry Grattan, In the Irish Parliament, in 1780 and 1782. Never before published* (London: J. Ridgway, 1821), p. 45.

49 Gerard O'Brien, 'The Grattan Mystique', in *Eighteenth-Century Ireland*, 1 (1986), pp. 191–4.

50 *First Report of the Commissioners on Education in Ireland*, House of Commons Papers 1825, xii, app. no. 221, p. 555; P.J. Dowling, *The Hedge Schools of Ireland* (Dublin: Talbot Press, 1935), p. 156; Dáithí Ó hOgain, *The Hero in Irish Folk History* (Dublin: Gill and Macmillan, 1985), p. 96.

51 P[atrick] Knight, *Erris in the 'Irish Highlands' and the 'Atlantic Railway'* (Dublin: M. Keene, 1836), p. 122. Knight's 'Preface', p. vi, indicates that the work was 'written chiefly in the year 1832' and Barret is recorded, p. 121, as having died 'about sixteen or eighteen years since', hence about 1815.

52 These stories are discussed at length

by Mackie L. Jarrell, '"Jack and the Dane": Swift Traditions in Ireland', in *'Fair Liberty was all His Cry': A Tercentenary Tribute to Jonathan Swift*, ed. A. Norman Jeffares (London: Macmillan, 1967), pp. 311–41; see also Ó hOgain, pp. 87–99.

53 George-Monck Berkeley, *Literary Relics . . .* , p. liv, which is apparently the first appearance of this story in English (1789); a later English version appears in Patrick Kennedy, 'Inedited Memoirs of Dean Swift', *The Banks of the Boro: A Chronicle of the County of Wexford* (London: Simpkin, Marshall, 1867), p. 213. See also Jarrell, p. 318n.

54 Kennedy evidently supplies the earliest version in English: *Banks of the Boro*, p. 214; see also Jarrell, p. 330n.

55 Ryan, 'Swift', in *Biographia Hibernica* (London: J. Warren, 1821), 2: 578, 587, 589.

56 William Monck Mason, *The History and Antiquities of the Collegiate and Cathedral Church of St. Patrick . . .* (Dublin: W. Folds for the Author, 1820), p. 242n.

57 Ibid., pp. 335n, 346–7.

58 For example by M. M'Dermot, *A New and Impartial History of Ireland from the Earliest Accounts to the Present Time* (London: J.M. Gowan, 1823), 4: 14.

59 W.C. Taylor, *History of the Civil Wars of Ireland* (Edinburgh: Constable, 1831), 2: 251.

60 William Goodhugh, *The English Gentleman's Library Manual: or a Guide to the Formation of a Library of Select Literature . . .* (London: For the Author, 1827), p. 140.

61 Rev. W. Harris et al., 'Swift', in *The Oxford Encyclopaedia* (Oxford: Bartlett and Hinton, 1828), 6: 784.

62 Jameson, *Loves of the Poets* (London, 1829); repr. as *Memoirs of the Loves of the Poets . . . Second Edition* (London: H. Colburn and R. Bentley, 1831), pp. 267–8.

63 John Mitford, 'Life of Swift', in *The Poetical Works of Jonathan Swift* (London: W. Pickering, 1833), 1: ix–cviii.

64 J.E. Bicheno, *Ireland, and its Economy: Being the Result of Observations made in a Tour through the Country in the Autumn of 1829* (London: J. Murray, 1830), pp. 159, 138.

65 E.H. Orpen, *An Authentic Exposure of Irish Affairs . . .* (London: J. Hatchard, 1835), p. 35.

66 William Cobbett, 'Repeal of the Union', in *Political Register*, 17 May 1834, repr. in *Cobbett in Ireland: A Warning to England*, ed. Denis Knight (London: Lawrence and Wishart, 1984), p. 263. Cobbett was responding to a leader in the *Morning Chronicle* (London), 26 April 1834, in which Swift was cited as an authoritative witness to Irish conditions in his day.

67 William Cobbett, electoral address of 5 February 1820, quoted in *The Life of William Cobbett, Second Edition* (London: F.J. Mason, 1835), p. 235.

68 Francis Sylvester Mahony, 'Dean Swift's Madness: A Tale of a Churn', in *Fraser's Magazine*, 10 (July 1834), pp. 29–30.

69 As early as November 1830, at a gathering of religious at Clongowes well before his own ordination, Mahony had displayed an antipathy to O'Connell that may date even earlier. See 'Biographical Introduction', in *The Works of Father Prout (The Rev. Francis Mahony)*, ed. Charles Kent (London: G. Routledge, 1881), p. xiii.

70 Mahony, p. 20.

71 See T.W. Moody et al., eds, *New History of Ireland*, Vol. 5 *Ireland under the Union I, 1801–70*, ed. W.E. Vaughan (Oxford: Clarendon Press, 1989), pp. 173 ff.

72 Mahony, p. 20n.

73 Ibid., p. 27.

74 Ibid.

75 Lord Mahon, *History of England from the Peace of Utrecht to the Peace of Aix-la-Chapelle* (London: J. Murray, 1836–54), (7 vols), 1: 69.

76 Ibid., 1: 70.

77 Ibid., 2: 95.

78 Ibid., 2: 101.

79 T.P. Courtenay, *Memoirs of the Life, Works and Correspondence of Sir William Temple, Bart.* (London:

Longman, 1836), 2: 140.

80 T.B. Macaulay, *Edinburgh Review*, 68 (October 1838), p. 178.

81 George Cunningham, 'Jonathan Swift', in *Lives of Eminent and Illustrious Englishmen* (Glasgow: A. Fullerton & Co., 1836), 5: 191–9.

82 Thomas Carlyle, *Lectures on the History of English Literature* (delivered 1838; first published London: Ellis and Elvey, 1892), pp. 168–9.

83 [Le Fanu], 'Original Letters – Swift – No. 1', in *Dublin University Magazine*, 12 (September 1838), p. 271.

84 [W.C. Taylor], 'Memoirs of Dean Swift', in *Gulliver's Travels* (London: Scott, Webster and Geary, 1839), pp. ix, xiii.

85 W.C. Taylor, 'Biographical Notice', in *Travels into Several Remote Nations of the World, by Lemuel Gulliver . . .* (London: Hayward and Moore, n.d. ('Preface' dated 'May 1, 1840', p. 8)), p. xlviii.

86 In his 1840 edition of the *Travels*, considering Swift's misanthropy, Taylor echoed Scott in observing that 'the state of society at that time in Ireland was well calculated to inspire the worst opinions of human nature', and continues that the country presented 'a faction of petty tyrants and a nation of trampled slaves . . . the party of the ascendancy regarded persecution as a toy, or plaything, and made human suffering an inhuman sport', p. xxxix.

87 Joe Spence, 'Nationality and Irish Toryism: The Case of the *Dublin University Magazine*, 1833–52', in *Journal of Newspaper and Periodical History*, 4, no. 3 (Autumn 1988), p. 9.

88 'Gallery of Illustrious Irishmen, No. xi – Swift', in *D.U.M.*, 15 (May 1840), p. 540.

89 *D.U.M.*, 15 (June 1840), p. 653.

90 R.F. Foster, *Modern Ireland: 1600–1972* (London: Allen Lane, 1988), p. 306.

91 *D.U.M.*, 15 (February 1840), p. 144.

92 *D.U.M.*, 15 (March 1840), p. 341.

Chapter 5

1 See Joe Spence, 'Nationality and Irish Toryism: The Case of the *Dublin University Magazine, 1833–52*' in *Journal of Newspaper and Periodical History*, 4, no. 3 (Autumn 1988), p. 4.

2 See Henry Grattan (Jr), *Memoirs of the Life and Times of the Rt. Hon. Henry Grattan* (London: H. Colburn, 1839–43), 1: 10–11, for his addition of Lucas to those his father had invoked as the ancestors of Irish patriotic agitation, and 1: 81–3 for his treatment of Lucas as Swift's particular heir.

3 Thomas Davis, 'The Young Irishmen of the Middle Classes', in *Essays Literary and Historical*, ed. D.J. O'Donoghue (Dundalk: W. Tempest, 1914), pp. 7–8.

4 [? Thomas Davis], 'English Appropriation of Irish Intellect', in *The Nation*, 26 November 1842, p. 106.

5 For a discussion of cultural homogenization as centripetal policy which in turn provokes centrifugal reaction, see William Bloom, *Personal Identity, National Identity and International Relations* (Cambridge: University Press, 1990), pp. 142–6.

6 [? Thomas Davis], 'Letters of a Protestant on Repeal, No. II', in *The Nation*, 31 December 1842, p. 185.

7 [Speech of Councillor Atkinson, 2 March 1843], in *The Nation*, 4 March 1843, p. 333.

8 [? Thomas Davis], 'A Patriot Parliament', in *The Nation*, 1 April 1843, p. 392.

9 [? Thomas Davis], 'Our National Language', in *The Nation*, 1 April 1843, p. 394.

10 [? Thomas Davis], 'An Irish Party', in *The Nation*, 15 April 1843, p. 424.

11 *Ibid.*

12 [? Thomas Davis], 'Abolition of the Lord Lieutenant', in *The Nation*, 18 May 1844, p. 504.

13 Anon., 'National Gallery No. III. Thomas Furlong', in *The Nation*, 11 March 1843, p. 348.

14 Anon., 'Popular Education', in *The Nation*, 27 July 1844, p. 664.

15 [Richard Lalor Shiel, address to the jury, 27 January 1844], *Dublin Evening Post*, 27 January 1844, p. 2.

16 [James Whiteside, Address to the jury, 1 February 1844], *Dublin Evening Post*, 3 February 1844, p. 3.

17 [? Thomas Davis], 'The Betrayed Protestants', in *The Nation*, 25 January 1845, p. 248. William Saurin, who was among the prosecutors of the United Irishmen in 1798, is included here (following Tone!) presumably because of his opposition to the Union in 1799–1800, though he had taken this stand because he feared that the Union would weaken Protestant Ascendancy.

18 Lord Brougham, *Historical Sketches of Statesmen who flourished in The Time of George III. Third series* (London: C. Knight and Co., 1843), 3: 371–2.

19 Robert Chambers, *Cyclopaedia of English Literature* (Edinburgh: W. and R. Chambers, 1844), 1: 547.

20 Thomas De Quincey, reviewing 'Schlosser's Literary History of the Eighteenth Century', in *Tait's Edinburgh Magazine*, 14 (September 1847), p. 577.

21 William Howitt, 'Swift', in *Homes and Haunts of the Most Eminent British Poets* (London: R. Bentley, 1847), 1: 207.

22 Anon., *The Life and Writings of Jonathan Swift . . . Interspersed with Several Amusing Anecdotes of this Celebrated Irishman* (Dublin: J. McCormick, 1844).

23 Daniel O'Connell [address of 9 September 1844], in *The Nation*, 14 September 1844, p. 772.

24 *The Nation*, 22 February 1845, p. 330.

25 *The Nation*, 7 June 1845, p. 561.

26 *The Nation*, 2 August 1845, p. 698.

27 Denis Florence MacCarthy, *The Poets and Dramatists of Ireland* (Dublin: James Duffy, 1846), 1: 130–1.

28 *The Book of the Poets . . . with an Essay on English Poetry* (London: J.J. Chidley, [1846]), pp. xxix–xxx.

29 John Forster MS. 48.E. 25, no. 1555, Victoria and Albert Museum, London.

30 T.F. Meagher, speech of 13 January 1847, *The Nation*, 16 January 1847, p. 229.

31 'Preface', in *Irish Political Economy* (Dublin: Irish Confederation, 1847), pp. iii–iv.

32 Anonymous report, *The Nation*, 24 July 1847, p. 668; P.A. S[illard], *The Life of John Mitchel* (Dublin: J. Duffy, 1889), pp. 128–9.

33 Anonymous review, *The Nation*, 27 March 1847, p. 394.

34 Anonymous review of works on Marlborough, *Dublin Review*, 26 (May 1849), p. 125.

35 *Biographical Sketches of Eminent British Poets . . . intended for Teachers, and the Higher Classes in Schools* (Dublin: Commissioners of National Education in Ireland, 1849), p. 235. Compiled by Maurice Cross, according to TCD catalogue.

36 See [Elizabeth Jane Brabazon], *Outlines of the History of Ireland for Schools and Families* (Dublin: Curry, 1844, repr. 1847), p. 313; Townsend Young, *Outlines of the History of Ireland for Schools and Families* (Dublin: Hodges & Smith, 1848), pp. 173–4.

37 W.R. Wilde, 'Some Particulars respecting Swift and Stella, with Engravings of their Crania; together with some notice of St. Patrick's Hospital', in *Dublin Quarterly Journal of Medical Science*, 3 (May 1847), pp. 384–434; 4 (August 1847), pp. 1–33.

38 W.R. Wilde, *The Closing Years of Dean Swift's Life* (Dublin: Hodges and Smith, 1849), pp. 71–2.

39 Ibid., p. 4.

40 [John Anster, reviewing Wilde], *Dublin University Magazine*, 33 (March 1849), p. 376; Anster is identified as the reviewer in *The Wellesley Index to Victorian Periodicals, 1824–1900*, ed. W.E. Houghton and J.A. Slingerland (Toronto: University Press, 1966–89), vol. 4, p. 277.

41 Wilde, *The Closing Years . . . Second Edition* (Dublin: Hodges and Smith, 1849), pp. 68–71.

42 [John Anster], 'Swift and his Biographers', in *North British Review*, 11

(August 1849), p. 362; Anster is identified as the reviewer in *Wellesley Index*, 1: 673.

43 R.S. Brooke, 'A Pilgrimage to Quilca in the year 1852; with some Account of the "Old Belongings" of that Place', in *Dublin University Magazine*, 40 (November 1852), p. 515. Though the article is merely signed 'B.', the author is identified as Brooke in *Wellesley Index*, 4: 288.

44 Ibid., p. 516.

45 James Wills, 'Jonathan Swift, Dean of St. Patrick's', in *Lives of Illustrious and Distinguished Irishmen* (Dublin: Macgregor, Polson & Co., 1852), 4, part 2: 416.

46 Ibid., p. 417.

47 Ibid., p. 440.

48 [Samuel Phillips], 'The Amours of Dean Swift', in *The Times*, 3 October 1850, p. 3.

49 W.M. Thackeray, *The English Humourists of the Eighteenth Century* (London: Smith, Elder, 1853), pp. 14–16.

50 Ibid., p. 30.

51 Ibid., pp. 32–3.

52 Ibid., p. 11.

53 Ibid., p. 40.

54 Ibid., p. 54.

55 Anonymous [Review of Thackeray], in *The Critic, or London Literary Journal*, 15 July 1853, p. 374.

56 Anon., 'A Picture of Swift by Thackeray', in *Hogg's Instructor*, 1 (July 1853), p. 79.

57 [John Eagles], 'Thackeray's Lectures – Swift', in *Blackwood's Edinburgh Magazine*, 74 (October 1853), pp. 496–7, 509–10. The review is reprinted in Eagles's *Essays Contributed to Blackwood's Magazine* (Edinburgh: Blackwood, 1857), pp. 212–65.

58 David Masson [review of Thackeray], in *British Quarterly Review*, 20 (October 1854), p. 551.

59 James Hannay, *Satire and Satirists* (London: D. Bogue, 1854), p. 151.

60 T.B. Macaulay, *The History of England from the Accession of James the Second* (London: Longman et al., 1849–55), 4: 115, 1: 370.

61 Walter Bagehot, 'The First Edinburgh Reviewers', in *National Review*, 1 (October 1855), pp. 280–1; though contributed anonymously, the article is reprinted in Bagehot's *Literary Studies*, ed. R.H. Hutton (London: Longmans, 1879).

62 Thomas Irwin, 'Swift', in *Versicles* (London: Bosworth and Harrison, 1856), p. 98.

63 Alexander Andrews, *History of British Journalism* (London: R. Bentley, 1859), pp. 115–16.

64 Thomas D'Arcy McGee, *A History of the Attempts to Establish the Protestant Reformation in Ireland* (Boston: P. Donahoe, 1853), pp. 215, 217.

65 Christian Brothers, *Historical Class-Book* (Dublin: W. Powell, 1859), p. 574.

66 Martin Haverty, *The History of Ireland* (Dublin: J. Duffy, 1860), p. 687.

67 George Craik, *A Compendious History of English Literature* (London: Griffin, Bohn and Co., 1861), 2: 216–17. Craik was Professor of English Literature at Queen's College, Belfast.

68 W.E.H. Lecky, *The Leaders of Public Opinion in Ireland* (London: Saunders, Otley & Co., 1861), pp. 42, 43, 59, 51.

69 Thackeray, p. 15.

70 Lecky, p. 48.

71 Ibid., p. 57.

72 W.J. O'Neill Daunt [review of Lecky], in *Cork Examiner*, 7 February 1862, p. 3.

73 See Donal McCartney, 'Lecky's *Leaders of Public Opinion in Ireland*', in *Irish Historical Studies*, 14 (September 1964), pp. 122–4.

74 Letter from J.A. Fox to W.E.H. Lecky, 4 February 1890, TCD MSS. (Lecky) 1827–36/574, quoted in McCartney, p. 140.

75 Goldwin Smith, *Irish History and Irish Character* (Oxford: J.H. and Jas. Parker, 1861), p. 138.

76 Charles Grant, *The Last 100 Years of English Literature* (Jena: Fr. Fromman; London: Williams and Norgate, 1866), p. 7.

77 Thomas Arnold, *A Manual of English Literature* (London: Longman, Green,

et al., 1862), pp. 160–1.

78 W.F. Collier, *A History of English Literature* (London: T. Nelson, 1862), pp. 285–6. For its indebtedness to Thackeray, Collier's criticism was derided a few years later as 'most nauseating Thackeray-and-water' by William Mackay: 'The Mad Dean', in *New Monthly Magazine* (September 1870), p. 346.

79 James Whiteside, 'The Life and Death of the Irish Parliament', in *Lectures delivered before the Dublin Young Men's Christian Association . . . during the Year 1863* (Dublin: Hodges, Smith & Co., 1864), p. 89.

80 W.H. Flood, *Historical Review of the Irish Parliaments* (London: J. Kenny, 1863), pp. 69–71.

81 Thomas D'Arcy McGee, *A Popular History of Ireland* (New York: Sadlier, 1864), 2: 617.

82 J.F. Waller, 'Life of Jonathan Swift', in *Gulliver's Travels* (London: Cassell, Petter and Galpin [1864]), p. xlii.

83 Anon., 'Three Cynical Spectators: Gulliver – Candide – Teufelsdrockh', *D.U.M.*, 67 (January 1866), p. 72.

84 William Allingham, 'Rambles: Moor Park and Swift', *Fraser's Magazine*, 76 (November 1867), pp. 651–2.

85 Isaac Butt, *The Irish People and the Irish Land* (Dublin: John Falconer; London: W. Ridgeway, 1867), pp. 62–3; George Sigerson, *History of the Land Tenures and Land Classes of Ireland* (London: Longmans, 1871), pp. 127–8.

86 John Mitchel, *The History of Ireland from the Treaty of Limerick to the Present Time* (Dublin: J. Duffy, 1869), 2: 76, 79, 81, 94.

87 Ibid., 2: 94.

88 Thadeus O'Malley, *Home Rule on the Basis of Federalism* (London: Ridgeway, 1873), p. 106.

89 J.A. Froude, *The English in Ireland in the Eighteenth Century* (London: Longmans, Green and Co., 1872), 1: 500.

90 Thomas Burke, *English Misrule in Ireland* (New York: Lynch, Cole and Meehan, 1873), p. 129. Burke was

visiting America at the time, and the book assembles his public lectures opposing Froude.

91 M[ary] F[rances] C[usack], *An Illustrated History of Ireland* (London: Longmans *et al.*, 1868), pp. 529–30.

92 [A.M. Sullivan], *The Story of Ireland* (Dublin: A.M. Sullivan [1868]), p. 494.

Chapter 6

1 F.H. Friswell, *Essays on English Writers* (London: Samson Low, Son and Marston, 1869), pp. 217–18.

2 Anthony Trollope, *Thackeray* (London: Macmillan, 1879), p. 158.

3 D. Laing Purves, 'Life of . . . Swift', in *The Works of Jonathan Swift* (Edinburgh: Nimmo, 1869), p. 30.

4 [C.H. Pearson], 'Swift', in *North British Review*, 51 (January 1870), p. 326 (Pearson is identified as the author in *The Wellesley Index to Victorian Periodicals, 1824–1900*, ed. W.E. Houghton, J.H. Slingerland (Toronto: University Press, 1966–89), vol. 1, p. 694; [Abraham Haywood], reviewing Stanhope's *History of England*, *Quarterly Review*, 129 (July 1870), p. 25 (Haywood is identified as the author in *Wellesley Index*, 1: 752).

5 William Mackay, 'The Mad Dean', in *New Monthly Magazine*, 147 (September 1870), pp. 352–3.

6 Anon., 'Odds and Ends about Dean Swift', in *Englishwoman's Domestic Magazine*, 16 (January 1874), p. 7.

7 For example reviews of Forster by [John Wilson], *Quarterly Review*, 141 (January 1876), p. 50 (Wilson is identified as the author in *Wellesley Index*, 1: 758); G.W. Forrest, *Temple Bar*, 46 (February 1876), p. 255; [James Thomson], *Cope's Tobacco Plant*, 1: no. 73 (April 1876), p. 886, repr. in Thomson's *Essays and Phantasies* (London: Reeves & Turner, 1881), p. 281. John Paget, after reviewing Forster in *Blackwood's Edinburgh Magazine*, 119 (May 1876), pp. 527–44 as vastly superior to his predeces-

sors, criticized one of the latter particularly in 'Swift and Macaulay', in *Blackwood's*, 120 (November 1876), pp. 521–36; Paget is identified as the author of both pieces in *Wellesley Index*, 1: 144–5.

8 *Dublin University Magazine*, 87 (January 1876), p. 118; the anonymous reviewer nonetheless considers Swift 'a politician of easy virtue' (p. 123) during his English career.

9 Albert D. Vandam, *Amours of Great Men* (London: Tinsley Brothers, 1878), 2: 156.

10 Stanley Lane-Poole, 'Swift and Ireland', *Fraser's Magazine*, n.s. 24 (September 1881), p. 400.

11 Matthew Arnold, 'Preface', in *Letters, Speeches and Tracts on Irish Affairs by Edmund Burke* (London: Macmillan, 1881), pp. v–vii.

12 C.G. Walpole, *Short History of the Kingdom of Ireland* (London: Kegan Paul, Trench & Co., 1882), p. 368.

13 Henry Craik, *The Life of Jonathan Swift* (London: John Murray, 1882), pp. 335–9.

14 Leslie Stephen, *Swift* (London: Macmillan, 1882), pp. 148, 167.

15 Stephen, p. 149.

16 J.C. Bucknill, 'Dean Swift's Disease', in *Brain: A Journal of Neurology*, 4 (January 1882), pp. 493–506.

17 John Churton Collins, 'Jonathan Swift', in *Quarterly Review*, 153 (April 1882), pp. 377–430; 'Dean Swift in Ireland', in *Quarterly Review*, 156 (July 1883), pp. 1–56; *Jonathan Swift: A Biographical and Critical Study* (London: Chatto and Windus, 1893).

18 Edward Dowden (review), *The Academy*, 22 (30 September 1882), pp. 233–4.

19 Collins, 'Dean Swift in Ireland', pp. 1–2.

20 Collins, 'Jonathan Swift', p. 268.

21 O'Neill Daunt, 'Ireland in the Time of Swift', in *Dublin Review*, 3rd Series, 9 (October 1883), pp. 349, 367.

22 W.A. O'Conor, *History of the Irish People* (Manchester: Abel Heywood, n.d. [NLI accessions stamp dated 1883]), 2: 153, 154, 159, 167.

23 Emily Lawless, *Ireland* (London: Unwin, 1888), pp. 318–19; first published as *The Story of the Nations*, no. 10 (London: Unwin, 1885).

24 J.H. McCarthy, *An Outline of Irish History from the Earliest Times to the Present Day* (London: Chatto and Windus, n.d. [1883]), p. 66.

25 Charles Gavan Duffy, *A Bird's-Eye View of Irish History* (Dublin: J. Duffy, 1882), pp. 174–5.

26 Christopher Page Deane, *A Short History of Ireland* (London: Elliot Stock, 1886), p. 79; see also Arthur J. Dadson, *A Short Sketch of English Misrule in Ireland* (London: Swan Sonnenschein, Lowery & Co., 1887), p. 54.

27 John Redmond (speech of 29 November 1886), *Historical and Political Addresses, 1883–1897* (Dublin: Sealy, Bryers & Walker, 1898), pp. 122–4.

28 See Donal McCartney, 'Lecky's *Leaders of public opinion in Ireland*', in *Irish Historical Studies*, 14 (September 1964), pp. 127–31.

29 Gladstone, 'Lessons of Irish History in the Eighteenth Century', in *Handbook of Home Rule*, ed. James Bryce (London: Kegan Paul, 1887), p. 266.

30 John Bowles Daly, *Ireland in the Days of Dean Swift* (London: Chapman and Hall, 1887), pp. 6, 7, 11, 14, 17.

31 Ibid., p. 11.

32 William Rooney, 'Illustrious Irishmen' (delivered to the Irish Fireside Club, 1889), quoted by Philip Bradley, in 'Introduction', to Rooney's *Poems and Ballads* (Dublin: M.H. Gill [1901]), p. xviii.

33 W.K. Sullivan, 'From the Treaty of Limerick to the Establishment of Legislative Independence', in *Two Centuries of Irish History, 1691–1870*, intro. J. Bryce (London: Kegan Paul, 1888), pp. 47–8; John Ferguson, *Three Centuries of Irish History* (Glasgow: Cameron, Ferguson, n.d. [c. 1898]), p. 62.

34 Standish O'Grady, *The Story of Ireland* (London: Methuen, 1894), pp. 176–7.

35 See Duke of Argyll, *Irish Nationalism: An Appeal to History* (London: J.

Murray, 1893); T. Dunbar Ingram, *A Critical Examination of Irish History* (London: Longmans, 1900).

36 O'Neill Daunt, *Cathechism of the History of Ireland* (Dublin: J. Duffy, n.d. [c. 1890]), p. 124; James Hay, *Swift: The Mystery of his Life and Love* (London: Chatto and Windus, 1891); J.C. Collins, *Jonathan Swift: A Biographical and Critical Study* (London: Chatto & Windus, 1893); Gerald Moriarty, *Dean Swift and His Writings* (London: Seeley, 1893); Richard Ashe King, *Swift in Ireland* (London: Unwin, 1895); W. O'Connor Morris, *Ireland, 1494–1868* (Cambridge: Cambridge University Press, 1896), pp. 219–20; William Rooney, *Prose Writings* (Dublin: M.H. Gill, 1909), pp. 2–3, 97.

37 W.E.H. Lecky, *A History of Ireland in the Eighteenth Century* (London: Longmans, 1892), 1: especially 448–58.

38 A.J. Balfour, 'Biographical Introduction', in *The Works of George Berkeley, D.D.*, ed. George Sampson (London: Bell, 1897), 1: liii–lvi.

39 Joseph Glynn, 'Biographical Sketches of Eminent Irishmen: Jonathan Swift', in *Dublin Journal*, 1 (November 1887), pp. 268–9; P.W. Joyce, *A Concise History of Ireland* (Dublin: Gill and Son, 1893), pp. 236–8.

40 W.B. Yeats, letter to the *Daily Express* (London), 8 March 1895. Similarly, 'Swift, Burke, and Goldsmith . . . hardly seem to me to have come out of Ireland at all,' letter to the *Daily News* (London), 11 May 1904, p. 4.

41 W.B. Yeats, 'The New Irish Library', in *The Bookman*, 10 (June 1896), p. 83.

42 W.B. Yeats, 'The Tables of the Law', in *The Savoy*, no. 7 (November 1896), p. 84, where he may have remembered King's description of Swift as 'a good hater', in *Swift in Ireland* (London: Unwin,1895), p. 50.

43 To Clery, Swift was one of 'the true representatives of our genius, in so far as it has taken form in English': 'Irish Genius in English Prose', a paper read at University College, Dublin, in 1899, published in Clery's *Dublin Essays* (Dublin: Maunsell, 1919), p. 85.

44 D.P. Moran, 'The Pale and the Gael', in *New Ireland Review*, 11, no. 4 (June 1899), p. 232; the essay was reprinted in Moran's *The Philosophy of Irish Ireland* (Dublin: J. Duffy, 1905), pp. 32–51.

45 Ibid., pp. 230, 232.

46 Ibid., p. 233.

47 Donal McCartney, 'Hyde, D.P. Moran and Irish Ireland', in F.X.Martin, ed., *Leaders and Men of the Easter Rising* (London: Methuen, 1966), p. 47, notes that Moran maintained that he launched *The Leader* shortly afterwards to 'put a little fight' into the Gaelic League.

48 Anon. (reviewing *Unpublished Letters of Dean Swift*, ed. G.B. Hill), *Daily Express* (Dublin), 11 March 1899, p. 3.

49 See Richard P. Davis, *Arthur Griffith and Nonviolent Sinn Fein* (Dublin: Anvil Books, 1974), pp. 4–7.

50 *United Irishman*, 4 March 1899, p. 2.

51 See Arthur Griffith, *The Resurrection of Hungary: A Parallel for Ireland* (Dublin: James Duffy & Son, 1904), p. 86.

52 Arthur Griffith, 'Parnell', in *Sinn Fein*, 7 October 1911, p. 3.

53 See Arthur Griffith, *When the Government Publishes Sedition*, Tracts for the Times, no. 4 (Dublin: Irish Publicity League, 1915), p. 2.

54 James Connolly, *Labour in Irish History* (1910; repr. Dublin, Maunsel, 1917), pp. 22–3; Justin McCarthy, *Ireland and Her Story*, Story of the Empire Series (London: H. Marshall & Son, 1903), pp. 109–10; E.A. D'Alton, *History of Ireland* (London: Kegan Paul, 1906), 2: 536–9.

55 Goldwin Smith, *Irish History and the Irish Question* (New York: McClure, Phillips & Co., 1905) pp. 109, 111. Cf. *Irish History and Irish Character* (Oxford: Parker, 1861), pp. 137–8.

56 The Swift section was accordingly omitted when *The Leaders* was revised for a third and final edition in 1903.

57 Temple Scott, 'Introduction', in *The Drapier's Letters, The Prose Works of Jonathan Swift* (London: G. Bell and Sons, 1903), 6: x–xi.

58 Anon., 'Odds and Ends about Dean Swift', in *Englishwoman's Domestic Magazine*, 16 (February 1874), pp. 63–5.

59 Lady Wilde, 'Stella and Vanessa', in *Notes on Men, Women and Books* (London: Ward & Downey, 1891), pp. 85–111.

60 John Todhunter, *The Black Cat* (London: Henry & Co., 1895), p. 49. The play was staged the previous year.

61 [Samuel Phillips], 'The Amours of Dean Swift', in *The Times*, 3 October 1850, p. 3.

62 Leon de Wailly and Louis Ulbach, *Le Doyen de Saint-Patrick. Drame en Cinq Actes* (Paris, 1862).

63 [Eveleen Bell as] Mrs Hugh Bell, *The Dean of St Patrick's* (London: Edward Arnold, 1903).

64 G. Sidney Paternoster, ' "Jonathan Swift" Dean of St Patricks' typescript MS. catalogued as LCP 1923/32, British Library. I am indebted to Professors Cheryl Herr and Mary Thale for helping me to locate this play.

65 [Letter from Yeats to Lady Gregory, 24 January 1913], in Donald T. Torchiana and Glenn O'Malley, eds, 'Some New Letters from W.B.Yeats to Lady Gregory', *A Review of English Literature*, 4, no. 3 (July 1963), pp. 20–1.

66 *Irish Times*, 24 January 1913, p. 6.

67 *Sinn Fein*, 1 February 1913, p. 1; *The Irish Citizen*, 1 February 1913, p. 294. Although both these papers were strongly political, neither criticized the play for its lack of attention to Swift's Irish politics.

68 *The Irish Citizen*, 1 February 1913, p. 294.

69 D.J. O'Donoghue, 'Swift as an Irishman', in *Irish Review*, 2 (June 1912), p. 209.

70 Ibid., p. 210.

71 D.J. O'Donoghue, 'Swift as an Irishman. III', *Irish Review*, 2 (August 1912), p. 331.

72 D.J. O'Donoghue, 'Swift as an Irishman. II,' *Irish Review*, 2 (July 1912), p. 259.

73 Phillip Lee, 'Dean Swift', in *Journal of the Ivernian Society*, 21 (October 1913), p. 5.

74 Arthur Griffith, 'Preface' to John Mitchel, *Jail Journal* (Dublin: Gill, 1914), pp. x, xiii, xxix.

75 Michael MacDonagh, 'Ireland Ablaze in 1724', in *Irish Monthly*, 43 (December 1915), p. 762.

76 Anon., *Dean Swift on the Situation* (Dublin: Cumann na mBan Central Branch, 1915), p. 3.

77 *Dean Swift on the Situation*, p. 4.

78 Christian Brothers, *Irish History Reader* (Dublin: Gill, 1916), p. 243.

79 Padraig Pearse, *Ghosts* (Tracts for the Times, no. 10) (Dublin: Whelan & Son, 1916), p. 15.

80 Mary Hayden and George Moonan, *A Short History of the Irish People* (Dublin: Talbot Press, 1921), p. 384.

81 Swift MacNeill, *The Constitutional and Parliamentary History of Ireland till the Union* (Dublin: Talbot Press, 1917), p. 82; Patrick Lennox, 'Swift, The Irish Patriot', in *Catholic Educational Review*, 14 (November 1917), pp. 289–99; Maurice Dalton, *Catholic Bulletin*, 8 (August 1918), pp. 387–9.

82 Charles Whibley, *Jonathan Swift: The Leslie Stephen Lecture*, delivered 26 May 1917 (Cambridge: University Press, 1917), p. 26.

83 C.H. Firth, 'The Political Significance of Gulliver's Travels', in *Proceedings of the British Academy*, 9 (1919–20), p. 250.

84 Ibid., p. 251.

85 [Timothy Corcoran] 'Donal MacEgan', 'Jonathan Swift and Ireland', in *Catholic Bulletin*, 14 (April 1924), p. 300. The pseudonym is identified as Corcoran's in Brian Murphy, 'The Canon of Irish Cultural History; Some Questions', in *Studies*, 77 (Spring 1988), p. 82, n. 17.

86 'MacEgan', pp. 300–5; also the same author's 'Jonathan Swift and "The Savage Old Irish" ', in *Catholic Bulletin*, 14 (June 1924), pp. 501–6.

87 Firth, p. 269.

88 Dom Patrick Nolan, 'Protection the Only Policy', in *Catholic Bulletin*, 14 (June 1924), p. 507.

89 W.F.P. Stockley, 'Swift as an Irish Writer: The Whole Truth', in *Irish Ecclesiastical Record*, 5th series, vol. 27 (February 1926), pp. 127–47.

90 [Timothy Corcoran] 'MacEgan', 'A Note on Detraction', in *Catholic Bulletin*, 16 (March 1926), p. 302.

91 Stephen Gwynn, *Ireland* (London: E. Benn, 1924), p. 110.

92 Eleanor Hull, *A History of Ireland and Her People* (London: Harrap, 1926), pp. 201–5.

Chapter 7

1 Milton Voight, *Swift and the Twentieth Century* (Detroit: Wayne State University Press, 1964) provides a useful survey: pp. 155–63; Hermann J. Real and Heinz J. Vienken have discussed the vogue more recently in 'Psychoanalytic Criticism and Swift: The History of a Failure', in *Eighteenth-Century Ireland*, 1 (1986), pp. 127–41.

2 Stuart Gilbert seems to have been the first to call broad attention to Swift's influence: *James Joyce's Ulysses* (London: Faber and Faber, 1930, repr. Harmondsworth: Penguin, 1963), p. 31. Later critics to notice it include Richard M. Kain, *Fabulous Voyager: James Joyce's Ulysses* (Chicago: University Press, 1947, repr. New York: Viking, 1959), p. 193; Stanley Sultan, *The Argument of Ulysses* (Columbus: Ohio State University Press, 1964), p. 291; and Robert H. Bell, *Jocoserious Joyce: The Fate of Folly in Ulysses* (Ithaca: Cornell University Press, 1991), p. 65.

3 The critical ground was broken in this area by Mackie L. Jarrell, 'Swiftiana in *Finnegans Wake*', in *ELH*, 26 (June 1959), pp. 271–94, which remains a fruitful introduction to Swift's presence in the novel, as is James S. Atherton's discussion in *Books at the Wake* (London: Faber, 1959), pp. 114–23.

4 Mary Colum, *Life and the Dream* (Garden City, NY: Doubleday, 1947), p. 287; first published in 1928.

5 Henry Mangan, 'Clio in Ireland', in *O'Connell School Centenary Record* (Dublin: Christian Brothers, 1928), pp. 59, 61.

6 W.B. Yeats, 'Introduction', in *The Midnight Court* (London: Cape, 1926), p. 6n.

7 Lady Gregory, *Kiltartan History-Book* (London: Unwin, 1926), p. 56.

8 Arthur Power, 'A Contact with Yeats', in *Irish Tatler and Sketch*, 74, no. 3 (December 1964), p. 34; repr. in E.H. Mikhail, ed., *W.B. Yeats: Interviews and Recollections* (London: Macmillan), p. 191.

9 C.E. Lawrence, 'Swift and Stella: A Dialogue', in *the Cornhill Magazine*, n.s. 60 (June 1926), pp. 672–81. That Yeats at least knew of Lawrence's play is suggested by Mary Fitzgerald: 'Out of a Medium's Mouth: The Writing of *The Words upon the Window-Pane*', in *Colby Library Quarterly*, 17, no. 2 (June 1981), pp. 61–73.

10 Arthur Power, *The Drapier Letters* and *Her Ladyship – the Poet – and the Dog: Two One-Act Plays* (Dublin: Talbot Press, 1927), pp. 3–33.

11 Ibid., p. 5.

12 Ibid., p. 32.

13 Power, 'A Contact with Yeats', p. 34.

14 Arthur Power, 'Artistic Life in Paris and Dublin in the Nineteen Twenties', unpublished typescript, pp. 257–9; I am indebted to Ulick O'Connor for acquainting me with this memoir, and to Roderic Power, the son of the late Arthur Power, for permission to quote from it.

15 Power, 'Artistic Life', pp. 257, 260.

16 W.B. Yeats, 'The Words upon the Window Pane: A Commentary' (Part I), in *Dublin Magazine*, 6 (October–December 1931), pp. 5–19; 'The Words . . . A Commentary, Part II', *Dublin Magazine* 7 (January–March 1932), pp. 11–15; the first part is dated 'November 1930,' the second, 'November 1931'; repr., *Wheels and*

Butterflies (London: Macmillan, 1934), *Explorations* (New York: Macmillan, 1952).

17 Yeats, 'Commentary' (Part I), p. 6.
18 Ibid., p. 6.
19 Ibid., pp. 10–11.
20 Ibid., p. 13.
21 Ibid., p. 6.
22 Ibid., p. 10.
23 Among the most fruitful discussions of this development are C.H. Sisson, 'Yeats and Swift', in *Agenda*, 9, nos 4–10, no. 1 (Autumn/Winter double issue, 1971), pp. 34–8; Adele Dalsimer, 'Yeats's Unchanging Swift', in *Eire-Ireland*, 9, no. 2 (1974), pp. 65–89; Douglas N. Archibald, 'The Words upon the Window-Pane and Yeats's Encounter with Jonathan Swift,' in *Yeats and the Theatre*, ed. Robert O'Driscoll and Lorna Reynolds (London: Macmillan, 1975), pp. 176–214; and Michael Steinman, *Yeats's Heroic Figures* (London: Macmillan, 1983), pp. 103–51.
24 Yeats, 'Commentary' (Part I), pp. 6–7.
25 W.B. Yeats, 'The New Irish Library', in *The Bookman*, 10 (June 1896), p. 83.
26 Yeats, 'Commentary' (Part I), p. 6.
27 Yeats, 'Commentary', (Part II), p. 15.
28 See Joseph Hasset, *Yeats and the Poetics of Hate* (Dublin: Gill and Macmillan, 1986), especially, pp. 81–2.
29 Archibald, p. 187.
30 Richard Cave, 'Dramatising the Life of Swift', in Masaru Sekine, ed., *Irish Writers and the Theatre* (Gerrards Cross: Colin Smythe, 1986), p. 25.
31 Lord Longford, *Yahoo: A Tragedy in Three Acts* (Dublin: Hodges Figgis, 1934). See also John Cowell, *No Profit but the Name: The Longfords and the Gate Theatre* (Dublin: O'Brien Press, 1988), p. 95.
32 Longford, p. 61.
33 Hilton Edwards, 'Production', in *The Gate Theatre Dublin*, ed. Bulmer Hobson (Dublin: Gate Theatre, 1934), p. 37.
34 Quoted in Cowell, p. 96.
35 W.D. Taylor, *Jonathan Swift: A Critical Essay* (London: Peter Davies,

1933), p. 167.
36 Joseph Hone, 'Ireland and Swift', in *Dublin Magazine*, 8 (July–September 1933), pp. 9–17.
37 Stephen Gwynn, *The Life and Friendships of Dean Swift* (London: Thornton Butterworth, 1933), pp. 228, 229, 235.
38 Mario Rossi and Joseph Hone, *Swift, or The Egotist* (London: Gollancz, 1934), pp. 47, 253.
39 Eamon de Valéra, 'The Values of the Spirit,' *Speeches and Statements*, ed. Maurice Moynihan (Dublin: Gill and Macmillan, 1980), p. 232. Swift was not alone among Irish patriots to be so narrowly characterized: even Wolfe Tone merely 'left us one of the most delightful autobiographies in literature', p. 232.
40 [Timothy Corcoran] 'Dermot Curtin', 'Our Gaelic Democracy', in *Catholic Bulletin*, 23 (July 1933), pp. 559–60. This pseudonym is attributed to Corcoran in Brian Murphy, 'The Canon of Irish Cultural History: Some Questions', in *Studies*, 77 (Spring 1988), p. 82, n.17.
41 [Timothy Corcoran] 'Donal MacEgan,' 'Stephen Gwynn on Jonathan Swift,' in *Catholic Bulletin*, 23 (December 1933), p. 1004.
42 Daniel Corkery, 'Ourselves and Dean Swift', in *Studies*, 23 (June 1934), p. 210.
43 Charles Whibley, *Jonathan Swift: The Leslie Stephen Lecture*, delivered 26 May 1917 (Cambridge: University Press, 1917), p. 26.
44 Corkery, p. 213.
45 Aodh de Blacam, *A First Book of Irish Literature* (Dublin: Talbot Press, 1934), p. 150.
46 Aodh de Blacam, 'The Other Hidden Ireland', in *Studies*, 23 (September 1934), pp. 439–54.
47 Joseph Hone, 'Berkeley and Swift as National Economists', in *Studies*, 23 (September 1934), pp. 421–32; postscript, p. 432.
48 Daniel Corkery, 'The Nation that was not a Nation', in *Studies*, 23 (December 1934), pp. 615, 621.
49 Anon., *Catholic Bulletin*, 24 (Novem-

ber 1934), pp. 869, 871–2; the author was probably the editor, Fr Corcoran.

50 Sean O'Faolain, *King of the Beggars* (New York: Viking, 1938), pp. 13–38.

51 Sean O'Faolain, 'Daniel Corkery', in *Commonweal*, 25 (6 November 1936), p. 36.

52 Sean O'Faolain, *The Irish: A Character Study* (Harmondsworth: Penguin, 1947).

53 Emmet Larkin, 'A Reconsideration: Daniel Corkery and His Ideas on Cultural Nationalism', in *Eire-Ireland*, 8 (Spring 1973), p. 46.

54 Ernest Boyd, *Ireland's Literary Renaissance* (New York: Knopf, 1922), p. 7.

55 Lawrence McCaffrey, 'Daniel Corkery and Irish Cultural Nationalism', in *Eire-Ireland*, 8 (Spring 1973), p. 39.

56 Corkery, 'Ourselves and Dean Swift', p. 207.

57 See Robert Hogan, *After the Irish Renaissance* (Minneapolis: University of Minnesota Press, 1967), p. 54.

58 Paul Vincent Carroll, 'The Substance of Paul Vincent Carroll', in *New York Times*, 30 January 1938, sec. x, p. 1.

59 Denis Johnston, 'The Mysterious Origins of Dean Swift', in *Dublin Historical Record*, 3, no. 4 (June–August 1941), p. 81.

60 See Joseph Ronsley, 'A Check-list of Denis Johnston's Writings', in *Denis Johnston: A Retrospective*, ed. Joseph Ronsley (Gerrards Cross: Colin Smythe, 1981), p. 255.

61 Cave, p. 29.

62 Hilton Edwards, 'Denis Johnston', in *The Bell*, 13, no. 1 (October 1946), p. 16.

63 Johnston outlined the theory further in a lecture to the Old Dublin Society in 1941, published as 'The Mysterious Origins of Dean Swift', in *Dublin Historical Record*, 3 (1941), pp. 81–97; he advanced it in greatest detail with *In Search of Swift* (Dublin: Allen Figgis, 1959).

64 D.E.S. Maxwell, *A Critical History of Modern Irish Drama* (Cambridge: University Press, 1984), p. 126.

65 Voight briefly reviews the treatment of Johnston's theory at the hands of the scholars in *Swift in the Twentieth Century*, p. 187, n. 64. Introducing the final version of his play, Johnston noted the difficulty of pressing the theory against 'a formidable lobby of scholarship, entrenched for over two hundred years behind a barricade of print': *Selected Plays of Denis Johnston*, intr. Joseph Ronsley (Gerrards Cross: Colin Smythe; Washington: Catholic University of America Press, 1983), p. 259.

66 Johnston, *Selected Plays*, p. 260.

67 P.S. O'Hegarty, 'Jonathan Swift, Irishman', in *The Bell*, 10 (September 1945), p. 488.

68 R. Wyse Jackson, 'Jonathan Swift, 1745–1945', in *Irish Press*, 19 October 1945, p. 2.

69 Anon., 'The Dean', in *The Irish Times*, 19 October 1945, p. 3.

70 'Press Owes Debt to Dean Swift', in *The Irish Times*, 19 October 1945, p. 3.

71 Denis Johnston, 'Jonathan Swift: 1667–1745. A Bicentenary Tribute', in *The Irish Times*, 20 October 1945, p. 2.

72 Edwards, p. 16. The revision, titled 'Weep for the Cyclops', was broadcast on BBC Television on 21 August 1947; see Ronsley, 'Check-list of Denis Johnston's Writings', p. 261.

73 J.J. Hogan, 'Bicentenary of Jonathan Swift', in *Studies*, 34 (December 1945), p. 505.

74 Frank O'Connor, 'Ireland', in *Holiday*, December 1949, p. 48.

75 Frank O'Connor, *Munster, Leinster and Connaught* (London: Robert Hale, [1950]), p. 15.

76 Roger Chauviré, *History of Ireland*, trans. Earl of Wicklow (Dublin: Clonmore and Reynolds, 1952), p. 80.

77 Christopher Preston, *A School History of Ireland* (Dublin: Brown and Nolan, n.d.), pp. 71–2.

78 P.S. O'Hegarty, *A History of Ireland under the Union, 1801–1922* (London: Methuen, 1952), p. 15.

79 James Carty, *A Class-Book of Irish History* (London: Macmillan, 1956), 3: 157.

80 T.W. Moody and F.X. Martin, eds,

The Course of Irish History (Cork: Mercier Press, 1967), pp. 205, 221.

81 See Paul A. Doyle, *Paul Vincent Carroll* (Lewisburg: Bucknell University Press, 1971), p. 107; the play was published as *Farewell to Greatness*, ed. Robert Hogan (Dixon, California: Proscenium Press, 1966).

82 Le Brocquy, *A View on Vanessa: A Correspondence with Interludes for the Stage* (Dublin: Dolmen Press, 1967).

83 Roger McHugh, 'The Woven Figure: Swift's Irish Context', in *University Review* (Dublin), 4, no. 1 (Spring 1967), p. 35.

84 'Swift: A Commemorative Supplement issued with the Irish Times, 22nd March 1967'.

85 Printed as, respectively, *Jonathan Swift, 1667–1967: A Dublin Tercentenary Tribute*, ed. Roger McHugh and Philip Edwards (Dublin: Dublin Press, 1967); *Swift Revisited*, ed. Denis Donoghue (Cork: Mercier Press, 1967).

86 Denis Johnston, 'The Year of Jonathan Swift', in 'Swift: A Commemorative Supplement', p. i. For an Irish audience on a celebratory occasion Johnston was himself circumspect, though in an American review of Oliver Ferguson's *Jonathan Swift and Ireland* a few years earlier he had likened an 'attempt to portray [Swift] as an Irish Patriot in the contemporary sense' to filming '*Ivanhoe* in terms of an anti-Norman resistance movement': 'The Trouble with Swift', in *The Nation*, 196, no. 4 (26 January 1963), pp. 73–4. In a lecture intended for delivery during the 1967 tercentenary but instead published the following year, Johnston returned to Swift's inconsistencies, arguing for their source in a distaste for the fleshly that he shared with the Irish at large: 'Swift of Dublin', in *Eire-Ireland*, 3, no. 3 (Fall 1968), pp. 38–50.

87 R. Wyse Jackson, 'The Places that Hold Memories', in 'Swift: A Commemorative Supplement', p. iv.

88 Frank O'Connor, *A Short History of Irish Literature: A Backward Look*

(New York: Capricorn Books, 1967), p. 121. This work is a revision of O'Connor's lectures at Trinity College in 1965.

89 Austin Clarke, *Poems 1967–1974*, ed. Liam Miller (Dublin: Dolmen Press, 1974), pp. 458, 459–60. For other evidences that Swift was Clarke's model see Robert F. Garratt, '"Aware of my Ancestor": Austin Clarke and the Legacy of Swift', in *Eire-Ireland*, 11, no. 2 (1976), pp. 92–103.

90 Eugene McCabe, *Swift* (author's typescript), p. 31. I am indebted to Eugene McCabe for making a typescript of this unpublished play available to me and allowing me to quote from it.

91 I am indebted to Ulick O'Connor for making a typescript of this unpublished play available to me.

92 'Guinness as Swift', in *The Times*, 16 August 1976, p. 9.

93 Keith Walker, 'Rational Grotesque', in *TLS*, 3 July 1981, p. 755.

94 I am indebted to Tom MacIntyre for making a typescript of this unpublished play available to me.

95 Tom MacIntyre, 'In Search of Three Swifts', in *Books Ireland*, no. 101 (March 1986), p. 36.

96 Tom MacIntyre, 'Swift, Stella and Vanessa', in *Cara*, 17, no. 4 (July–August 1984), pp. 44–52.

97 MacIntyre, 'In Search of Three Swifts', p. 37.

98 Ibid., p. 36.

Epilogue

1 Andrew Carpenter, 'Jonathan Swift', in *The Field Day Anthology of Irish Writing* (Derry: Field Day, 1991), 1: 327.

2 Cheryl Herr, 'The Erotics of Irishness', in *Critical Inquiry*, 17, no. 1 (Autumn 1990), p. 6.

3 Andrew Carpenter, 'Double Vision in Anglo-Irish Literature', in *Place, Personality and the Irish Writer*, ed. Andrew Carpenter (Gerrards Cross, Bucks.: Colin Smythe, 1977), p. 174.

4 P.F. Sheeran, 'Colonists and Col-

onized: Some Aspects of Anglo-Irish Literature from Swift to Joyce', in *Yearbook of English Studies*, 13 (1983), p. 115.

5 Arguing briefly, in his 'Answer to several letters sent me from unknown hands', for the benefit of using English in Ireland, mainly for commercial purposes, Swift recommended: 'It would be a noble achievement to abolish the Irish language in this kingdom': *Prose Writings*, 12: 89.

Select Bibliography

I. Editions of Swift's Works

Eighteenth- and nineteenth-century

[Faulkner, George, ed., with Swift's supervision], *The Works of J.S., D.D., D.S. P.D.* (4 vols), Dublin: G. Faulkner, 1735; augmented in later years and issued in various editions and formats.

Hawkesworth, John, ed., *The Works of Jonathan Swift, . . . with Some Acount of the Author's Life and Notes . . .* by John Hawkesworth (6 vols), London: C. Bathurst, *et al.*, 1755.

Scott, Walter, ed., *The Works of Jonathan Swift . . . and A Life of The Author* (19 vols), Edinburgh: A. Constable, 1814.

Sheridan, Thomas, ed., *The Works of the Rev. Dr. Jonathan Swift, . . .* (17 vols; first is 'A Life . . .'), London: W. Strahan, *et al.*, 1784.

Twentieth-century

Davis, Herbert, *et al.*, eds, *The Prose Works of Jonathan Swift* (16 vols), Oxford: Basil Blackwell, 1939–68.

McMinn, Joseph, ed., *Swift's Irish Pamphlets: An Introductory Selection*, Gerrards Cross: C. Smythe, 1991.

Williams, Harold, ed., *The Correspondence of Jonathan Swift* (5 vols), Oxford: Clarendon Press, 1963–5.

——, *The Poems of Jonathan Swift.* (3 vols), Oxford: Clarendon Press, 1937, rev. 1958.

Woolley, James, ed., *The Intelligencer* [by Swift and T. Sheridan], Oxford: Clarendon Press, 1992.

II. Commentaries and References, mainly biographical

Eighteenth-century

[Amory, Thomas], *Memoirs of Several Ladies of Great Britain. Interspersed with Literary*

Reflexions . . . , London: J. Noon, 1755.

Anon., 'Character of Jonathan Swift, D.D., Dean of St. Patrick's, Dublin', *European Magazine*, 18 (November 1790), pp. 329–35.

Anon., 'Some Outlines of the Character of Dr. Swift', *Dublin Magazine*, 2 (December 1763), pp. 713–17; repr. *European Magazine*, 18 (September 1790), pp. 182–5.

Berkeley, George-Monck, *Literary Relics . . . To which is prefix'd, An Inquiry into the Life of Dean Swift*, London: C. Elliot, *et al.*, 1789.

['C.M.P.G.N.S.T.N.S.'], 'Anecdotes of Dean Swift and Miss Johnson', *Gentleman's Magazine*, 27 (November 1757), pp. 487–91.

Delany, Patrick, *Observations upon Lord Orrery's Remarks on the Life and Writings of Dr. Jonathan Swift*, London: W. Reeve, 1754.

Dilworth, W.H., *The Life of Dr. Jonathan Swift, Dean of St. Patrick's, Dublin*, London: G. Wright, 1758.

Johnson, Samuel, *Lives of the English Poets*, ed. G.B. Hill (3 vols), Oxford: Clarendon Press, 1905.

[?Nichols, John, ed., noting Swift], *The Tatler*, London: Nichols, 1786, 5: pp. 142n.–145n.

Orrery [John Boyle, fifth], Earl of, *Remarks on the Life and Writings of Dr. Jonathan Swift*, London: A. Millar; Dublin: G. Faulkner, 1752.

Pilkington, Laetitia, *Memoirs . . .* (3 vols), London: R. Griffiths, 1748–54.

Swift, Deane, *An Essay upon the Life, Writings and Character, of Dr. Jonathan Swift*, London: C. Bathurst, 1755.

Ware, James, *The Writers of Ireland. In two Books*, written in Latin, trans. with addns, Walter Harris . . . Dublin: S. Powell, 1745.

Nineteenth-century

Anon., 'Gallery of Illustrious Irishmen. No. XI. Swift', *Dublin University Magazine*, Part I, February 1840, pp. 131–44; Part II, March 1840, pp. 333–44; Part III, May 1840, pp. 538–56; Part IV, June 1840, pp. 634–61.

Anon., *The Life and Writings of Jonathan Swift . . .* Dublin: J. McCormick, 1844.

Anon., 'Odds and Ends about Dean Swift', *Englishwoman's Domestic Magazine*, 16 [(January 1874), pp. 6–8; (February 1874), pp. 63–5].

Anster, John, 'Swift and his Biographers', *North British Review* 11 (August 1849), pp. 337–68.

Beddoes, Thomas, *Hygeia: Or Essays Moral and Medical . . .* (3 vols), Bristol: J. Miller for R. Philips, 1803.

Brooke, R.S., 'A Pilgrimage to Quilca in . . . 1852 . . .', *Dublin University Magazine*, 40 (November 1852), pp. 509–26.

Bucknill, J.C., 'Dean Swift's Disease', *Brain: A Journal of Neurology*, 4 (January 1882).

Courtenay, Thomas Peregrine, *Memoirs . . . of Sir William Temple* (2 vols), London: Longman *et al.*, 1836.

[Macaulay, T.B., reviewing Courtenay's *Temple*], *Edinburgh Review*, 68 (October 1838), pp. 113–87.

Craik, Henry, *The Life of Jonathan Swift*, London: J. Murray, 1882.

Forster, John, *Life of Jonathan Swift*, London: J. Murray, 1875.

Glynn, Joseph, 'Biographical Sketches of Eminent Irishmen. VIII. Jonathan Swift', *Dublin Journal*, 1 (November 1887), pp. 268–9.

Hay, James, *Swift: The Mystery of his Life and Love*, London: Chapman and Hall, 1891.

Jameson, Anna, *Memoirs of the Loves of the Poets . . .* (2 vols), London: R. Bentley, 1831.

King, Richard Ashe, *Swift in Ireland*, London: T.F. Unwin, 1895.

Nichols, John Bowyer, *Illustrations of the Literary History of the Eighteenth Century* (8 vols), London: J.B. Nichols, 1817–58.

Ryan, Richard, *Biographia Hibernica* (2 vols), London: J. Warren, 1821.

Stephen, Leslie, *Swift*, London: Macmillan, 1882.

Thackeray, W.M., *The English Humourists of the Eighteenth Century*, London: Smith, Elder, 1853.

Waller, John Francis, 'Life of Jonathan Swift', *Gulliver's Travels*, London: Cassell *et al.* [1864].

Wilde, W.R., 'Art. XIII. Some Particulars respecting Swift and Stella . . . ', *Dublin Quarterly Journal of Medical Science* [3 (May 1847), pp. 384–434; 4 (August 1847), pp. 1–33].

——————, *The Closing Years of Dean Swift's Life*, Dublin: Hodges & Smith, 1849.

Wills, James, 'Jonathan Swift, Dean of St. Patrick's', *Lives of Illustrious and Distinguished Irishmen*, Dublin: Macgregor, Polson, 1852, 4, part 2: 331–443.

[Wilson, C.H., ed.], *Swiftiana* (2 vols), [London:] R. Phillips, 1804.

Twentieth-century

Doody, Margaret Anne, 'Swift among the Women', *Yearbook of English Studies*, 18 (1988), pp. 68–92.

Downie, J.A., *Jonathan Swift: Political Writer*, London: Routledge, 1984.

Ehrenpreis, Irvin, *Swift: The Man, His Works and the Age* (3 vols), Cambridge, MA: Harvard University Press, 1962–83.

Ferguson, Oliver, *Jonathan Swift and Ireland*, Urbana: University of Illinois Press, 1962.

Gwynn, Stephen, *The Life and Friendships of Dean Swift*, London: Thornton Butterworth, 1933.

Johnston, Denis, *In Search of Swift*, Dublin: Figgis, 1958.

——————, 'The Mysterious Origin of Dean Swift', *Dublin Historical Record*, 3, No. 4 (June–August 1941), pp. 81–97.

McMinn, Joseph, *Jonathan Swift: A Literary Life*, London: Macmillan, 1991.

Nokes, David, *Jonathan Swift: A Hypocrite Reversed*, Oxford: Clarendon Press, 1985.

Rossi, Mario M. and Joseph Hone, *Swift, or The Egoist*, London: V. Gollancz, 1934.

Sun, Phillip Su Yue, *Swift's Eighteenth-Century Biographies*, unpublished doctoral dissertation, Yale University, 1963.

III.   References and Commentaries, mainly historical, literary or political

Eighteenth-century

Anon., *An Answer to the Proposal for the Universal Use of Irish Manufactures . . .* , Dublin, 1720.

Anon., *A Dialogue between Dean Swift and Tho. Prior. Esq.* . . . , Dublin: G. and A. Ewing, 1753.

Anon., *A Letter from Aminadab Firebrass, Quaker Merchant, to M.B. Drapier*, Dublin: J. Harding, [1724].

Anon., *A Letter from a Gentleman in the Country to his son in the College of Dublin* [and *Letter II. From a Gentleman*, etc.], Dublin: O. Nelson, 1752; *Letter III* [and *Letter IV*] *from a Gentleman in the Country*, etc., Dublin, 1753.

Anon., *A Letter from a Primate to a Pretender* . . . *And a Letter from Dean Swift to George F—k—r*, [Dublin, 1754].

Anon., *A Letter to a Member of the H[ous]e of C[ommon]s of I[RELAND]*, *on the Present Crisis of Affairs in that Kingdom*, London: R. Scot, 1753.

Anon., *A Letter to the Examiner, Suggesting Proper Heads for Vindicating his Masters*, London: J. Moore, 1714.

Anon. ['Philostelus'], *A Letter to the Right Honourable Sir Ralph Gore* . . . , Dublin, 1732.

Anon. [?Paul Hiffernan], *A Dish of Chocolate for the Times*, Dublin, 1754.

Anon., *An Essay on Preferment*, Dublin, 1736.

Anon. ['A.R. Hosier'], *A Poem to the Whole People of Ireland, Relating to M.B. Drapier*, [Dublin:] E. Sadlier, 1726.

Anon., *A Young Lady's Complaint for the Stay of Dean Swift in England*, Dublin: G. Faulkner, 1726.

Anon., *All's out at LAST; Or, See who has been in the wrong*, Dublin, 1714.

Anon., *Dean Swift's Ghost, To the Citizens of Dublin, Concluding with a Word particularly to the Weavers*, Dublin, 1749.

Anon., *Dr. S—t's Real Diary* . . . , London: R. Burleigh, 1715.

Anon. [?Sir Thomas Barnet], *Essays Divine, Moral and Political* . . . *By the author of A Tale of a Tub* . . . , London: 1714.

Anon. ['T. Taylor'], *Lucas Refuted: or Liberty Supported* . . . , Dublin: H. Garland, 1749.

Anon., *Magdalen – Grove: Or, A Dialogue Between the Doctor and the Devil* . . . , London: J. Carrett [1714].

Anon., *Neck or Nothing: Or, The History of Queen Robin* . . . , Part I. London, M. Budenell; repr. Dublin, 1714.

Anon., 'On Dean Swift', *Gentleman's Magazine*, 9 (October 1739), p. 574.

Anon. [as 'Obadiah Tithepig'], *Pastor Evangelicus: A Poem*, Dublin: H. Fitzpatrick for G. Folingsby, 1795.

Anon., *Poem on the Dean of St. Patrick's Birth-Day* . . . , [Dublin:] J. Gowan, 1726.

Anon., *Proceedings of the Catholic Meeting of Dublin* . . . *on* . . . *October 31, 1792* . . . , Dublin: H. Fitzpatrick, 1792.

Anon., *Remarks on Two Letters signed Theatricus and Hibernicus*, . . . *in the Dublin Journal* . . . , Dublin, 1754.

Anon., *Some Account of the Irish*, By J.S., D.D., D.S. P.D., London: M. Cooper, 1753.

Anon., *Swift's Jests: Or, a Compendium of Wit and Humour* . . . , London: H. Dell, 1759.

Anon. comp., *The Beauties of Swift: or, the Favourite Offspring of Wit and Genius*, London: J. Kearsley, 1782.

Anon., *The Case of the Stage in Ireland* . . . , Dublin, London; repr. J. Coote [1758].

Anon., *The Comic Miscellany* (2 vols), London: M. Cooper, 1756.

Anon., *The Draper's APPARITION to G—e F—r*, A New Poem, Dublin, 1745.

Anon., *The Enigmatical Court: Or, A KEY to the High-German Doctor . . .* , Part I, London, printed; repr. Dublin: G. Risk, 1714.

Anon., *The First Lines of Ireland's Interest in the Year 1780*, Dublin: R. Marchbank, 1780.

Anon., *The Justice and Necessity of Restraining the Clergy in their Preaching*, London: J. Roberts, 1715.

Anon., *The Review. Being a Short Account of the Doctrine . . . [of] the C[our]t Advocates . . .* , Dublin, 1754.

Anon., 'To the Author of the Dublin Journal', *Dublin Journal*, 1–4 February 1734, 1.

Anon. [as 'Hibernicus'], 'To Mr. Faulkner', *Dublin Journal* 25–8 April 1752, p. 2.

Anon. [as 'Patricius'], *Tyranny Display'd. In a Letter from a Looker-On . . .* , Dublin, 1754.

Browne, John, [Letter to G. Faulkner, 14 February 1750], *The Works of Dr Jonathan Swift . . .* , London: W. Bowyer, *et al.*, 14: 1–4.

[Campbell, Thomas], *A Philosophical Survey of the South of Ireland . . .* , Dublin: W. Whitestone, *et al.*, 1778.

Campbell, Thomas, *Strictures on the Ecclesiastical and Literary History of Ireland . . .* , Dublin: L. White, 1789.

[?Chesterfield, Philip Dormer Stanhope, Earl of], *The Drapier's Letter to the Good People of Ireland*, Dublin, 1745; also *The Drapier's Second Letter to the Good People of Ireland*, Dublin, 1745.

Chesterfield, Philip Dormer Stanhope, Earl of, *Miscellaneous Works*, ed. M. Maty (3 vols), Dublin: Watson, *et al.*, 1777.

Coxe, William, *Memoirs of the Life and Administration of Sir Robert Walpole . . .* (3 vols), London: Cadell & Davies, 1798.

Crawford, William, *A History of Ireland from the Earliest Period, to the Present Time . . .* (2 vols), Strabane: J. Bellew, 1783.

Curry, John, *An Historical and Critical Review of the Civil Wars in Ireland . . .* (2 vols), Dublin: L. White, 1786.

[Curry, John], *Observations on the Popery Laws*, Dublin: T. Ewing, 1771.

Drennan, William, *The Drennan Letters*, ed. D.A. Chart, Belfast: Stationery Office, 1931.

Eden, William, *A Letter to the Earl of Carlisle . . .* Dublin: R. Marchbank, 1779.

Ewing, George and Ewing, Alexander, *An Attempt to Answer Mr. George Faulkner's Extraordinary Appeal to the Public*, [Dublin: G. and A. Ewing, 1758].

Faulkner, George, [answer to query] *Dublin Journal*, 29 September–2 October 1744, p. 2.

——, [campaign for a Swift monument: selective references] *Dublin Journal* 9–12 November 1745, p. 2; 6–9 August 1748, p. 2; 21–5 March 1749, p. 2; 5–8 August 1749, p. 2; 21–5 January; 25–8 January; 1–4 Feburary; 4–8 Feburary; 22–5 Feburary; 29 Feburary–3 March 1752; 14–17 March; 17–21 March; 21–4 March 1752; 9–13 January 1753, p. 1; 4–7 February 1758, p. 2; 19–22 November 1763, p. 1; 13–17 December 1763, p. 2.

——, *An Appeal to the Public*, Dublin: G. Faulkner, 1758.

——, [description of Co. Mayo Swift commmemmoration] *Dublin Journal*, 12–15 May 1753, p. 1.

——, [obituary of Swift] *Dublin Journal*, 19–22, October 1745, p. 1.

Fielding, Henry, *The Covent-Garden Journal*, ed. G.E. Jensen (2 vols), New Haven: Yale University Press, 1915.

Forman, Charles, *A Defence of the Courage, Honour and Loyalty of the Irish Nation* . . . sixth edn London, printed; repr. Dublin: E. Rider, 1736.

[Jones, Henry], *The Bricklayer's Poem*, Dublin, 1745.

La Touche, James Digges, *A Second Address to the Citizens of Dublin* Dublin: P. Wilson, 1749.

Lewis, Richard, *The Dublin Guide: Or A Description of the City of Dublin* . . . , Dublin [1787].

———, *The Pleasing Moralist: or, Polite Philosopher* (2 vols), Dublin [1775].

Lucas, Charles, *The Political Constitutions of Great-Britain and Ireland Asserted and Vindicated* . . . (2 vols), London, 1751.

[MacNally, Leonard], *The Claims of Ireland and the resolutions of the Volunteers Vindicated* . . . , London: J. Johnson, 1782.

Minute Book, Meetings of Chapter, Cathedral Church of St. Patrick, Dublin, (1764–92).

Molyneux, William, *The Case of Ireland's Being Bound by Acts of Parliament in England, Stated*, Dublin: A. Long and H. Hawker, 1749.

Mullala, James, *A View of Irish Affairs* . . . (2 vols), Dublin: T. Henshall, 1795.

Oldmixon, John, *The History of England during the Reigns of King William and Queen Mary, Queen Anne, King George I* . . . , London: T. Cox et al., 1735.

Pilkington, Laetitia, *et al.*, *The Celebrated Mrs. Pilkington's Jests; or the Cabinet of Wit and Humour* . . . , second edn, London: W. Nicoll, 1764.

Pilkington, Matthew, *Poems on Several Occasions*, London: T. Woodword, et al., 1731.

[Reynardson, Francis, as] 'Timothy Brocade', *A Genuine EPISTLE from M[atthe]w P[rio]r, Esq; at Paris, To the Reverend J—n S—t, D.D. at Windsor* . . . , London, 1715.

[Reynardson, Francis], *An Ode to the Pretender*, London: M. Foster, 1713.

Sandys, Michael, *A Letter to the Right Honourable Henry Grattan, on the State of the Labouring Poor in Ireland*, Dublin: B. Dugdale, 1796.

Sharp, R., *A Letter to the People of Ireland: On the Present State of the Kingdom* . . . Dublin, 1755.

[Smedley, Jonathan], *An Hue and Cry after Dr. S—t; Occasioned by a True and Exact Copy of Part of his Own Diary* . . . second edn, London: J. Roberts, 1714.

[Smedley, Jonathan], *Gulliveriana* . . . , London: J. Roberts, 1728.

Smollett, Tobias, *A Complete History of England* (4 vols), London: J. Rivington and J. Fletcher, 1757–8.

Somerville, Thomas, *The History of Great Britain during the Reign of Queen Anne*, London: A Strahan et al., 1798.

Tone, Theobald Wolfe, *Life of Theobald Wolfe Tone* . . . , edited by his son (2 vols), Washington: Gales & Seaton, 1826.

[Wilkes, John], *The North Briton*, London: G. Kearsley, 1762.

[Witherall, Richard], *A New Song Sung at the Club at Mr. Taplin's[,] The Sign of the Drapier's Head in Truck-Street*, Dublin, 1724.

Nineteenth-century

[Allingham, William as] 'Patricius Walker', 'Rambles: Moor Park and Swift', *Fraser's Magazine*, 76 (November 1867), pp. 638–53.

Andrews, Alexander, *The History of British Journalism* (2 vols), London: R. Bentley, 1859.

Anon., *Joe Miller's Jest Book, Forming a Rich Banquet of Wit and Humour . . .*, London: J. Smith, 1833.

Anon., *Joe Miller's New Irish Jest Book, being an Everlasting Fund of Amusement . . .*, Dublin: G.P. Warren, n.d.

Anon., 'Letters of Swift', *Daily Express* (Dublin), 11 March 1899, p. 3.

Anon., 'Our Periodical Literature', *The Nation*, 20 March 1847, p. 378.

Anon., 'Popular Education', *The Nation*, 27 July 1844, p. 664.

Anon., [report of Cllr Atkinson, debate in Dublin Corporation] *The Nation*, 4 March 1843, p. 333.

Anon., 'Three Cynical Spectators: Gulliver – Candide – Teufelsdrockh', *Dublin University Magazine*, 67 (January 1866), pp. 64–75; (February 1866), pp. 184–97.

Arnold, Thomas, *A Manual of English Literature*, London: Longman, et al., 1862.

Bagehot, Walter, 'The First Edinburgh Reviewers', *National Review*, 1 (October 1855), pp. 253–84.

Berwick, Edward, *A Defence of Dr. Jonathan Swift . . . in answer to . . . the Edinburgh Review*, London: J. Nichols & Son, 1819.

Bicheno, J.E., *Ireland, and its Economy. Being the result of Observations made in a Tour through the Country in . . . 1829*, London: J. Murray, 1830.

[Brabazon, Elizabeth Jane], *Outlines of the History of Ireland for Schools and Families . . .* second edn, Dublin: Curry, 1847.

Burdy, Samuel, *The History of Ireland from the Earliest Ages to the Union*, Edinburgh: D. Stevenson, 1817.

Burke, Thomas, *English Misrule in Ireland. A course of Lectures . . . in reply to . . . Froude*, New York: Lynch, et al., 1873.

Butt, Isaac, *The Irish People and The Irish Land*, Dublin: J. Falconer, 1867.

Carlyle, Thomas, *Lectures on the History of Literature delivered . . . April to July 1838*, ed. J. Reay Greene, London: Ellis and Elvey, 1892.

[Christian Brothers], *Historical Class-Book . . .*, Dublin: W. Powell, 1859.

Collier, William Francis, *A History of English Literature . . .*, London: T. Nelson, 1862.

Collins, John Churton, 'Jonathan Swift', *Quarterly Review*, 153 (April 1883), pp. 377–430; 156 (July 1883), pp. 1–55.

Croker, John Wilson, *A Sketch of the State of Ireland Past and Present*, Dublin: M.N. Mahon, 1808.

[Curran, J.P.], *Forensic Eloquence. Sketches of Trials in Ireland . . . [and] papers Illustrating the History and Present State of that Country*, Baltimore: G. Douglas, 1804.

Cusack, Mary Frances, *An Illustrated History of Ireland: From the Earliest Period*, London: Longmans, Green, 1868.

Daly, John Bowles, *Ireland in the Days of Dean Swift*, London: Chapman and Hall, 1887.

Daunt, W.J. O'Neill, *Ireland and her Agitators*, Dublin: J. Mullany, 1867.

———, 'Ireland in the Time of Swift,' *Dublin Review* third ser. 9 (October 1883), pp. 337–70.

[Davis, Thomas], 'Abolition of the Lord Lieutenant', *The Nation*, 18 May 1844, p. 504.

[Davis, Thomas], 'An Irish Party', *The Nation*, 15 April 1843, p. 424.

[Davis, Thomas], 'A Patriot Parliament', *The Nation*, 1 April 1843, pp. 392–3.

[?Davis Thomas], 'English Appropriation of Irish Intellect', *The Nation*, 26 November 1842, p. 106.

[?Davis, Thomas as], 'A Protestant', 'Letters of a Protestant on Repeal, No. II', *The Nation*, 31 December 1842, p. 185.

[Davis, Thomas], 'Our National Language', *The Nation*, 1 April 1843, p. 394.

[?Davis, Thomas], 'The Ballad Poetry of Ireland', *The Nation*, 2 August 1845, p. 698.

[?Davis, Thomas] 'The Betrayed Protestants', *The Nation*, 25 January 1845, p. 248.

[?Davis, Thomas] 'The Speeches of Grattan', *The Nation*, 22 February 1845, p. 330.

Davis, Thomas, 'The Young Irishmen of the Middle Classes', *Essays Literary and Historical*, ed. D.J. O'Donoghue, Dundalk: W. Tempest, 1914.

Deane, Christopher Page, *A Short History of Ireland*, London: E. Stock, 1886.

de Wailly, Leon, [as trans.] *Stella and Vanessa. A Romance of the Days of Swift* [trans. Lady Duff-Gordon], London: R. Bentley, 1853 [first published 1850].

Duffy, Charles Gavan, *A Bird's-Eye View of Irish History*, Dublin: J. Duffy, 1882.

Duhigg, B.T., *History of the King's Inns . . .* , Dublin: J. Barlow, 1806.

Duignan, Patrick [speech to the Irish House of Commons, 5 February 1800] *Parliamentary Register for 1800*, (Dublin), p. 234.

Ferguson, John, *Three Centuries of Irish History . . .* , Glasgow: Cameron, Ferguson [?1898].

Flood, Warden, *Memoirs of the Life and Correspondence of the Rt. Hon. Henry Flood, M.P. . . .* , Dublin: J. Cumming, 1838.

Friswell, James Hain, *Essays on English Writers*, London: Samson Low et al., 1869.

Froude, James Anthony, *The English in Ireland in the Eighteenth Century* (3 vols), London: Longman, Green, 1872.

Gladstone, W.E. 'Lessons of Irish History in the Eighteenth Century', *Handbook of Home Rule*, ed. J. Bryce, London: Kegan Paul, 1887, pp. 262–80.

Gordon, James, *A History of Ireland . . .* (2 vols), Dublin: J. Jones, 1805.

Grattan, Henry, *Speeches . . . in the Irish Parliament in 1780 and 1782*, ed. James Grattan, London: J. Ridgway, 1821.

——, *Speeches . . . In the Irish, and in the Imperial Parliament*, ed. Henry Grattan, jr (4 vols), London: Longman, et al., 1822.

Grattan, Henry, jr, *Memoirs of the Rt. Hon. Henry Grattan* (5 vols), London: H. Colburn, 1839–43.

Gregory, W., *The Picture of Dublin being a Description of the City and a Correct Guide . . .* , Dublin: J. and J. Carrick [1811].

Hannay, James, *Satire and Satirists. Six Lectures*, London: D. Bogue, 1854.

——, 'Thackeray on Swift', *Temple Bar*, 21 (October 1867), pp. 322–30.

Haverty, Martin, *The History of Ireland, Ancient and Modern*, Dublin: J. Duffy, 1860.

Hazlitt, William, *Lectures on the English Poets*, London: Taylor and Hessey, 1818.

Jeffrey, Francis [review of Scott's edition], *Edinburgh Review*, 27 (September 1816), pp. 1–58.

Joyce, P.W., *A Concise History of Ireland*, Dublin: Gill, 1893.

Kennedy, Patrick, *The Banks of the Boro: A Chronicle of the County of Wexford*, London: Simpkin, Marshall, 1867.

Knight, Patrick, *Erris in the 'Irish Highlands', and the 'Atlantic Railway'*, Dublin:

M. Keene, 1836.

Lane-Poole, Stanley, 'Swift and Ireland,' *Fraser's Magazine*, n.s. 24 (September 1881), pp. 385–400.

Lawless, Emily, *The Story of the Nations: Ireland*, London: T.F. Unwin, 1885.

Lecky, W.E.H., *A History of Ireland in the Eighteenth Century* (3 vols), London: Longmans, Green, 1892.

———, *Leaders of Public Opinion in Ireland*, London: Saunders, Otley, 1861.

Leeper, Alexander, *Historical Handbook to the Monuments, Inscriptions &c of the . . . Cathedral Church of St. Patrick, Dublin*, Dublin: Hodges et al., 1878.

[Le Fanu, W.S.], 'Original Letters – Swift – No. 1', *Dublin University Magazine*, 12 (September 1838), pp. 269–72.

Lockhart, J.G., *Memoirs of the Life of Sir Walter Scott* (7 vols), Edinburgh: R. Cadell, 1837.

MacCarthy, Denis Florence, *The Poets and Dramatists of Ireland*, Dublin: J. Duffy, 1846.

McCarthy, Justin H., *An Outline of Irish History from the Earliest Times to the Present Day*, London: Chatto & Windus [1883].

Macaulay, T.B., *The History of England from the Accession of James the Second* (4 vols), London: Longman, et al., 1849–55.

M'Dermot, M[artin], *A New and Impartial History of Ireland from the Earliest Accounts to the Present Time* (4 vols), London: J.M'Gowan, 1820–23.

McGee, Thomas D'Arcy, *A History of the Attempts to establish the Protestant Reformation in Ireland . . .* , second edn, Boston: P. Donahoe, 1853.

———, *A Popular History of Ireland . . .* (2 vols), New York: D. & J. Sadlier, 1864.

Mahon [Philip Stanhope], Lord, *History of England . . .* (7 vols), London: J. Murray, 1836–54.

[Mahony, Francis, as 'Fr. Prout'], 'Dean Swift's Madness. A Tale of a Churn,' *Fraser's Magazine*, 10 (July 1834), pp. 18–32.

Mason, William Monck, *The History and Antiquities of the Collegiate and Cathedral Church of St. Patrick, near Dublin . . .* , Dublin: W. Folds, 1820.

Meagher, T.F. [speech to the Irish Confederation] *The Nation*, 13 January 1847, p. 229.

Mitchel, John, *The History of Ireland from the Treaty of Limerick to the Present Time*, Dublin: J. Duffy, 1869.

———, *Jail Journal* [preface by A. Griffith], Dublin: M.H. Gill, 1914.

———, 'Preface', *Irish Political Economy*, Dublin: Irish Confederation, 1847, pp. iii–vi.

[Moore, Thomas], *Memoirs of Captain Rock, the celebrated Irish Chieftain . . .* , London: Longman, et al., 1824.

Moran, D.P., 'The Pale and the Gael', *The New Ireland Review*, 11 (June 1899), pp. 230–44.

Morgan [Sydney (Owenson),], Lady, *The Book of the Boudoir* (2 vols), London: H. Colburn, 1829.

Moriarty, Gerald P., *Dean Swift and his Writings*, London: Seeley [1893].

Morris, William O'Connor, *Ireland, 1494–1868*, Cambridge: University Press, 1896.

[Musgrave, Richard], *Strictures upon An Historical Review of the State of Ireland by Francis Plowden . . .* , London: F. and C. Rivington, 1804.

O'Connell, Daniel [speech to Repeal Association], *The Nation*, 14 September 1844,

p. 772.

O'Conor, Matthew, *The History of the Irish Catholics from the Settlement in 1691* . . . , Dublin: J. Stockdale, 1813.

O'Conor, W.A., *History of the Irish People*, Manchester: A. Hayward [1883].

O'Grady, Standish J., *The Story of Ireland*, London: Methuen, 1894.

O'Keefe, John, *Recollections* . . . (2 vols), London: Colburn, 1826.

Orpen, E.H., *An Authentic Exposure of Irish Affairs* . . . , London: J. Hatchard, 1835.

[Paget, John], 'Swift and Lord Macualay', *Blackwood's Edinburgh Magazine*, 120 (November 1876), pp. 521–36.

[Pearson, C.H.], 'Swift', *North British Review*, n.s. 12 (January 1870), pp. 325–60.

[Philips, Samuel], 'The Amours of Dean Swift,' *The Times*, 3 October 1850, p. 3.

Plowden, Francis, *An Historical Review of the State of Ireland* (2 vols), London: C. Rowarth for T. Egerton, 1803.

Ponsonby, George [speech to the Irish House of Commons, 5 February 1800] *Parliamentary Register for 1800* (Dublin), p. 168.

Purves, D. Laing, 'Life of Jonathan Swift', *The Works of Jonathan Swift*, Edinburgh: D. Nimmo, 1869, pp. 1–40.

Redmond, John, *Historical and Political Addresses, 1883–97*, Dublin: Sealy, *et al.*, 1898.

Sheil, Richard Lalor [address to jury], *Dublin Evening Post*, 27 January 1844, p. 2.

Sigerson, George, *History of the Land Tenures and Land Classes of Ireland*, London: Longmans, 1871.

Smith, Goldwin, *Irish History and Irish Character*, Oxford: J.H. and J. Parker, 1861.

[Sullivan, A.M.], *The Story of Ireland*, Dublin: Sullivan [1868].

Sullivan, W.K., *et al.*, *Two Centuries of Irish History, 1691–1870*, intro. J. Bryce, London: Kegan Paul, Trench, 1888.

Taafe, Denis, *An Impartial History of Ireland* . . . (4 vols), Dublin: J. Christie, 1809–11.

[Taafe, Denis], *A Vindication of the Irish Nation, and particularly its Catholic Inhabitants, from the Calumnies of Libellers*, Part I. Dublin: J. Fletcher, 1801.

Taylor, W.C., *History of the Civil Wars of Ireland* . . . (2 vols), Edinburgh: A. Constable, 1831.

Todhunter, John, *The Black Cat*, London: Henry, 1895.

Trollope, Anthony, *Thackeray*, London: Macmillan, 1879.

Vandam, Albert D., *Amours of Great Men* (2 vols), London: Tinsley, 1878.

Walpole, Charles George, *A Short History of the Kingdom of Ireland*, London: Kegan Paul, Trench, 1882.

Whiteside, James [address to jury], *Dublin Evening Post*, 3 February 1844.

———, *Lectures delivered before the Dublin Young Men's Christian Association* . . . , Dublin: Hodges, Smith, 1864.

Wilde [Jane Francesca] Lady, *Notes on Men, Women and Books*, London: Ward & Downey, 1891.

Wright, G.N., *An Historical Guide to the City of Dublin* . . . , London: Baldwin, *et al.*, 1825.

Wyon, Frederick William, *The History of Great Britain during the Reign of Queen Anne* (2 vols), London: Chapman and Hall, 1876.

Yeats, W.B., 'The New Irish Library', *The Bookman* 10 (June 1896), pp. 83–4.

———, 'Rosa Alchemica,' *The Savoy*, no. 2 (April 1896), pp. 56–70.

———, 'The Tables of the Law,' *The Savoy*, no. 7 (November 1896), pp. 79–87.

Twentieth-century

Anon., 'Books and Booksellers', *Daily News* (London), 29 April 1904, p. 4.

Anon., 'Guinness as Swift', *The Times* 16 August 1976, p. 9.

Anon., 'Press Owes Debt to Dean Swift', *Irish Times*, 20 October 1945, p. 1.

Anon., 'The Dean', *Irish Times*, 19 October 1945, p. 3.

Bartlett, Thomas, *The Fall and Rise of the Irish Nation: The Catholic Question, 1690–1830*, Dublin: Gill & Macmillan, 1992.

—— , 'The Origins and Progress of the Catholic Question in Ireland, 1690–1800', *Emergence and Endurance: Catholics in Ireland in the Eighteenth Century*, ed. T.P. Power and Kevin Whelan, Dublin: Irish Academic Press, 1990, pp. 1–19.

Bartlett, Thomas, and D.W. Hayton, eds, *Penal Era and Golden Age: Essays in Irish History, 1640–1800*, Belfast: Ulster Historical Foundation, 1979.

Bell, [Eveleen, as] Mrs Hugh, *The Dean of St. Patrick's: A Play in Four Acts*, London: E. Arnold, 1903.

Berwick, Donald M., *The Reputation of Jonathan Swift, 1781–1882*, Philadelphia, 1941.

Bloom, William, *Personal Identity, National Identity and International Relations*, Cambridge: University Press, 1990.

Breeze, George, comp., *Society of Artists in Ireland: Index of Exhibits, 1765–80*, Dublin: National Gallery of Ireland, 1985.

Brown, Terence, 'After the Revival: The Problem of Adequacy and Genre', *The Genres of the Irish Literary Revival*, ed. Ronald Schliefer, Norman, OK: Pilgrim, 1980.

Carpenter, Andrew, 'Double Vision in Anglo-Irish Literature', *Place, Personality and the Irish Writer*, ed. A. Carpenter, Gerrards Cross: C. Smythe, 1977, pp. 173–89.

Carroll, Paul Vincent, *Farewell to Greatness. A Three Act Drama based on the Life and Loves of Dean Jonathan Swift*, Dixon, CA: Proscenium Press, 1966.

—— , *Shadow and Substance*, New York: Random House, 1937.

—— , 'The Substance of Paul Vincent Carroll', *New York Times*, 30 January 1938, sec. 10, p. 1.

Cave, Richard Allen, 'Dramatising the Life of Swift', *Irish Writers and the Theatre*, ed. M. Sekine, Gerrards Cross: C. Smythe, 1986, pp. 17–32.

Chauviré, Roger, *History of Ireland*, trans. Earl of Wicklow, Dublin: Clonmore and Reynolds [1952].

Christian Brothers, *Irish History Reader*, Dublin: Gill, 1916.

Clare, Anthony, 'Jonathan Swift, Mental Illness and the Irish', unpublished, Jonathan Swift Annual Lecture, St Patrick's Cathederal, 1991.

Clery, Arthur, *Dublin Essays*, Dublin: Maunsel, 1919.

Coleborne, Bryan, *Dean Swift and the Dunces of Dublin*, unpublished Ph.D. thesis, National University of Ireland, 1982.

Connolly, James, *Labour in Ireland; Labour in Irish History; The Re-Conquest of Ireland*, intro. R. Lynd, Dublin: Maunsel, 1917.

[?Corcoran, Timothy], 'Berkeley and Swift in "Studies", September 1934', *Catholic Bulletin*, 24 (November 1924), pp. 868–71.

—— , 'The "Hidden Ireland" of the "Protestant Gaels"', *Catholic Bulletin*, 24 (November 1924), pp. 871–3.

[Corcoran, Timothy, as] Donal MacEgan, 'Ingenious Bigotry', *Catholic Bulletin*, 14

(July 1924), pp. 593–600.

[Corcoran, Timothy, as] Donal MacEgan, 'Jonathan Swift and Ireland', *Catholic Bulletin*, 14 (April 1924), pp. 300–305.

———, 'A Note on Detraction', *Catholic Bulletin*, 16 (March 1926), pp. 300–6.

[Corcoran, Timothy, as] Dermot Curtin, 'Our Gaelic Democracy: Teaching the Lessons of its History', *Catholic Bulletin*, 23 (July 1933), pp. 587–92.

[Corcoran, Timothy, as] Donal MacEgan, 'Stephen Gwynn on Jonathan Swift', *Catholic Bulletin*, 23 (December 1933), pp. 1000–1004.

Corkery, Daniel, 'Ourselves and Dean Swift', *Studies*, 23 (June 1923), pp. 203–18.

———, 'The Nation that was not a Nation', *Studies*, 23 (December 1934), pp. 611–22.

Cowell, John, *No Profit but the Name: The Longfords and the Gate Theatre*, Dublin: O'Brien Press, 1988.

[Craig, Maurice, ed.], *The Legacy of Swift: A Bi-Centenary Record of St. Patrick's Hospital*, Dublin: Three Candles, 1948.

Crawford, Robert, *Devolving English Literature*, Oxford: Clarendon Press, 1992.

Cruise O'Brien, Conor, 'Irishness', *Writers and Politics*, London: Chatto & Windus, 1965, pp. 97–100.

Cumann na mBan, *Dean Swift on the Situation*, National Series, No. 3, Dublin: Cumann na mBan, 1915.

Dalsimer, Adele, 'Yeats's Unchanging Swift', *Eire-Ireland*, 9, no. 2 (1974), pp. 65–89.

D'Alton, E.A., *History of Ireland . . .* (3 vols), London: Kegan Paul, *et al.*, 1906.

Dalton, Maurice, 'Dean Swift', *Catholic Bulletin*, 8 (August 1918), pp. 387–89.

Davis, Richard, *Arthur Griffith and Non-Violent Sinn Fein*, Dublin: Anvil, 1974.

———, *The Young Ireland Movement*, Dublin: Gill & Macmillan, 1987.

Deane, Seamus, *A Short History of Irish Literature*, London: Hutchinson, 1986.

———, *Celtic Revivals: Essays in Modern Irish Literature, 1880–1980*, London: Faber, 1985.

——— ed., *The Field Day Anthology of Irish Writing* (3 vols), Derry: Field Day, 1991.

de Blacam, Aodh, *A First Book of Irish Literature . . .*, Dublin: Talbot Press, 1934.

———, 'The Other Hidden Ireland', *Studies*, 23 (September 1934), pp. 439–54.

de Valera, Eamon, 'The Values of the Spirit', *Speeches and Statements*, ed. Maurice Moynihan, Dublin: Gill and Macmillan, 1980, pp. 230–33.

Donoghue, Denis, ed., *Swift Revisited*, Cork: Mercier, 1968.

Dowling, Patrick John, *The Hedge-Schools of Ireland*, Dublin: Talbot Press, 1935.

Eagleton, Terry, Jameson, Frederic, and Said, Edward W., *Nationalism, Colonialism and Literature*, intro. S. Deane, Minneapolis: University of Minnesota Press, 1990.

Edwards, Hilton, 'Denis Johnston', *The Bell*, 13, no. 1 (October 1946), pp. 7–18.

Elliott, Marianne, *Wolfe Tone: Prophet of Irish Independence*, New Haven and London: Yale University Press, 1989.

Fabricant, Carole, *Swift's Landscape*, Baltimore: Johns Hopkins University Press, 1982.

Firth, C.H., 'The Political Significance of Gulliver's Travels', *Proceedings of the British Academy*, 9 (1919–20), pp. 237–59.

Flanagan, Thomas, 'A Discourse by Swift, A Play by Yeats', *University Review* (Dublin) 5, vol. 1 (Spring 1968), pp. 9–22.

Garratt, Robert F., ' "Aware of my Ancestor": Austin Clarke and the Legacy of Swift', *Eire-Ireland*, 11, no. 2 (1976), pp. 92–103.

Gogarty, Oliver St John, 'Swift as a Human Being', *Atlantic Monthly*, 186 (October 1950), pp. 54–6.

———, 'The Enigma of Dean Swift', *Intimations*, New York: Abelard Press, 1950, pp. 81–97.

Gregory, [Augusta] Lady, *The Kiltartan History-Book*, London: T.F. Unwin, 1926.

Griffith, Arthur [leader], *United Irishman*, 4 March 1899, p. 2.

———, 'Parnell', *Sinn Fein*, 7 October 1911, p. 3.

———, *The Resurrection of Hungary: A Parallel for Ireland*, Dublin: J. Duffy, 1904.

———, *When the Government Publishes Sedition*, Dublin: Irish Publicity League [1915].

Gwynn, Stephen, *Ireland*, London: E. Benn, 1924.

Hayden, Mary and Moonan, George A., *A Short History of the Irish People . . .* , Dublin: Talbot Press, 1921.

Hayton, David, 'Anglo-Irish Attitudes: Changing Perceptions of National Identity Among the Protestant Ascendancy in Ireland', *Studies in Eighteenth-Century Culture*, 17 (1987), pp. 145–57.

Herr, Cheryl, 'The Erotics of Irishness', *Critical Inquiry*, 17 (Autumn 1990), pp. 1–34.

Hickey, Des, and Smith, Gus, *A Paler Shade of Green*, London: L. Frewen, 1972.

Higgins, Ian, *Swift's Politics: A Study in Disaffection*, Cambridge: University Press, 1994.

Hill, Jacqueline R., 'The Intelligentsia and Irish Nationalism in the 1840s', *Studia Hibernica*, 20 (1980), pp. 73–109.

Hobson, Bulmer, ed., *The Gate Theatre, Dublin*, Dublin: Gate Theatre, 1934.

Hogan, J.J., 'Bicentenary of Jonathan Swift, 1667–1745,' *Studies*, 34 (December 1945), pp. 501–10.

Hogan, Robert, *After the Irish Renaissance*, London: Macmillan, 1968.

Hone, J.M., 'Berkeley and Swift as National Economists,' *Studies*, 23 (September 1934), pp. 421–32.

———, 'Ireland and Swift', *Dublin Magazine*, 8 (July–September 1933), pp. 9–17.

Hull, Eleanor, *A History of Ireland and her People* (2 vols), London: G. Harrap [1926].

Hunt, Hugh, *The Abbey: Ireland's National Theatre, 1904–79*, New York: Columbia University Press, 1979.

Ingram, T. Dunbar, *A Critical Examination of Irish History . . .* (2 vols), London: Longmans, Green, 1900.

Irish Times Supplement, 'Swift', *Irish Times*, 22 March 1967.

Jackson, R. Wyse, 'Jonathan Swift, 1745–1945', *Irish Press*, 19 October 1945, p. 2.

Jarrell, Mackie L., ' "Jack and the Dane": Swift Traditions in Ireland', in *'Fair Liberty was all his Cry': A Tercentenary Tribute to Jonathan Swift*, ed. A.N. Jeffares, London: Macmillan, 1967, pp. 311–41.

Johnston, Denis, *Dramatic Works*, ed. J. Ronsley (3 vols), Gerrards Cross: C. Smythe, 1977–92.

———, 'Jonathan Swift: 1667–1745. A Bicentenary Tribute', *Irish Times*, 20 October 1945, p. 2.

———, 'Swift of Dublin', *Eire-Ireland*, 3 (Fall 1968), pp. 38–50.

———, 'The Trouble with Swift', *The Nation*, 196, no. 4 (26 January 1963), pp. 73–6.

Kelly, James, 'The Genesis of "Protestant Ascendancy": The Rightboy Disturbances of the 1780s and their Impact on Protestant Opinion', in *Parliament, Politics and People: Essays in Eighteenth-Century Irish History*, ed. Gerard O'Brien, Dublin: Irish

Academic Press, 1989, pp. 93–127.

———, *Prelude to Union: Anglo-Irish Politics in the 1780s*, Cork: University Press, 1992.

Kinane, Vincent, *The Dublin University Press in the Eighteenth Century*, unpublished fellowship thesis, Library Association of Ireland, 1981.

Lammey, David, 'The Free Trade Crisis: A Reappraisal', in *Parliament, Politics and People: Essays in Eighteenth-Century Irish History*, ed. Gerard O'Brien, Dublin: Irish Academic Press, 1989, pp. 69–92.

Larkin, Emmet, 'A Reconsideration: Daniel Corkery and his Ideas on Cultural Nationalism,' *Eire-Ireland*, 8 (Spring 1973), pp. 42–51.

Le Brocquy, Sybil, *Cadenus*, Dublin: Dolmen, 1962.

———, *A View on Vanessa: A Correspondence with Interludes for the Stage*, Dublin: Dolmen, 1967.

Lee, Phillip G., 'Dean Swift', *Journal of the Ivernian Society*, 21 [(October 1913), pp. 5–23; (December 1913), pp. 98–107].

Leerssen, J.Th., *Mere Irish and Fíor-Ghael*, Amsterdam: Benjamins, 1986.

Leighton, C.D.A., *Catholicism in a Protestant Kingdom*, Dublin: Gill & Macmillan, 1994.

Lennox, P.J., 'Swift, the Irish Patriot', *Catholic Educational Review*, 14 (November 1917), pp. 289–99.

Leventhal, A.J., 'The Dean among his Friends', *Irish Times*, 20 October 1945, p. 2.

Longford [Edward A.H. Pakenham], Earl of, *Yahoo: A Tragedy in Three Acts*, Dublin: Hodges, Figgis, 1934.

Lovic, James Allen, *Yeats's Epitaph: A Key to Symbolic Unity in his Life and Work*, Washington: University Press of America, 1982.

Lustick, Ian, *State-Building Failure in British Ireland & French Algeria*, Berkeley: Institute of International Studies, 1985.

McCabe, Eugene, *Swift*, author's unpublished typescript.

McCaffrey, Lawrence, 'Daniel Corkery and Irish Cultural Nationalism', *Eire-Ireland*, 8 (Spring 1973), pp. 35–41.

McCartney, Donal, 'James Anthony Froude and Ireland: An Historiographical Controversy of the Nineteenth Century', *Irish University Review*, 1 (Spring 1971), pp. 238–57.

———, 'Lecky's *Leaders of public opinion in Ireland*', *Irish Historical Studies*, 14 (September 1964), pp. 119–41.

———, *W.E.H. Lecky: Historian and Politician, 1838–1903*, Dublin: Lilliput Press, 1994.

[McCartney, Donal, as] Donald MacCartney, 'The Writing of History in Ireland, 1800–30', *Irish Historical Studies*, 10 (1957), pp. 347–62.

McCormack, W.J., 'Vison and Revision in the Study of Eighteenth-Century Irish Parliamentary Rhetoric', *Eighteenth Century Ireland*, 2 (1987), pp. 7–35.

MacDonagh, Michael, 'Ireland Ablaze in 1724', *Irish Monthly*, 43 (December 1915), pp. 749–66.

McDowell, R.B., 'Swift as a Political Thinker' in *Jonathan Swift 1667–1967: A Dublin Tercentenary Tribute*, ed. Roger McHugh and Philip Edwards, Dublin: Dolmen, 1967, pp. 176–86.

McHugh, Roger, 'The Woven Figure: Swift's Irish Context', *University Review*, (Dublin) 4, no. 1 (Spring 1967), pp. 35–52.

MacIntyre, Tom, 'In Search of three Swifts', *Books Ireland* (March 1986), pp. 36–7.

——, 'Swift, Stella and Vanessa', *Cara*, 17, no. 4 (July–August 1984), 44–52.

——, *The Bearded Lady*, unpublished rehearsal typescript, Abbey Theatre.

McMinn, Joseph, 'A Weary Patriot: Jonathan Swift and the Formation of an Anglo-Irish Identity', *Eighteenth-Century Ireland*, 2 (1987), pp. 103–13.

MacNeill, J.G. Swift, *The Constitutional and Parliamentary History of Ireland till the Union*, Dublin: Talbot Press, 1917.

Mangan, Henry, 'Clio in Ireland', *O'Connell School Centenary Record*, Dublin: Christian Brothers, 1928.

Maume, Patrick, 'The Propulsive Course of Epics: the Making of The Hidden Ireland', unpublished paper, delivered to the Eighteenth-Century Ireland Society, conference 7 March 1993.

Maxwell, D.E.S., *A Critical History of Modern Irish Drama, 1891–1980*, Cambridge: University Press, 1984.

Maxwell, D.E.S., 'Swift's Dark Grove: Yeats and the Anglo-Irish Tradition', *W.B. Yeats 1865–1965 Centenary Essays*, ed. Maxwell and S.B. Bushrui, Ibadan: University Press, 1965, pp. 18–33.

Mercier, Vivian, *The Irish Comic Tradition*, Oxford: Clarendon Press, 1962.

——, 'Swift and the Gaelic Tradition', *'Fair Liberty was all his Cry': A Tercentenary Tribute to Jonathan Swift*, ed. A.N. Jeffares, London: Macmillan, 1967, pp. 279–89.

Merriman, Brian, *The Midnight Court and the Adventures of a Luckless Fellow*, trans P.A. Ussher; intro. W.B. Yeats, London: J. Cape, 1926.

Montag, Warren, *The Unthinkable Swift: The Spontaneous Philosophy of a Church of England Man*, London: Verso, 1994.

Moody, T.W. and W.E. Vaughan, eds, *A New History of Ireland*, vol. 4, *Eighteenth-Century Ireland*, Oxford: Clarendon Press, 1986.

Moore, J.N.P., *Swift's Philanthropy*, Dublin: St Patrick's Hospital [1967].

Murphy, Brian, 'The Canon of Irish History: Some Questions', *Studies*, 77 (Spring 1988), pp. 68–83.

Murphy, Seán, 'Charles Lucas and the Dublin Election of 1748–49', *Parliamentary History*, 2 (1983), pp. 93–111.

——, 'The Dublin Anti-Union Riot of 3 December 1759', *Parliament, Politics and People: Essays in Eighteenth-Century Irish History*, ed. Gerard O'Brien, Dublin: Irish Academic Press, 1989, pp. 49–68.

National Gallery of Ireland, *Swift and his Age: A Tercentenary Exhibition, 1667–1967*, Dublin: National Gallery, 1967.

O'Brien, Gerard, *Anglo-Irish Politics in the Age of Grattan and Pitt*, Dublin: Irish Academic Press, 1987.

——, 'Illusion and Reality in Late Eighteenth-Century Irish Politics', *Eighteenth-Century Ireland*, 3 (1988), pp. 149–55.

O'Brien, William, *Edmund Burke as an Irishman*, Dublin: Gill, 1924.

——, *Recollections*, London: Macmillan, 1905.

O'Connor, Frank, 'Ireland', *Holiday*, 6 no. 6 (December 1949), pp. 34–7, 40–41, 44–5, 48–9, 51–3, 56–60, 62–3.

——, *Leinster, Munster and Connaught*, London: R. Hale [1950].

——, *A Short History of Irish Literature: A Backward Look*, New York: Capricorn, 1967.

O'Connor, Ulick, 'The Dark Lovers (A Play about Jonathan Swift and Stella)', author's unpublished typescript.

O'Donoghue, D.J., 'Swift as an Irishman', *Irish Review*, 2 (June 1912), pp. 209–14; (July 1912), pp. 256–63; (August 1912), pp. 305–11.

O'Faolain, Sean, 'Daniel Corkery', *Commonweal*, 25 (6 November 1936), pp. 35–7.

———, *King of the Beggars: A Life of Daniel O'Connell*, New York: Viking, 1938.

O'Hainle, C.G., 'Neighbours in Eighteenth-Century Dublin: Jonathan Swift and Seán Ó Neachtain', *Eire-Ireland*, 21 no. 4 (1986), pp. 106–21.

O'Hegarty, P.S., *A History of Ireland Under the Union, 1801–1922*, London: Methuen, 1952.

———, 'Jonathan Swift: Irishman', *The Bell*, 10 (September 1945), pp. 478–88.

Ó hOgain, Daithi, *The Hero in Irish Folk History*, Dublin: Gill and Macmillan, 1985.

Ó Tuathaigh, Gearoid, 'Gaelic Ireland, Popular Politics and Daniel O'Connell', *Galway Archeological and Historical Society Journal*, 34 (1974–5), pp. 21–34.

Paternoster, G. Sidney, '"Jonathan Swift" Dean of St. Patrick's: A Play in Four Acts', unpublished typescript, British Library MS/LCP 1923/32.

Pearse, P.H., *Ghosts*, Tracts for the Times, No. 10, Dublin: Whelan & Son, 1916.

Power, Arthur, 'Artistic Life in Paris and Dublin in the Nineteen Twenties', unpublished typescript, in custody of Ulick O'Connor.

———, *The Drapier Letters and Her Ladyship – the Poet – and the Dog. Two One Act Plays*, Dublin: Talbot Press, 1927.

Rawson, C.J., ed. *Swift*, London: Sphere, 1971.

Real, Hermann J. and Vienken, Heinz J., eds, *Proceedings of the First Muenster Symposium on Jonathan Swift*, Munich: W. Fink, 1985.

Rodino, Richard H., and Hermann, J. Real, eds, *Reading Swift: Papers from the Second Muenster Symposium on Jonathan Swift*, Munich: W. Fink, 1993.

Rollins, Ronald. G. 'Enigmatic Ghosts of Swift in Yeats and Johnston', *Eire-Ireland*, 18, no. 2 (Summer 1983), pp. 103–15.

Rooney, William, *Poems and Ballads*, intro. Philip Bradley, Dublin: M.H. Gill [1901].

———, *Prose Writings*, intro, S. MacManus, Dublin: M.H. Gill [1909].

Scott, Temple, 'Introduction', *The Drapier's Letters. The Prose Works of Jonathan Swift*, vol. 6 London: G. Bell, 1903, pp. ix–xiv.

Sheeran, P.F., 'Colonists and Colonized: Some Aspects of Anglo-Irish Literature from Swift to Joyce', *Yearbook of English Studies*, 13 (1988), pp. 97–115.

Sheldon, Esther K., *Thomas Sheridan of Smock Alley*, Princeton: University Press, 1967.

Shorter, Clement [letter] *Daily News* (London), 4 May 1904.

Simms, J.G., *Colonial Nationalism, 1698–1776*, Cork: Mercier, 1976.

Sisson, C.H., 'Yeats and Swift', *Agenda*, 9, nos 4–10, no. 1 (double issue, Autumn–Winter 1971), pp. 34–8.

Smith, Goldwin, *Irish History and the Irish Question*, New York: McClure, Phillips, 1905.

Spence, Joe, 'Nationality and Irish Toryism: The Case of the *Dublin University Magazine*', *Journal of Newspaper and Periodical History*, 4, no. 3 (Autumn 1988), pp. 2–17.

Stockley, W.F.P., 'Swift as an Irish Writer: The Whole Truth', *Irish Ecclesiastical Record*, fifth ser. 27 (February 1926), pp. 127–47.

Strickland, Walter George, *A Dictionary of Irish Artists*, Shannon: Irish University Press, 1968; orig. pub. 1913.

Torchiana, Donald T., 'Jonathan Swift, the Irish and the Yahoos: The Case Reconsidered', *Philological Quarterly*, 54 (1975), pp. 195–212.

——, *W.B. Yeats and Georgian Ireland*, Evanston: Northwestern University Press, 1966.

——, and Glenn O'Malley, 'Some New Letters from W.B. Yeats to Lady Gregory', *Review of English Literature*, 4 (July 1963), pp. 9–47.

Ua Murchada, Domhnall, *Sean-Aimsireacht*, Dublin: Stationery Office, 1939.

Vance, Norman, *Irish Literature: A Social History*, Oxford: Basil Blackwell, 1990.

——, 'Celts, Carthaginians and Constitutions: Anglo-Irish literary relations, 1780–1820', *Irish Historical Studies*, 22 (1981), pp. 216–38.

Voight, Milton, *Swift and the Twentieth Century*, Detroit: Wayne State University Press, 1964.

Walker, Keith, 'Rational Grotesque', *Times Literary Supplement*, 3 July 1981, p. 755.

Whibley, Charles, *Jonathan Swift: The Leslie Stephen Lecture*, Cambridge: University Press, 1917.

Woolley, James, *Swift's Later Poems: Studies in Circumstances and Texts*, New York: Garland, 1988.

Wyatt, Anne, 'Froude, Lecky and "the humblest Irishman"', *Irish Historical Studies*, 19 (1974–5), pp. 261–85.

Yeats, W.B., 'The Best Book from Ireland', *Daily News* (London), 11 May 1904, p. 4.

——, 'The Words upon the Window Pane. A Commentary', *Dublin Magazine*, 6 (October–December 1931), pp. 5–19; 7 (January–March 1932), pp. 11–15.

——, *The Words upon the Window Pane: A Play in One Act, with notes upon the Play and its Subject*, Dublin: Cuala Press, 1934.

Index